Planting Empire, Cultivatir

Planting Empire, Cultivating Subjects examines the stories of ordinary people to explore the internal workings of colonial rule. Chinese, Indians, and Malays learned about being British through the plantations, towns, schools, and newspapers of a modernizing colony. Yet they got mixed messages from the harsh, racial hierarchies of sugar and rubber estates and cosmopolitan urban societies. Empire meant mobility, fluidity, and hybridity, as well as the enactment of racial privilege and rigid ethnic differences. Using sources ranging from administrative files, court transcripts and oral interviews to periodicals and material culture, Professor Lees explores the nature and development of colonial governance, and the ways in which Malayan residents experienced British rule in towns and plantations. This is an innovative study demonstrating how empire brought with it both oppression and economic opportunity, shedding new light on the shifting nature of colonial subjecthood and identity, as well as the memory and afterlife of empire.

Lynn Hollen Lees is Professor of History Emerita at the University of Pennsylvania and a Past President of the Urban History Association. She has written extensively on cities and social history in Europe and elsewhere Her recent publications include *The Solidarities of Strangers: The English Poor Laws and the People, 1700–1948* (1998), *Cities and the Making of Modern Europe, 1750–1914* (2007) with Andrew Lees, and *Global Society: The World since 1900* (2013) with Pamela K. Crossley and John W. Servos. She has received fellowships from the Guggenheim Foundation, the American Council of Learned Societies, the National Endowment for the Humanities, and the Rotary Foundation. She has been an exchange professor at University College London, the Catholic University of Leuven Belgium, and the University of Diponegoro in Indonesia.

Planting Empire, Cultivating Subjects

British Malaya, 1786–1941

Lynn Hollen Lees

University of Pennsylvania

CAMBRIDGE
UNIVERSITY PRESS

CAMBRIDGE
UNIVERSITY PRESS

University Printing House, Cambridge CB2 8BS, United Kingdom

One Liberty Plaza, 20th Floor, New York, NY 10006, USA

477 Williamstown Road, Port Melbourne, VIC 3207, Australia

314-321, 3rd Floor, Plot 3, Splendor Forum, Jasola District Centre, New Delhi - 110025, India

79 Anson Road, #06-04/06, Singapore 079906

Cambridge University Press is part of the University of Cambridge.

It furthers the University's mission by disseminating knowledge in the pursuit of education, learning and research at the highest international levels of excellence.

www.cambridge.org
Information on this title: www.cambridge.org/9781108732086
DOI: 10.1017/9781139814867

© Lynn Hollen Lees 2017

First published 2017
First paperback edition 2019

A catalogue record for this publication is available from the British Library

Library of Congress Cataloging in Publication data
Names: Lees, Lynn Hollen, author.
Title: Planting empire, cultivating subjects : British Malaya, 1786–1941 / Lynn Hollen Lees, University of Pennsylvania.
Description: Cambridge, United Kingdom ; New York, NY : Cambridge University Press, [2017] | Includes bibliographical references and index.
Identifiers: LCCN 2017018418 | ISBN 9781107038400 (alk. paper)
Subjects: LCSH: Malaya – History – British rule, 1867–1942. | Plantations – Malaysia – Malaya – History. | Agriculture and politics – Malaysia – Malaya – History. | Cosmopolitanism – Malaysia – Malaya – History. | Imperialism – Social aspects – History.
Classification: LCC DS596 .L44 2017 | DDC 959.5/103–dc23
LC record available at https://lccn.loc.gov/2017018418

ISBN 978-1-107-03840-0 Hardback
ISBN 978-1-108-73208-6 Paperback

For my friends in the Perak Oral History Project,
the Perak Heritage Society, and the Perak Academy,
who taught me to love Malaysia.

Contents

Figures

Maps and Tables

Maps

Tables

Acknowledgements

This book has had a long gestation because it required that I broaden my skills to include expertise in Southeast Asian history. As I moved more deeply into the project and spent time in Malaysia, I realized all too clearly what I did not know and would have to learn. Years passed, but they were productive ones. This book could not have been written without the aid of archivists and librarians on several continents. Staff at the Arkib Negara Malaysia, the National Archive and National Library of Singapore, the National University of Singapore, the National Archive in London, the British Library, the Bodleian Library, the London School of Economics, the archive of the School of Oriental and African Studies, Rhodes House, the Cambridge University Library, the Huddersfield Public Library, the county archives of Buckinghamshire, Cumberland, and West Yorkshire, the American Philosophical Society, and the Library of Congress have been of great help. Their endless patience and willingness to find sources has been invaluable. Special thanks go to John Pollock, Andrea Gottschalk, and Lee Pugh from Van Pelt Library at the University of Pennsylvania, whose assistance with books and images has been indispensable. In Ipoh, Malaysia, the Old Andersonian Club, St Michael's Institution, the Anglo-Chinese School, and the SMK Convent School allowed me to see school records, photographs, and students' publications. Several undergraduate and graduate students assisted this project along the way, tackling particular newspapers or other sources. Kacey Baker, Jason Berry, Shefali Chandra, D'Maris Coffman, Andrew Loh, Tania Mohd. Nor, Caroline Ong, Saadia Toor, and Wicky Tse took time from their own work to help me, and I benefitted from their many talents.

I would not have been able to write *Planting Empire, Cultivating Subjects* without the collaboration of my friends in Malaysia, to whom I have dedicated this book. The Perak Academy not only sponsored me for a research visa, but they gave me office space and library access during my many visits to Ipoh. The interest of its members and their local support opened doors and launched conversations. The Perak Heritage Society introduced me to the small towns of Perak as well as to their superb food. Eager historians of their locality, my collaborators in the Perak Oral History Project found fascinating subjects, conducted interviews, and then videotaped and transcribed conversations. They took me to their schools, clubs, and libraries, where I was welcomed warmly. The hours I have spent with Chee Wai Kheng, Angela Lim, Tan Yap Pau, Chong Fong Loon, Ho Tak Ming, Mohd. Jaki Mamat, Chan Kok Keong, Cheng Yeok San, and David Foon Hoong Seng have been a pleasure, and their help was invaluable. Law Siak Hong and Mohd. Taib bin Mohamed and his family virtually adopted me, becoming guides-in-chief to the intricacies of Malaysian history and material culture. Their endless enthusiasm for learning more about British Malaya has enriched both my work and my life. I am grateful to Ian Anderson not only for creating IpohWorld, a superb online archive of local history, but also for his willingness to share sources and insights about Malaysia during my visits to Ipoh. Over very good meals in Penang and Kuala Lumpur, Khoo Salma Nasution, Abdur-Razzaq Lubis, Gareth Richards, and Henry Barlow helped me think through knotty problems. At an early stage in my project, Dr Paul Kratoska offered encouragement and excellent advice. Chew Joo Leong, Elwyn Chew and Khoo Eng Yow taught me about the Chinese communities in Batu Kawan and Taiping, and I am grateful for their help.

Conversations with colleagues and friends sharpened my arguments and widened my perspectives. Lee Cassanelli, Sandra Barnes, Nancy Farriss, Steve Feierman, and Sumathi Ramaswamy – all veterans of Penn's Ethnohistory Seminar – forced me to engage with anthropologists. Kathy Brown, Eve Troutt Powell, Barbara Savage, Siyen Fei, Vanessa Ogle, Ben Nathans, Ramya Sreenivasan, and Teren Sevea raised welcome questions and pushed me to clarify statements. Ann Farnsworth Alvear taught me the best practices of oral history and read parts of my manuscript. Friends whose work in Asian history I greatly admire – particularly Debjani Bhattacharyya, Ulbe Bosma, Frances Gouda, Lillian Li, Sue Naquin, Robert Nichols, and Howard Spodek – provided inspiration through example and pointed out problems.

Over the past several years, parts of my argument have been presented in many settings, and I am grateful to listeners for their questions. I benefitted from comments at seminars at Indiana University, Merton College, Cambridge University, the University of Glasgow, and the Rutgers Center for Historical Analysis, as well as the University of Pennsylvania's Economic History Forum and the History Department's Annenberg Seminar. Audiences at the European Social Science History Conference, the Institute for Historical Research, the Mid-Atlantic Conference on

British Studies, the Pacific Coast Conference on British Studies, the Anglo-American History Conference, the American Association of Asian Studies, and Swarthmore College helped me to refine my ideas. Weaving together the strands of what I originally intended to be two manuscripts forced me to rework arguments multiple times. Seth Koven, Andrew Lees, Craig Lockard, and Jennifer Sessions read drafts of this manuscript, and their perceptive and detailed comments led me in new directions. I am immensely grateful to them all. In the congenial setting of the Delaware Valley British Studies Seminar, I presented work in progress, which members gently took apart and then helpfully put back together. The intellectual style of that group, particularly that of its co-director Seth Koven, has been a constant source of intellectual stimulation and insight.

Research grants from the American Philosophical Society and a faculty research grant from the School of Arts and Sciences at the University of Pennsylvania made possible early trips to Malaysia. A welcome sabbatical leave from the University of Pennsylvania facilitated trips to British archives. Their confidence in my project when it was still in its infancy has been much appreciated. My forays into the history of plantations led me also to productive conversations with the families of planters who worked in Malaya and with the heirs of the Ramsden family. Anne and Hunter Crawford shared memories and photographs of the Penang Rubber Estates with me, and Ruth Rollitt let me read the unpublished memoirs of her uncle, Werner Michael Iverson. The late Phyllida Gordon-Duff-Pennington welcomed me to the family archive in Muncaster Castle and opened her collection of Ramsden photographs and letters. Iona and Peter Frost-Pennington were similarly gracious, leading me and my husband into Muncaster Castle attic rooms to search for additional photographs and papers.

It has been a pleasure to work with Cambridge University Press. Michael Watson has been supportive of this project since he first learned of it several years ago. His flexibility and good advice have solved problems and maintained my morale. Anonymous readers gave good advice, and I thank them. Heidi George's help in the final stages of manuscript preparation has been invaluable, and working with her has been a pleasure. Transformation of my text into a printed volume has been expertly handled by Bronte Rawlings and Anubam Vijayakrishanan, whose painstaking work is appreciated. Short sections of the text have been reworked from articles already published in the *Business History Review*, the *Journal of British Studies*, and *Urban History*. I thank the editors of those periodicals for permission to draw from those essays.

As this project comes to an end, I find myself in a different intellectual space from the one where I began. The shift from studying European urban history to that of Southeast Asia and the addition of oral history to my repertoire have been exciting. Along the way, my husband Andrew has not only read multiple drafts of what I have written, but he has never complained about my many absences and workaholic habits. I thank him for his constant support, tolerance, and good humour.

Glossary

adat	local customs as practised by Muslim communities
bumiputera	lit: "sons of the soil"
changkol	hoe used for weeding
chettiar	South Asian moneylender
Chulia	Tamil Muslims
dhoti	South Asian male's garment, a cloth wrapped around waist and legs
Foochow	speaker of Foochow dialect, immigrant from Fujian province in China
gharry	horse-drawn cab or carriage
gurdwara	Sikh place of worship
haj, haji	pilgrimage to Mecca, pilgrim to Mecca
Hakka	speaker of Hakka dialect, immigrant from South China
Hokkien	speaker of Hokkien dialect, immigrant from Fujian province in China
Jawi Peranakan	locally born, Malay-speaking Muslims of mixed South Asian and Malay ancestry
kampong	village
kang	agricultural community in Malaya, chartered by Sultan
kangany	South Indian labour recruiter and gang boss
kangchu	head, usually Chinese, of a river mouth settlement of planters in Johor
kapitan China	headman of a Chinese community
kaum muda	Muslim reformist movement active in the 1930s
Kerajaan	lit: "that which pertains to a raja," government
kongsi	a Chinese partnership, labour gang, or share-holding group, sometimes applied to the illegal brotherhoods called "secret societies" by the British
madrasa	Muslim religious school
munshi	language teacher

nasi lemak	Malay rice dish made with coconut milk
orang asli	lit: "original people," aborigine
orang kaya	lit: "wealthy people," persons of high status
padang	parade ground or playing field
penghulu	headman of a Malay sub-district
rakyat	the "people," peasantry
shroff	money changer or banker, usually South Asian
sing-song girls	Chinese females who entertained wealthy men in urban clubs
Sufi	follower of an ascetic and mystical style of Islam
Teochew	speaker of Teochew, immigrant from Guangdong province of China
Thaipusam	Tamil Hindu festival celebrated at the full moon in January or February
tindal	South Asian foreman
toddy	alcoholic drink made by fermenting the flowers of the coconut palm
towkay	wealthy Chinese trader or businessman
tuan	lit: "lord, master" used by Asians to address European males
vakil	attorney or agent

Abbreviations

AHR	*American Historical Review*
APS	American Philosophical Society
JAS	*Journal of Asian Studies*
JIA	*Journal of the Indian Archipelago*
JMBRAS	*Journal of the Malaysian Branch of the Royal Asiatic Society*
JSBRAS	*Journal of the Straits Branch of the Royal Asiatic Society*
JSEAS	*Journal of South East Asian Studies*
MBRAS	Malaysian Branch of the Royal Asiatic Society
PRE	Penang Rubber Estates
PSE	Penang Sugar Estates

Introduction

When Francis Light, a middle-aged captain of the Bengal Marine and an employee of the East India Company, sailed to Penang Island in July of 1786, he saw uncultivated land where wild cattle, deer, and hogs outnumbered the few human beings. Sultan Abdullah of Kedah had agreed to lease the island to the East India Company in return for cash and potential support against his Siamese and Burmese enemies. Within a few days of Light's arrival, marines began clearing the land, and a stream of new settlers – Chinese, Indian Muslims, and Christians of unspecified ethnicity – arrived from Kedah on the mainland, the first of hundreds who quickly put down roots in the new port. Traders built houses near the newly erected Fort Cornwallis, which was soon staffed by over 100 officers and troops. In the 1780s, the East India Company acted as an arm of the British government, which added the company's territorial possessions to its empire. Convict labourers sent from India helped to build the settlement. The story of British colonial rule in Malaya weaves tales of private capital with those of state power in a common search for economic development.[1]

Telling the tale, however, of British Malaya in terms of Francis Light's landing on a relatively empty island erases much of its early cast of characters. Chinese, Tamils, Arabs, Malays, and Eurasians, not just the East India Company, built the colony on Penang Island. Empire in Malaya is a tale of mixed origins and many peoples who together constructed a multi-cultural society under the umbrella of British overlords. If the story began with traders, sailors, and sultans, it continued with soldiers, labourers, convicts, and adventurers who sniffed opportunities in the relative weakness of local elites. The history of British Malaya was intertwined with the histories of India, China, the Netherlands Indies,

---

[1] Marcus Langdon, *Penang: the Fourth Presidency of India 1805–1830*, Vol. 1, *Ships, Men, and Mansions* (Penang: Areca Books, 2013), pp. 7, 190–193; on the importance of convict labour to British colonies, see Anand A. Yang, "Indian Convict Workers in Southeast Asia in the late Eighteenth and early Nineteenth Centuries," *Journal of World History*, Vol. 14, No. 2 (2003), pp. 179–208.

and the Arabian Peninsula, as well as of the British Isles; thousands of immigrants into Malaya remained tied via imaginations and identities to far-off places.

This book explores the transnational movements that shaped British Malaya and its peoples. It asks how and to what extent British colonial rule in Malaya permitted, and indeed fostered, cross-cultural exchanges and learning. Its analysis rests on a social history of plantations and towns in the economically developing areas of the Malaya peninsula, grounding the experience of individuals in their communities. The main characters are workers, managers, merchants, teachers, and officials who planted empire on the peninsula and who became British subjects as a result. Their stories illuminate small-scale distributions of power which shaped the multiple allegiances of people who functioned within imperial networks. Colonialism operated locally, despite its transnational dynamics and global framework.

When European traders first sailed to the Malay Archipelago, they encountered a fragmented political world of sultanates and local chiefdoms which vied for power and control of long-distance trade. Hundreds of islands and the western shore of the Malay Peninsula sheltered a shifting group of entrepôt states organized around ports and river valleys. The practice of Islam and use of the Malay language tied them together, although local customs (*adat*) varied. Muslim rajas, who had ritual authority rather than effective political power, entrusted the work of government to ministers drawn from local aristocratic lineages or chieftains. Since eldest sons did not automatically inherit fathers' titles and families were very large, rival claimants to thrones and offices connived to defeat opponents and sent their armed followers into action. The Sultanate of Melaka – seized by the Portuguese in 1511, by the Dutch in 1641, and then by the British in 1795 – was one of the most powerful of these courts, located in the peninsula's most important port and one of its only towns. In the pre-colonial period, it was the central place where foreign merchants traded textiles for spices and where they waited for shifts in the monsoon winds that made possible travel to India and to China.[2] Its multi-ethnic community of traders adapted quickly to its foreign conquerors and changes of regime. British control spread from Penang in 1786 to Melaka and then to Singapore in 1819.

When the British moved officially into Malaya in the late eighteenth century, towns on the peninsula were few and far between. During the

---

[2] Barbara Watson Andaya and Leonard Y. Andaya, *A History of Malaysia*, 2nd ed. (Houndsmill, Hampshire: Palgrave, 2001), pp. 34–38; Anthony C. Milner, *The Malays* (Chichester: Wiley-Blackwell, 2008), pp. 18–19

remained separate. In contrast, T. N. Harper has written of polyglot, cosmopolitan cities, whose residents learned to switch among cultural codes and styles rather than remain segregated. Even if Malaya can be called a "pluralist" society, the term "hybrid" is also apt because it captures the cultural mixing that took place, particularly in the colonies' towns and cities.[11] Thinking in terms of separated cultural worlds ignores the mutual learning and regular interactions that took place in schools, shops, theatres, and offices. Colonial rule had boundaries that were not only flexible, but also permeable in many settings, although inequalities of power twisted interactions in fundamental ways.

Racial categories constituted powerful dividing lines in European-ruled empires, shaping both individual imaginations and the institutions of civil society. Europeans' beliefs in the superiority of their own kind and culture were reinforced by legal separations, which were undermined by the day-to-day accommodations necessary in a multi-cultural society and by the alternative images that groups held of themselves. In Malaya, where colonial rulers argued for the existence of "racial harmony," many happily embraced segregation, while others were comfortable within the hybridized world which colonialism had helped to create. In the longer run, of course, it is clear that the awareness of differences overwhelmed the forces of integration. All of the colonized societies of South and Southeast Asia have found it difficult in the post-colonial world to maintain societies in which multiple ethnic groups are successfully and permanently integrated as citizens of a single nation-state. Instead, divisions along the lines of religion, ethnicity, and caste have continued to disrupt political life, occasionally producing riots and bloodletting in India, Sri Lanka, Burma, Indonesia and Malaysia. The question of how multiple communities deal with one another is still with us. The Malay Peninsula offers a geographically confined but exceptionally heterogeneous space in which to analyse how British colonizers viewed and managed social differences.

Colonial officials controlled not only multiple peoples, but also multiple environments. A colony that began with the port town of Penang grew to include plantations, farms, mines, forests, villages, and the city of Singapore, each of which developed distinctive institutions and legal controls. As imperial subjects moved from plantation to town or from village to port city, they experienced very different repertoires of rule. From the perspective of colonized subjects, imperialism was never monolithic. As subjects moved, they shifted their experience of empire. A Tamil

[11] T. N. Harper, "Empire, Diaspora and the Languages of Globalism, 1850–1914," in A. G. Hopkins, ed., *Globalization in World History* (London: Pimlico, 2002), pp. 141–166; J. S. Furnivall, *Netherlands India: A Study of Plural Economy* (Cambridge: Cambridge University Press, 1944)

labourer on a rubber estate lived in a hierarchical, segregated, paternalist environment. Work was controlled by Europeans and South Asian foremen who enforced norms of productivity and subservient conduct. Yet if that labourer moved to a small town, he had to negotiate the local labour and housing markets on his own. While he had to watch out for the colonial police, local employers were predominantly Chinese, and he had to learn to deal with them. The Chinese not only owned most stores but also ran the bars, brothels, gambling halls, theatres, and opium shops. The few state employees in evidence were, for the most part, Asians, who used family connections to supplement the authority of the colonial state. On plantations, the imposition of British rule was direct and prescriptive of everyday actions, while in the towns it was indirect and masked by alternative systems of authority. Municipal laws and divided sovereignties, rather than managers and foremen who carried rattan sticks, set the rules of the game.

Empire could be practised in different ways, therefore, and the strength of its bite depended on the local repertoire of rule. The key concept for understanding British Malaya or any other particular part of the British Empire, therefore, is colonialism – foreign presence in and direct domination of a particular place – rather than imperialism, which refers to foreign rule irrespective of occupation and local exercise of power.[12] A focus on colonialism directs attention to colonized peoples and to their experiences, rather than to an empire's rulers. How were the many groups that lived on the Malay Peninsula controlled, and how did they respond to British dominance? Imperial subjects participated in their own transformation, and the process cannot be understood from an imperial and central vantage point.

At the same time that European states expanded their control of land in Southeast Asia, political and ideological revolutions in North America and Western Europe destabilized the rationale for imperial rule. When, in the late eighteenth century, armies of citizens ousted monarchs and championed nationalism, a rhetoric of universal rights spread in the Americas and in Europe. The new language of rights enabled anyone – whether male or female, black or white, slave or free – to claim the protections of representative government and to assert their equality. The successful defeat of French armies by the ex-slave soldiers of St. Domingue and the creation of an independent Haiti in 1804 proved the liberating power of new ideas, and political elites had to adapt. How could empires be justified, if individuals ought to be free? Although classic liberal theorists such as John Locke argued in terms of universal human rights and liberties,

[12] See Ho, "Empire through Diasporic Eyes," p. 211.

labour depots in South India and with marketing agents in Hong Kong and Calcutta. The letters soon led me to other archives in London, Oxford, Cambridge, Cumberland, Yorkshire, Singapore, Kuala Lumpur, and Penang, each site representing more voices. I had stumbled upon an insider's view of a colonial capitalist enterprise as it operated in the global economy, and I then worked to find other vantage points for this study of colonial rule in Malaya.

How to move beyond British views and responses to those of other groups has been a major challenge. Colonial archives reveal much about the categories and practices of the colonizers, but their representations and silences also comment on encounters between the state and its subjects.[20] Traces of multiple voices appear, and marginal jottings record personal responses. Court cases from the Federated Malay States include statements in Malay and Chinese by bystanders, by the injured, and by the accused. In archival files, runaway Tamil labourers reveal their names and moments of agency. Even if not all subalterns speak, some have made recognizable marks through their actions and objections. Outside the archive, multiple sources shine a spotlight on the vanished worlds of British Malaya. Of particular value have been photographs, local newspapers, periodicals, material objects, and published memoirs, which offer glimpses into the day-to-day lives of Malays, Tamils, and Chinese before 1941. In Malaysia, evidence of the colonial past is easy to find; interpreting messages from its many fragments is much more difficult. My methods are primarily those of a social and economic historian influenced by dialogues with anthropologists, cultural historians, and historians of memory.

This book also draws upon interviews of Malaysians and Singaporeans who experienced British colonial rule. The Singapore National Archive's Oral History Centre, organized in 1979 with the purpose of preserving social memories, has collected interviews of people from multiple communities and social statuses. I have also used interviews recorded and transcribed by the Perak Oral History Project, which was established in 2008 under the auspices of the Perak Heritage Society and the Perak Academy. This group of local historians, which I helped to organize, began its work with inquiries into memories of the Japanese occupation and the Emergency years, but then broadened its scope to include the

---

[20] See Ann Laura Stoler, *Along the Archival Grain: Epistemic Anxieties and Colonial Common Sense* (Princeton: Princeton University Press, 2009); Carolyn Steedman, *Dust: The Archive and Cultural History* (New Brunswick: Rutgers University Press, 2002); Gyatri Chakravorty Spivak, "Can the Subaltern Speak?," in Cary Nelson and Lawrence Grossberg, eds., *Marxism and the Interpretation of Culture* (Urbana: University of Illinois Press, 1988).

pre-war period. Those interviewed agreed to have their remarks recorded, transcribed, and preserved for use by scholars. These conversations were not casual events, but sessions for which they carefully prepared. Most of the people questioned were long-time residents of Perak, friends of members of the project who arranged and usually attended the interviews. Most of these interviews were conducted in English, since it serves as the common language of the group. When, however, a subject chose to use Malay or Tamil, a translator assisted the conversation when necessary, and the interview was translated into English after it was transcribed. The people questioned were in no sense a random selection of those who had lived under British rule in western Malaysia: they were articulate survivors, most of whom had built good lives for themselves after independence. While not part of a Malaysian elite, most had become teachers, managers, or local officials. Even the former plantation workers whom I interviewed had moved into positions of relative comfort. All were asked to reconstruct their memories of social life and consciousness after exposure not only to World War II but also to decades of films, television shows, books, and conversations about Malaysia in the twentieth century, topics on which there is no unified set of opinions or discourses. All of those interviewed had spent years listening to multiple voices and alternative formulations about the Malaysian past and its cast of characters. When they spoke to the video camera, they were engaging with an unknown, wider audience, telling tales that they had selected themselves. They were "composing stories," which in turn helped them present a self with which they were comfortable. A second dynamic is that of relationship to actual and imagined audiences. People describe events which they think of interest to their listeners and which pick up on shared values and identities.[21] (When I interviewed Roman Catholic Malaysians in settings near their churches, their stories always emphasized the importance of church activities and religious ties. In more secular spaces, those questioned spoke far less about religion.) Oral histories do not give unmediated access to memory, but they present narratives constructed from selected recollections, familiar discourses, and social frameworks. They comment as much on the present as on the past. Nevertheless, their representations arise outside colonial archives and offer alternative views of colonial pasts.

Part I of this book discusses the nineteenth century, tracing the expansion of British control in Malaya through the development of plantation

---

[21] Penny Summerfield, *Reconstructing Women's Wartime Lives: Discourse and Subjectivity in Oral Histories of the Second World War* (Manchester: Manchester University Press, 1998), pp. 15–22

agriculture and through the urbanization of territories drawn into the Straits Settlements and the Federated Malay States. My story proceeds chronologically, although each chapter has a different theme and covers a broad swath of time. Chapter 1 uses the story of the Penang Sugar Estates and their Chinese competitors to explore how plantations transformed the land by using imported labour, operating under the protective umbrella of an increasingly complex administrative structure largely run by multilingual Asians. Chapter 2 explores the social world of plantations and the distinctions of race and gender that underlay its rigid hierarchies and inequalities. Economic development brought with it extensive urbanization, whose beginning Chapter 3 traces. Unlike the plantations, small towns created relatively open, hybridized spaces, whose schools, shops, and services brought inhabitants into contact with multiple cultures and sources of information. Chapter 4 contrasts the growing civil society that emerged among literate Asian men of middling status with the street culture of the day labourers, prostitutes, and rickshaw pullers. Sovereignty in the towns was fractured between the law-based administration of the colonial state and an underworld of brotherhoods and sworn associations that permeated the Chinese and Malay communities. Urban economies flourished along with the plantation and mining sectors, whose demand for labour exploded after the conversion to rubber production and rising exports.

Part II jumps forward into the twentieth century and ends in 1941 as the Japanese conquered British Malaya. Again, my story centres on plantations and towns, the primary settings of British rule on the peninsula. Chapter 5 looks at the rubber boom's impact on plantation colonialism and the growth of middling groups and smallholders who were drawn into a thriving consumer economy. During the 1920s and 1930s, Malayan towns became increasingly modernized with the growth of commercial entertainment and the expansion of education. Chapter 6 explores cosmopolitan urban culture and the overlapping language worlds of literate Malays, Chinese, and Indians. By the later 1930s, educated men had a choice of cultural and political domains with which they could identify, stretching far outside the boundaries of the colony. Chapter 7 raises the problem of urban governance in the context of continued divisions between formal colonial institutions and the informal power of Chinese societies and criminal gangs. Police power concentrated on street crime and gambling, keeping a careful distance from underground associations they could not control. Sovereignty remained divided, and residents had to negotiate among rival authorities. Chapter 8 explores the multiple political and social choices of people living in British Malaya and raises the question of alternative loyalties during the 1930s.

Although evidence of imperial allegiance is not hard to find, neither is interest in Indian and Chinese nationalism, Malay modernity, and Muslim reform movements. Nevertheless, contingent accommodation with the empire was possible for those who adopted a flexible notion of subjecthood and who found within the British Empire a way to combine their global ties and local advantages. Colonial rule accustomed growing numbers to a kind of performative Britishness and contextual allegiance to the British Empire that temporarily overcame ethnic and religious divisions. More strident anticolonial messages from trades unions and the Communist Party seemed relatively weak until the late 1930s, when demonstrations against Japanese expansion into China and strikes by plantation workers showed that mass mobilizations in defiance of colonial restrictions were possible. The epilogue of the book looks back over the era of British rule through the lens of memory, exploring how contemporary Malaysians understand the colonial past in light of present ethnic divisions. Nationalist narratives of resistance to colonial rule compete for attention with nostalgia for an imagined cosmopolitan past, where multiple types of belonging coexisted and the boundaries among communities were permeable.

The British Empire created a cosmopolitan polity on the Malay Peninsula, one where multiple peoples jostled for position in a frontier territory. Within British Malaya, plantations and towns existed as insular, but also connected worlds. Because racially compartmentalized, hierarchical plantations lay within walking distance from multi-ethnic, cosmopolitan towns, people in Malaya experienced multiple styles of imperial rule. In this mobile society, many residents became border-crossers, fluent in multiple languages and sets of cultural norms as they learned about the many forms that power took in a colonial setting. They also experienced alternative models of governance, some of which drew on British and Chinese systems of authority and others of which delegated formal sovereignty to Malay leaders. Subjects, rather than citizens, they had to decide to whom they owed allegiance and how they would accommodate themselves to the competing powers that nested within an authoritarian system. Individuals in the Straits Settlements and the Federated Malay States lived within a fractured space whose interstices could be exploited. Survival required cultural learning and adaptation to the multiple environments created by British officials as they planted a colony in Malaya and cultivated its inhabitants as British subjects.

Part I

The Nineteenth Century

Economics prompted the East India Company to put down roots in Southeast Asia as its trade with China grew. Easy access to Indian textiles and opium gave it profitable products to trade in Malaya, and the increasing power of the British Navy brought protection. British territorial power in Southeast Asia expanded quickly after Francis Light sailed to Penang Island in July of 1786. The Dutch turned over Melaka in 1795, and the Sultan of Kedah was forced to part with additional land in 1800, which became Province Wellesley. Then in 1819, Sir Thomas Stamford Raffles, another ambitious East India Company employee, leased Singapore Island from a local territorial chief to serve as a free-trade port. The carefully negotiated Anglo-Dutch Treaty of 1824 assigned the Malay Peninsula to the British as a "sphere of influence."[1] By the early nineteenth century, these separate towns and their hinterlands served as naval bases and ports of call for the India-China trade.

Multiple European and local rulers coveted more land and economic influence in Southeast Asia, but the British managed to consolidate and expand their authority in the early nineteenth century. Working through the East India Company, British administrators attacked and then administered the large and immensely rich island of Java from 1811 to 1816, annexing new land and raising taxes. Nevertheless, at the end of the Napoleonic Wars they returned Java to the Dutch, and in 1824 agreed via treaty to share local territory: the British gave up claims to Sumatra and the islands south of Singapore in return for a free hand on the mainland. In 1826, the British state successfully pressured the Thai government to settle outstanding border conflicts, trading recognition of Thai influence in the Northern Malay states (Kedah, Petani, Kelantan, and Terengganu) for secure borders with Burma and Thai acceptance of growing British power in the rest of the peninsula. In 1829, the

---

[1] Barbara Watson Andaya and Leonard Y. Andaya, *A History of Malaysia*, 2nd ed. (Houndsmill: Palgrave, 2001), pp. 111–112, 125; C. E. Wurtzburg, *Raffles of the Eastern Isles* (Singapore: Oxford University Press, 1984)

settlements of Penang, Melaka, and Singapore were merged into the Straits Settlements and run from India until 1867, when they became a separate colony. Governing authority of the Straits Settlements passed in 1858 from the East India Company to the British Colonial Office.[2]

British intrusion into western Malaya was limited until Penang and Singapore merchants, who had invested heavily in the region's tin mines, organized to ask for British protection of their investments. The Colonial Office ignored their repeated complaints about gang fights among the Chinese and mini-civil wars among the Malays, choosing not to intervene. Then a new Governor, Sir Andrew Clarke, arrived in the colony in 1873. He decided, after talking with leading investors and with the President of the Singapore Chamber of Commerce, that the British should act to keep the peace. Soon Clarke found a golden opportunity in Perak, where Raja Abdullah, who aspired to be the sultan, had been passed over by the chieftains who had the right to elect the new raja. Abdullah, who had long been an ally of leading British and Chinese investors in Perak tin mines, wrote to Clarke, offering to accept a British advisor in Perak if he were recognized as Sultan. Clarke happily accepted the bargain, negotiating the Pangkor Treaty in 1874 with Abdullah, who – at least in the English version of the treaty – obligated himself and his successors to accept a British Resident whose advice "must be asked and acted upon on all questions other than those touching Malay religion and custom." Clarke pressured the rulers in two other states, Selangor and Sungai Ujung, to accept similar deals.[3] Moreover, the Colonial Office accepted Clarke's decision, moving without objection into effective political control of the most economically developed areas of western Malaya.

The Pangkor Treaty gave the British – in their opinion, anyway – the right to control the political, legal, economic, and financial affairs of Perak, although Perak's Sultan formally continued in place. The treaty set a pattern that was later extended to the remaining territories of Negeri Sembilan (1887) and Pahang (1888), all of which were loosely unified with Perak and Selangor as the Federated Malay States in 1896. Although each state supposedly remained independent with a "sovereign" ruler, British Residents made all the important decisions and controlled the civil service, police, tax collection, and all non-Islamic courts. A Resident-General based in Kuala Lumpur coordinated the separate

[2] M. C. Ricklefs, *A New History of Southeast Asia* (Houndsmill Hampshire: Palgrave Macmillan, 2010), pp. 142, 151, 187–188; Sir Frank Swettenham, *British Malaya: An Account of the Origin and Progress of British Influence in Malaya* (London and New York: John Lane, 1907), pp. 81–82

[3] Andaya and Andaya, pp. 147–154, 157–158; Ricklefs, pp. 175–176; Khoo Kay Kim, *The Western Malay States, 1850–1873* (Kuala Lumpur: Oxford University Press, 1972)

state governments. Technically a system of indirect rule, the administrations of the Federated Malay States closely resembled those of the directly ruled Straits Settlements, whose Governor was also the High Commissioner of the other British controlled areas. In both colonies, District Officers, who worked with Malay and Chinese headmen, supervised local affairs.[4]

British political control of Malaya went hand in hand with rapid economic development, spurred by heavy British and Chinese investments. Trade and production grew rapidly as international demand for primary commodities exploded. Since membership in the British Empire brought easy access to world markets, industrial agriculture seemed a sure economic bet, particularly after massive state spending on roads and railways improved land transportation. Malay customary rules for land tenure were annulled and replaced by a European system of land registration, leasing, and sale, clearing the way for massive transfers to outsiders. Entrepreneurs turned more and more land into sugar, pepper, and coffee plantations, tin mining increased in scale, and rubber cultivation spread. Towns multiplied. The Malayan frontier beckoned to risk-takers, whether they were Chinese, British, European, South Asian, or Malay. Ethnicity mattered less than connections and cash, and capital rushed into Malaya from multiple sources. A sweet smell of prosperity beckoned immigrants and reconciled local people to the new and thriving colonial economy.

The expansion of colonial control has often been told as a story of heroic resistance against foreign intrusions, resulting in bloody repression. That story does not describe the Malayan experience, where opposition was relatively weak and short lived. To be sure, some Malays fought against the British seizure of power. The first British Resident of Perak, J. W. W. Birch, was stabbed to death by a group of Malay chiefs while he was bathing in a river a few months after his arrival. The exact reasons for the attack are still debated, but Birch had moved to take over tax collection and had sheltered runaway slaves, insisting that Malay rulers had to accept British policies. Moreover, the British governor had threatened the Perak Sultan with deposition if he opposed British control of finances and legal matters. The British responded to Birch's murder with massive force. Not only did they convict and hang three of the culprits, but they also sent Sultan Abdullah and several other chieftains into exile. At least 1,500 soldiers arriving from Hong Kong and India pursued the conspirators and spent six months quashing minor rebellions in nearby states. The availability of well-armed troops in the region, as well as British ships to

[4] Ricklefs, pp. 176–177; Andaya and Andaya, pp. 185–186

transport them, meant that resistance by small bands of mercenaries was futile.

For the rest of the century, armed attacks on the British were limited. After the British had manoeuvred the Pahang sultan to accept a British agent charged to open up the territory to "commerce and civilization," continued disputes over power and rights in that state led to the brief Pahang War, an intermittent campaign of ambushes and minor skirmishes. One of the regional chiefs, Abdul Rahman, launched an uprising in 1891 to defend his own position as well as to oppose British policies, and he found some local allies. Nevertheless, Sikh troops brought in from nearby states eventually defeated the rebels, some of whom were exiled and others amnestied. By combining direct repression with generous pensions to Malay rulers and territorial lords, the British consistently dampened opposition and negotiated peace. Yet violence and opposition come in multiple forms, many of which left little trace in national records. The expropriation of land, corporeal punishment, and forced labour could be brutal and were deeply resented, even if they did not produce rebellions. Peasants could argue with state officials, squat illegally on vacant land, or challenge rent payments. Labourers could feign sickness, strike, or run away. The absence of open resistance is not evidence for social harmony or uncontested acceptance of colonial rule. Court cases, newspaper reports, arrest records, and local legends testify to a muted but continued undercurrent of opposition to the social order administered by the British.

By the end of the nineteenth century, British imperial jurisdiction extended far into Malaya and deep into local settlements. Much of the western peninsula had been drawn into a profitable export economy that brought very unequally distributed costs and benefits. The extension of British colonial control required taming the land and its peoples, a process which involved many Chinese, Tamils, Sikhs, Arabs, Malays, and relatively few British officials and settlers. Part I of this book looks at the starkly contrasting styles of British colonial rule that developed on the plantations and in the towns of western Malaya.

were quickly put to work building bridges, roads, and simple police stations, which gave administrators a visible presence in the new British territory.[9] All signalled security to a wave of enthusiastic planters, whose estates produced spices, coconuts, indigo, and tapioca for the global as well as the regional market.

A rhetoric of progress through colonial cultivation underlay the dreams of early British travellers as they crossed Malayan terrain via elephants, looking for adventures and opportunity. Taming the land, they thought, would require the intertwining of empire with export agriculture. Europeans in the area in the 1830s insisted that British-ruled enclaves differed from Malay-governed states not only in political security, but also in their prospects for development. Thomas John Newbold, an officer in the Madras Light Infantry posted to Melaka in 1832, contrasted the attractive, well-run port towns of Penang and Melaka with Perak's "straggling villages" surrounded by jungle and the thick forests of Sungei Ujong in nearby native states. Elephant tracks, rather than proper roads, linked interior settlements. In Newbold's view, "cultivation" and industry came not from Malays but from outsiders: Chinese immigrants, Bugis from Sulawesi, and Minangkabau from Sumatra. Local population was scanty, since many had fled the "despotic" rule of the rajas and occasional threats from the kingdom of Siam.[10] His hope was that if British control were extended, these backward places could be modernized too. While on a mission to Perak in 1826, James Low pronounced the soil "extremely fertile" and the climate "favourable for the production of sugar, indigo, and other tropical plants," although he thought that Malays were incapable of carrying out such projects themselves. Low recommended "the example and protection of a civilized and humane European nation to ameliorate their condition and ... to induce settled aims of industry."[11] The military officers posted from India to Malaya enthusiastically supported the extension of British rule, and they identified empire with export agriculture. Their own entrepreneurial activities demonstrated easy shifts from governance to plantation ownership. Focusing on the Penang Sugar Estates and their neighbours, this chapter explores the dependence of plantations on the colonial state.

---

[9] The East India Company transported convicts from India to Penang and Singapore from 1800 to 1858. This export of unfree labour parallels the British government's practice of exiling felons to North America and Australia during roughly the same period. Anand A. Yang, "Indian Convict Workers in Southeast Asia in the Late Eighteenth and Early Nineteenth Centuries," *Journal of World History*, Vol. 14, No. 2 (2003), pp. 179–208

[10] T. J. Newbold, *Political and Statistical Account*, Vol. 2, pp. 23–25, 28, 75

[11] James Low, "Observations of Perak," *Journal of the Indian Archipelago and Eastern Asia*, Vol. 4 (1850), pp. 497–498, 504

Planting Sugar

The prospect of cheap land and a job also drew immigrants to Malaya from South China, where periodic famines, floods, and high rents gave labourers ample reason to emigrate. Unlike the British government, which encouraged emigration to its colonies, the Qing state tried in the eighteenth century to enforce exit controls, but was unable to do so effectively. After 1728, imperial laws required merchants to have trading licences and to post bond to guarantee their return. Permanent settlement overseas was tolerated at best, and the state offered no protection to the adventurous men willing to travel for work. This was an era, however, of limited border controls and no passports, so the stream of Chinese coming to Penang did so unofficially as part of an ethnic diaspora regulated by kin networks and merchant organizations.[12]

Chinese immigrant farmers started sugar growing in Malaya as early as 1810.[13] Bringing with them agricultural techniques from South China, Teochew farmers from Guangdong moved into coastal areas of Province Wellesley, transforming muddy lowlands near the sea into cane-growing fields.[14] The largest group settled in Batu Kawan, an isolated area of mangrove swamps surrounded by water; they used simple tools and hand labour to grow cane, which they then crushed in bullock-driven rolling mills. The resulting juice was immediately boiled, clarified, drained, and dried to produce a rough grade of brown sugar for sale in the region. James Low estimated that by 1835 they had opened about 900 acres to sugar planting. Khaw Loh Hup, a Teochew immigrant, arrived as a poor apprentice in Batu Kawan and within a few years earned enough to buy his own property there and later to buy more property in the Krian district. His eldest son, Khaw Boo Aun, expanded the family sugar business in both Province Wellesley and Perak, and quickly became a powerful figure among the local Teochew.[15] The family was in the right place at

---

[12] Adam M. McKeown, *Melancholy Order: Asian Migration and the Globalization of Borders* (New York: Columbia University Press, 2011), pp. 29, 37–38

[13] *Penang Gazette*, 4 September 1841, quoted in Tan Kim Hong, "Chinese Sugar Planting and Social Mobility in Nineteenth Century Province Wellesley," *Malaysia in History: Journal of the Malaysian History Society*, Vol. 24 (1981), p. 25

[14] James Low, who worked for the East India Company in the Straits Settlements for over twenty years, estimated that by 1835 over 2,000 Chinese worked on sugar plantations in central and southern Province Wellesley, growing cane and processing it into refined sugar with simple crushing mills, boiling pans, and clarifiers. Low, *British Settlement*, p. 49; Sucheta Mazumdar, *Sugar and Society in China: Peasants, Technology, and the World Market* (Cambridge: Harvard University Press, 1998); Tan, "Chinese Sugar Planting," pp. 24–38

[15] Tate, *RGA History*, pp. 18, 114–116; Lee Kam Hing and Chow Mun Seong, eds., *Biographical Dictionary of the Chinese in Malaysia* (Petaling Jaya: Pelanduk Publications, 1997), pp. 57, 59–60

the right time: sugar prices were rising, the region was relatively empty, and land was cheap to rent. In the early days of the industry, small loans and savings were enough to launch a Chinese-style plantation, which required little more than hand tools, boiling pots, and a draft animal to help crush the cane.[16]

Europeans followed in the footsteps of the Chinese. The Penang-based Brown family of spice planters opened a sugar estate in the southern part of Batu Kawan in 1846, initially using Chinese labour, boiling equipment from India, and a factory foreman trained in Mauritius.[17] These men launched a new industry at a favourable moment in a plausible place. Caribbean sugar producers found African labour much harder to obtain after the British stopped the trans-Atlantic slave trade in 1807, and they lost their comparative advantage in the sugar industry after the formal end of slavery in the British Empire in 1838. Shortly thereafter, Parliament ended West Indian tariff privileges, permitting sugar grown in Mauritius, India, and, later, Bengal and all its dependencies, to enter the British market on the same terms as Caribbean sugar.[18] Sniffing the scent of opportunity, would-be planters searched for new sugar-growing land. The Malay Peninsula was one of the territories they chose. Joseph Balestier, who from 1837 served as the American Consul in Singapore, quickly became both a booster of export agriculture and a planter himself, opening a sugar estate on the island.[19] He and several of the other leading planters there, including Governor Murchison, constituted themselves as the Singapore Agricultural and Horticultural Society to encourage the growing of export crops. Their paeans of praise for plantations were similar to those of James Low, based more to the north. Another active booster was Leonard Wray, who had been a planter in Jamaica and Bengal and who came to Malaya in the 1840s looking for land. He soon became a spokesman for a burgeoning sugar industry. If planters could find low-cost labour and import the latest technology for their factories and fields, he predicted that they could "produce sugar at a rate as cheap as (if not cheaper than) any planter in the world." In the Malayan future, he envisaged rectangular fields crossed by canals and cultivated with steam ploughs. Steam engines would drain the swamps and power refineries.

---

[16] Tan, "Chinese Sugar Planting," p. 33; Tate, *RGA History*, p. 117

[17] Low, *British Settlement*, p. 49; Donald Davies, "Roughing It in the Sugar Estates," *The Sunday Gazette*, 27 August 1972

[18] Adam Hochschild, *Bury the Chains: Prophets and Rebels in the Fight to Free an Empire's Slaves* (Boston: Houghton Mifflin, 2005); J. H. Galloway, *The Sugar Cane Industry: An Historical Geography from Its Origins to 1914* (Cambridge: Cambridge University Press, 1989), pp. 121–130

[19] J. Balestier, "View of the State of Agriculture in the British Possessions in the Straits of Malacca," *Journal of the Indian Archipelago*, Vol. 2 (1848), p. 141

His book, *The Practical Sugar Planter: a Complete Account of the Cultivation and Manufacture of Sugar-Cane*, went through several editions, advising landlords of the best techniques and equipment.[20] With the demand for sugar rising, adventurers of many sorts turned swamps into sugar plantations, albeit without much machinery. Joseph Donadieu, who came from Mauritius looking for contract coolies, stayed to open up the Jawi and Val d'Or estates.[21] By 1850, planters in Melaka, Singapore, Province Wellesley, and northern Perak had begun to try their luck with sugarcane along the west coast of the Malay Peninsula, and the industry was launched internationally under the protective umbrella of the British Empire. What these planters had in common was a taste for adventure and an optimism about the gains to be had from bringing "jungle" land into cultivation. They were hard men who did not mind getting dirty to turn a profit. The sheltering umbrella of empire offered planters, whatever their nationality, cheap land, police protection, and access to the British market. British control fostered a multi-ethnic group of planters and labourers who remade the Malayan landscape as they cleared fields and planted cane.

Absentee landlords offered an alternative model to the small-scale estates of European adventurers and Chinese immigrants. Edward Horsman (1807–1876), a Member of the British Parliament, became the largest investor and sugar grower in West Malaya during the 1850s. Horsman, a Liberal politician who had ambitions much bigger than his trust-fund income would support, began to look in the 1840s for promising investments at a time when the Malayan sugar industry was being promoted by local planters. Perhaps his interest was piqued by his elder brother, I. D. Horsman, who had worked for the East India Company and who had explained strategies for trading with Asia.[22] He also knew men in London who had gotten rich on the profits of Caribbean sugar estates. Working through an attorney in Penang, Horsman bought land in Province Wellesley from the East India Company, amassing almost 12,000 acres by 1857. The core of his holdings (see Map 1.1) consisted of six estates – Caledonia, Krian, Victoria, Golden Grove, Jawi, and Val d'Or – the latter two having been opened up by Donadieu, whose holdings had been sold after pirates murdered him in 1850. Horsman contributed borrowed capital but little else to his estates, being much more

[20] (London: Smith, Elder and Co., 1848), pp. 133, 139
[21] Tate, *RGA History*, p. 116; Davies, "Roughing It in the Sugar Estates
[22] I. D. Horsman Letters, "I. D. Horsman to Mr. Mercer," 4 November 1841, 30 November 1841, 28 December 1841, D/RA/A/3E/12 (Buckinghamshire Record Office)

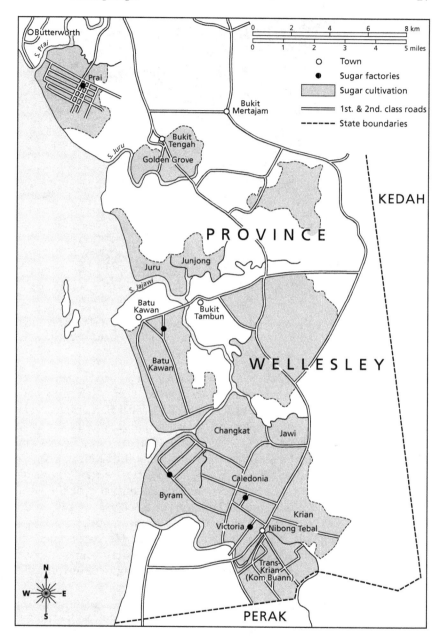

Map 1.1 Sugar Estates and Small Towns in Province Wellesley, 1897

Figure 1.1   Caledonia plantation sugar mill, Province Wellesley, c. 1863.
Labourers fed cane into the metal rollers, turned by a steam engine.

interested in his political career than in agriculture.[23] Sugar production
was merely an investment for Horsman, and he seems never to have
learned much about either the business or the Straits Settlements. The
London banking house of Baring and Co. handled his accounts, exported
equipment, and managed sales in London. A Penang firm, Brown and
Co., served as agent in the Straits Settlements, shipping sugar and rum to
Asian and European destinations. Chinese labourers, working in gangs
run by local Teochew labour bosses, cleared the land and planted and
harvested the cane. Indian contract labourers and Malays worked on the
estates too. A well-equipped factory under European supervisors produced refined white sugar and rum (see Figure 1.1). Horsman remained
an absentee owner, leaving himself and his business in the hands of local
managers, foremen, and refiners, whom he never dealt with directly.[24]

[23] Edward Horsman served in Parliament from 1836 virtually continuously until his death
in 1874. He served as Chief Secretary for Ireland and a member of the Privy Council from
1855 to 1857, and led opposition to the Liberal Reform Bill of 1866. Edward Horsman,
Dictionary of National Biography, pp. 1281–1282
[24] Tan, "Chinese Sugar Planting," p. 29; Edward Horsman, "Accounts, 1853–1854,"
"Accounts, 1868," D/RA/A/SE/25 (Buckinghamshire Record Office); James William
Norton Kyshe, ed., *Cases Heard and Determined in her Majesty's Supreme Court of the*

Horsman's estates were by far the largest in the area, and they set the standard for the "modern" Malayan plantation at the time. When the Prince of Wales visited the Straits Settlements in 1870, he spent a night at the Caledonia plantation, being entertained and taken out hunting by the general manager. The prince stayed in the manager's bungalow, a long building with a palm leaf roof and a wide veranda. He would have been able to see the factory chimney above the cane fields and to sniff the heavy smell of burnt sugar in the humid air as he stalked snipe and quail in the fields.[25] Edward Horsman's social position in England was enhanced by the estates, but he never found sweet prosperity. He had borrowed heavily to finance his purchases of land and machinery, discovering belatedly that profits usually did not cover his costs and interest payments. Soon after he bought the estates, the Crimean War drove up shipping rates and taxes. Between 1855 and 1868, the plantations ran up large overdrafts at Barings, and Horsman had to ask his wealthy brother-in-law, Sir John William Ramsden, repeatedly for money to pay off debts. Luckily for him, Ramsden was one of the largest landlords in Britain and was willing to guarantee Horsman's loans. Ramsden not only owned estates in Yorkshire and Scotland, but also had inherited the land on which the textile town of Huddersfield lay; its expanding rent roll went directly into his pockets. Ramsden family money and collateral kept the plantations afloat until 1874, when Horsman went bankrupt and turned over the title to the plantations to Ramsden as part of a general settlement of his debts.[26]

British Malaya

Horsman's agents had not made him rich, but they had transformed the southern half of Province Wellesley into a vast sugar plantation. By 1874, over 2,000 labourers from South India, South China, and Java cleared, planted, and harvested Horsman's fields. Chinese served as clerks and weigh masters in his offices and factory, while a German ran the refineries, and British men bossed all the rest.[27] Similar groups of men worked on

Straits Settlements, 1808–1884, Vol. 3: *Magistrates' Appeals* (Singapore: Singapore and Straits Printing Office, 1886), pp. 16–17

[25] "The Duke of Edinburgh at Penang," *Illustrated London News*, 5 February 1870, Issue 1579, p. 135

[26] "Letter E. Horsman to J. W. Ramsden," 26 September 1854, D/Pen/Hors/No. 6; "Letter, Dalgety DuCroz & Co., to Edward Horsman," 14 March 1868, D/Pen/Hors/No. 7.; "Letter J. W. Ramsden to E. Horsman," 22 December 1870, D/Pen/Hors/No. 8; "Declaration by way of Charge and Indemnity," 25 June 1876, D/Pen/Hors/ No. 10 (Cumbria Record Office, Whitehaven)

[27] "Labour returns, 1874–1875," in Appendix to "Report to the Rt. Hon. Edward Horsman, MP on his Sugar Estates at Penang," Turquand, Young & Co., London, September, 1875, pp. 61–63, D/Pen/Malaya/17/1 (Cumbria Record Office, Whitehaven)

the nearby Batu Kawan, Prye, and Trans-Krian estates. Collectively, they had drained swamps and built bungalows and barracks. They cut canals for drainage and transport, dividing the land into rectangular, homogenous fields. Within and around the estates, land had been repurposed and repopulated by a multi-lingual crew of male immigrants, dedicated to making money through industrial agriculture, aided and abetted by the British state. Owners and managers, whatever their birthplace, exploited land and labour using international networks. Industrial agriculture in Malaya was both a global enterprise and a colonial one. In 1859, the Straits Settlements administration glowingly described the sugar estates to other officials and the local audience of English-speakers: "Each factory may be considered as a centre from which civilization, with its attendant advantages, is diffused throughout the neighbourhood ... The labourers employed upon the different estates are well paid and otherwise cared for; and the whole, as a scene of well applied industry, forms a pleasing contrast to those districts which have not yet been benefited by the introduction of European skill, energy, and capital."[28] The official point of view coupled paternalist benevolence and private profit making, seeing both as agents of local improvement. No one asked the workers, however, for their opinions.

The benefits of European "energy" are hard to detect in the Batu Kawan and Horsman estates today, which seem relatively isolated. Travel to them from Penang begins with a leisurely ferry ride from Georgetown across the straits and then a drive south through coconut plantations and roads bordered with oil palms. Batu Kawan village, a collection of small shophouses surrounding a Chinese temple called Peace for Ten Thousand Generations, dedicated to Xuan Tian Shang Di, the God of War, lies on an unmarked road between the Jajawi and Tengah rivers. It is nested within oil palm fields and the grey concrete of rising industrial estates.[29] A rutted overgrown lane leads to the shell of an abandoned manager's bungalow with empty windows and broken tile floors. Several miles to the south, between the small town of Nibong Tebal and the Krian River, thousands of acres of oil palm trees cover the land that once was the Horsman estates of Caledonia and Victoria, hiding the remaining manager's house and the sites of earlier factories and offices.

The current obscurity of these places belies their earlier importance and connectedness. Each of these estates was in regular communication via land, water, and wire with other places in the British Empire, from

[28] Straits Settlements, "Annual Report for 1859–1860," in Robert L. Jarman, *Annual Reports of the Straits Settlements, 1855–1941* (Archive Editions, 1998), Vol. 1, p. 223
[29] I would like to thank Mr Chew and Elwyn Chew for their tour of Batu Kawan and for information on its temple.

London to Hong Kong. From the 1850s, managers and workers travelled frequently by steam launches and bullock carts to and from the Penang Harbour. Letters could be sent from the government-run post office in Nibong Tebal to Penang, where Peninsular and Oriental Line vessels picked up mail regularly. The laying of submarine cables from Europe to India in 1870 and then quickly on to Penang and Singapore brought the peninsula into a fast global communications network, which reached local post offices as telegraph lines spread inland. It was this government-sponsored and subsidized communications network that enabled the plantations to survive as international businesses, taking advantage of their position within the British Empire. The support of the British state for export agriculture was both substantial and consistent. A discussion of the Penang Sugar Estates will demonstrate some of the forms that it took.

A Colonial Planter Digs In: John William Ramsden and the Penang Sugar Estates

The classic story of a successful businessman centres on individual merit. Extraordinary intelligence and talent combined with hard work and determination allow a handful of people to rise to the top as a result of their personal qualities. Malcolm Gladwell reminds us, however, of the importance of several other factors: patronage and parentage, time, place, and culture.[30] People achieve extraordinary things in part because of when and where they were born, because of the institutions and helpers surrounding them, and because of the cultural advantages they inherited. This was definitely the case for Malayan sugar growers and manufacturers, who flourished during the relatively short window of time between the ending of slavery in the older sugar colonies of the British Caribbean and the rise of large-scale sugar production in Europe, Cuba, Java, and Hawaii later in the century. As the geography of world sugar production was reorganized, the British Empire offered planters comparative advantages: imperial infrastructures, the security shield of the British Navy and the Indian Army, and the huge size of the British imperial market. Those who bet on Malaya as a venue for sugar production did so because of its location within the British Empire and because of their enthusiasm for its land and climate.

In 1874, Sir John William Ramsden took over his brother-in-law's plantations. A baronet and Member of Parliament, he knew virtually nothing about Southeast Asia or sugar cultivation, but unlike Edward Horsman, he was curious enough to learn and soon became involved in

---

[30] Malcolm Gladwell, *Outliers: The Story of Success* (New York: Little, Brown and Co., 2008), p. 19

their management. The London solicitors, Turquand, Young & Co., advised him that the estates needed reorganization, better management, and expansion in order to make money.[31] Ramsden accepted their advice and threw his influence and capital into turning the plantations into a profitable business for himself and his heirs. Although he never visited Malaya, John Ramsden remained sufficiently impressed by the company's prospects that he regularly advanced money to managers so that they could expand his landholdings. Not only did they obtain adjoining tracts in Province Wellesley, but by 1900, the company had secured from the government several thousand acres in the Krian area and in southern Perak. Penang Sugar Estate agents also bought land in Johore and Kedah, and they negotiated to buy Batu Kawan, Prye, and at least one of Khaw Boo Aun's estates.[32] As the Empire expanded in western Malaya, so did Ramden's holdings, which reached 44,000 acres by 1914. In his obituary, the *Straits Echo* claimed that he had "a larger and more valuable interest than any other European in landed property in British Malaya."[33] Ramsden used the institutions and networks of the British Empire to build a successful international agribusiness, one that depended upon colonial control of land and labour.

Sir John Ramsden was a "gentlemanly capitalist" with deep pockets, discipline, and patience. Owner of 150,000 acres of land in Great Britain, he had plenty of collateral to back his Malayan projects, as well as a rising need to supplement an income that depended heavily on agricultural prices and rents, which fell sharply in the United Kingdom during the depression of 1873–96. Educated at Eton and Trinity College Cambridge, Ramsden can be called a "broad-acred baronet," a man who oversaw multiple estates in Scotland and Yorkshire, as well as Bulstrode in Buckinghamshire, which his wife inherited from her father, the twelfth Duke of Somerset.[34] A practical, energetic man, Ramsden preferred

---

[31] Turquand and Young, "Report on the Sugar Estates, 1875"

[32] "Letter J. Arnold to J. Turner, 12 November 1897," Vol. 24, section 1; "Letter John Turner to J. Arnold, 6 May 1898," Vol. 24, section 2; "Letter J. Turner to R. G. Watson, Secretary of Government, Perak, 2 Sept., 1898," and "Letter John Turner to J. Arnold, 9 Sept. 1898," Vol. 25, section 2, in Penang Sugar Estates Company, Ltd., "Letters and Papers," Coll. Misc. 0373 (Archive, London School of Economics); "Letter Waterson Simons & Co. to J. Turner, 3 Nov., 1898," and "Letter J. Turner to J. Arnold, 4 April 1899" and "Letter R. G. Watson, Acting Secretary to the Government of Perak, to J. Turner, 16 Nov. 1898," in Straits Sugar Company, "Letters and Papers of the Straits Sugar Company," Vol. 1, n.p., Mss. 644.1 p. 19 (APS)

[33] "Death of Sir John Ramsden: A Great Landowner," *The Straits Echo Mail Edition*, 17 April 1914 (West Yorkshire Archive, Leeds)

[34] The phrase is from P. J. Cain and A. G. Hopkins, *British Imperialism: Innovation and Expansion 1688–1914* (London: Longman, 1993), p. 44. Also, Donald Southgate, *The Passing of the Whigs, 1832–1886* (London: Macmillan, 1962), p. 97

Figure 1.2 Sir John William Ramsden and his family at Bulstrode, their estate in Buckinghamshire, c. 1899

hunting, riding, and fishing to London society, and he spent much time worrying about his rents and the condition of his estates. Sugar cultivation allowed him to diversify his holdings at a time when imperial investments paid more than domestic ones, and he seems to have enjoyed thinking about tropical agriculture, albeit from a distance.[35] From the age of 43, he built the Penang plantations into his life, treating them as a family estate, one of a group which collectively supported the Ramsdens' income, social position, and political power (see Figure 1.2). "High farming" was a classic avocation of the English gentry, and Ramsden seems to have preferred it to high politics, which he had tried as a young man, but not excelled in.[36]

[35] For information on the comparative profitability of imperial investments, see Lance E. Davis and Robert A. Huttenback, *Mammon and The Pursuit of Empire: The Political Economy of British Imperialism, 1860–1912* (Cambridge, UK: Cambridge University Press, 1987).

[36] Elected to Parliament in 1853 at age 22, John William Ramsden served as Under-Secretary for War for 10 months in 1857 and 1858, being appointed on the strength of two good speeches in the House of Commons, kinship with the Dundas and Fitzwilliam families, and his reputation as a gentleman. This was his one experience of high office, although he sat in the House of Commons for most of the period until 1886, voting with

Making the plantations profitable was a decades-long process involving London and Penang managers, colonial officials, and field workers, all operating under the oversight of British institutions and British law. In 1876, Ramsden arranged for incorporation of the business as the Penang Sugar Estates, Ltd., with a declared capital of £250,000 and a head office in London. Whenever additional funds were needed for new equipment or for additional land, he simply borrowed more money from British insurance companies. His loans were secured by his Huddersfield rents, which easily covered his interest payments.[37] This pattern of finance continued until after 1900, when the capital needs of several new plantations and a shift from sugar to rubber cultivation convinced him to adopt more conventional forms of raising money. As he bought more land, several new companies were floated on the London stock exchange, and a limited number of friends, army officers, widows, and Straits businessmen were allowed to buy shares.[38] In each case, however, Ramsden kept over 50 per cent for himself and his son, John Frecheville Ramsden. Those outside his immediate family remained passive investors without any power. The Penang Sugar Estates and its daughter companies were his hobbies, and he took pride in setting policies and giving advice.

John Ramsden and his managers were determined to do well in the global sugar business, and by various measures they succeeded. From its beginnings, the Penang Sugar Estates was one of the largest and most technologically sophisticated of the European-owned sugar producers in Malaya. Its original landholdings dwarfed the typical Chinese-owned sugar estate of 500 acres or less, and they were several times the size of competing European firms. A European visitor in the 1880s remarked that six of the nine large sugar estates in Province Wellesley were owned by the Penang Sugar Estates, making them the largest single producer of sugar in the region. Their refineries, touted as "the last word in modernity," also processed the canes of smaller producers. Around 1900, the Penang Sugar Estates in Province Wellesley produced about 5,500 tons of sugar annually, which

the Liberals. He ended his career as a strong Unionist, breaking with the Liberals over their reformist policies on Ireland. See Sir George Douglas and Sir George Dalhousie Ramsay, Eds., *The Pamure Papers* (London: Hodder and Stoughton, 1908), Vol. 2, pp. 376–377; Michael Stenton, Ed., *Who's Who of British Members of Parliament*, Vol. 1, 1832–1885 (Hassocks Sussex: Harvester Press, 1976), p. 323.

[37] John William Ramsden, "Penang Estate Financial Accounts, 1876–1882," D/Pen/Malaya/1/8, D/Pen/Malaya/ 1/6 (1882) (Cumbria Record Office Whitehaven), and Ramsden Collections 8/2, "Yearly Accounts, 1861–1895/96," Box 45 (West Yorkshire Archive, Leeds)

[38] BT 31/191391/106499 (National Archive London)

amounted to roughly 15 per cent of the total amount of sugar exported that year from the entire Malay Peninsula.[39]

Penang Sugar Estates, Ltd. was an international company that depended upon networks created within the British Empire for its operations. It had an owner who remained in Yorkshire and Scotland most of the time, a London secretary and directors, sales agents operating in Penang, a general manager who lived on the Caledonia estate in Province Wellesley, and a crew of assistants and overseers divided among the separate plantations. A tiny head office in the City of London, staffed by a clerk, a hired secretary, and a company director (E. M. Underdown) handled routine administrative details and correspondence, collecting and transmitting data on prices, markets, and shipping. In addition, it recruited all the European staff, made decisions about production technology, and purchased supplies and equipment. It relayed Ramsden's decisions about long-term business strategy and interfered constantly in small operational details, although daily decisions remained under the control of plantation managers and overseers. Face-to-face contacts between British directors and those who grew the cane and produced the sugar were rare. Although growing numbers of steamboats combined with the opening of the Suez Canal in 1869 cut sailing times and distances between London and Singapore dramatically, a trip between those two cities still took about a month around 1880.[40] The length and cost of the voyage meant that supervisory visits took place about once a decade, a situation that imposed only modest restraints upon plantations' middle management. Letters sent by the imperial mail service were the fragile but steady channel of communication between the British owners and Malayan employees. The management of Penang Sugar rested on a boundless faith in the global transferability of European agricultural and engineering knowledge. Farming and refining techniques from Caribbean plantations would apply to Southeast Asia; land management insights from Yorkshire estates would work in Malaya; Scottish-built machinery could be introduced in the tropics with little change. Malaya was "virgin land" that could be

---

[39] "Travel and Colonization: A Five Years' Sojourn in Province Wellesley," *The Field, the Country Gentleman's Newspaper*, 3 July 1880, p. 39. Tan, "Chinese Sugar Planting," *Malaysia in History*; Tate, *The R. G. A. History*, pp. 122–126. The amount of profit generated by the company is difficult to calculate, but an audit done in 1882 announced a 4.4 per cent return annually on Ramsden's initial investment. Lynn Hollen Lees, "International Management in a Free-Standing Company: The Penang Sugar Estates, Ltd., and the Malayan Sugar Industry, 1851–1914," *Business History Review*, 81 (Spring 2007), pp. 27–57

[40] Adam W. Kirkaldy, *British Shipping: Its History, Organization, and Importance* (New York: 1970, reprint of 1914 ed.), pp. 127–128, 132–136, 600

transformed into a British garden with an imported combination of machinery, chemistry, and agronomy.

The sugar business depended upon far-flung, active networks of exchange. The stream of letters sent after 1876 by company employees every two weeks between London and Penang testifies to a constant circulation of information within the company, and it triggered international flows of commodities. Newspapers and books flowed into the estates by post while money orders went out to India, China, and the Netherlands Indies. After 1882, telephones linked the estates to a Penang office and local police stations. A north-south railway opened several station stops on Penang Sugar land in 1900, permitting easy travel from Prai to northern Perak, and later, to Singapore.[41] Managers, staff, and field workers used these networks, not only to move to the plantations, but also to retreat from them and to retain contacts with kin and country.

The daily operation of the estates depended upon far-flung networks of supply. The estates bought rice from Calcutta and Burma, spirits from Scotland, and tea from India. Managers ordered a billiard table from London. They bought bicycles, telephones, and typewriters from local agents who imported them from Europe. When cane plants in the fields became diseased, managers consulted European botanists and imported different varieties of cane from Fiji, Mauritius, Queensland, and Java. They corresponded with H. E. Ridley of the Singapore Botanic Gardens, who sent seeds and seedlings, which he in turn drew from the network of imperial gardens stretching from Kew across the Atlantic and Indian Oceans.[42] The sugar factories at Caledonia and the other company estates used Glasgow-made refining equipment brought by ship to Penang and installed by Scottish engineers. German sugarboilers and Dutch agronomists advised them on refining and planting techniques.[43]

Once sugar was produced, finding the best prices globally remained a challenge. Long-distance communication remained slow because managers found cable transmissions too expensive. Letters had to suffice,

[41] "Annual Report of the Straits Settlement for 1885," in Jarman, *Annual Reports*, Vol. 3, p. 91; *The Singapore and Straits Directory for 1900* (Singapore: Fraser and Neave, Ltd., 1900), p. 231; "Fifty Years of Railways in Malaya, 1885–1935," *The Far Eastern Review* (April 1936), Vol. 32, pp. 157–158

[42] "Travel and Colonisation: A Five Years' Sojourn in Province Wellesley," *The Field: the Country Gentleman's Newspaper*, 3 July 1880, p. 3; "Letter of Joseph Sargant to John Arnold, 1 December 1899," in Penang Sugar Estates Company Ltd., "Letters and Papers," Vol. 26, Coll. Misc. 0373 (Archive, London School of Economics); see also Richard Drayton, *Nature's Government: Science, Imperial Britain, and the "Improvement" of the World* (New Haven: Yale University Press, 2000).

[43] "Letters J. Arnold to J. Turner, 14 October 1898, 8 December 1898, 14 April 1899," in Penang Sugar Company Estates, Ltd., "Letters and Papers," Vol. 25, Coll. Misc. 0373 (Archive, London School of Economics)

even for the all-important price comparisons between European and Asian markets. Using newspaper stories, mailed reports from local agents, and gossip in the ports, company agents sent cargoes where they guessed that prices were highest. Shipments regularly went to London, Singapore, Rangoon, and Calcutta. A fail-safe destination was the huge Jardine Matheson factory in Hong Kong, which took lower grades of semi-processed sugar from growers in South China and the Straits Settlements to refine it into a high-grade product for urban consumers.[44] Although local demand for white sugar was growing, large-scale Malayan producers wanted to feed a global sugar craving, and imperial communication and distribution networks helped them do it.

Helping Hands of the Imperial Government

Despite their rhetoric of free labour and free enterprise, plantations in British Malaya demanded and received substantial support from the colonial government. Land rights and many of their workers came through official channels, but more broadly, the business required the infrastructures of empire. Managers used government-built roads, bridges, telegraphs, and post offices. They relied on state law courts, police, doctors, and colonial hospitals to keep their workers on the plantations and to keep them healthy. British rule surrounded the estates with a penumbra of infrastructures and approval. Through effective lobbying, estate managers turned government policies to their advantage, but they learned to conform, even if grudgingly, to the weak paternalist structures enacted into law. The state and local plantations created interlocking structures of cooperation, which translated imperial power into colonial rule.

Colonial governance in the Straits Settlements began as a branch of the government of India, which until 1858 was formally under the control of the East India Company. Penang was run from Calcutta, as were Melaka and Singapore. After these towns, which had become known as the Straits Settlements in 1826, were separated from India in 1867, the Colonial Office in London took over its administration. Its first local officials not only worked for the company, but also served in the British Army in India. Sir George Leith, who had participated in the campaigns against Tippoo Sultan in 1795 and worked his way up to the rank of Captain in a Madras-based infantry regiment, was appointed as the Lieutenant Governor

[44] Mazumdar, *Sugar and Society*; see also H. C. Prinsen Geerligs, *The World's Cane Sugar Industry: Past and Present* (Manchester: Norman Rodger, 1912)

between 1800 and 1803.[45] Their combination of military and commercial connections set the tone for a trader-friendly regime that depended heavily upon urban police forces in its early years.

State building began with the appointment of a Superintendent (1786–1799), later replaced by a Lieutenant-Governor (1800–1805) and Governor (1805–1946). In Penang from 1800, Committees of Assessors selected by the Lieutenant Governor or Governor from among rich European and Asian settlers advised on important policy decisions. A Police Department enforced the laws and patrolled the streets. A Recorder's Court, first established in 1807, administered the common law, both civil and criminal, on Penang Island and, later, in Province Wellesley. Aided by appointed Justices of the Peace, British recorders, councillors, and district officials held courts daily in settlements throughout the area. British administrators and military men hired police, constructed jails, and welcomed army units from India. Since colonial spaces required infrastructures, a small public works department soon took on the duty of constructing and repairing bridges, roads, and public buildings.

By 1850, when detailed reports began to be published, colonial administration had expanded to include tax collecting, postal and medical services, and modest support for Christian churches. In 1846 in Province Wellesley near the sugar estates, the government stationed an assistant resident, Captain Hay Ferrier of the Madras Native Infantry, who served as both Chief Magistrate and Superintendent of Police, aided by a small staff of Eurasian and Asian clerks and translators, tax collectors, a resident apothecary, and a crew of convicts who worked on construction jobs.[46] This establishment expanded by 1875 to include multiple police stations, courts, and jails, adding also a surveyor, a hospital, and land and coroner's offices.[47]

Public order and public works got the lion's share of attention and support until late in the century, when growing amounts of money and attention went toward public health and education. Two surgeons trained in Britain and their staff of South Asian and Eurasian apothecaries and vaccinators ran three public hospitals and several dispensaries; they also examined Indian labourers at plantation hospitals. Similar medical

[45] Nordin Hussin, *Trade and Society in the Straits of Melaka: Dutch Melaka and English Penang, 1780–1830* (Singapore: NUS Press, 2007), p. 239

[46] Jarman, "Annual Report for 1855–1856," in Jarman, *Annual Reports*, Vol. 1, pp. 3–4, 7, 10, 54–59; *The Straits Times Almanac, Calendar and Directory for 1846* (Singapore: Straits Times Press, 1846), pp. 29–39

[47] *The Straits Calendar and Directory for the Year 1865* (Singapore: Commercial Press, 1865), pp. 3–8; *The Colonial Directory of the Straits Settlements for 1875* (Singapore: Mission Press, 1875)

establishments were organized in other parts of the Straits Settlements and the Protected Native States.[48] In 1883, the Straits Settlements' governor announced his intention to bring "the native races in our country districts into closer contact with the Government." People who had experienced colonial authorities primarily as police and tax collectors, he hoped, would soon see officials "as taking an interest in their general welfare ... as friends and advisors."[49]

Since authorities were determined not to tax trade or to levy high rents, they turned to consumption taxes for money to support this fast-growing army of officials. Their gaze fell on the entertainments and pleasures of the local Asian populations: opium, gambling, betel nut, and locally brewed liquor. Public auctions sold monopoly rights to sell these goods in return for set annual payments to the colonial government. The profits from these revenue farms, which were run by syndicates of wealthy Chinese, gave the colonial state guaranteed and growing revenue. The financial viability of the Straits Settlements, therefore, rested on an alliance between the Chinese revenue farmers and British administrators, primarily at the expense of Chinese labourers.[50]

By the 1880s, local people had encountered colonial authorities in multiple settings, but a growing number of those authorities had Asian faces and were the multi-lingual assistants of British bosses. Malaya was not a settlement colony, and there were too few Europeans to staff its many courts, police stations, jails, and hospitals. Delegation to Asian subordinates made colonial government and international business possible, and it created a growing group of middling status – educated men whose income, aspirations, consumption patterns, and identities distinguished them from the masses of labourers, miners, and farmers, as well as the few elite families who had inherited high rank within their own cultures. Social theorists would include them as part of the middle classes. This group was of sociological importance in colonial settings, as well as in European countries. Scholars studying the British Empire have used the labels of "collaborator" or "compradore" to describe these people of middling status, although neither captures the hybridity, the multiplicity of loyalties, and the growing self-confidence of this group, whose political importance grew over time. By-products of colonial rule, these multi-lingual men both helped to build plantation colonialism and, later, also

[48] Leonore Manderson, *Sickness and the State: Health and Illness in Colonial Malaya, 1870–1914* (Cambridge: Cambridge University Press, 1996), pp. 128, 143–144
[49] "Address of his Excellency the Governor Sir Frederick Aloysious Weld to the Legislative Council, 6 July 1883," in Jarman, ed., *Annual Reports*, Vol. 2, p. 627
[50] Hussin, *Trade*, pp. 237–239, 241, 253–255; Carl A. Trocki, *Opium and Empire: Chinese Society in Colonial Singapore, 1800–1910* (Ithaca: Cornell University Press, 1990)

helped to undermine it.[51] They mediated the daily operations of the Empire and the rigid hierarchies established by the British, which proved impossible to maintain in practice.

The power of colonial authorities was rooted in their effective control of land. In a territory where virtually anyone could take possession of a parcel by clearing it, the East India Company and, later, British administrators in the Straits Settlements and Protected Native States, introduced European forms of land tenure and private property. Systems of communal use and shifting cultivation fell victim to a pattern of individual ownership, certified by legal titles registered with the state. It took decades, however, to organize the new system and to gain acceptance of its ground rules. To attract settlers into Penang and Singapore after their founding, the early governors granted land in perpetuity to friends and would-be cultivators, but soon decided they had been overly generous, attempting to restrict the sizes of plots and to tax them effectively. Nevertheless, through protests and passive resistance, planters effectively blocked East India Company attempts to introduce more stringent land codes and to substitute long leases for outright ownership. In Melaka, administrators had to contend with Dutch land grants and their recognition of local Malay custom and rulers' rights, which slowed changes in that area. During the 1850s, however, a proper land survey was carried out in the Straits Settlements, permitting the accurate recording of boundaries, and a uniform land policy for the colony was finally imposed. It provided agricultural investors with secure tenure and cheap land. As other parts of the peninsula passed into British control, planters, well organized in lobbying groups, helped to work out land policies, participating fully in the 1896 conference that produced a land code for the Federated Malay States.[52]

John Ramsden and his agents learned how this land policy actually operated when they took over Edward Horsman's estates. They found that boundaries were not clearly set and titles were lacking. Although existing deeds specified that if one-quarter of the holding was not cleared

---

[51] Ronald Robinson, "Non-European Foundations of European Imperialism: Sketch for a Theory of Collaboration," in Roger Owen and Bob Sutcliffe, *Studies in the Theory of Imperialism* (London: Longman, 1972), pp. 117–142; see also Ulbe Bosma and Remco Raben, *Being "Dutch" in the Indies: A History of Creolisation and Empire, 1500–1920* (Athens: Ohio University Press, 2008); Henrike Donner, ed., *Being Middle-Class in India: A Way of Life* (London: Routledge, 2011).

[52] Tate, *RGA History*, pp. 29–38, 185. The 1896 code provided for surveying and registration of claims, with moderate requirements that one-quarter of the land be cultivated by the fifth year of a grant. Quit-rents and other costs could be negotiated with state governments. See also "Annual Report for 1855–6," in Jarman, *Annual Reports*, Vol. 1, p. 11.

and cultivated within five years, land reverted to the state, Ramsden's agents negotiated, and the governor signed, updated legal titles to 15,753 acres in 1875. The estates then fostered a lively local land market. Local Malays and Chinese bought parcels from the estates and sold off some of their holdings to the Penang Sugar Estates, allegedly "clamouring for titles" to land received. What before had taken place informally now had to be registered, measured, and approved by the state. Papers were precious. When, in 1887, estate managers found their deeds in an open safe, mildewed and half eaten by ants, they had to reregister their holdings – a slow and expensive process, which must have been much more difficult for non-Anglophone Malays and Chinese.[53] As the estates expanded, managers negotiated with state governments in Perak, Johore, and Selangor for more land on advantageous terms, having no qualms about moving into indirectly ruled areas. While land codes set the parameters, government agents could adjust quit rents, taxes, and customs duties to their or to the estates' advantage. After hard bargaining in 1898 and 1899, Penang Sugar Estates agents bought tracts that totalled more than 13,500 acres in lower Perak near Teluk Anson. They acquired what became the Rubana and Gedong estates for only $2 per acre (a small sum in Straits dollars), which could be paid over ten years as they cleared and cultivated it. Not only was the grant in perpetuity, but there were no annual taxes or quit rents to pay for land planted in sugar. Moreover, the government pledged to keep export duties low.[54]

While any would-be planter, whatever his resources, could apply for land, the European estates had more capital and greater political support from colonial administrators than did Chinese or South Asian proprietors. Frank Swettenham, who spent twenty-five years helping to administer Perak and Selangor, was an enthusiastic supporter of "liberality" toward landowners and "all those willing to risk their capital and health in a new country." In his view, European planters, men "of the right sort," if encouraged would be able to turn "unexplored and inhabited jungle" into flourishing fields of coffee, sugar, tea, and other tropical products.[55]

[53] "Report on the Sugar Estates, 1875," pp. 61–63, D/Pen/Malaya/17/1; "Letter from J. MacDonald to J. Ray, 18 October 1884," Vol. 2, p. 218; "Letter J. Low to J. Ray, 4 October 1884," Vol. 11, p. 209; "Letter J. Low to J. Ray, 12 May 1887," Vol. 13, pt. 2, p. 161, in PSE, "Letters and Papers," Mss 644.1 p.19 (APS)

[54] "Letter R. G. Watson, Acting Secretary of Perak to J. Turner, 16 November 1898," Vol. 24, n.p., in Penang Sugar Estates Company, "Letters and Papers" (Archive, London School of Economics); The Singapore and Straits Directory for 1904 (Singapore: Fraser & Neave, 1904), pp. 488–489

[55] Frank Swettenham, who served as resident in Perak and Selangor during the years 1875–1876, 1882–1884, 1889–1895 and Governor General of the Federated Malay States between 1896 and 1901, was one of the most consistent supporters of plantation agriculture in Malaya, judging it to be better for the region than tin mining.

Province Wellesley and the large, modern plantations there became poster children for the success of this policy.

Over time, imperial rule of the Straits Settlements produced a self-satisfied administrative elite. In the eyes of the appointed officials, British control was successful and benign. The Governor, Sir Frederick Weld, bragged to a London audience in 1884, "Happy is the colony which keeps free from little wars, successfully and noiselessly rules four or five different races, carries out great public works as fast as labour and means of supervision will permit, and yet has surplus revenue to lend and invest, and such a colony is the . . . the Straits Settlements."[56] These comments communicated no sense of irony or self-doubt, and they set a congratulatory tone for British rhetoric.

Finding Workers to Till the Fields

Economic development depended upon far more than owners and land titles for its success. Someone had to do the work, and managers looked to global empires to find labourers because the cost of tempting local workers into their fields was more than they were willing to pay. After slavery became illegal in the British Empire, planters in Caribbean and Indian Ocean colonies negotiated with the government of India and British officials in London to set up an international system of indentured labour to replace the unfree workers they had lost. Shipments of convicts from British India already had set a precedent for the use of South Asians in work gangs throughout the Empire. Between 1830, when the first shipments of Indian farm hands went to the island of Réunion, and 1920, when this state-sponsored export of unfree labour was ended, at least two million people bound by long-term contracts to a single employer left India to take on foreign labouring jobs. This flow of workers represented an effort to "regulate labour on a global and transnational scale" by imperial states.[57] In 1857, European proprietors on Penang

F. A. Swettenham, "British Rule in Malaya" in Paul H. Kratoska, *Honorable Intentions: Talks on the British Empire in South-East Asia Delivered at the Royal Colonial Institute, 1874–1928* (Singapore: Oxford University Press, 1983), p. 188.

[56] Sir Frederick A. Weld, "The Straits Settlements and British Malaya," quoted in Paul H. Kratoska, ed., *Honorable Intentions*, p. 43

[57] The similarities of indentured and convict labour have been pointed out by Clare Anderson, "Convicts and Coolies: Rethinking Indentured Labour in the Nineteenth Century," *Slavery and Abolition*, Vol. 30, No. 1 (2009), pp. 93–109; see also David Northrup, *Indentured Labor in the Age of Imperialism, 1834–1922* (Cambridge: Cambridge University Press, 1995), pp. 156–157. Rachel Sturman suggests that arrangements for indentured labour be considered as part of international human rights campaigns; see "Indian Indentured Labor and the History of International Rights Regimes," *AHR*, Vol. 119, No. 2 (2014), p. 1465.

island and in Province Wellesley reminded the Straits government that they were "dependent for all the ordinary heavy work of cultivation, as well as for most kinds of skilled labour, on the natives of China and India, ... [and] natives of Java and other Eastern Islands."[58] European planters, who had rigid ideas about the wages they would pay and the control needed over labour, insisted that Malays were neither interested in nor suited for the work of sugar growing.[59] They also saw the Malay Peninsula in the nineteenth century as virtually uninhabited. The idea of *Terra nullius*, endorsed by Locke in his account of America's aboriginal emptiness, had long justified British imperial confiscation; but in this case, such claims were not far-fetched. Scholars estimate that in 1800 the overall density of the Malay Peninsula was only 3.4 persons per square kilometre, only one-tenth that of South Asia then, and Malayan population growth rates remained low through the early nineteenth century, depressed by local wars and disease.[60] People, rather than land, remained the scarce resource.

But Malaya lay at the centre of a vast migration zone stretching west across the Bay of Bengal and east through the South China Sea, in which movement intensified after 1850. Adam McKeown calculates that between 48 and 52 million people moved from India and southeastern China into Southeast Asia, the South Pacific, and the Indian Ocean rim between 1846 and 1940. In this region, emigration was a family strategy designed for survival in territories where poverty, famine, disease, and political troubles combined to limit economic opportunities for many, and where long-distance trade had flourished for centuries. Within this zone, the Malay Peninsula was a popular destination. Possibly 11 million Chinese, mostly men from Guangdong and Fujian provinces, sailed from Swatow, Amoy, and Hong Kong to the Straits Settlements, and then several million of these went on to Sumatra; at least 4 million Indians came to the Malay peninsula, arriving by the thousands every year in the

---

[58] "Regine vs. Willans," in James William Norton Kyshe, ed., *Cases Heard and Determined in Her Majesty's Supreme Court of the Straits Settlements, 1808–1884*, Vol. 3: *Magistrates' Appeals* (Singapore: Singapore and Straits Printing Office, 1886), pp. 17–18

[59] This was normal practice in the industry. The early sugar estates on Caribbean islands put African slaves into their fields, replacing them in the later 1830s with Indian and Chinese indentured workers. Planters in Mauritius, Australia, Hawaii, and Fiji imported contract labourers from India, Japan, and the South Pacific. See Walton Look Lai, *Indentured Labor, Caribbean Sugar: Chinese and Indian Migrants to the British West Indies, 1838–1918* (Baltimore, 1993); Marina Carter, *Servants, Sirdars, and Settlers: Indians in Mauritius, 1834–1874* (Delhi: Oxford University Press, 1995); David Northrup, *Indentured Labor in the Age of Imperialism, 1834–1922* (Cambridge: Cambridge University Press, 1995)

[60] Anthony Reid, *Southeast Asia in the Age of Commerce, 1450–1680*, Vol. 1: *The Lands below the Winds* (New Haven: Yale University Press, 1988), table 2, p. 14

century before World War II.[61] They travelled along well-established routes as sojourners, moving into active labour markets and returning home as they were able. Much of this movement was circular until the 1920s, when growing numbers settled permanently in British Malaya.[62]

This constant flow of people along "self-reproducing grooves" was encouraged movement, not random travel by individuals. Thousands of brokers, merchants, and ship captains, paid by the head for their charges, made money by recruiting new migrants not only to Malaya but also to the Caribbean, Ceylon, Mauritius, and Natal. Stories abound of deception and kidnapping, but many emigrants also faced coercion from family to earn elsewhere, and others wished to escape a variety of disappointments and local frustrations. Madras officials noticed that after the failure of the monsoon rains in 1853, many grain farmers in the region left their land, looking for work overseas.[63] A Madras government report accused recruiters in 1870 of "representing, in bright colours, prospects of enrichment and advance" and generally misleading ignorant, illiterate people, but officials found it difficult to prosecute cases of suspected fraud because those involved generally asserted their willingness to emigrate and had already accepted money and food from the labour brokers. One group of unhappy emigrants wrote in 1843 to the Madras Emigration Agent. Who had helped them write the petition and direct it to the proper person is unclear. "We are poor and distressed people mostly cultivators of the interior countries, resolved to embark for Mauritius for the purpose of bettering our circumstances ... There are nearly 70 maistries (recruiters), deputies, under maistries and collectors in men and women, the whole from Pondicherry come for the sole purpose of this traffic. They are all old hands who have robbed many thousands of poor fellows." They complained that they had been cheated of the money advanced to them, locked up, and "shipped off without the means of putting one quarter of a rupee into the hands of parting friends and relatives who come from distant places to bid us farewell."[64] Despite

[61] Adam McKeown, "Global Migration, 1846–1940," *Journal of World History*, Vol. 15, 32 (June, 2004), pp. 156, 158; Adam McKeown, "Conceptualizing Chinese Diasporas, 1842–1949," *Journal of Asian Studies*, Vol. 58, No. 2 (May 1999), pp. 317–319
[62] Sunil S. Amrith, *Migration and Diaspora in Modern Asia* (Cambridge: Cambridge University Press, 2011), pp. 37, 49. Marina Carter estimates that at least two-thirds of all Indian indentured labourers did not return to India; many of this group died before they could return. See Marina Carter, *Voices from Indenture: Experiences of Indian Migrants in the British Empire* (London: Leicester University Press, 1996), p. 56.
[63] Marina Carter and Khal Torabully, *Coolitude: An Anthology of the Indian Labour Diaspora* (London: Anthem Press, 2002), p. 30
[64] Madras Public Consultations #248/4, March–April 1843, quoted in Carter, *Voices from Indenture*, pp. 69–70

their outrage, they presented themselves as intentional migrants, leaving with the knowledge of families. They objected not to leaving India but to extortion and to their mistreatment. Lies and forced detention are familiar themes in surviving depositions of labourers and their folksongs. "Oh recruiter, your heart is deceitful, your speech is full of lies" charges an Indian song, recorded in Fiji.[65]

British officials in India and the Straits Settlements helped to create a demographic imbalance among migrants. When Indian administrators signed labour migration agreements with British Guiana, other West Indian colonies, and Fiji, they stipulated that 40 women had to be sent for every 100 males (28 per cent), but they did not insist that such a clause be included in the Emigration Act of 1877 for the Straits Settlements. Each colony was free to make its own deals, and Straits authorities and plantation managers seem not to have worried about the comparative lack of South Asian females arriving as indentured workers. Moreover, the Madras Protector of Emigrants disparaged those women who passed through his port: "No female of good character emigrates, except with her husband, father, mother or some very near relation," and he suspected "bogus marriages and recent liaisons," concocted by women who had been prostitutes or "kept women" before setting sail. Remarking that syphilis was one of the "chief diseases" from which coolies suffered, A. M. MacGregor, the Protector of Indian Immigrants, recommended that females be "properly examined on arrival, for there have been several instances of Syphilis being communicated by new women."[66] Those charged with safeguarding emigrants' welfare saw women as creators of social problems, rather than as workers with rights. In Malaya, the colonial government did not try to use the indenture system to engineer family formation and the reproduction of workers.

Indian women ready and willing to sail away to a distant plantation were hard to find. Rural Indian women were commonly children when they married, and the 1883 Indian Immigration Act required that

---

[65] See Carter, *Voices from Indenture*; V. P. Vatuk, "Protest Songs of East Indians in British Guiana," *Journal of American Folklore*, Vol. 77 (1964), pp. 220–235; B. V. Lal, "Approaches to the Study of Indian Indentured Emigration with Special Reference to Fiji," *Journal of Pacific History*, Vol. 15.1 (1980), p. 68.

[66] Carter and Torabully, *Coolitude*, p. 52; "Report by the Principal Civil Medical Officer, Straits Settlements, Regarding the State of the Hospital at Batu Kawan Estate," *Straits Settlements Paper Laid before the Legislative Council*, No. 41, p. cccxxxiii; "Report on Indian Immigration for the year 1880," 12 April 1881, Straits Settlements, *Paper Laid before the Legislative Council*, No. 10, p. 70; Manderson, *Sickness*, p. 178; see also Philippa Levine, *Prostitution, Race, and Politics: Policing Venereal Disease in the British Empire* (New York: Routledge, 2003).

husbands had to give permission for wives to emigrate. Recruiters were instructed to verify a women's marital status before she was accepted as a contract labourer, and after 1883 colonial police checked stories when possible. Nevertheless, famines, family problems, widowhood, and poverty pushed women out of their households and onto the roads.[67] Ratna's story reflects similar ones, unrecorded: "My man left the house after he had been rebuked by my father-in law. I took my child and went looking for him in Ajodaji . . . I was told that my husband had gone to Calcutta. I went to Calcutta by train to search for him . . . I was told that he had already left two or three days earlier. I went to the wharf and . . . some people took my son off me and threatened me. I was put into the depot with my child and stayed there for two or three days before embarking on the ship."[68] She spent the rest of her life in Fiji on a sugar plantation. When outside their village and family structures, women like Ratna were easily exploited. Her desire to find her husband and to keep her son led her to agree to go to Fiji, and none of the officials supposedly monitoring her move interfered. Although in many ways a victim, Ratna developed the ability to survive on her own and to tell her story.

An advertisement from the recruiting firm of Ganapathy Pillay and Co. in the South Indian port of Negapatam in 1890 painted plantation work in Malaya in favourable colours. It promised "coolies" willing to go to Province Wellesley a wage of $3.60 per month [12 cents per day], free houses, medical care, fuel, and garden land, if they bound themselves for three years. It announced an advance of $1 and a month's worth of free food after arrival, describing a benign environment with a relatively low cost of living. Province Wellesley, they said, was "quite similar to our own places, and comfortable," a region where "many of our own countrymen are working on each estate." The ad neglected to mention that wages were paid only for tasks completed on full days worked, and that employers deducted about $2.20 per month for rice rations and passage costs, while levying fines for minor offences. While the very healthy, energetic, and obedient might earn enough to feed and clothe themselves decently, the average worker lost so many days from sickness, exhaustion, bad weather, or refusal to work that his monthly take-home pay was well below the estimated cost of living after deductions for passage costs and other debt. In addition, workers owed their employers a total of six days of work per week for thirty-six months, and their contracts were legally extended until

---

[67] Gaiutra Bahadur, *Coolie Woman: The Odyssey of Indenture* (Chicago: University of Chicago, 2014), pp. 26–28

[68] Ratna lived until at least 1979, when she told her story to a newspaper reporter. See *Fiji Sun*, 19 March 1979, pp. 8–9, quoted in Marina Carter, *Voices from Indenture*, p. 83.

they had completed them.[69] In practice, this meant that months of unrelenting hard toil left "coolies" in debt to their employers with little choice but to remain as nominally "free" labourers on plantations. Contracts were therefore open-ended in terms of time and repayment owed, reproducing the debt bondage of the Tamil countryside.

The contrast between the terms of a plantation labour contract and what was available on the open market in the Straits Settlements or the Native Protected States during the second half of the nineteenth century was extreme. Plantation wages for free workers around Penang were about 20 cents per day, while they rose to between 25 and 30 cents per day in the Native Protected States and Singapore, sometimes with free housing included. Later in the century, jobs building the railroad pushed wages even higher. Chinese workers had contracts of no more than one year, and they could earn $42 per year plus free food at mines in Perak and Selangor, as compared to $30 per year plus free food on an estate.[70] By leaving a plantation and moving a few miles into another jurisdiction or state, contract workers could therefore escape their debts and earn significantly more money; this information was common knowledge in British Malaya.[71] The plantation system had built into it two opposing tendencies: on the one hand, it entrapped contract workers in virtual debt peonage; on the other, it produced huge incentives for labourers to break their legally binding contracts and flee to the more favourable free markets nearby. This contradictory logic, in fact, reinforced the strength of British colonial rule in rural areas. The penal regime of the plantations maintained profits and productivity, while escape routes for the adventurous and the troublesome kept the system from exploding.

Direct testimonies from individuals about recruitment and travel to Malaya are rare. They met public officials in public settings where

---

[69] Plantation managers, defending their good treatment of their workers, told the 1890 Labour Commission that the average "coolie" completed and was paid for only 20.5 work days a month, which would have brought a male labourer in his first year $2.46 per month from which deductions for passage and food were taken. Since monthly living costs in Province Wellesley were estimated to be at least $2.40, workers went even more heavily in debt to their employers so that they could eat. The first year was the most difficult. By the third year of a contract, wages automatically rose to 14 or 15¢ for males, producing monthly incomes of $3.08, and the $12.00 legally capped cost of passage would have been paid off, but food costs and other debts remained. Straits Settlements, *Report of the Labour Commission of 1890* (Singapore: Government Printing Office, 1891), pp. 43–44, 52–56.

[70] *Report of the Labour Commission of 1890*, pp. 21, 46–47

[71] Even the Protector of Immigrants commented in 1880 that "Coolies have everything to gain and nothing to lose by desertion" because deserters could avoid paying their debts and earn higher wages. See Straits Settlements, A. M. MacGregor, "Report on Indian Immigration for the Year 1880," *Paper Laid before the Legislative Council*, 12 April 1881, No. 10, p. 68.

complaints could easily have brought retribution.[72] The Labour Commission of 1890 spoke to one estate labourer in Province Wellesley who said he was told that he could join his brother in Burma and to another who said he had been promised clerical, not field work. But at the same time, Rathan, a Tamil labourer working for the colonial government in South Perak, said that "he had been induced to leave his country with the promise of getting land to live on and cultivate and he had not been disappointed."[73] Tamils were aggressively prodded to emigrate, even if they were not literally deceived about what lay in store for them. In 1870 and 1871, indentured workers bound to Malaya were recruited primarily in Tamil Nadu coming from the districts of Tanjore, Tiruchirapalli, Madurai, Salem, and Coimbatore, areas inland from the port of Negapatam, from which they sailed. Indian government officials pressured Straits authorities and recruiters to work only in the Madras area because the earliest contract labourers to the peninsula had been Tamil speakers from that region, and they argued that all would benefit from having workers be able to communicate with one another and to work among kin and friends. Creating migration chains seems to have been official policy.[74] No systematic records of the caste backgrounds of these immigrant workers survived, but employers complained strongly about the many cooks, weavers, and other artisans unfitted for hard fieldwork who frequently were sent to their plantations.

A significant although unknown proportion of immigrant workers moved directly into debt bondage in Malaya in order to pay the costs of their passage. In a parallel movement across the Bay of Bengal, thousands of Chulias, Tamils, and Bengalis sailed to Penang and Singapore by contracting themselves to employers who agreed to pay for their passage. An itinerant labour force in South India was growing in the mid-nineteenth century under the pressures of British revenue policies and growing commercialization in South India. If already on the road to Madras looking for work, men were easy marks for labour recruiters, who promised good wages abroad. Brokers rounded up those who agreed to be indentured, locked them in labour depots, and then marched them onto departing ships, charging a fee for each passenger; a second set of middlemen took over in Penang and Singapore, housing and feeding immigrants until they signed contracts with employers, who repaid the

---

[72] Written records about the individual indentured workers going to Malaya seem not to have survived, but the group was similar to the Tamils who left South India for Mauritius and the Caribbean. For some of their testimonies, see Carter, *Voices*.

[73] Quoted in David Chanderbali, *Indian Indenture in the Straits Settlements, 1872–1910* (Leeds: Peepal Tree, 2008), pp.84, 108; *Report of the Labour Commission of 1890*, "Inspection Visits," p. 15.

[74] Chanderbali, *Indentured*, p. 106

many middlemen.[75] Between 1866 and 1910, a minimum of 250,000 Indian indentured labourers sailed to ports in the peninsula, and probably twice that number arrived under informally organized assisted passage schemes.[76] Managers sent trusted Tamil foremen (kanganies) to their home villages to find new workers, who contracted to repay passage costs from wages earned.[77] These labour foremen successfully lured tens of thousands of Indian labourers to Malayan plantations.

Chinese emigrants found themselves similarly trapped. Although some could raise money for their tickets, most emigrants from South China travelled via the "credit-ticket" system set up by coolie brokers in the ports. They financed the trips of "Chue Tsai" or "piglets," who were herded onto ships and after arrival held in lodging houses until a future employer was found to pay off the various recruiters. These emigrants then had to reimburse their bosses for passage costs.[78]

Chinese credit-ticket passengers found themselves drawn into and held within a Chinese community through membership in powerful sworn brotherhoods, clan and surname associations. These migrants lived together and worked together in gangs, under the thumb of foremen who spoke their same dialect and who handled negotiations with employers.[79] Unlike the South Asian population, these workers were shielded from the gaze of the state by headmen and by their communal associations. In effect, they were indirectly ruled, controlled more closely by their compatriots than by the colonial state. The government commission that investigated immigration in 1876 claimed that "the Government knows little or nothing of the Chinese ... and the immense majority of them know still less of Government."[80] In contrast, South Asians, who moved primarily to sugar and rubber plantations, were heavily monitored after 1870 by British colonial authorities, who inspected, interviewed, photographed, and listed them. Relatively few independent social organizations bound them

---

[75] Northrup, *Indentured Labor*, p. 53; Carter, *Voices from Indenture*, p. 66
[76] K. S. Sadhu, *Indians in Malaya: Some Aspects of Their Immigration and Settlement* (Cambridge, 1969), pp. 304–310; Drabble, *Economic History*, p. 67
[77] Chanderbali, *Indentured*, p. 117; Amrith, *Crossing*, p. 118
[78] Sunil S. Amrith, *Migration and Diaspora in Modern Asia* (Cambridge: Cambridge University Press, 2011); David Ludden, *Peasant History in South Asia* (Princeton: Princeton University Press, 1985), pp. 92–93; W. L. Blythe, "Historical Sketch of Chinese Labour in Malaya," *Journal of the Malayan Branch of the Royal Asiatic Society*, Vol. 20, No. 1 (1947), pp. 68–74
[79] Amrith, *Migration*, pp. 41–44; Kaoru Sugihara, ed., *Japan, China and the Growth of the Asian International Economy, 1850–1949* (Oxford: Oxford University Press, 2005)
[80] Straits Settlements, "Report of the Committee Appointed to Consider and Take Evidence upon the Condition of Chinese Labourers in the Colony," *Papers Laid before the Legislative Council*, 3 November 1876, p. ccxliv

together. When the Colonial Office took over administration of the Straits Settlements in 1867, sailing from India to Penang or Singapore suddenly became "emigration" rather than an internal trip from one part of British India to another. Existing Indian regulations did not mention Malaya as a legal destination for contract labourers leaving the country. No one noticed the illegality until 1870, when W. J. Hathaway, the man who administered the South Indian district of Tanjore, went public with the charge that recruiters regularly kidnapped local people, selling the women into prostitution and the men into coolie jobs. He then blocked all further labour emigration to the Straits Settlements. The resulting uproar soon spread to Penang and Singapore, where planters and colonial officials denounced the charges and began their own investigations. After much sound and fury, the government of India struck a deal with the Straits Settlements by which emigration would again be legal, in return for strict regulation of indentured workers' recruitment, transportation, wages, diet, contract, and treatment – new rules intended to protect them while satisfying the insatiable need for plantation labourers. After 1876, recruiters had to be listed and licensed, and they had to bring all potential labourers to depots in Negapatam or Madras for a government medical examination and a personal interview to ensure that they were willing and well-informed emigrants. Although contract labour was a global system within which specific destinations brought comparative advantages, recruiters gave would-be emigrants little or no information about their alternatives. Indian indentured labourers in Malaya received lower wages than their counterparts in Ceylon, Mauritius, or Caribbean colonies, and they had higher passage costs to repay. Overall, Tamil migrants in Malaya had fewer economic opportunities than Indians who chose to go to either Ceylon or Burma, and the trip was longer, as well as more expensive.[81] But migrants generally followed in the footsteps of kin and friends, and many of those relatives had already chosen Malaya.

Once transported to a second labour depot, in either Penang or Singapore, they were interviewed again. Contracts were signed and scrutinized to see that they met the requirements for minimum wages, maximum hours and terms of service. Workers also had to accept their liability for the entire amount of their recruitment and passage. The Straits Government grudgingly agreed to appoint and pay for an Emigration Agent and a Protector of Emigrants, who were jointly responsible for ensuring that laws were enforced and the workers fully informed of their rights and obligations. As in other British colonies around the world, Straits officials directly monitored the recruitment, transportation, and

[81] Chanderbali, *Indentured*, pp. 108–111

assignments of South Asian indentured workers, and they continued their oversight of them on plantations. The system of indentured migration represented not only a global system of labour transference and control but also an extension of colonial rule at the local level, which accepted the premises of workers' dependence and the state's responsibility for social welfare.[82]

Scrutiny of the Chinese took place only after their arrival in Malaya. Although it was much less intrusive than the monitoring of South Asian indentured workers, the colonial state took on some welfare responsibilities for Chinese immigrants. A Labour Ordinance of 1877 created the Chinese Protectorate, whose head examined Chinese contract labourers to guarantee their willingness to work in British Malaya; he also oversaw their contracts and conditions.[83] Most of these examinations had to have been perfunctory. Hundreds of workers arrived simultaneously to be processed within a few hours by a single British official. Shortly after he arrived in Singapore in 1883, William Evans, an aspiring civil servant of twenty-three, was sworn in as a magistrate and justice of the peace so that he could sign the labour contracts for the Chinese emigrants who flooded daily into his office. Evans, who admitted he could not understand what they were saying, had the role of witnessing each man sign his mark on a printed form, and then moving on to the next.[84] The system was designed to allow workers to object to their contracts, but its speed and workers' lack of information undermined its effectiveness.

Sir Frederick Weld, Governor of the Straits Settlements, announced in 1881, "I am convinced that the [Native States] have a great future, if we can give them population."[85] To advance this process, the Straits Settlements and Protected Native States partially subsidized the fares of contract labourers after 1887, and these governments administered the Negapatam emigration depot after 1890.[86] However many labourers sailed into Straits ports every year, they were not enough, and employers did not like most of those they did hire. They complained that the men were weak, sick, and untrained in farm labour. J. M. Vermont, the

[82] Chanderbali, *Indentured*, pp. 87–100; Sturman, "Indian Indentured Labor," p. 1457

[83] Chanderbali, *Indentured*, pp. 87–100; Tate, *RGA History*, pp. 155, 162. "Report of the Committee Appointed to Consider and Take Evidence upon the Condition of Chinese Labourers in the Colony," *Papers Laid before the Legislative Council of the Straits Settlements*, 3 November 1876, pp. 443–483

[84] "Letter William Evans to Sam Evans," 22 June 1883; "Letter William Evans to Mrs. Evans, 26 April, 1883," Evans Papers, PPMS 11, Box 1, file 1 (SOAS Archive, London)

[85] Government support for contract labour increased via subsidies to steamship companies; Straits Settlements, "Address of His Excellency Governor Sir Frederick Aloysius Weld, K. C. M. G. at a Meeting of the Legislative Council, 11 October, 1881," in "Annual Report for 1881," Jarman, editor, *Annual Reports*, p. 486

[86] Tate, *RGA History*, p. 166

manager of the Batu Kawan plantation, was the most outspoken. He described newcomers as "ignorant of all work, prone to laziness." J. Lamb of the Prye estate blamed workers' frequent hospitalizations and generally bad health on their poor diets in India and China. It was then aggravated by their eating too much after arrival.[87] After extensive interviews with planters, the Labour Commission of 1890 described the supply of Indian labour as "of insufficient quantity, defective quality, and [burdened by a] heavy cost of importation." But all wanted more of this allegedly unsatisfactory lot![88]

Official policy was to satisfy the local demand for labour. Planters' continued demand for more labourers eventually led them in 1907 to fund a government-administered Tamil Emigration Fund, which would subsidize workers' recruitment and transportation costs, leaving them debt free and effectively raising their take-home pay.[89] This change in the financial basis of contract labour directly benefitted Tamil emigrants. During the course of the century, more and more South Asian workers arrived without advance labour contracts or debts, putting them in a position to negotiate better conditions. Even if planters remained dissatisfied because they often lacked enough workers to till their own fields, the colonial government had by 1911 effected a significant expansion in the total supply of labour throughout Malaya. Their aim to convert birds of passage to a settled population was successful. The peninsula's population quadrupled between 1800 and 1911, growing from 500,000 to 2,300,000.[90] More emigrants remained in Malaya, and they benefitted too from the rising wages and better working conditions that obtained when plantations shifted from sugar to rubber production in the twentieth century.

Staffing the Penang Sugar Estates depended upon migration chains that linked the plantations to Scotland, the Caribbean, India, and China. Arthur Morrison, who managed the plantations for both Edward Horsman and John Ramsden until 1884, learned the sugar business in Demerara, a region of British Guiana, now Guyana, as did many other Malayan planters, including John Turner and William Duncan, who ran the estates from 1889 through 1921. Turner and Duncan, who moved from Keith in Scotland to Demerara in their late teens to work in the sugar

---

[87] Straits Settlements, "Letter from Mr. Lamb to the Protector of Immigrants, 10 February, 1879," and "Letter from J. M. Vermont to the Protector of Immigrants, 8 June 1879," in *Papers Laid before the Legislative Council by Command of His Excellency the Administrator*, No. 23 (24 July 1879) (Singapore: Government Printing Office, 1879), pp. cxli–cxlii, cclx

[88] *Report of the Labour Commission of 1890*, pp. 1, 14, 17, 42

[89] Chanderbali, *Indentured*, p. 122

[90] *Report of the Labour Commission of 1890*, p. 68; Drabble, *Economic History*, p. 90

Figure 1.3 Overseer and Tamil labourers transporting sugar cane, West Malaya, 1907

industry, kept in touch, as did Morrison, with former associates and friends, whom they occasionally tried to recruit for the company.[91] Assistant managers for the estates normally came from the Aberdeen area of Scotland. As the supply of workers willing to indenture themselves for three years of painfully hard labour dwindled, managers sought to hire workers who already had ties to company employees, occasionally sending Tamil and Chinese overseers back to their home villages. These men tempted kin and neighbours, with some success, to come and work with them on short-term contracts, set up so that they did not have to clear a debt from their passage money.[92] Penang Sugar followed this strategy from the 1880s into the 1920s. The resulting labour gangs, whose members knew their foremen, formed social units of relatively mobile people who, after they returned home, could advise others about the burdens and benefits of plantation work. The long-term heavy movement of men and

[91] "Planters Past and Present: the Hon. Mr. Wm. Duncan," *The Planter*, Vol. 1, No. 2 (September 1920), p. 1; "Minutes of Evidence: Testimony of Mr. J. Turner," *Report of the Labour Commission of 1890*, p. 85, q. 1428; "Letter A. Morrison to J. Ray, 28 March 1883," in PSE, "Letters and Papers," Vol. 9, p. 205, Mss. 644.1 p19 (APS); "Tali Ayer Rubber," *Straits Times*, 3 December 1921, p. 2
[92] Chanderbali, *Indentured*, pp. 116–118

women into the plantations of the Straits Settlements and Federated Malay States moved from the novel to the familiar, as particular groups and villages in South India built a certain comfort level with migration to Malayan ports and estates.

Penang Sugar Estate managers worried constantly about being able to hire enough workers. In the spring of 1885, its field workforce consisted of 1,789 Tamils, about 600 Chinese, and 37 Javanese.[93] Most of the South Asians they employed were indentured workers from coastal areas in Tamil Nadu south of Madras, sent by the recruiting firms of Ganapathy Pillay and Co. and Adamson McTaggert, which operated out of the port of Negapatam. Javanese pilgrims in Jeddah were another possible source of supply because many needed money to finance their return trip from Jeddah. When that strategy of recruitment failed, the company turned periodically to the Netherlands Indies government, which permitted a relatively small number of Javanese to sign labour contracts and which mandated relatively high wages. The normal cost in the 1880s for hiring a Javanese field hand to serve an eight-month contract was around $37, to which monthly wages around $8 were added, over twice the rate for Indian labourers. While estate managers complained about the terms, they worked with an agent in Semarang who could arrange longer contracts and lower wages, as long as their transport was provided for free.[94]

The Penang Sugar Estates normally hired Chinese workers through Province Wellesley shopkeepers and labour brokers, although they tried unsuccessfully to set up their own networks in southwestern China. A lengthy campaign in 1889 to import workers through Bradley & Co. agents in Swatow was disastrous: many in the first group to arrive deserted, allegedly under pressure from local shopkeepers, who had been cut out of their recruitment, and from their families, who charged that the men had been kidnapped and sold into slavery. To calm protests in China, the Penang Sugar Estates had to pay compensation to relatives and send back all the remaining recruits along with a trusted Teochew headman, whose job it was to give the estates a good report and deny all the charges.[95]

---

[93] "Letter J. MacDougall to J. Ray, 9 March 1885," in PSE, "Letters and Papers," Vol. 11, p. 331–334, Mss 644.1 p19 (APS)

[94] *Report of the Labour Commission of 1890*, pp. 34–35; "Letter A. G. Morrison to J. Ray, 27 August 1881," Vol. 8, p. 101; "Letter Adam Stewart to John Turner, 16 April, 1896" Vol. 16, p. 273, in PSE, "Letters and Papers," Mss 644.1 p19 (APS)

[95] *Report of the Labour Commission of 1890*, pp. 12–13; "Letter J. Turner to J. Arnold, 19 March, 1890," Vol. 16, p. 255; "Letter J. Turner to J. Arnold, 30 April 1890," Vol. 16, pp. 267–268, "Letter J. Turner to J. Arnold, 22 May 1890," Vol. 16, p. 276, in PSE, "Letters and Papers," Mss 644.1 p19 (APS)

Defining the Coolie

It is important to remember that plantation managers thought of their Asian labourers as "coolies." The word coolie had multiple origins and associations, all of them negative. In the late sixteenth century and there-after, Portuguese travellers in Asia referred to labourers as Culé or Culi, a word borrowed from sea captains who used it for the dockers and porters they employed. By the later seventeenth century, the word "coolie" had transferred into English, probably derived from either kūli, a Tamil word meaning wages for menial work, or from Kuli, the name of an aboriginal tribe in Gujarat whose members were thought to be thieves. In the multi-lingual port cities of Asia, words easily overleapt language barriers and gained a place in many vocabularies. Whatever the derivation, well before the British arrived in Malaya the word was used by Europeans to describe Asian workers of few skills and low status.[96]

The key point is not the origin of the word but the attached cultural meanings of inferiority and incapacity, which put "coolies" at the bottom of local social hierarchies and justified their treatment. For the Anti-Slavery Society in Britain, coolies were "helpless and ignorant," as unaware of the dangers that awaited them as indentured labourers as earth-lings would be of life on the moon. Coolies were cast as victims – easily duped, docile, ambitionless men who were easy marks for dishonest recrui-ters and employers.[97] They were said to lack the energy to resist abuses and to defend their own interests. Commissioners inquiring into the condi-tions of labour in British Malaya in 1890 quoted earlier descriptions of arriving coolies as "naked, diseased, and poverty-stricken," men "of the lowest class" who could not take care of themselves. Alleged coolie weakness helped to justify colonial rule at the same time that it legiti-mated limitations of workers' rights. The colonial government took the position that "the coolie must be protected" by a vigilant state which would compensate for migrants' vulnerability.[98] Rather than seeing emi-grant labourers as "free," the British state used the excuse of their alleged

---

[96] OED (1971), "Coolie"; Hugh Tinker, *A New System of Slavery: the Export of Indian Labour Overseas 1830–1920*, 2nd ed. (London: Hansib Publishing Ltd., 1993), pp. 41–43; Jan Bremen and Val Daniel point out that the two Indian derivations together fused a money payment and a disreputable person, reinforcing the unity of a human being and a wage. See Jan Bremen and E. Valentine Daniel, "Conclusion: The Making of a Coolie," *Journal of Peasant Studies* Vol. 19, No. 3–4 (April/July 1992), pp. 268–269

[97] Carter and Torabully, *Coolitude*, pp. 50–51

[98] *Report of the Labour Commission of 1890*, p. 18; W. E. Maxwell, "The Malay Peninsula: Its Resources and Prospects, 18 November, 1891," in Kratoska, *Honorable Intentions*, p. 148

incapacity to control their movements and working conditions.[99] The indenture system shifted discussion of bound labour from a discourse about human rights to one of working conditions. The legitimacy of contract labour could then be assured by appropriate state regulation to ensure humane treatment. This argument justified an elaborate system of paternalist protections whose adequacy could then be debated by employers, medical doctors, and workers. Above them all stood British officials who ranked continued immigration and employers' rights well above those of plantation labourers. Protective legislation was part of a Liberal style of governance, and many would-be reformers within India and Malaya accepted its premises, choosing to lobby for improved conditions for indentured workers rather than abolition of the system.

British officials and major planters in the Straits Settlements also took a dim view of coolie character and capacities. In 1879, J. Lamb, manager of the Prye Estate, complained to the Protector of Immigrants of the numbers of "utterly useless characters" recognizable by their "very low, often semi-idiotic type of physiognomy" in every gang of new recruits. T. Irvine Rowell, the Principal Civil Medical Officer of the Straits Settlements called coolies in Province Wellesley men of "very inferior intellect," and members of the 1890 Labour Commission concluded that coolies cared "little or nothing for cleanliness or ordinary sanitary precautions." Moreover, they drank too much.[100] J. M. Vermont, the manager of Batu Kawan plantation who had worked in Province Wellesley since the mid-1840s and who served on the 1890 Labour Commission, described new recruits to Batu Kawan as "ignorant of all work, prone to laziness," and he feared that government inspections led to "over-pampering" and would produce men "unfit to work, helpless, without resources, hospital loafers, vagrants useless to themselves and the Colony." When charges of heavy floggings on his estate continued, Vermont complained of

---

[99] Indentured and contracted labourers in the British Empire were overseen by the state in an early example of international labour regulation. Rather than seeing the system as merely coercive, scholars have suggested that government intervention represented an effort to construct a humane international labour system. That it failed to provide appropriate protections does not undercut the point about its origins. See Robert J. Steinfeld, *Coercion, Contract, and Free Labour in the Nineteenth Century* (Cambridge: Cambridge University Press, 2001); Rachel Sturman, "Indian Indentured Labor and the History of International Rights Regimes," *AHR*, Vol. 119, No. 5 (December 2014), pp. 1438–1465

[100] Straits Settlements, "Letter from Mr. J. Lamb to the Protector of Immigrants," in *Papers Laid before the Legislative Council by Command of His Excellency the Administrator, 10 February, 1879*, No. 23, p. cxlii; "Report by the Principal Civil Medical Officer, Straits Settlements, Regarding the State of the Hospital etc. at Batu Kawan Estate," Straits Settlements; *Paper Laid before the Legislative Council by Command of His Excellency the Administrator, 12 December 1879*, No. 41, p. cccxxxv; *Report from the Commission on Labour, 1890*, p. 47. Evidence, p. 111

"unprincipled coolies," men "getting to think they ought to be paid wages whether they work or not," men who reacted to discipline by deserting, making "false charges," or "firing growing crops, houses or sheds containing valuable property so as to get a long term of imprisonment and thus be off their contract."[101] In his opinion, coolies resembled disloyal Irish peasants, rather than the docile, helpless figures of official rhetoric. By 1890, Vermont had become one of the senior planters of Province Wellesley, and after he was appointed to the Legislative Council of the Straits Settlements, he had a powerful forum for his strong views on plantation discipline and coolie incapacity.

Plantation workers bore not only their coolie label, but also rigid classifications by race and by gender. Awareness of ethnic diversity was not new in the pluralist societies of Southeast Asia, of course, and cities throughout the region had long housed foreign merchants, soldiers, and sailors, whose presence could trigger conflict and resentment. But Malay served as a lingua franca, allowing communication, and intermarriage fostered limited assimilation. The Baba Chinese of Melaka and Penang blurred the lines between Chinese and Malay, and Muslim Indian-Malay marriages produced the Jawi Peranakan group. Then, during the nineteenth century, Europeans brought into Malaya narrower definitions of race and hierarchical classifications of peoples. Racial categories were thought to signal not only biological differences but also innate capacities. For physiognomists, cranial and facial differences translated into character traits, and Social Darwinists used what they saw as evolutionary differences between races to justify imperial conquests.[102] The language of race and practice of racial segregation became more open in Malaya late in the nineteenth century, as some Europeans insisted on increased social distance between themselves and Asians. Separate carriages "For Europeans Only" appeared on the Selangor Railway during the 1890s, and non-Europeans were barred from the Malayan Civil Service after 1904.[103]

---

[101] Straits Settlements, "Letter J. M. Vermont to F. H. Gottlieb, Protector of Immigrants, 8 June, 1879," and "Report on Indian Immigrants," *Paper Laid before the Legislative Council by Command of His Excellence the Administrator, 22 August, 1879*, No. 30, p. cclx; Straits Settlements, "Complaints of Ill-treatment of Indian Immigrants on the Batu Kawan and Golden Grove Estates in Province Wellesley," in *Paper Laid before the Legislative Council by Command of His Excellency the Governor, 29 December, 1881*, No. 38, p. 363

[102] Charles Hirschman, "The Making of Race in Colonial Malaya: Political Economy and Racial Ideology," *Sociological Forum*, Vol. 1, No. 2 (1986), pp. 330–361; L. Perry Curtis, *Apes and Angels* (Washington, DC: Smithsonian Institution Press, 1971), pp. 8–14; Henrika Kuklick, *The Savage Within: The Social History of British Anthropology, 1885–1945* (Cambridge: Cambridge University Press, 1991); Christine Bolt, *Victorian Attitudes to Race* (London: Routledge & Kegan Paul, 1971)

[103] John Butcher, *The British in Malaya 1880–1941* (Kuala Lumpur: Oxford University Press, 1979), pp. 98, 107

Censuses of British Malaya, which had originally tallied "nationalities," began in 1891 to substitute the word "race" for that category when discussing the groups to be counted, and the transition to classification by "race" was completed by 1911. While the earliest listings of peoples were largely alphabetical, the census of 1891 substituted a pecking order of groups that loosely followed anthropologists' ideas of human evolution: Europeans stood at the top, to be followed by Eurasians, Chinese, Malay, Tamils and other Indians, and then the rest of the world, alphabetized but grouped as "Other." While dozens of ethnicities were recognized, they were subsumed into races and ranked according to their relative position on popular evolutionary trees of human descent and progress.[104]

Stereotypes of each ethnic group that linked culture, character, and capacity circulated widely within the European community in Malaya. In one of the most popular handbooks about the colony designed for travellers and newcomers, Mrs Reginald Sanderson contrasted the "indolence of the Malays" with the "untiring" energy of Teochews. Hylams were "smart and industrious," and like all Chinese, had exceptional "power of endurance." She identified poor Tamils as Klings, "a name given to the lowest classes of native immigrants," and she thought them "patient and enduring." Telegus had less stamina and got sick easily, while Bengalis were "indolent."[105] Each group had its essential character, as well as assigned slots in the local economy. Chinese workers pulled rickshaws or dug in the mines; Teochews cleared the jungle and took on heavy labouring jobs, the most degraded becoming herdsmen "barely clothed in strange fragments of rags." Bengalis held soft jobs, such as watchmen. Each race was fitted by character and temperament into an appropriate place. In the discussions of the 1890 Labour Commission, contract workers were "coolies," given different treatment and tasks according to the capabilities of their ethnic groups; as one witness explained, "each race is good at its own kind of work, and both [Chinese and Tamil] are necessary on an estate." Particularly useful, however, was the Tamil labourer, because "he is a British subject, accustomed to British rule, [and] is well behaved and docile."[106] Planters did not hire individual workers to clear land or cut cane. They hired gangs of Tamils or Teochews who had collective functions and identities, which maintained the racial and work

---

[104] Charles Hirschman, "The Meaning and Measurement of Ethnicity in Malaysia: An Analysis of Census Classifications," *Journal of Asian Studies*, Vol. 46, No. 3 (1987), pp. 555–582

[105] Mrs Reginald Sanderson, "The Population of Malaya," in Arnold Wright and H. A. Cartwright, *Twentieth Century Impressions of British Malaya* (London: Lloyd's Great Britain Publishing Company, 1908), pp. 122–123. See also Syed Hussein Alatas, *The Myth of the Lazy Native* (London: Frank Cass, 1977)

[106] *Report of the Labour Commission of 1890*, p. 66; and Minutes of Evidence, p. 123

hierarchies of the plantations. In Anthony Stockwell's analysis, the British in Asia saw local people first as "members of a distinct community and only secondly as individuals."[107] Publicly defined racial categories underlay European perceptions of Asian populations and came into play in decisions about hiring. While all Asians were denigrated, they could be divided into fine-grained categories to justify the different roles they were assigned.

Racial categories, when fused with coolie status, could also trigger a deep set of emotions within planters that linked back to other places and times. Consider this account of a sugar estate in the Straits written by a European assistant manager around 1898. Lamenting the absence in Malaya of the sentimental glow that surrounded "the negro's life" on a slave plantation and the "happy times" conjured by their work songs, he portrayed Indian "dusky labourers" mustered before dawn, "jabber-jabbering" in an unknown tongue. Order was supplied by the assistants who called out the names of the workers and certified their presence. Then "those dusky imps glide away in a single file to their respective fields, looking as they go like the body of a gigantic snake turning and twisting as they travel onwards." More reptile than human, they had a collective identity, arriving in "batches" and deserting in groups. The assistant could understand nothing of what they said. He found their music annoying and their religious practices ridiculous. Only those "Klings" who had served in the West Indies and been disciplined to grow vegetables in their spare time seemed worthy of his approval.[108] His plantation was racially divided and hierarchically organized, rigid in its disrespect for labourers, who could not quite fill the shoes of the slaves they replaced.

Plantation colonialism was a modern, global hybrid. Built with assumptions carried over from the Caribbean sugar growers, revised by colonial administrators who believed in an interventionist state, which for the most part neglected workers' needs, it brought together state and society in a harsh, hierarchical environment whose practices shaped British rule in Malaya.

The Colonized Landscape

Outsiders arrived in Malaya not only to possess the land, but also to remake it. Where travellers in 1820 found jungle and elephant trails,

[107] A. J. Stockwell, "The White Man's Burden and Brown Humanity: Colonialism and Ethnicity in British Malaya," *Southeast Asian Journal of Social Science*, Vol. 10, No. 1 (1982), pp. 54, 56
[108] "Sugar Planting Life in the Straits Settlements," by an Assistant, *The Straits Chinese Magazine*, Vol. 2, No. 5 (1898), pp. 54–57

their successors in the 1880s saw roads, houses, estates, and settlements. Perak, earlier the "abode of crocodiles" and tigers, had acquired irrigated rice fields and plantations. Coastal lowlands once covered by mangrove trees and tidal swamps were stripped and filled and planted. Men levelled the forest for firewood to feed factory furnaces, and arrow-straight drainage canals divided numbered fields into rectangles. Maps registered the road lines, towns, and river-spanning bridges, which migrants who flooded into the region named and organized into their own imaginative landscapes.

The countryside was colonized not only by physical possession, but also through cultural appropriation. Newcomers often re-named the land, imprinting onto it their pasts and dreams of the future, but whose words carried the most weight? The earliest estates named by Edward Horsman were Victoria for his Queen and Caledonia, the Roman name for the Scottish Highlands, where he went annually to hunt and fish and where most of the company's assistant managers were born. John Ramsden called his first new plantation Byram, after the name of his Yorkshire estate. The main road from Nibong Tebal to Caledonia is still called Jalan Byram or Byram Street. Other owners chose to commemorate Bristol, Harvard, and Halifax. With these gestures, areas perceived as jungle acquired the sound of home. Field workers had less power to publicly label the land, but they could give it their own titles, asserting territorial control in a more private way. Chinese farmers in Province Wellesley re-named local places as their numbers mounted, inventing their own words for towns, hills, and important places. For them, Victoria Road was Red Earth Road. Teochews called Bukit Mertajam "Foot of the Great Mountain" since it resembled a hill near Swatow. They substituted "washing clothes bridge" and "betel nut bridge" for unfamiliar European or Malay names. "European's plantation," "foreigner's well," and "foreigner's bridge" signalled their sense of distance from particular places.[109] Their temples along riverbanks and in their villages of settlement marked out sacred spaces where they housed images of their gods, brought offerings, and came to pray, creating community in the process.[110] Tamil migrants had their own

---

[109] William H. Newell, "Chinese Place Names in Province Wellesley," *Journal of Tropical Geography*, No. 19 (1964), pp. 58–61. See also S. Durai Raja Singam, *Port Weld to Kuantan* (Kuala Lumpur: Malayan Printers, 1939).

[110] Kwan Yin (the goddess of Mercy) and Kwan Ti (the god of war) were among the most common deities in early Straits Settlement temples; Yen Ching-hwang, *A Social History of the Chinese in Singapore and Malaya 1800–1911* (Singapore: Oxford University Press, 1986), pp. 10–12. See also Susan Naquin, *Peking: Temples and City Life, 1400–1900* (Berkeley: University of California Press, 2000).

names for places, which circulated within their community.[111] They selected trees to be holy sites, where they set up small shrines in their shade. Early examples, which continue to be venerated, exist on the Batu Kawan estate and near the Mariyamman temple in Nibong Tebal. Just as they built tennis courts for their British employees, plantation managers allocated estate land for Hindu temples, which became community centres and the sites of annual celebrations. The resulting mélange of styles and references marked British Malaya as a distinctive and fractured space, one where juxtaposed, contending layers of meaning signalled differences, as well as attempts to accommodate and understand them.

[111] Singam, *Port Weld*, pp. 4, 6

2   Body Politics in a Plural Society

On 20 November 1857, a South Asian male labourer named Chivatean signed, or more likely made his mark on, a contract to work for a year at Edward Horsman's Val d'Or estate, a not-very-profitable inland plantation in Province Wellesley. The contract obligated Chivatean to work in the fields to repay from his wages a debt of between 10 and 12 Straits dollars, the cost of his trip from South India. In December 1857, he decided to ignore his contract and to run away. The estate had no fence around it, and there were better paid jobs available in Penang or nearby villages, a fact that he presumably knew. Unfortunately Chivatean did not leave Penang and Province Wellesley, and he remained within the jurisdiction of the Penang court. Val d'Or's British manager, Duncan Pasley, immediately went to a local police magistrate, John Rogers Alexander, and asked for a warrant for Chivatean's arrest. With the warrant in hand, local police sought and arrested the labourer. A magistrate promptly found him guilty of "absconding from the said Estate" and sent him to the Penang House of Correction for two months. When released, Chivatean adamantly refused to go back to the estate and to complete his term of service. He could not be persuaded (or coerced) to change his mind. The irate plantation manager then lodged a formal complaint against him for breach of contract, which resulted in Chivatean's re-arrest and another court hearing. To the great surprise of the manager and his lawyer, the justice of the peace and police magistrate, William Willans, released Chivatean again, arguing that a person could not be punished twice for violating the same contract. Willans' ruling effectively gave the labourer freedom, debt-free. If Chivatean had immediately moved about twenty miles to the east, north, or south, he would have arrived in what was then Malay-ruled territory, out of British jurisdiction. Unfortunately for him, Chivatean remained within Province Wellesley.

Chivatean's story continued for another year, as other voices and interests weighed in on the local court's decision. A sizeable group of local estate owners, which included Chinese and "other Natives" as well as the leading British planters, petitioned the court to reconsider its decision. Warning that "the safety and protection of the agricultural interests" as well as "the general prosperity of the Settlement" were at stake, they demanded that the local magistrates compel "the specific fulfilment of contracts to labour for hire, for, unless these are enforced, the cultivation of the principal staples of the Settlement will become gradually abandoned." Their appeal went quickly to the Supreme Court of the Straits Settlements, which ruled in May of 1858 in favour of the plantation owners and against Chivatean, laying down the principle that a first conviction under a contract was "no bar to . . . conviction under the same Statute for a second absenting" and presumably also for a third or fourth such offence.[1] There is no record of whether or not he returned to Val d'Or. What matters is that a crucial principle was established in local labour law that would last for the rest of the century. "Coolies" could be convicted repeatedly for absconding from estates to which they owed unpaid debts or labour time.

Chivatean's story opens a window into the world of post-slavery plantations, as it was constructed in the Straits Settlements in the mid-nineteenth century. Not only did the labourer find it easy to escape from an estate, but Chivatean, with the aid of a sympathetic magistrate, successfully defended himself against his employer – for a time. He knew that the colony offered jobs other than plantation labour. Local planters needed a constant supply of low-wage workers, which they believed they could not obtain locally, and they made clear their dependence on the colonial state for coercion of indentured employees to complete contracts. At issue, in their eyes, was the viability of export agriculture, which could not survive unprotected. For them, a free market system was neither desirable nor sustainable. Colonial magistrates probed these arguments and eventually accepted them on the basis of centuries-old English laws that gave employers great power over their apprentices and domestic workers. Since unfree labour in England had been ratified by Parliament, they said that the same rules should obtain in the country's colonies. The justices admitted that jurisdiction over the Asian residents of Penang and Province Wellesley had originally been delegated by the British to the headmen of each community, who would have blocked the applicability of British laws to Chivatean's case. Yet over time, they decided, English law had been more broadly imported into the colony, and the principles of the English Master and Servant laws covered Asian

---

[1] James William Norton Kyshe, "Regine v. Willans," *Cases Heard and Determined in Her Majesty's Supreme Court of the Straits Settlements (1808–1854)* (Singapore: Singapore and Straits Printing Office, 1886), Vol. 3, pp. 17–42

residents. Unless an employer had released a worker from his or her contract, they were bound to complete it unless the state decided that the contract was void – an action which it refused to take. Indirectly, they recognized the state's duty to oversee the workers' welfare, but they offered neither definitions of that task nor proposed limits on employers' powers.[2] Employers had to bring cases of absconding workers into a British court, and the Chinese plantation owners at this time were unlikely to do so, having alternative mechanisms for contract enforcement. The regulatory role of the state remained weak and essentially undefined. Nevertheless, the justices' response recognized that colonial law and, by extension, the colonial state incorporated contradictory imperatives: workers could be coerced, but they also needed to be protected. At the heart of plantation colonialism in Malaya was a conflict generated by the welfare functions of the colonial state grafted onto a system of labour management with its roots in slavery.

Plantation colonialism in Malaya during the nineteenth century rested on the possession of workers' bodies, as well as their time and labour, an ownership ratified by British law and enforced in its colonial courts. Until legally freed from their contracts' obligations, labourers became the property of their estates, to be commanded, often confined, and punished virtually at will. Water surrounded the Batu Kawan plantations, which a ferry linked to the mainland. In 1890, estate workers complained that watchmen guarded the ferries, and without a manager's pass they were refused rides across the river. Several workers whose debts had not been cleared had been forced to remain for several years beyond their original indenture contract.[3] Even more constraining were conditions on the Saga estate in Negeri Sembilan, where the housing lines were surrounded by a 10-foot fence, and workers were confined from 6 PM until the morning muster.[4] In extreme cases, the desire to control labourers' bodies led directly to locking them up. To be sure, their contracts guaranteed them certain rights and wages, but they owed much in return, and they lost important liberties for the time of their indentures. On the plantation, they became "coolies," who faced flogging, fines, or jail time if they did not obey orders and complete their contracts. This system operated, however, within narrow spatial limits. Workers were bound to particular

[2] Kyshe, "Regine v. Willans," *Cases*, Vol. 3, pp. 17–42
[3] Straits Settlements, *Report of the Commissioners of Inquiry into the State of Labour in the Straits Settlements and Protected Native States*, 1890 (Singapore, 1890), p. 22
[4] Federated Malay States, *Report of the Commission Appointed to Enquire into the Conditions of Indentured Labour in the Federated Malay States*, 1910, [Papers laid before the Federal Council] #11 of 1910, pp. 14, 35

plantations; police and court systems had jurisdictions only within their colony or state. Governance and space were tightly linked. Moving across an open border from Province Wellesley to Perak or from Province Wellesley to Kedah was easily done. A different life lay only a few miles down the road. The sugar estates typified one style of colonial rule: that of a harsh, racially organized paternalism, designed to keep wages low and workers quiet. At the same time, imperial governance also proclaimed through its oversight of the indenture system an interest in subjects' welfare. Officials specified standards and then inspected ships and estates to guarantee their adoption.

But how much protection was actually provided? The nineteenth century was a time of rising expectations, and objections to conditions on plantations regularly surfaced among both Europeans and Asians. William Cowan, Acting Protector of Chinese for the states of Selangor, Negeri Sembilan, and Pahang, denounced the indenture system in 1890 as "disguised slavery." Twenty years later, he still held this opinion, despite rising wages and improved conditions.[5] Was the enactment of minimum standards sufficient to make contract labour a politically acceptable system in an empire that had embraced trade unions, factory legislation, and old age pensions for English workers but rejected them for colonial subjects? Europeans did not agree on what standards should apply, and indentured workers as well as reformers kept pushing for more concessions. Judges and magistrates gave contradictory rulings in the case of Chivatean. His status and expectations were significantly higher in a Straits Settlements town than on a plantation, and he knew it. Both the spatial and the social organization of the sugar estates trapped their workers in ways that were questioned increasingly as the century progressed.

Space and Social Place on the Plantation

Colonial rule reworked the space of western Malaya into an orderly landscape that mirrored the tight social discipline cultivated by plantations. Sugar estates developed in lowland, riverside areas of western Malaya, where there were few natural boundaries other than rivers to mark borders, and internally differentiated spaces were laid out and then assigned to particular ethnic groups or occupations. Managers divided holdings into rectangular units, and they often appropriated choice riverside sites for their bungalows and sports ground. Workers' housing

[5] Federated Malay States, *Report of the Commission Appointed to Enquire on the Conditions of Indentured Labour*, 1910, p. 27

normally lay near the sugar factory or paths into the fields, places that offered easy access to work sites and where they could be observed. The state soon built a modern infrastructure that connected plantations and the growing towns. Step by step, a network of roads and canals channelled people and products north toward Penang or south to Singapore. Both entry and exit became easier as transportation services, and eventually a railway, linked major ports to production sites.

The Field: the Country Gentleman's Newspaper, described Province Wellesley in 1880 in its "Travel and Colonisation" column. Its author praised the east-west and north-south roads, which turned the territory from "unbroken jungle" to "a healthy cultivation."[6] Between the roads were plantations, themselves divided into numbered fields. Colonial rule and settlement redrew local geography, replacing wilderness with an industrialized agriculture organized to maximize production and minimize the variations of the natural world. Labourers drained the marshes and embanked rivers. Managers shot wild animals. After he took possession of his plantations, the company sent Sir John Ramsden crude drawings of the estates, depicted as long lines of rectangles divided by drainage ditches, boating canals, and roads.

Plans of the Nova Scotia Estate, laid out by Ramsden's employees for sugar production in 1899, show the land with its full complement of buildings in 1913 (see Map 2.1). A central road ran through the plantation, leading to the towns of Teluk Anson on the east and Bagun Datoh to the west, from which a branching road led north past a hospital, a Hindu temple, and workers' housing to the Perak River and the core of the estate. The road ended at the riverside, where a factory, an office, and the large manager's bungalow dominated the complex, which was unfenced, like most plantations.

On Nova Scotia Estate, assistant managers and other European employees shared large, airy bungalows surrounded by shade trees and flowers. They could walk to a tennis court, a club, and a cricket ground. As estates developed, their managers moved from simple attap-roofed, wooden structures to imposing houses with plastered columns, shaded verandas, shuttered windows, and broad staircases. By late in the nineteenth century, rattan or teak furniture, rugs, pillows, and pictures brought comfort and a sense of European style to sitting and dining rooms. Managers had indoor bathing rooms amply supplied with water and their own dressing rooms, as well as multiple servants who cooked, washed, and cleaned for them. They could retreat from the tropical sun

[6] "A Five Years' Sojourn in Province Wellesley," *The Field: The Country Gentleman's Magazine*, 3 July 1880, p. 39

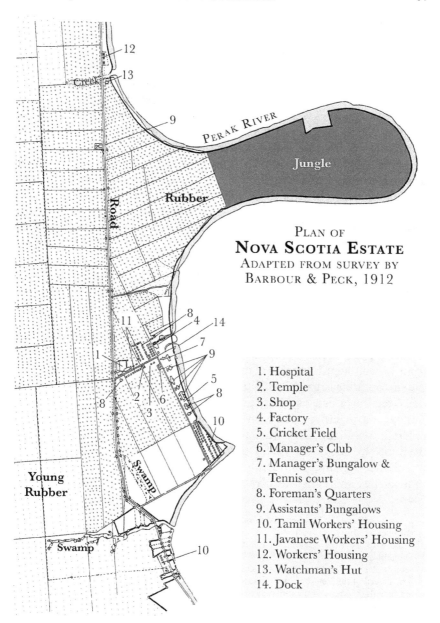

PLAN OF
NOVA SCOTIA ESTATE
ADAPTED FROM SURVEY BY
BARBOUR & PECK, 1912

1. Hospital
2. Temple
3. Shop
4. Factory
5. Cricket Field
6. Manager's Club
7. Manager's Bungalow &
   Tennis court
8. Foreman's Quarters
9. Assistants' Bungalows
10. Tamil Workers' Housing
11. Javanese Workers' Housing
12. Workers' Housing
13. Watchman's Hut
14. Dock

Map 2.1 Plan of Nova Scotia Estate, 1912

into large, shaded spaces, where comfortable chairs, clean water, and cool drinks were ready to hand.[7] Farther to the east of the manager's bungalow were the smaller houses for the European assistant managers, engineers, and medical personnel. Sizes and facilities varied with status. Assistants and engineers had many of the same privileges as their bosses, although several would share a single structure and the cost of cook, laundryman, and water carrier. Their quarters were less imposing and sparsely furnished with little more than a bed, mosquito net, table, chair, and wardrobe.[8] Yet they too had dining and sitting rooms and indoor bathing. They also had access to a billiard table, reading room, and social club from which Asian employees, no matter what their rank, were excluded.[9]

Unequal access to resources was built into plantation life. Teams of servants ran plantation bungalows, providing clean, white clothes and large, cooked meals, as well as looking after plants and grounds. Surviving budgets for European, mid-ranking employees showed sizable expenses for household staff, whose presence brought status along with service. Tinned food, whiskey, and wine could be bought in town shops, where markets offered a range of local fruit, vegetables, and chicken. After 1880, refrigerator ships from New Zealand and Australia brought high-grade frozen meat to ports around the empire.[10]

A set of photos sent to Sir John Ramsden around 1875 helped him visualize the estates. European men, dressed all in white, stand tall in front of well-kept bungalows, moving out of those enclosed spaces into the surrounding sugar fields. A group of male managers drawn from six of the company's estates, perhaps together for a meeting or a drink on Sunday, sit together talking on a well-kept lawn in front of a bungalow at Krian (see Figure 2.1). Mr Bacon, the Golden Grove manager, lounges deep into his chair. Mr Pasley of Val d'Or has hooked his thumbs in his waistband, looking confidently at his friends. Several sport luxuriant moustaches and chin whiskers. Their hair is carefully cut and combed.

---

[7] Peter and Waveney Jenkins, *The Planter's Bungalow: A Journey down the Malay Peninsula* (Singapore: Editions Didier Millet, 2007)

[8] "Letter O. B. Pike, Caledonia Estate to the Penang Sugar Estates Co., London, 12 December, 1907" in Penang Sugar Estates, "Copy Book of Letters," Film, No. 5634, section 2/15 (Singapore, National University of Singapore Library)

[9] The Board of the Penang Sugar Estates told the General Manager in 1891 that we "quite agree with the views you express as to the grave mischief which might arise from Overseas mixing too familiarly with drivers and other coloured subordinates." "Letter John Turner to J. Arnold, 26 August, 1891," Vol. 17, p. 105; "Letter J. Arnold to J. Turner, 25 September, 1891," Vol. 18, p. 12, in PSE, "Letters and Papers," Mss 644.1 p19 (American Philosophical Society)

[10] Lady Birch, "Diary for 1896," Mss Ind Ocn. 354, Box 1 (Rhodes House, Oxford). J. M. Gullick, *They Came to Malaya* (Singapore: Oxford University Press, 1993), pp. 88–89, 144; *Perak Pioneer*, 2 June 1897, p. 2

Figure 2.1 Managers of the Penang Sugar Estates relaxing together, c. 1875

All are wearing slightly different tailored jackets and bow ties, and a white brimmed hat has been dropped onto the grass. They seem comfortable with themselves and in charge of their environment. The dress coats of Mr Wilson from Krian and Mr Lamb from the Prye plantation signal that this is not a workday, and several of the managers brought sticks or canes. These evoke both the dress of an urban gentleman and overseers' weapons and badges of authority in the fields.

A small group of Eurasians and Chinese who worked as clerks, book-keepers, and carpenters blurred the rigid economic divide between management and labour. It is not clear where they lived, although they seemed to have houses for their families somewhere on the sugar estates. They were not, however, welcome in Europeans' social spaces. This middling group crossed boundaries of place as well as language, moving on and off the plantation at will. Augustin Francis Nicholas, remembered by his family as a ship captain from Brazil, came to Penang with his brother at the latest by 1866. He married four times and fathered twelve children, two of whom were born on Victoria estate in 1880 and 1884, when he was an overseer there. Their mother, Louise Mary Rangel, who married Nicholas at age fifteen, came from a well-connected Roman Catholic Eurasian family based in Melaka with ties to Singapore. Nicholas lived intermittently in Penang, where his brother became a police commissioner.[11] By the early twentieth century, a handful of Eurasian and Chinese clerks, engineers, and overseers from Province Wellesley estates served as jurors in the Penang magistrate's court alongside European and Asian elites. The chief clerk on the Caledonia estate around 1900, Yeoh Poh Chuan, wore a queue until the Qing dynasty fell, but he combined it with a western-style suit, signalling dual cultural loyalties. In addition to his house on Caledonia, he owned a house in Penang, where some of his children were born. His second son, Yeoh Teik Swee began working at a Caledonia office after he finished his education at the Penang Free School and Victoria Institution in Kuala Lumpur.[12] He could have been empaneled alongside the many European assistant managers, or possibly Vincent Michael D'Souza, a Eurasian engineer employed at Batu Kawan estate. Eurasian families had broad networks extending to local towns as well as to plantations in the area. Their positions entitled them to respect, and their incomes moved them into the ranks of the propertied. They travelled, educated their children at the best schools in Malaya, and married them to other families of similar status, remaining in the area for several generations. With one foot in local towns and another in the plantations, they were both urban and rural, multilingual and broadly connected to other places and cultures. They had cultural similarities to both bosses and workers, but did not fit easily into the social categories of plantation colonialism. They occupied a middle space in the plantation hierarchy, bordering on and mediating between managers and labourers.[13]

---

[11] Personal communication from Julian Nicholas about the Nicholas/Rangel family and their genealogy, 3 March 2003. I would like to thank Julian Nicolas for sending me information about his great-great grandfather and great grand-aunts.

[12] List of Qualified Jurors, Penang 1904, *Straits Settlements Government Gazette*, 23 December 1904; posted as www.oocities.org/tfoenander/penangjurors.htm, 30 October 2009. Personal communication about her great grandfather from Lim Chooi Lian, 12 March 2009. I would like to thank Lilly Lim for her family story.

[13] "Letter John MacDonald to J. Ray, 4 October 1884," Vol. 11, p. 209; "Letter J. Low to J. Ray, 2 February 1887", Vol. 13, Part 2, p. 50, in PSE, "Letters and Papers," Mss 644.1

Overseers lived near their workers, who were segregated by ethnic group. Tamils and Javanese similar, lived in separate areas south of the factory. Workers' houses, the so-called "coolie lines," signalled low status through their size and design. The Labour Commission of 1890 visited multiple estates in Province Wellesley and Perak and found labourers living in single-storey, mud-floored structures made of palm leaves or attap, sometimes with walls of mud and stick. Constructed in long rows, these structures lacked ventilation and light, having only entrance doors and sometimes a hole in the rear wall. Most had an outside veranda where cooking was done and a surrounding drainage ditch to help keep the structure dry during rainstorms. Interiors could be divided into rooms or left as single open spaces. Inspectors objected only to extreme over-crowding. One estate regularly assigned six people to a 10-by-10-foot room, while others put multiple married couples into a single room or mixed couples and single men. The larger European-owned estates seem to have invested more in their housing. On the Caledonia and Byram plantations, workers' quarters were made with brick walls, although they still had mud floors; married couples had separate rooms. Inspectors, however, found some Caledonia workers sleeping in an attic over a veranda where cooking was done, and they complained of the rising smoke as well as the "very dark" structures where all of the ventilation holes had been blocked up. Javanese lived in a "large attap building subdivided by partitions," while the Chinese men had a large, one-roomed hut with mosquito-curtained beds. The Batu Kawan plantation provided three types of mud-floored, attap barracks. Some were divided into separate rooms for married couples, and a large room, guarded by watchman at night, was set aside for unmarried women. Newer structures grouped 45 men together dormitory style, each with a separate sleeping platform. The smaller, older barracks, each housing twenty-five men, had a single sleeping platform along one side. Employers in Selangor in the mid-1890s were advised that "double lines – i.e. lines two rooms broad each facing on to a veranda – will be found much more economical than the long singular lines, besides being dearer to the heart of the gregarious cooly."[14] Workers lived cheek-by-jowl, hearing one another's coughs

---

p19 (APS). Teh Seong, who worked for the Penang Sugar Estates for 35 years as clerk, cranny, and rent-collector, bought plantation land for his family's burial ground, and John Sargant, his manager, tried to get his widow a company pension; "Letter J. Sargant to J. Turner, 14 June 1894," Vol. 20, p. 131, in PSE, "Letters and Papers," Mss 644.1 p19 (APS)

[14] Straits Settlements, *Labour Commission of 1890*, Appendix B: "Visit No. 5, Visit No. 6, and Visit No. 11," pp. 8–9, 13–14; *Selangor Journal*, 1894, No. 6, p. 90, quoted in R. N. Jackson, *Immigrant Labour and the Development of Malaya, 1786–1920* (Kuala Lumpur, 1961), p. 105

and curses, in structures designed for sleeping rather than waking hours. Their living spaces were public and shared – veranda, temple, field, and barrack – in contrast to the Europeans' private, relatively empty bungalows.

A local photographer captured the images of plantation workers as they stood outside a warehouse on one of the Penang Sugar Estates. Production spaces were their territory. The Tamils, bare chested with wrinkled, rather dirty dhotis wrapped around their waists, clutch heavy hoes or changkols; they look down or away from the camera (see Figure 2.2). Their overseer sports a plaid sarong, white turban and white long-sleeved shirt; he holds a cane, as do all the other foremen. A bunch of cut and trimmed sugar stalks

Figure 2.2 Tamil work gang, Penang Sugar Estates, c. 1875. The overseer, dressed in a white turban and jacket, stands in front.

is propped against the wall, a sign of the work team's current labour. In their half-nakedness they resemble the Chinese, who were photographed grouped around a basket, bucket, and rake. Their muscles bulge and their skin glistens. Conical straw sunhats distinguish them from turbaned Malays and Javanese. The long queue of the overseer reaches down to his waist, and he leans slightly on a stick as he gazes directly at the camera. These photos juxtapose leisure and work, individuality and community, authority and subservience, identifying the men of the plantation either with management or with labour, and then subdividing the latter into the boss and his gang, whose territory is a warehouse, not a home.

The Penang Sugar Estate labourers had names and social links, even if they were thought irrelevant by the photographer and the manager who mailed the pictures to London. When Tamils signed indenture contracts, the Indian Immigration Agent recorded their names, as well as those of their fathers, their villages, their religions, and their castes. Photographs were compulsory after 1888 in Perak for all who had contracts longer than 6 months.[15] Although these documents seem not to have survived for contract workers in Malaya, examples from Mauritius show formally dressed men and women, whose migration histories, names, and origins were meticulously recorded. Those few contract labourers who have told their own stories located themselves precisely in geographic and social space. "I am Rahman Khan, son of Mohammad Khan … an Afghan pathan, who was a lieutenant in Jalal Khan's army." He describes his father's work and movements that led him to establish a family in Bharkhari village in the United Provinces and gives the names, brief histories, and residences of three generations of kin, before recounting the circumstances that led him to emigrate at the age of 24.[16] The complexity of such stories did not filter through to the plantation managers or owners, who operated with a reductionist vision of employees; their castes and local affiliation disappeared into the designation, Kling or Tamil. At best, assistants called workers by name at morning musters and identified those reported to the magistrate for desertion or who had died in the estate hospital. Estate work has to have been a levelling experience for Tamil immigrants, who were recruited as individuals and then crammed into barracks with strangers. Sharing living spaces, latrines,

[15] *Perak Government Gazette*, 12 October 1888, p. 74
[16] Marina Carter, *Voices from Indenture: Experiences of Indian Migrants in the British Empire* (London: Leicester University Press, 1996), pp. 183–227. Jeevan Prakash, *Autobiography of an Indian Indentured Labourer Munshi Rahman Khan (1874–1972)*, Translated by Kathinka Sinha-Kerkhoff, Ellen Bal and Alok Deo Singh (Delhi: Shipra Publications, 2005), pp. 26–27. See also Gaiutra Bahadur, *Coolie Woman: The Odyssey of Indenture* (Chicago: University of Chicago Press, 2014).

and food forced them to transgress the rules of caste. To survive, they had to adapt. Although labourers shared a common language, the specificities of village, social group, and family vanished when no others shared those memories and networks.

Before wages began to rise around 1900, most contract labourers could not afford enough food to stay healthy during the first two years of their contracts because of the debts they had to repay. In any case, who would do the cooking and purchasing? Since virtually all adults, male and female, spent their days in the fields, someone had to cook at the end of the day. Would the few women be pushed into this role? Might there have been rotations or joint meals? Given limited space and facilities, sharing would have been efficient and communal, at least within single work gangs or barracks, but did caste relations permit it? Managers wanted to control what workers ate, but workers were said to "consider it a punishment" not to be able to choose their own food. A trip to a village store brought conversation, different sights, and at least meagre entertainment. The alternative was a company shop. Most plantations provided a set amount of uncooked rice at cost, but then deducted its price from earnings, and managers were furious if they caught workers selling the allocation. In 1891, Penang Sugar proudly announced it had established an estate store, where prices were fair and quality controlled, but this followed upon decades of having stores run by overseers or their friends, who took rake-offs and supplied very little. Overall in the region, company stores helped keep workers in debt. Unindentured workers and the more experienced contract labourers took up garden plots to grow their own vegetables.[17] Food was another marker of plantation inequality, which produced low-level conflict over how and what workers ate.

Although employers were obligated to supply workers with sufficient and "wholesome" water, the colonial government seems not to have set clear standards of water hygiene and safety during the nineteenth century. When visiting estate hospitals in Province Wellesley in 1879, the chief medical officer of the Straits Settlements did not test local water supplies nor worry much about their quality, despite acknowledging "bowel complaints" as one of the "usual diseases" encountered among patients. Water purity was not on the agenda of the 1890 Labour Commission, even though it did worry about standards for medical care and housing.

By the late nineteenth century, both doctors and estate managers worried about the safety of drinking water, but they generally lacked the

---

[17] "Letter J. Turner to J. Arnold, 20 May 1891," Vol. 17, pp. 260–261, in PSE, "Letters and Papers," Mss 644.1 p19 (APS); Straits Settlements, *Labour Commission of 1890*, Evidence, pp. 86, 93

knowledge and the funding to provide a potable supply. Although European public health experts had known since the mid-nineteenth century that cholera was a water-borne disease and that its cure was filtration or boiling, these were not options easily implemented on isolated sugar plantations for hundreds or even thousands of people. Small clay filtration jars that blocked bacilli but permitted a flow of water molecules were used in Malaya by 1900, but they were expensive and not designed to provide a mass supply.[18] Sir John Ramsden and the London directors ordered managers to go well beyond the letter of the law: "Considerations of humanity and expediency alike require a perfectly untainted water supply, and lines which are not open to the criticism of even the most captious critic." They were happy to foot the bill. Estate managers concentrated their efforts on piping in what they considered to be "clean" water from nearby towns and rivers, installing standpipes next to workers' housing, but this was a flawed solution.[19] The Batu Kawan estate, which had comparatively high rates of gastro-intestinal diseases and fevers, installed a broad system of filtration only in 1909, but what system they used is unclear.[20] Despite periodic inspections and the multiplication of estate and state hospitals, faulty sanitation and polluted water meant high death rates for plantation workers until the 1920s.

The ultimate proof of plantation inequality lay in its mortality rates. In the twenty-five years of Penang Sugar Estate letters sent to London, they reported no deaths of managers or assistants, although they mentioned periodic cases of "fever" and other illnesses among their British employees. In contrast, the annual death rate for South Asian labourers in 1911 was 49.8 per thousand in Perak, 60.3 per thousand in Selangor, 195.6 per thousand in Negeri Sembilan, and 109.5 per thousand in Pahang, and

[18] The Pasteur–Camberland filter was developed in 1884, and examples dating from around 1900 have survived in Ipoh, Perak. Some Chinese urban workers' clubs invested in them, as did wealthy merchants. See www.sciencemuseum.org.uk/broughttolife/objects/display.aspx?id=5268 (Site downloaded on 31 January 2013).

[19] "Letter J. Arnold to J. Turner, 9 September 1892," Vol. 19, p. 6; "Letter J. Arnold to J. Turner, 24 March 1893," Vol. 19, p. 47; "Report of Government Analyst's Office, Singapore to Penang Sugar Estates, 22 July 1892," Vol. 19, pp. 107–109, in PSE, "Letters and Papers" Mss 644.1 p19 (APS)

[20] Straits Settlements, "Report by the Principal Civil Medical Officer, Straits Settlements on the hospital, etc. at Batu Kawan Estate," *Papers Laid before the Executive Council by Command of His Excellency the Administrator*, No. 41, 12 December 1879, pp. 339–341; David Chanderbali, *Indian Indenture in the Straits Settlements* (Leeds: Peepal Tree, 2008), pp. 188–191. Both in the 1870s and then around 1900, diarrhoeal diseases were among the major reasons for hospital admission and death, not only in the Straits Settlements but in Selangor and Negeri Sembilan where 50 per cent of deaths in 1899 were attributed to dysentery and bowel complaints; see Lenore Manderson, *Sickness and the State* (Cambridge: Cambridge University Press, 1996), pp. 28, 36–42, 152, 261–262.

these rates would have been higher in the nineteenth century. Compare these numbers to the death rate per thousand males in England and Wales in 1911, which had fallen to well below 10 per thousand for men between the ages of 15 and 44, the age range of estate labourers. Sugar plantations were death traps for their manual workers. Mortality rates on single estates rose to staggering levels during outbreaks of cholera or smallpox. Anopheles mosquitoes bred in the drainage ditches and swampy land. The Chief Medical Officer for the Federated Malay States in 1914 reported that on average each plantation labourer was treated nine times *each year* for malaria attacks![21] Sir Frank Swettenham, British Resident of Perak, confidently attributed "the sickness of the Tamil coolies to their bad physical state on arrival, to the unwholesome stuff they insist upon eating, and to the fact of their being unused to and unprepared for the condition of their work here."[22] In other words, the labourers had only themselves to blame for their mortality.

South Asian workers received the bulk of managerial attention. Staff interaction with Chinese and Javanese labourers was even more limited because of Europeans' inability to speak a wide range of appropriate Asian languages or dialects. While managers had to learn Malay and some Tamil, they did not study Chinese dialects or Javanese. In any case, the polyglot and polylingual plantations would have defeated the most avid language learner. As an alternative, they delegated control of work gangs to foremen of the same ethnic group, who kept records, superintended labourers in the fields, and received their wages. Between managers and their Chinese labourers stood the overseers or heads of the kongsi work groups, whose activities they found very difficult to monitor. This division of authority mirrored the layered sovereignty of the colony as a whole.

The social world of Chinese labourers turned inward toward the multiple organizations that grouped them according to dialect, family network, or native place. Those who left South China took with them familiar precedents and forms, adapting them to new environments, whether in the United States, Peru, or Southeast Asia.[23] Chinese emigrants to Malaya moved into an environment already highly organized by the earlier Chinese merchant diaspora. Dialect associations multiplied in Penang after 1800, and clan groups were organized, both soon spreading into the towns and villages of Malay states. Responding to the needs of immigrants, these groups founded temples, clubhouses, and kongsis or

---

[21] Manderson, *Sickness*, pp. 134, 136; B. R. Mitchell and Phyllis Dean, *Abstract of British Historical Statistics* (Cambridge: Cambridge University Press, 1962) pp. 36–39
[22] Straits Settlements, *Labour Commission of 1890*, Evidence, p. 91
[23] Adam McKeown, *Chinese Migrant Networks and Cultural Change: Peru, Chicago, Hawaii, 1900–1936* (Chicago: University of Chicago Press, 2001)

welfare societies, within which newcomers could bond with those who spoke their same dialect and had ties to the same villages and lineages. Belonging brought companionship, some small security, and contact with Chinese lineage customs and rituals. These brotherhoods, essentially fictive kin, enrolled, mustered, defended, and remembered even their poorer members. Generally controlled by the richer merchants and men with local political power, they helped labourers find work and shelter, trading protection in return for support.

The political roles of similar associations in China and the criminal activities of some of them terrified the British, however, who branded them all "secret societies," guilty of anti-social behaviour until proven innocent. Although in 1889 membership was criminalized in all but social and welfare organizations deemed harmless by the government, the banned as well as the permitted survived to organize the social life of Chinese in Malaya.[24] Koh Seang Tatt, one of the richest and best connected of the Penang Chinese merchants and the holder of the Penang opium and alcohol farms in the 1870s, employed Chinese immigrants in Penang and on estates. For each newly arrived worker, he had to pay the Teochew Kongsi a dollar, which each worker had to repay to him through wage deductions, but he added, "For this, the man is received into the Congsee [Kongsi] and the man is looked after if he gets into difficulties."[25] The 1890 Labour Commission charged that many of the Chinese labour importers were secret society headmen, who exploited their position to control workers, sending them to estates where they lived in a kongsi house "far from the main buildings . . . practically free from supervision," except by their overseer. They worked out contract details, kept all the accounts, assigned all tasks, and paid the men, effectively insulating them from their European employers. They would have been bi-lingual, speaking Malay with assistants and other managers. In 1890, the Commissioners knew of no estate which employed a Chinese-speaking European assistant. Managers were incapable of communicating with Chinese workers, and might not even know their names.[26] Leaders of the Chinese labour gangs

---

[24] Yen Ching-hwang, *A Social History of the Chinese in Singapore and Malaya 1800–1911* (Singapore: Oxford University Press, 1986); Irene Lim, *Secret Societies in Singapore* (Singapore: Singapore National History Museum, 1999); Victor Purcell, *The Chinese in Malaya* (London: Oxford University Press, 1948), Chapter 8, pp. 155–173; Tan Kim Hong, *The Chinese in Penang: A Pictorial History* (Penang: Areca Books, 2007), p. 49. See also Wilfred Blythe, *The Impact of Chinese Secret Societies in Malaya: A Historical Study* (London: Oxford University Press, 1969).

[25] Straits Settlements, "Report of the Committee Appointed to consider and take Evidence upon the Condition of Chinese Labourers in the Colony, 1876," *Papers Laid before the Legislative Council*, 3 November 1876, p. cclxxxii

[26] Straits Settlements, *Labour Commission of 1890*, pp. 20, 22, 26. PSE managers made similar complaints to the London office in 1887, and their efforts later in the decade to

and the kongsis kept their mostly Teochew members within their own social spaces, away from the daily demonstrations of hierarchy and control enacted in the fields and near the factory. Managers had far less power over the bodies of their Chinese workers than over their Indian ones, and this fact made them deeply uneasy.

Plantation people were socially and spatially segregated into groups which exhibited their assumed dissimilarity through dress codes, housing styles, leisure activities, and diets. Differences of class, income, and ethnicity took on visible forms as one moved from comfortable bungalows to rows of workers' shacks and from the European-only club to toddy shops, where Tamils bought cheap coconut liquor. Hindu temples guarded South Asian sacred spaces, while Europeans and Chinese exercised their greater freedom of movement to visit churches and temples in the adjoining towns. This spatial and cultural segregation continued in the fields, where each group had a carefully defined role to play in cane cultivation. Managers and contracts mandated tasks, which were then enforced by internal and external disciplines.

Women in a Masculine World

A sugar plantation was a masculine world, organized by men for production, not reproduction. While a few women did move to the sugar estates, either as indentured or as free workers, their presence was marginal and their utility defined as cheap labour. Colonial records omit their names and silence their voices, speaking of and not to them. Women's presence has to be inferred and imagined, told indirectly through their silences and the responses of others. But they were scarce, not absent. Their meagre numbers shaped the sexual mores of the plantations, and their low status and limited options made them easy targets. Immigration records reveal how many arrived, and censuses set those numbers in a comparative context, giving the bare bones of a story. But that is the place to begin.

The sojourner populations from Southeast China were predominantly male, as were the credit-ticket passengers who came to work in Malayan tin mines or plantations. Women were supposed to remain in China with kin and children. When Straits Settlements authorities recorded the sex distribution of Chinese immigrants in 1881 and 1882, females accounted for only 3.5 per cent of the total. This tiny percentage was typical among Chinese who emigrated: women made up only 1 per cent of the flow of

hire Chinese workers directly from Swatow stemmed from efforts to re-establish control over Chinese employees; "Letter Thompson Low to James Ray, 15 September 1887," Vol. 14, p. 197, in PSE, "Letters and Papers," Mss 644.1 p19 (APS)

workers from China to Latin America and the Caribbean during the nineteenth century. The Chinese Exclusion Act, which was enacted in 1882, prohibited labourers from bringing their wives with them into the United States. Females, in fact, made up 5 per cent or less of the Chinese population recorded in the United States censuses between 1880 and 1900.[27] Although South Asian women constituted about 30 per cent of all South Asian emigrants around 1895, few went to Malaya, because emigration agreements to that colony did not mandate their presence. No systematic count of South Asian women was made until 1867–1869, when between 11 and 15 per cent of annual arrivals were registered as female. The proportion fell to 9 per cent in 1900.[28] Women in the Straits Settlements and the Malay states of the peninsula were unevenly distributed among ethnic communities. Given the limited amount of intermarriage among ethnic groups that seems to have occurred at that time, the ability to form a local family and to raise children was restricted among the Chinese and South Asian labouring populations.

In contrast, Chinese merchants and British managers had families, as did Malays, who made up the majority of the residents of the Malay states in the mid-nineteenth century. Chinese tin miners, coolies, and European assistant managers were normally bachelors, unless they left spouses in the country from which they came. Hindus who stayed in Malaya sometimes arranged a marriage with a woman from their home village who might be able to join them. Among the Chinese and the Tamils of the Province, only 14 and 9 per cent, respectively, were female in 1860, and these proportions were lowest in the central district dominated by the sugar plantations.[29] Around 1870, Governor Ord of the Straits Settlements noted in a dispatch to London that planters thought family immigration was not desirable: women lost time in the fields when nursing or heavily pregnant, and they were less good field workers in any case. Family housing would have to be provided, and dependents cared for. Since they instructed overseers and agents about the sort of worker they wanted, managers had some control over the demographic balance of their labour forces. They clearly valued production over procreation. Women on the Ramsden plantations were seen by the head office and general managers as workers, not wives or mothers. The tally sent regularly to the London office in

[27] Dirk Hoerder, *Cultures in Contact: World Migrations in the Second Millennium* (Durham: Duke University Press, 2002), p. 379; McKeown, *Chinese Migrant Networks*, p. 31
[28] Robert L. Jarman, editor, "Annual Report for 1883," *Annual Reports of the Straits Settlements, 1855–1941* (Chippenham Wiltshire: Archive Editions, 1998), Vol. 2, p. 645; Kernal Singh Sadhu, *Indians in Malaya: Some Aspects of their Immigration and Settlement (1786–1957)* (Cambridge: Cambridge University Press, 1969), Appendix 3, pp. 310–313
[29] Jarman, "Annual Report for 1859–1860," *Annual Reports*, Appendix V, p. 244–245

the 1880s and 1890s divided labourers by ethnicity, not gender, but it also included data on losses, counting those who were in jail, sick, missing, or pregnant or nursing and therefore not available for work. Women became important through their absences, and reproduction was a liability, rather than an asset. The number removed from the fields at any given time, however, was small. At Caledonia plantation, where a total of 1686 workers were employed in July 1890, only 31 or 1.8 per cent were not in the fields because of the demands of producing or rearing children.

The few children born on the estates faced an uphill battle for survival. About a quarter of the infants born in the Straits Settlements in the early twentieth century died before their first birthday. Poor nutrition, unsanitary conditions, and inferior medical care meant high infant mortality. In addition, the company did not employ any midwives in its estate hospitals, and the colonial state did not begin to train midwives for its hospitals until after 1905. Throughout the nineteenth century, women of all ethnic groups relied on untrained Malay *biden*, or traditional birth attendants, who did not use antiseptic procedures when delivering babies or cutting umbilical cords.[30] Women on the sugar estates, where male wages during the nineteenth century were not high enough to support a family, had to go back to work quickly, leaving babies with a child minder, assigned by the managers to watch infants and toddlers, while parents were in the fields. Malayan plantations during the nineteenth century did not facilitate either child bearing or child rearing.

Although intermarriage among Europeans and Asians was rare, the possibility of inter-racial sex worried the European males who ran the colony. British colonial officials who travelled widely in the Federated Malay States before 1914 claimed that both planters and government employees in the rural areas commonly had Asian mistresses. Richard Winstedt, long-time Director of Education in the Straits Settlements and Federated Malay States, presented the situation of European men in Malaya in the following terms: "No home life, no women friends, no libraries, no theatres or cinemas, not always [a] big enough community for bridge or tennis, no motor-cars, no long walks on account of that labyrinth of trackless jungle; was it any wonder that the white exile took to himself one of the complaisant, amusing, good-tempered and good mannered daughters of the East?" Winstedt wanted plantation civil society to resemble that of suburban London or Brighton. For him, a male

---

[30] "Fortnightly Accounts, 19 July 1890," Vol. 16, p. 399 in PSE, "Letters and Papers," Mss 644.1 p19 (APS); The infant mortality rate in the Straits Settlements ranged between 231 and 271 per thousand births in the years between 1901 and 1914. See Manderson, *Sickness*, pp. 44, 55, 204–206.

Orientalist dream became the one viable solution to the social isolation of the planters.[31] When representatives of the Board of Directors of the Penang Sugar Estates arrived in 1888, they were scandalized to find that three of the middle level staff had Tamil concubines. As they saw it, these liaisons not only made good management impossible, but they corrupted assistants who had gone native and lost personal discipline. They were outraged by reports that Mr Lease, who worked in the factory, allegedly showed up for breakfast in a sarong, and spent the middle of the day in his bungalow reading and being fanned by a servant! In 1890, a similar case surfaced. Edward Bratt, an assistant manager admitted to his employers that he and the government magistrate with whom he shared a bungalow kept Tamil mistresses. He threatened to quit his job if the company did not give him the right to control his private life. Yet when pressured, he pledged to change his ways and asked for permission to marry a woman from home, which was the only solution to his wish for companionship that the company found acceptable.[32]

What was at issue was not only disapproval of inter-racial sex, but the blurring of cultural boundaries and the loss of European and managerial control. Quintin Hogg, a sugar merchant and Christian philanthropist who had been sent to Province Wellesley to evaluate conditions on the Penang Sugar Estates, blamed its labour problems on competition for women's sexual favours:

I say unhesitatingly that such intercourse is most prejudicial to the well-being of the Estates. The majority of the rows & disturbances which take place are as you must well know caused by jealousies & intrigues arising there from. Moreover you almost invariably find that the friends & relatives of the favorite concubine get promoted to positions of trust on the estate. The effect of course is disastrous. The estate is robbed to furnish presents wherewith to buy the favour of the prostitute in question, & every branch of the service on the property suffers as the employees feel that the road to promotion does not depend upon the faithful discharge of their duties but on their currying favour with this woman.[33]

Hogg saw Tamil women as polluters of the plantation, little more than prostitutes or thieves. His attack on the women deflected attention from the uneven sex ratios on the plantation and managers' virtually

---

[31] John Butcher, *The British in Malaya 1880–1941* (Kuala Lumpur, Oxford University Press, 1979), pp. 200–201; Richard Olaf Winstedt, *Start from Alif; Count from One, an Autobiographical Mémoire* (Kuala Lumpur: Oxford University Press, 1969), p. 18

[32] "Letter T. Low to J. Ray, 23 June 1888," Vol. 14, p. 366; Letter "T. Low to J. Ray, 21 July 1888," Vol. 14, p. 376, in PSE, "Letters and Papers," Mss 644.1 p19 (APS)

[33] "Letter Q. Hogg to J. Ray, 25 October 1889," Vol. 16, pp. 189–193, in PSE, "Letters and Papers," Mss 644.1 p19 (APS)

unchallenged power over their employees. In his opinion, problems of labour relations resulted not from managerial coercion or incompetence but from sexual jealousy and the flawed morality of Tamil women, who were neither given names nor asked to tell their stories.

Even when Tamil women spoke, they were not heard. In 1891, a Tamil woman named Arlamalu tried to get medical aid for her husband Rengasamy, a plantation worker, who had a bad case of dysentery. After three days she took him to the house of their overseer, Kandarsammy, and asked his wife for help. When they were told to leave, Arlamalu got a cart and pushed her husband to the nearest hospital. There a Chinese attendant refused them admittance because they lacked an official letter from an employer. They then sat outside the hospital for two days while the hospital continued to ignore their appeals. No inquiry would have been made, but a local magistrate asked Mr Webber, the irascible plantation manager for whom the couple worked, why he had not sent his sick coolies to the hospital earlier. To defend himself, he promptly charged the hospital's medical officer, Munnameah, with neglecting his duty to admit Rengasamy and other sick workers. An irate Munnameah promptly sued Mr Webber for slander and public defamation of character. Munnameah won his suit, despite the evidence given against him by the two women. The court reasoned that such a serious charge could not be proven by "the simple uncorroborated statement of a Kling woman ... The defendant is perfectly cognizant with the image of Tamils, [he] is a Tamil speaker. That he should have relied on this one statement is extraordinary, for without exception there is hardly a race equal to the lower class of Tamils for lying and abuse."[34] End of story. The issue of appropriate medical care and oversight faded away in the face of colonial assumptions about Tamils' inherent mendacity. Such charges deflected onto Tamil women the blame for the failure of the colonial state to safeguard workers' welfare.

When women did emerge from the shadows – only briefly to be sure – they did so as victims. They were sometimes considered as property, in effect bought and sold. A Selangor government tax collector, Mr McCarthy, was dismissed by the British resident in 1885 after a Tamil named Ibrahim complained that his wife was living with Mr McCarthy until he repaid a loan of 20 dollars. After an investigation, British officials determined that McCarthy had given Ibrahim 20 dollars for his permission to take his wife as a mistress. They ordered the note to

---

[34] Batang Padang, District Office Files, "Notes of the Case: Munnameah vs. W. Webber, Slander, 4.7.91," BP 104/91; "Munnameah: Action against Mr. Webber for certain Statements made by him, 2.5.91," BP 165/91 (Arkib Negara, Kuala Lumpur)

be destroyed and the wife to be returned, although her opinion in the matter seems not to have been solicited.[35]

Readers of the *Perak Pioneer*, an English-language newspaper published between 1896 and 1912, relished the "Police News" column, which reported on the colourful transgressions of local Asians. Headlines all too often featured violence against women. "The Kling (Tamil) who murdered his girl wife remains at large." "Kling named Allapitchay was charged on the 21st. with abducting a girl of 13 years old named Segupi from her home." "A Kling was charged before Mr Stephens today for threatening to stab his wife; he was bound over to keep the peace for 6 months in the sum of 25 dollars." Reporters generally blamed male jealousy and brutality, which was allegedly provoked by flirtatious or unfaithful females. Women had a scarcity value on the plantations, but single ones could not be effectively independent. They earned too little to support themselves, and as emigrants they had lost the protections given in India by kin, caste, and village group. At the bottom of the plantation hierarchy, they lived in a brutal world where neither the state nor plantation management would protect them.[36]

Work Disciplines on the Plantations

Industrial agriculture strove for uniformity of product and output, which was easier to achieve in factories than in fields. European companies imported steam engines, multi-roller mills, and furnaces whose temperatures and speeds could be controlled, allowing them to refine techniques that were tested in laboratories and systematically compared for results. On the larger sugar estates, steam engines, vacuum pans, centrifuges, and triple-effect furnaces overseen by European engineers and chemists substituted for the relatively simple methods of Chinese cane farmers, who relied on buffalos and stone rollers to crush the cane and iron boilers and on clay jars to process the juice (see Figure 1.1). In the large factories by the end of the nineteenth century, electrical lighting permitted round-the-clock operation, letting managers not worry much about human biological rhythms and limitations. At least at the end of the sugar-making process, managers had a sense of control and comparative advantage.[37] But before the machines

[35] Selangor Secretariat Files, KL 610/85 (Arkib Negara, Kuala Lumpur)
[36] See Gaiutra Bahadur, *Coolie Woman*, pp. 124–125
[37] D. J. M. Tate argues that European sugar manufacturers quickly gained an advantage in sugar processing because of their access to capital, technology, and information from other producing areas, while Chinese sugar growers retained at least equality in the area of cultivation because of their access to cheap labour and familiarity with locally appropriate methods; D. J. M. Tate, *The RGA History of the Plantation Industry in the Malay Peninsula* (Kuala Lumpur: Oxford University Press, 1996), pp. 118–119. See also James

could be pressed into service, cane had to be grown and transported to the mills, and both the plants and their caregivers proved much more difficult to handle. The effort to use workers as if they were machines played a major part in the creation of plantation colonialism, but it was bound to fail. Human bodies tire, sicken, or rebel. Cane could be destroyed by too much or too little rain, by infections and infestations. Sugar manufacture was a risky business, and the Malayan industry struggled to compete with lower-cost growers in Cuba, China, and Java, as well as beetroot sugar producers in Europe. Companies saw heavy discipline and low wages as survival strategies, whose costs were displaced onto the workers.

Sugar growing in Malaya required the repurposing and reconfiguration of the land. Since plantations were located along tidal rivers near the sea, new estates had to be drained and desalinated. Workers first built dykes or dams to prevent sea water from backing up into the many small creeks and inlets that led inland. They next stripped away the trees and plants and dug both a network of drainage canals and another deeper set for navigation. Wooden sluice gates allowed water to pass out through the dykes at low tide and as the water rose blocked it from moving back into the fields. As rain leeched through the soil, lowering its salt content, cultivation could begin. Men used hand hoes or changkols to dig shallow furrows, 6 feet apart and 120 feet long, where they planted cane tops. During the twelve to fourteen months that it took canes to mature, women weeded the fields and men cultivated the soil. Then, when juice and sugar levels reached their peaks, men stripped, cut, and transported cane to the mill. To grow a second crop, workers removed the heavily rooted lalang grasses that spread quickly in open areas, and then replanted new cane tops.[38]

The frustrations of cane growing in Malaya were unending. Not only did the weather intervene in the form of drought or downpour to stunt crops and decrease sugar content, but destructive funguses sometimes spread like wildfires. Rats ate the cane, and beetles tunnelled into it. Certainly, managers tried hard to tame local nature. They kept shifting varieties of cane and fertilizers; they imported ferrets to kill rats and discussed plant diseases with agronomists. But fixes were short-term and never produced the uniformly favourable results planters desired. James Scott argues that monocultures are "more fragile" and "more vulnerable to the stress of disease and weather than polycultures." Moreover, the search for the highest yields using uniform methods and identical plants runs up against

C. Jackson, *Planters and Speculators: Chinese and European Agricultural Enterprise in Malaya, 1786–1921* (Kuala Lumpur: University of Malaya Press, 1968), pp. 130–133, 145–146

[38] Jackson, *Planters*, 130–131; H. C. Prinsen Geerligs, *The World's Cane Sugar Industry: Past and Present* (Manchester: Norman Rodger, 1912), pp. 70–71

the complex interrelationships of species, particularly in the tropics, where soils are thin and biodiversity is great.[39] Nature in the tropics was not easily tamed. Most importantly, the work itself was nasty and unrelenting. However far away the field, gangs marched there in the very early morning and marched back in the mid-afternoon. Shade and cool water were always in short supply. Ten hours in the hot sun swinging a heavy hoe or a parang against heavy stalks exhausted even the strongest. Straw sandals and skimpy coarse cotton offered little protection against stones, insects, or knife-sharp leaves. Mosquitoes bred in stagnant water, spreading malaria and dengue fever. Workers needed much inner discipline, rein-forced by outer compulsion, to carry on. They could not match the relentless productivity of the juice-extracting and processing factories, which could, and in the opinion of managers *should*, be fed constantly with an ample supply of uniform canes.

In the early days of sugar cultivation, when Chinese immigrants domi-nated the industry, European planters simply handed over tracts of uncleared land to a Chinese headman, who assembled a work gang from his dialect group and signed a contract for a year's worth of their labour. For a set rate per month, they drained and cleared land and then planted, weeded, and cut canes for transport to the mill. Estates advanced money to cover tools, food, and a mud and palm-leaf cabin, whose cost was then repaid from the value of the sugar produced. In bad years, workers deserted and gangs failed to repay their debts. Moreover, the Chinese had access to land in Perak where they could grow sugar on their own, if they could raise some capital.[40] Chinese immigrants, given their ties to local merchants and clan associations, had resources unavailable to South Asian workers. European owners were kept at a distance, and they had limited power over Chinese employees.

Although this system of subcontracting continued, the larger estates took on a new risk by moving into cane production themselves, recruiting South Asians, Javanese, and Chinese to work in gangs under the control of assistant managers or Asian headmen.[41] The Penang Sugar Estates

[39] James C. Scott, *Seeing Like a State: How Certain Schemes to Improve the Human Condition Have Failed* (New Haven: Yale University Press, 1998), pp. 21, 274, 292–295; Lynn Hollen Lees, "International Management in a Free-Standing Company: The Penang Sugar Estates, Ltd., and the Malayan Sugar Industry 1851–1914," *Business History Review*, 81 (Spring 2007), pp. 42–44

[40] Leonard Wray, *The Practical Sugar Planter* (London: Smith, Elder and Co., 1848) pp. 126–127; "Letter A. Morrison to J. Ray, 11 April, 1883," Vol. 9, p. 212 in PSE, "Letters and Papers," Mss 644.1 p19 (APS)

[41] W. L. Blythe, "Historical Sketch of Chinese Labour in Malaya," *Journal of the Malayan Branch of the Royal Asiatic Society* 20, Pt. 1 (1947): 64–114; *Labour Commission of 1890,* pp. 9–14

worked through labour associations, or kongsis, to which they advanced money in payment for each worker's time. Kongsi headmen kept the books, paid the crews, and generally took care of discipline and work assignments. Labourers were attached to them, rather than to the plantations. Debt, commonly expanded through opium sales, helped keep members under the headman's thumb. When the District Office of Batang Padang in Perak investigated Heng Taihin Kongsi in 1890, it found that two of the contract workers had remained in their jobs for ten years and another for seven years because they had never cleared their debts. The office ordered new accounts to be made up, and those who had served at least three years were declared free to leave.[42] This would have permitted these individuals to move to better-paying jobs as independent labourers in the larger villages or towns.

The state's oversight of Chinese workers was minimal. Hubert Berkeley, who eventually became a District Officer in charge of a large territory in northern Perak, spent his early years in that state as a junior magistrate and police inspector. Although he regularly inspected local kongsis, his mandate was only to see that they had correctly registered all their workers and make sure that any other residents had proper permits. As long as bodies were accounted for, they were normally the business of the kongsis, whose methods were ignored.[43]

In the fields, bosses divided work among ethnic groups. On Batu Kawan estate in 1890, Chinese cleared the land and cut cane, while Tamils were assigned to plant, cultivate, and weed. On Byram plantation, Javanese indentured men did preliminary clearing, but Tamils handled the fieldwork. Managers hired local Malays sometimes for specific, limited jobs, such as clearing one field or digging a drain, although they would not sign on for regular employment at the wages offered. Gangs of Javanese or Tamil women were given the lighter tasks of weeding or stripping cane of old leaves. Most of the cultivation and cane transport was done by Tamils, although estates continued to employ indirectly controlled Chinese work gangs.[44]

Work may have been differentiated by ethnic groups, but everyone awakened to the clanging of a factory gong at 5:00 or 5:30 AM. Sleepy workers rolled out of bed, searching for food and water in the early

---

[42] Batang Padang, District Office Files, "Statements of various Chinese Tindals and Coolies of Heng Tailhin Congsee at Chendriang," 28 March 1890, No. 102/90, Register A 72 (National Archive, Kuala Lumpur)

[43] "Office Diary, Hubert Berkeley, 1888," 15 November 1888, 2 December 1888, 15 January 1889, RCS/RCMS 103/1/2 (Royal Commonwealth Society Collection, Cambridge University Library)

[44] Straits Settlements, *Report of the Labour Commission, 1890*, Appendix B, Evidence, pp. 110–111, 123

morning haze. More clangs, and people poured out from barracks into the muster ground, men and women in separate lines. Assistants and foremen with roll books marched down the rows, calling out workers' names so that they could check off those present and record the absent, for whom they would have to account. By 6:00 AM or so, foremen marched their gangs out to specific fields, and assistants retreated to breakfast before riding out by bike or horse to meet the teams. They and the foremen then assigned each worker his or her daily quota, an act that bred conflict and resentment.[45] Who would get the hardest soil to till? Who would be given the thickest patch of weeds? Overseers had great power to reward some and punish others. The task, rather than time, was the unit of measurement. To be paid for the day, workers had not only to show up but to complete whatever task was assigned in order to be credited for the day's work. Managers insisted these assignments were easily done, but workers complained they were too hard to finish. In any case, the planters' own evidence in 1890 shows that labourers were credited on average with only twenty days work per month, rather than the mandated twenty-seven, indicating that one-quarter of their time was normally spent either completing the previous day's tasks or not working because of illness or some other reason.[46] Maximum productivity was never achieved, despite direct orders, fines, and caning. Labourers succeeded in reducing their work requirement through their unwillingness, or physical inability, to finish what was demanded.

The Immigration Ordinance of 1876 stipulated six days of fieldwork per week, each day no more than 10 hours long.[47] Later in the century, however, this was reduced to 9 hours, with the recommendation that Sunday labour be stopped. Estate factories did not take holidays during harvesting, however, and it is clear that as late as 1890 managers tried to recruit men for Sunday work, generally unsuccessfully, by paying overtime. The Penang Sugar Estates abandoned Sunday work a few years later, after admitting failure in their efforts to compel labourers to spend six full days in the fields. Although the work day stretched officially from 6:00 AM until mid-afternoon, the end of the day was variable. Labourers took a long break at midday, when the sun was at its height, and they

[45] An Assistant, "Sugar Planting," *Straits Chinese Magazine* (1898), Vol. 2, p. 55
[46] Straits Settlements, *Report of the Labour Commission of 1890*, p. 56
[47] The Governments of India and of the Straits Settlements were part of an international movement toward regulating indenture as a labour system that would safeguard the welfare of labourers. Although early legislation set low standards, they established precedents that would carry forward into the era of the International Labor Organization and League of Nations. See Rachael Sturman, "Indian Indenture Labor and the History of the International Rights Regime," *AHR*, Vol. 119, No. 5 (December, 2014), pp. 1439–1465.

could rest and eat, if they had food with them. Meanwhile, assistants went back to their bungalows for a bath, lunch, and possibly a nap until the afternoon work shift. The day wound down in the late afternoon, when workers marched back to their barracks and the assistants adjourned to tennis, drinks, and perhaps an evening at their club.[48]

The issue of how a plantation could control its workers' bodies never disappeared. Overseers and assistants watched in the fields and lived near the lines, always in earshot. They could dock wages, fine, or hit the non-compliant with a cane. Fieldwork, therefore, created endless confrontations between demanding overseers and unhappy labourers. But people in the fields had their own strategies of self-protection. They could slow the pace of work, stay away from the fields claiming illness, or run away. Unauthorized trips to town or to a village toddy shop could bring brief interludes of freedom. The weak are not without weapons.[49]

The labour needs of the Penang Sugar Estates constantly expanded, in part because many labourers died, deserted, or refused to renew their indentures every year. The company, which employed around 1,800 workers in 1880, needed about 3,000 in 1890, 4,000 in 1910, and 5,000 in 1913.[50] Both state labour inspections and court reports acknowledged high rates of desertion from plantations throughout the region. Slightly more than 11 per cent of the indentured Indian labourers absconded from their plantation employers in the Straits Settlements in 1880, and an average of 13 per cent deserted annually between 1902 and 1910.[51] Compare those numbers with 1889 reports from the Caledonia plantation, which lost 27 per cent of its indentured workers in that year. At the same time, the Byram estate admitted that 21 per cent of its indentured workers had deserted and another 7 per cent were "absent without leave."[52] A high proportion of the company's workers treated the estates as way stations en route to elsewhere, rather than as a long-term job. Without the continued importation of new workers, plantation colonialism in Malaya was not a sustainable system.

---

[48] An Assistant, "Sugar Planting," pp. 55–57
[49] James C. Scott, *Weapons of the Weak: Everyday Forms of Peasant Resistance* (New Haven: Yale University Press, 1985)
[50] "Fortnightly Returns, 1888–1889," Vol. 15, pp. 335, 345, 385; in PSE, "Letters and Papers," Mss 644.1 p19 (APS); "General Report from W. Duncan, 23 Sept., 1910," p. 10, in Ramsden Papers Relating to the Sugar and Rubber Companies in Malaya, Microfilm 5633 (National University of Singapore)
[51] Jackson, *Immigrant Labour*, p. 113
[52] "Letter Mr. Low to J. Ray, 23 January 1889," Vol. 15, p. 195; "Letter Mr. Low to J. Ray, 5 March 1889," Vol. 15, pp. 209–210; "Fortnightly Mail Reports: Caledonia and Byram Estates," Vol. 17, pp. 340, 368, in PSE, "Letters and Papers," Mss 644.1 p19 (APS)

Sugar growing demanded much of its field hands, whether they toiled in Cuba, Fiji, or Southeast Asia. Brutal work and miserable pay could hold only those who had no viable alternatives. Many made the decision to escape, just as Chivatean had done in 1857. In Malaya, roads elsewhere were blocked not by fences but by watchful foremen and by police constables who chased runaways and enforced contracts. Ethnic divisions of labour, arising from racial stereotypes, reinforced separations widespread in local communities. British governance on the plantations demonstrated its power primarily through penal sanctions and segregation, setting a pattern for the colony as a whole.

The Dual Role of the State

Colonial governance on Malayan plantations took on two contradictory forms. Most obvious was direct disciplining of workers' bodies as they carried out their daily tasks in the fields. Behind the power of the foremen and managers lay the authority of the colonial state and its police, who sent workers to jail for non-compliance with their contracts. At the same time, imperialists insisted that British rule would civilize subject peoples and bring them direct benefits. The indenture system mandated state oversight of emigrant labourers, which was defined in terms of their welfare. To that end, the importation of European biomedicine became an important strategy of imperial rule. The government of India appointed sanitary officers in several provinces after 1864, and colonial doctors there expanded state oversight of daily life through its anti-cholera campaigns. In an effort to lower death rates, hospitals were built in the larger Malayan towns during the nineteenth century, and the Straits Settlements mounted mass vaccination drives after 1870.[53] Municipalities in British Malaya invested in sanitation as a key infrastructure of governance. In compliance with state directives, plantations hired medical staff and built their own hospitals, which were periodically visited by colonial medical inspectors. Colonial governance deepened its control of labour through its mandate to safeguard workers' welfare, as well as through penal sanctions.

British estate owners and managers agitated for the government's help controlling workers, while at the same time they worked to minimize state interference on plantation spaces. The Directors of the Penang Sugar Estates complained to the Colonial Office in 1883 that overregulation of emigrants by the Indian government "hampered and discouraged" the

[53] Thomas R. Metcalf, *Ideologies of the Raj, The New Cambridge History of India*, Vol. 3, Part 4 (Cambridge: Cambridge University Press, 1994), pp. 176–177; Manderson, *Sickness*, pp. 15, 46, 48–49

movement of workers into the Straits, and they threatened that in the event of any additional "impediment placed in the way of freedom of contract, and the engagement of free labour in an easy and natural manner, the Company's Estates [would] sooner or later be rendered practically unworkable." Freedom of contract for them, however, meant contract enforcement, with non-compliance punishable by jail terms at hard labour. They joined a large group of merchants and planters from the Straits Settlements who protested against changes in Straits labour laws proposed in 1882, which would have shortened contract terms to one year and replaced imprisonment with fines as the penalty for misconduct on estates. From their point of view, indentures were mutually advantageous agreements entered into freely by consenting adults, which governments had no right to restrict and which would be even more beneficial if they could be extended to five or more years. At the same time, they demanded that the government enforce any breach of contracts with jail time. Claiming that labourers viewed fines "with indifference," they demanded "*real* punishment" for any refusal to comply with work orders or contract terms.[54] Planters argued that it was essential to their businesses that they have an indentured, low-wage labour force bound by long-term contracts, and the Straits Government agreed with them. Although indentures for South Asians were temporary and therefore not slavery, they were a rigid form of unfree labour, which many were constrained to accept and which the British state encouraged and enforced in Malaya on terms much less favourable for workers than those available in the Caribbean.[55] Most importantly, colonial law codes in the Straits Settlements and the Federated Malay States mandated jail time for infringement of labour contracts. Estate labourers who deserted and were re-captured or those who refused to obey orders were taken before a British magistrate (normally a district officer) and locked up for periods between a few days and a few months. "Coolie catchers" – plantation employees, and police constables sent out as trackers – managed to arrest and bring back fewer than half of the runaways. Incentives to disappear were as great as the number of places outside the plantations in which to hide.

In September of 1879, Arthur Morrison, the general manager of the company reported to London that there had been a "riot" and a

[54] "Letter E. M. Underdown to A. Evelyn Ashley, M.P., 18 February 1883," CO 273/ 125, pp. 10–12 (National Archive, London)

[55] Straits Settlements, *Labour Report of 1890*; Carter, *Voices from Indenture*, pp. 1–42; Chanderbali, *Indian Indenture*, pp. 93–99; Hugh Tinker, *A New System of Slavery: The Export of Indian Labour Overseas 1830–1920*, 2nd ed. (London: Hansib Publishing Ltd., 1993)

subsequent strike on the Caledonia estate. After J. MacDougall, the Caledonia estate manager, had attempted to put the Immigration Ordinance "in force against a number of men who had failed to complete an ordinary day's work," a group of labourers objected. When MacDougall claimed his legal rights as mandated by contract, they attacked him, possibly throwing stones. He suffered a head wound, which became infected with tetanus, and was sent back to Britain for treatment. In the meantime, 150 workers refused to go back to work until the issue was settled. The triggering event was probably a threatened deduction from their daily wage. The 1876 law permitted fines to be levied if an overseer judged that a man had done "unsatisfactory work" on his daily task. Magistrates were supposed to decide such cases after weighing the evidence, and if they did not, the action was illegal. Attendance at court, however, removed men and managers from the fields, so estate staff normally took matters into their own hands. Although colonial officers in the Straits Settlements knew the practice was common, they did not enforce the letter of the law. The company's general manager was furious with his workers for the attack:

I much regret to say we are having a great deal of trouble with our Kling Coolies, who thanks to the injudicious treatment of the Officials under the new Immigration Ordinance are rapidly becoming almost unmanageable. So completely is all power of maintaining discipline taken out of our hands and centred in those of the Magistrates and Immigration Officers, that the Coolies are beginning to think that they can do as they like on the Estates and can do as much or as little work as they think fit ... A spirit of greater insubordination I have never known displayed by any body of men. For days they were perfectly unmanageable and though the Acting Lieutenant Governor of Penang came over to try his power among them, they simply placed him at defiance.

Morrison's fury toward unruly workers was matched by his anger at colonial officials, whom he perceived as too lax in their treatment of labourers, who perceived and could sometimes exploit the fault lines among the several authorities who attempted to discipline them. Although the company initially wanted to haul all the strikers into court and sue them for breach of contract, they eventually opted for relative moderation. They prosecuted only three men for assault, each of whom was sentenced to one month in jail and a $20 fine, approximately eight months' wages. Then each of the three was convicted of inflicting "grievous bodily hurt" and "unlawful assembly," which extended their jail sentences substantially. Mr Morrison reported happily: "The late disturbance has also had a good effect upon the Government Officials here and has opened their eyes to the fact that the Coolie is not quite so harmless and unsophisticated a being as they imagined, and that the planter has also need of some protection in dealing with them." Morrison needed the help of officials whom he regarded as naïve and relatively uninformed. In his opinion, only a hard line would preserve managerial power on the plantations. He noted that the sentences had a "very wholesome deterrent effect . . . I do not think that future trouble may be expected from them for a very long time to come." Moreover, the company continued to fine contract workers for performance that was judged to be unsatisfactory. Managers at Batu Kawan, Caledonia, and Golden Grove admitted in 1881 that they had continued to deduct 10 cents from the daily wage, which was only 12 or 14 cents, as a punishment for those contract workers whose efforts did not meet an unspecified standard.[56] The law and the magistrates helped the company win that particular fight, but reducing workers to starvation wages was not an effective long-term strategy for sustaining a plantation labour force of people with time-limited contracts.

Plantation managers and overseers pushed a continuing stream of labourers into the courts on charges of breach of contract, which arose from insubordination, absenteeism, and desertion. In 1880, 32 per cent of Indian immigrants working on Province Wellesley plantations were hauled into court and convicted of an offence against the Immigration Ordinance. Almost a third of the people jailed that year in Province Wellesley were Tamil labourers convicted of desertion.[57] In 1888, the proportions were similar: 30 per cent of the indentured Indian immigrants were convicted of breach of contract, and 31 per cent deserted, but it is not reported how many actually escaped and how many were eventually caught and jailed.[58] Kongsi overseers had the job of keeping Chinese workers in line and on the plantations, and they tended not to use British courts. Simply holding on to workers' bodies produced an ongoing struggle until late in the century, although the plantations had

---

[56] "Letter from A. Morrison to J. Ray," 18 September 1879, Vol. 6, pp. 70–71; "Letter A. Morrison to J. Ray, 16 November, 1879," Vol. 6, p. 94; "Letter A. Morrison to J. Ray, 29 November, 1879," Vol. 6, p. 101, in PSE, "Letters and Papers," Mss 644.1 p19 (APS); Chanderbali, *Indian Indenture*, pp. 169–170

[57] Straits Settlements, "Report on Indian Immigration for the Year 1880," *Paper Laid before the Legislative Council, 12 April 1881*, No. 10, p. 72. In 1888, The Straits Settlements "Annual Report for 1888" suggested that "coolie prisons" were needed in Province Wellesley, so that inmates could be used to work on the roads; Straits Settlements, "Annual Report for 1888," in Jarman, *Annual Reports*, Vol. 2, p. 388; see also Straits Settlements, "Annual Report for 1886," in Jarman, *Annual Reports*, Vol. 2, p. 187

[58] Straits Settlements, "Report on Indian Immigration for the Year 1880," p. 72; Straits Settlements, "Annual Report for 1888," in Jarman, *Annual Reports*, Vol. 3, p. 358. By 1900, anxiety about desertions and convictions lessened. Not only did later reports stop publishing those two numbers, but in 1899 the number of desertions was lower than in the previous two years and only eight people were "prosecuted for attempting to leave the Colony without a certificate"; Straits Settlements, "Annual Report for 1899," in Jarman, *Annual Reports*, Vol. 4, p. 469.

better weapons in the fight than did labourers. Planters fought hard to retain jail time at hard labour for breaches of contract, objecting to fines as weak and ineffective discipline.[59] But the meaning of endless trips to court is ambiguous. They signalled both continuing determination to discipline labourers and also workers' rejection of that discipline. Who won in the day-to-day struggles is not obvious. Managers accused labourers of preferring jail to field work because it was easier, and workers seem to have agreed with this damning assessment of the estates.

Planters also claimed the right to control workers' movements and superintend their free time. In 1884, MacDougall bragged to the London office that he had managed to almost stop desertions "by prohibiting the Coolies from going to the village on Sundays where they meet the crimps in the drinking shops. We supply all necessaries from the Godowns and have prohibited entrance to the estate to all outsiders without a pass."[60] A few estates locked their workers up at night, or, in the case of Batu Kawan, blocked labourers without a permit from taking ferries to the mainland. The total control of workers' time and bodies about which MacDougall dreamed remained a fantasy, however. Plantations were not and could not be closed spaces.

The major weapon wished for by sugar planters to block desertion, which many of them had used when working in Demerara or British Guiana, was a pass-law system. There, labourers needed a written permit, or pass, to be more than two miles away from the plantation to which they were bound. Such rules had come into force in Trinidad in 1846 and then been adopted more broadly in the British West Indies colonies, remaining in force through the rest of the century, but they had not been included in the legislation regulating contract labour in the Straits Settlements in 1876. When the economic development of Perak and Kedah took off in the 1880s and desertions on the estates increased, planters asked the governor of the Straits Settlements to introduce a similar system. Thomson Low, who managed the Penang Sugar Estates in 1888, commented: "At the Planters' interview with the Governor, I brought before him the desirability of making all Coolies, if not under Indenture, carry their Contract signed by whoever they served their Indenture period with; that they had fulfilled it; and that anyone failing to produce this ticket or a pass from the Estate ... should be arrested and prosecuted." Since the

[59] See "Letters E. M. Underdown to A. Evelyn Ashley, M.P., 13 February, 18 February 1883," CO 273/125, pp. 10–12 (National Archive, London)
[60] Walton Look Lai, *Indentured Labor, Caribbean Sugar: Chinese and Indian Migrants to the British West Indies, 1838–1918* (Baltimore: Johns Hopkins, 1993), pp. 64–65; "Letter J. MacDougall to J. Ray," 18 June 1884, Vol. 10, p. 409 in PSE, "Letters and Papers," Mss 644.1 p19 (APS)

colonial government sometimes hired runaway coolies to work on its road gangs, it was not eager to comply with their request. The governor politely refused, citing the need for general economic development and reminding the planters of the outcry against such a requirement when it had been recently introduced in Mauritius. He argued that it would be offensive to workers already in the colony and might deter future migrants. Planters did not let the matter rest, but repeated their demands before the 1890 Labour Commission, but again to no avail.[61] Even though colonial officials generally supported the planters, they sometimes recognized that the overall stability of the colony required protecting workers' right to mobility.

Although a formal pass system was not instituted in the Straits Settlements, efforts to track workers who escaped across state borders produced an informal one by 1890, which local officials could implement if they chose. A group of free Tamil workers decided in the spring of 1890 to leave jobs in southern Perak and walk to the state of Pahang, where they thought they would do better. Unfortunately, they were stopped by police and detained by order of J. Campbell, Magistrate and Collector in Ulu Selangor, because they had no proof that they were not runaway coolies. As he explained to his counterpart in Perak, the state of Selangor required passes for travelling Chinese and Tamils so that their routes could be tracked, and he would be most obliged if local Perak magistrates or headmen would provide migrants with official letters defining their status. British civil servants stated clearly that Perak had "no regulations ... requiring a Tamil to bear a pass or a ticket, as is the case with the Chinese," but they quickly agreed to provide those documents if Selangor authorities demanded them. A notice in English and Tamil soon circulated around the district telling would-be emigrants to Selangor that they should get letters from their local magistrate to protect them from detention. Although colonial magistrates, police, and Malay headmen in Perak disagreed about what local rules were, the default position was that Tamils and Chinese not on an estate or in a tin mine needed to establish their right to move freely.[62] The pass system in Malaya was never as extensive as that in the West Indies or in Natal, but its shadow hung over free Chinese and Tamils, who were automatically suspected of being runaways during the period when indenture

---

[61] "Letter Thomson Low to J. Ray, 8 June 1888," Vol. 14, pp. 343–344; "Letter T. Low to J. Ray, 9 January 1890," Vol. 15, p. 191, in PSE, "Letters and Papers," Mss 644.1 p19 (APS); Straits Settlements, *Labour Commission of 1890*, Appendix B, Evidence, p. 88

[62] Batang Padang, District Office Files, "Complaints of the Conduct of the Police," Native 20/89; "Detention of 27 Tamils who were on their way to Pahang," BP 90/90; "Pass given by Penghulu Toh Bias to one Lee Chin," BP 167/90 (National Archive, Kuala Lumpur)

and debt shaped the Malayan labour market.[63] The assumption built
into the informal pass system that workers' free movement required
surveillance and documentation reveals the strongly coercive and unfree
nature of the plantation labour market in British Malaya.[64]

Circulating within plantation colonialism, however, was a second
set of imperatives based upon the official view that the British government needed to – and eventually did – improve the physical well being of
colonized peoples. Moreover, the premise on which the indenture system rested was the acceptance of agreed-upon standards for workers'
welfare, which the British state pledged to enforce. Officials in the
Straits Settlements proclaimed their good intentions and successes as
often as possible. In 1872, the Governor, Sir Harry Ord, pledged that
the colony would meet all the standards set by the Indian government
for the treatment of Indian emigrants, which were levied "for the health
and safety of the coolie."[65] In 1884, Governor Frederick Weld pointed
to the building of hospitals and the ending of debt slavery as two of many
ways that imperial rule in the Straits Settlements had improved the lives
of ordinary people there. Indian labourers flocked to the colony, he
thought, for the sweetness of a life where they were "protected" and
where food, wages, and medical care were overseen for their adequacy.
Frank Swettenham, who advised the Sultans of Selangor and Perak
during the 1880s and 1890s and then became the first Resident
General of the Federated Malay States, claimed in 1896 that British
rule had made the population of Malaya "freer, healthier, wealthier, …
happier by far than when we went to them."[66] These men saw no
contradiction between economic development and labourers' welfare;
one complemented the other.

These statements by the colony's top officials empowered local doctors
and magistrates to protest what they saw as shocking conditions on
Malayan plantations. Starting in the 1870s, harsh attacks on some of
the Province Wellesley sugar estates were noted in official records and

[63] Lai, *Indentured Labor*, pp. 62–64; Tinker, *New System*, p. 107, 191, 272–273
[64] See Tinker, *New System*.
[65] After 1867, when the Straits Settlements was separated from British India, movement
between the two areas became international travel, which the Indian government had to
approve. Governor Ord of the Straits Settlements was one of the architects of the
regulatory system legislated in 1872 and 1876 for Indian immigrants. He accepted the
obligation to appoint an Emigration Agent and a Protector of Emigrants, and to establish
reception depots. Emigrant ships also had to be licensed and to meet government-set
standards for conditions and food supplied, regulations soon extended to treatment on
plantations. Chanderbali, *Indian Indenture*, p. 143.
[66] Paul Kratoska, *Honorable Intentions: Talks on the British Empire in South-East Asia
delivered at the Royal Colonial Institute 1874–1928* (Singapore: Oxford University
Press, 1983), pp. 64–65

local newspapers in India, Penang, and Singapore. Even before the appointment of a Protector of Immigrants in 1876, doctors, coroners, and magistrates in the colony spoke out about the neglect and mistreatment that they saw. In 1873, investigators probing the deaths of two fieldworkers, Ramsamy and Periaya, concluded that the men had been forced to work while seriously ill and that they were paid too little to feed themselves adequately. Shortly thereafter, the Acting Colonial Surgeon, Dr J. D. M. Coghill, reported that about 100 workers from the Malakoff Estate had been sent to the Butterworth Hospital, weak from diarrhoea, gangrene, and deep cuts from caning. Two workers soon died, and their emaciated bodies showed evidence of severe floggings. Although managers tried to block an investigation, police brought charges of "culpable homicide" against overseer I. I. Durnford and two foremen, Udumansa and Ponnen, as well as the manager, J. T. Thompson. All were convicted on the lesser charge of assault and given short prison sentences, but Governor Andrew Clarke remitted even that penalty for the two Europeans after they had served about a month in jail. The case forced observers to take sides, since investigators collected direct evidence of brutal beatings, overcrowded housing, and scanty food. This evidence was transmitted to the Colonial Office in London, which took no remedial action. Governor Clarke commented that he had "every reason to believe that much more satisfactory relations have been already established between the planters and their coolies, and that considerable improvements are being effected in their accommodation and treatment."[67] Everyone but the plantation labourers seemed content to look forward, rather than backward.

Optimism continued to shape dealings between planters and officials for the rest of the century, and neither the Colonial Office nor appointed governors and residents were willing to force planters to adopt a more generous definition of workers' welfare. When G. T. Hare, the Perak Protector of the Chinese, reported he had "no doubt that systematic cruelty has been carried on in [the sugar estates of Krian and Kurau] for years," he blamed overseers, not the planters, and merely called for more frequent inspections rather than wholesale reform.[68] The upper ranks of colonial officials offered only muted criticism of the planters, despite clear evidence of brutal treatment and starvation wages. Planters effectively

---

[67] Straits Settlements, "Ill Treatment of Coolie Laborers on certain Estates," 12 May 1874, CO 273/75, No. 7055; see also "Letter Clarke to Carnarvon," 25 December 1873, CO273/71 No. 397 (National Archive, London); Chanderbali, *Indian Indenture*, pp. 144–156

[68] "Annual Report on the Chinese Protectorate, Perak for the year 1898," 1342/1899 (National Archive, Kuala Lumpur)

shielded themselves from outside attack: their overseers both delivered the blows for their bosses and absorbed reformers' criticisms.

During the last quarter of the century, colonial authorities kept a somewhat tighter rein on sugar plantations. The Protector of Immigrants regularly inspected Indian labourers on the estates, and Colonial Surgeons visited estates weekly, transferring the seriously ill to government hospitals. Workers' welfare was defined in narrow, sanitary terms, however, and the medical care offered was rudimentary. In August of 1879, Batu Kawan estate reported 75 of its 900 workers on its sick list and in the hospital sheds. Most suffered from leg ulcers or gangrene resulting from infected cuts. Treatment seems to have consisted primarily of rest, better food, and water. The hospital was old but relatively clean, and the surgeon found it satisfactory. By 1890, it had three wards with wooden floors and a palm leaf roof, which were judged to be "in good order." Inmates all had blankets and separate beds. Time in hospital, however, gave labourers a chance to complain out of their overseers' hearing. One group of Batu Kawan workers in 1881 tried to shift the question from sanitation to flogging and working conditions, and in response Governor Frederick A. Weld appointed a group of senior Straits administrators to investigate. Although they found workers reluctant to complain publicly in front of one another, they heard tales of extortion and forced labour. One overseer was said to threaten "no work, no rice!" to get ill men out into the fields, and discontent seemed endemic on the estate. Since they turned up no serious problems on other estates in the area, they concluded that "the condition of the Indian Immigrants is such as to leave no reasonable ground for complaint." Nevertheless, they implicitly accepted the workers' charges, calling for shorter hours, limited fines and debts, and a month of allowed sick days. Commissioners accused planters of locking up flogged workers to prevent their being questioned by inspectors. Planters, however, refused to admit that current standards were too low and that workers were beaten. They recommended flogging labourers who would not work, and said, approvingly, that overseers commonly carried rattan canes "as a badge of office."[69] By 1881, sharp differences existed between planters' opinions of appropriate standards and those of government doctors, inspectors, and, more importantly, those of workers who protested overseers' cruelties and demanded their back wages.

---

[69] Straits Settlements, "Complaints of Ill-treatment of Indian Immigrants on the Batu Kawan and Golden Grove Estates in Province Wellesley," in *Paper Laid before the Legislative Council*, 29 December 1881, No. 38, pp. 363–376; Straits Settlements, *Labour Commission* of 1881, pp. 2–3; Chanderbali, *Indian Indenture*, pp. 158–159; Straits Settlements, *Labour Commission of 1890*, Appendix B, Visit No. 11, p. 13

This divide persisted through the rest of the century, as the Labour Commission of 1890 reveals. Dominated by planters, it focused primarily on their concern for labour recruitment and the need for healthy, well-qualified workers. But its members also presented evidence of debt bondage and floggings, which they refused to condone. Their report recognized "abuses," admitting that "coolies are not infrequently beaten and otherwise ill-treated by their Tyndals or headmen." Chinese estate owners, especially those in Batu Kawan, received the bulk of the criticism, which cleverly deflected attention from the standard operating procedures of the larger, European plantations. In any case, commissioners blamed the casual cruelty of plantation life on foremen and overseers, not on European managers. They suggested that estates employ Chinese speakers, who would be better able to monitor treatment of Chinese labourers. The issue of the abuse inherent in contract labour was ignored.[70] From the standpoint of the planters, indentured workers had freely chosen their lot, and a deal was a deal. Although official investigations made clear the systematic mistreatment of workers on multiple plantations, the governments of the Straits Settlements and the Federated Malay States remained unwilling either to set higher standards of treatment or to void their contracts.

In 1889, Chellappah, an overseer at Messrs Hill and Rathhorn's estate in the Batang Padang area of Perak, reported the death of a Tamil worker named Veerasamy. When the District Medical Officer, Mr Munnameah, investigated, he found the body curled in a foetal position, lying on dirty grass in an area once used to house cattle. He reported the cause of death as "starvation and general debility . . . and exposure to cold and rain." The doctor requested a summons be issued to Veerasamy's supervisor, Mr J. C. Ford, for "having neglected the deceased and not sending him to the hospital when he was sick."[71] But there is no record of prosecution or punishment. Both planters and the colonial state in Malaya defined workers' "welfare" narrowly during the nineteenth century. Although prodded to do more by medical doctors and labour inspectors, colonial officials offered scant protection for contract workers. The state normally interceded only to inquire whether workers understood and accepted their labour agreements and whether employers complied with negotiated, minimal levels for wages, housing, and medical care. Employers' wishes to keep labour costs low trumped any lingering doubts about the

---

[70] Straits Settlements, *Labour Commission of 1890*, pp. 22–23

[71] No information on the resolution of this case is included in the archive; Batang Padang, District Office Files, "Report on the death of a Tamil coolie at Messrs. Hill and Rathbone lines; Cause of death by neglect," 30 January 1889, Misc. 12/89 (National Archive, Kuala Lumpur)

adequacy of state intervention. No one brought forward issues that by the 1890s mobilized British workers – for example, an eight-hour day, pensions, accident insurance, and unemployment benefits.[72] In colonial Malaya, welfare remained a paternalist, minimalist concept, one imposed rather than negotiated. Those who rejected the official definition could protest in the fields, whisper to visiting doctors and inspectors, or run away. Not until the 1930s did sustained, collective responses occur.

***

Plantation colonialism in Malaya was a coercive regime which depended upon physical violence and cultural caricatures to sustain a rigid hierarchy of power and inequality reinforced by the colonial state. Gender and ethnicity created an ascribed status, which was mirrored in space occupied, costumes worn, and food consumed, while the state added penal sanctions to the canes and fines of overseers and managers. The imperial framework for indentured labour brought one layer of oversight, while international agro-business constituted another, both of which reinforced the bodily disciplines created by low pay and bruisingly hard work. Neither overarching structure gave workers more than an ascribed voice, and labourers fought back by running away and turning on one another.

Plantation colonialism with a core of unfree, heavily disciplined labour is not just a Malayan story. Industrial agriculture, supported on the backs of slaves, spread globally in the seventeenth century along with European empires, its growth barely slowed by the ending of slavery. State oversight of indentured labour became a global system during the nineteenth century, one whose rules were negotiated by central and colonial governments with planters' groups. Workers' human rights took second place to a narrow conception of their "welfare," which states enforced in an ineffective manner. The sugar story has been retold in terms of tea, coffee, and rubber, and with Dutch, French, Spanish, South African, or American owners.[73] Except in the nostalgic recollections of their owners,

---

[72] Lynn Hollen Lees, *The Solidarities of Strangers: the English Poor Laws and the People, 1700–1948* (Cambridge: Cambridge University Press, 1998); Marjorie Levine-Clark, *Unemployment, Welfare, and Masculine Citizenship: "So Much Honest Poverty" in Britain, 1870–1930* (Houndsmills: Palgrave MacMillan, 2015)

[73] Discussions of plantations and indentured labour in the nineteenth century are legion. Among the most important for Southeast Asia are Jan Bremen, *Taming the Coolie Beast: Plantation Society and the Colonial Order in Southeast Asia* (Delhi: Oxford University Press, 1989); James S. Duncan, *In the Shadows of the Tropics: Climate, Race and Biopower in Nineteenth Century Ceylon* (Aldershot: Ashgate, 2007); Vincent J. H. Houben, J. Thomas Lindblad, and others, *Coolie Labour in Colonial Indonesia: a Study of Labour Relations in the Outer Islands, c. 1900–1940* (Wiesbaden: Harrassowitz Verlag, 1999); John D. Kelly, *Hinduism, Sexuality, and Countercolonial Discourse in Fiji* (Chicago: University of Chicago

plantations are normally portrayed as coercive places, albeit with important variations in specific legal and political regimes. The central question to ask, however, is not how bad was life on particular sugar plantations in the nineteenth century, but how did those plantations fit within the larger global colonial regimes of which they were only a part. Colonial rule was not a unitary structure, but a mosaic made from various systems of governance in discrete environments. Labourers circulated internationally and locally among these sites, learning as they moved. In Malaya a worker could enter a separate colonial world by walking down a dusty road or crossing a tiny river. Chivatean would have been a free man with a better range of choices if he had travelled a few miles farther. Thousands of his co-workers managed to escape to alternative colonial environments, the most important of which existed in local towns. Asian owners and managers moved among urban and rural colonial regimes easily. Khaw Boo Aun and Augustin Francis Nicholas spent part of their lives on plantations and part in nearby towns where they learned how to function in the midst of layered sovereignties, open labour markets, and mingling ethnicities. British colonial rule in Malaya was a pluralist system where individuals experienced distinct styles of authority depending upon where they lived as much as who they were. Urbanization fundamentally altered the ways in which the population of the Malay Peninsula experienced colonial rule.

Press, 1991); Ann Laura Stoler, *Capitalism and Confrontation in Sumatra's Plantation Belt, 1870–1979*, 2nd ed. (Ann Arbor: University of Michigan Press, 1995); for the Caribbean and North America among many others, see Walton Look Lai, *Indentured Labor, Caribbean Sugar* (Baltimore: Johns Hopkins Press, 1993); Rebecca J. Scott, *Degrees of Freedom: Louisiana and Cuba after Slavery* (Cambridge, MA: Belknap Press, 2005).

3 New Towns on the Malayan Frontier

When Frank Swettenham, Assistant Resident for the Malay state of Selangor, trekked to Kuala Lumpur in 1875, he found a fledgling town centred on a market hall and gambling booths. The "palatial residence" of Yap Ah Loy, the Chinese headman or Kapitan China, served as a town office, as well as a quasi-hotel and restaurant. About 1,000 Chinese, who ran the shops, lived near their de facto ruler in small, mud-walled and palm-leaf houses, while 700 Malays resided at the other end of the settlement along the river, close to the mosque.[1] Kuala Lumpur was founded after 1857 as a market to supply a growing local population of tin miners. Raja Abdullah, a Malay chieftain based in the town of Klang, wanted to develop the area, so he sent a group of Chinese miners upstream and inland to open new tin mines under his protection. Hoping for captive customers, Mandailing traders from Sumatra joined Chinese Hakka merchants, vegetable gardeners, and pig farmers in a camp on the riverbank, linked to the mines by jungle paths. For the first few years of its existence, Yap Ah Loy ran the town in cooperation with Mandailing headmen. Yap Ah Loy collected and kept proceeds from the market and the gambling concession, while Abdullah made his money from customs duties on the area's tin mines. Together they formed the effective government of the locality. Only after 1880, when the British resident to the State of Selangor decided to live in Kuala Lumpur and make it the official capital, were British administrative offices added to its scaffolding of Chinese and Malay bosses.[2]

---

[1] P. L. Burns and C. D. Cowan, *Sir Frank Swettenham's Malayan Journals, 1874–1876* (Kuala Lumpur: Oxford University Press, 1975), p. 219

[2] After the British Governor, Sir Andrew Clarke, sent steam ships and soldiers into the Larut mining region of Selangor in 1874 to suppress piracy, Frank Swettenham was appointed the assistant resident for the State of Selangor. He took up residence in Langat with Sultan Abdul Samad, who signed an agreement with the British to accept and pay for a British resident. See J. M. Gullick, *A History of Kuala Lumpur, 1857–1939* (Singapore: Malaysian Branch of the Royal Asiatic Society, 2000), pp. 6–8, 20–32; Burns and Cowan, *Swettenham*, p. xxv.

The Kuala Lumpur story is typical for the west coast of Malaya in the nineteenth century. Villages settled by Chinese and various Muslim groups mushroomed quickly into small towns whose most powerful people were the male leaders of immigrant communities. They collected taxes and built roads, cooperating with the local Malay chiefs who controlled land and mining rights. Even before the British moved into the region, economic development triggered urbanization on the Malayan frontier. After the British moved into the state in 1874, they built colonial administrative structures around existing settlements and encouraged more urbanization. Towns became key sites for the imposition of colonial rule, physically close to the mines and plantations they served but socially and culturally a world apart from them. These settlements drew immigrants into competitive labour markets and showed newcomers an array of imported goods and technologies. Towns gave people choices of where to live, what to consume, and how to spend time unmonitored by their bosses. They provided places where petty capitalists could earn a living and where newcomers could literally taste, smell, and see the products of multiple cultures. They offered relatively open, well-connected spaces that enticed customers, rather than publicly regimenting residents. Inhabitants were still disciplined, but less directly and through delegation. During the nineteenth century, the urban style of British colonial rule operated more effectively through layered sovereignty than direct punishment. Although colonial police watched the streets and locked up offenders in newly built jails, Chinese headmen, Malay chiefs, and Muslim imams and judges continued to resolve local conflicts and enforce communal norms of behaviour. British urban officials demonstrated authority through their control of infrastructure and public health and by providing roads and clean water. British colonial rule in Malaya rested on a relatively weak state, but one whose subsidiary representatives exercised great power.

Urbanization in Malaya

British expansion in Malaya resulted in a network of small towns tightly linked to, but culturally distinct from, local agricultural settlements. Quite unlike the port-forts of Melaka and Penang, their purpose was not long-distance trade, but the collection and sale of locally produced goods and services. By the early 1830s, Province Wellesley had three large villages of about 300 houses each and several smaller ones. Batu Kawan, Bukit Mertajam, and Nibong Tebal, all early sites of production and local trade, were among them. James Low, who served as resident of Province Wellesley from 1827 to 1837, did a rudimentary census, counting over

2,000 Chinese, 1,000 "Chuliahs" and "Bengalese," and 500 Siamese in the district, many of whom lived in a handful of growing villages. Low identified over 4,000 people whom he called traders, weavers, "artificers," dealers, and hawkers, not members of the Malay agricultural population.[3] These thriving settlements had geographic names derived from the Malay words for river (sungei), mouth of river (kuala), hill (bukit), bay (teluk), quai (bagan), or other natural features generally linked to their waterside sites, but they were rooted less in the local landscape than in the economic needs of the larger towns and the international political economy.

The development of Bukit Mertajam, a small administrative centre and market town in the centre of Province Wellesley, shows how economic and political change went hand in hand. Before 1800, Malay and Thai farmers lived there in dispersed settlements. Then Chinese moved into the district, lured by the prospect of growing pepper, nutmeg, clove, and gambier for export to Europe. Penang builders also wanted stone from the Bukit Mertajam quarry. Bullock carts loaded with cargo soon lumbered along mud paths to the Juru River for trans-shipment to the coast. By the 1830s, both Chinese and European entrepreneurs had begun large-scale sugar cultivation nearby, drawing more immigrants into the district and helping to expand the central settlement. Within a few decades, road transportation improved, and the rivers became less useful because of soil erosion from the sugar cane fields. Soon the village of Bukit Mertajam became a central place for sending sugar, tapioca, and tin to the ports of Butterworth, Prai, and Penang. A railway linked the growing settlement to the west coast by 1899, and a north-south line that eased exports soon followed. Meanwhile, Straits administrators chose Bukit Mertajam to be a district capital. By the turn of the century, the drive for law and order had produced a police station, a magistrate's court, and a colonial administrative office, as well as a small hospital. Roman Catholic priests arrived and built a modest church to serve a Chinese congregation. By 1911, over 37,000 people lived in the Bukit Mertajam area, producing a density of more than 400 persons per square mile. The town of Bukit Mertajam, although small, offered the local rural population easy access to urban services and transportation. Its offices represented the colonial state, while its shops displayed a wide array of international goods.[4]

---

[3] Lim Heng Kow, *The Evolution of the Urban System in Malaya* (Kuala Lumpur: The University of Malaya, 1978), pp. 24–27

[4] R. D. Naidu, "A History of Bukit Mertajam," unpublished manuscript, 1994, Penang Public Library; Hayes Marriott, *Report on the Census of the Colony of the Straits Settlements taken on 10 March, 1911* (Singapore: Singapore Printing Press, 1911), Table 1, p. 9; *Singapore and Straits Directory for 1896* (Singapore, 1896), p. 173

Table 3.1 *Towns in Perak, 1891*

	Populations			
Towns	Malays	Chinese	Indians	Total
Taiping	411	8,764	3,549	13,304
Teluk Anson	1,204	1,368	606	3,373
Ipoh	407	2,389	340	3,184
Gopeng	278	2,144	426	2,870
Kamunting	18	2,383	202	2,608
Lahat	30	2,036	149	2,232
Batu Gajah	963	739	358	2,135
Tapah	807	561	180	1,630
Matang	308	812	164	1,289
Papan	113	1,076	29	1,218
Kuala Kangsar	208	400	292	952

Source: Lim Heng Kow, *The Evolution of the Urban System in Malaya* (Kuala Lumpur: The University of Malaya, 1978), p. 43

Urbanization in western Malaya outside the colony of the Straits Settlements proceeded slowly. The beginnings of an inland urban network began in Perak (Table 3.1) with the growth of tin mines, well before the British sent in residents to run the state. Chinese immigrants, brought in during the mid-1840s by the Malay entrepreneur Che Long Ja'afar, worked mines near hamlets that would soon become Kamunting and Taiping. By 1871, over 40,000 Chinese, divided into competing associations (Hai San and Ghee Hin), were said to live in the Larut district. F. McNair saw "long thatched buildings by the hundreds" in Taiping and Chinese shops in multiple, prosperous looking settlements.[5] In the Kinta valley, Papan began as a lumber town, but shifted to mining by the 1870s. Both Chinese and Mandailings, originally from Sumatra, lived there and dug for tin. They lived in the town but hired themselves out to local mine owners or prospected on their own. Gopeng, developed by the Mandailing Kulop Riau, grew quickly as Hakka miners flooded into the area in the 1870s. It became a largely Chinese town, effectively controlled by the Hakka leader Chung Keng Kwee (1821–1901), whom the British appointed as Kapitan China and to whom they leased various revenue farms, giving him effective control over local opium and alcohol

---

[5] Lim, *Evolution*, pp. 29–33; Ho Weng Hin, et al., *Returning Taiping: the Town of Tin, Rain, Commerce, Leisure, and Heritage* (Singapore: Centre for Advanced Studies in Architecture, National University of Singapore, 2010), pp. 12–13

Figure 3.1 Hugh Low Street, Ipoh, 1887

sales. By 1882, Gopeng was the leading town in the Kinta Valley, having more than 1,500 resident Chinese miners.[6] By the 1890s, the larger settlements had acquired a few public buildings and had begun to replace palm leaf huts with brick and wooden houses. Chinese and Indians formed majorities in the mining and market towns, while British administrative centres and ports, such as Batu Gajah, Taiping, and Teluk Anson, had larger Malay and European populations.

Decade by decade in both Province Wellesley and Perak, the larger villages prospered, as the need for their produce rose along with the ease of getting it to market. The economic development of the province fostered inland urbanization, producing small towns that served as central places for traders, farmers, and the estate populations (see Figure 3.1).

From their early days, Malayan towns were multi-ethnic communities where immigrant males had to learn to deal with one another. When

[6] Khoo Salma Nasution and Abdul-Razzaq Lubis, *Kinta Valley: Pioneering Malaysia's Modern Development* (Ipoh: Perak Academy, 2005), pp. 7, 129, 162; Dato' Dr Dolbani Bin Mijan, editor, *Papan: Pekan Perlombongan Tertua Lembah Kinta: Dari Perspektif Perancangan Bandar* (Taiping and Ipoh: Jabatan Perancangan Bandar dan Desa Perak Darul Ridzuan, 2014); Dato' Dr Dolbani Bin Mijan, *Gopeng: Pekan Warisan Perlombongan Bijih Timah: Dari Perspektif Perancangan Bandar* (Taiping and Ipoh: Jabatan Perancangan Bandar dan Desa Perak Darul Ridzuan, 2014)

Munshi Mohamed Ibrahim visited Klang in 1872, he estimated that there were around 3,000 inhabitants, whom he identified as "Arabs, Malays, English, Chinese, Eurasians, Southern Indians, Bengalis, Hindus and *peranakan* born in Penang, Malacca and Singapore." The few Europeans there, whom he derisively branded unemployed "drifters," took jobs as mercenary soldiers. The language teacher remarked on the town's all-male look, for he saw no women or children outdoors as he walked Klang's streets.[7] In 1880, respectable European men living in Province Wellesley were located in the port town of Prai or on local plantations.[8] They might visit places like Nibong Tebal or Bukit Mertajam, but they certainly would not settle in them. The men running town offices and shops were almost exclusively Chinese, South Asian, Sumatran, or Eurasian.

Since censuses taken in the nineteenth century in British Malaya usually did not tabulate occupations, little detailed information exists on small-town economies, but the Straits Settlements census of 1881 listed the different trades practised by the major ethnic groups in Province Wellesley.[9] If agricultural occupations and the few skilled trades needed on plantations are eliminated, the remaining trades indicate surprisingly complex urban economies. The towns housed teachers, doctors, dentists, and artists. There were imams, priests, and civil servants, as well as large contingents of Chinese clerks and Malay policemen. Tamils, Malays, and Chinese divided up urban commerce, and a few of each group got the elevated title of "merchant." Malays ran shops or sold food. Tamils operated eating houses or traded toddy, while some peddled a range of goods in small stores or on the streets. Chinese shopkeepers and dealers far outnumbered their South Asian or Malay competitors, and anyone wanting opium, pork, or spirits had to patronize them. Townspeople produced goods as well as selling them. Thousands of artisans comprised 12.3 per cent of the Province Wellesley's male population. Jewellers and goldsmiths needed wealthy town clienteles, as did actors and musicians. Carters and carriage builders operated from centrally located stables on town streets. Urban expansion required contractors, carpenters, brick

---

[7] Amin Sweeney and Nigel Phillips, *The Voyages of Mohamed Ibrahim Munshi* (Kuala Lumpur: Oxford University Press, 1975), pp. 74–75

[8] T. J. Keaghran, *The Singapore Directory for the Straits Settlements, 1877* (Singapore: Government Printing Office, 1877), pp. 28–29; "List of Penang Jurors," *Papers of the Legislative Council of the Straits Settlements*, 29 November 1881 (Singapore, 1881)

[9] *Census of Penang, Province Wellesley and the Dindings, 1881, Papers Laid before the Legislative Council of the Straits Settlements, 1881* (National University of Singapore)

makers, and builders of many sorts. Towns also housed specialized cake makers, bakers, and butchers. Weavers, dyers, tailors, and shoemakers abounded. Many of these men were self-employed or worked in small shops, where signs proclaimed their names and skills. They built local reputations along with their businesses.

Two urban networks developed on the Malay Peninsula: a northern one comprising Province Wellesley and Perak with Penang, Ipoh, and Taiping as major centres; and a southern system linking Selangor, Negeri Sembilan, and Johore, centring on Kuala Lumpur, Melaka, and Singapore.[10] The extension of the railway and trunk roads eventually linked the two systems. In territory outside the orbit of British control until 1909, the court city of Alor Star served as a central place for Kedah. In the eastern half of the peninsula, where production for export had not taken hold, the seaside ports of Kota Baru and Kuala Terengganu served as central places for the local trading and agricultural economy.[11]

The census of 1921 drew a more complete picture of the Malay Peninsula's surprising level of urbanization. In 1921, the census counted 27.7 per cent of the population of "British Malaya" (Federated Malay States and the Straits Settlements) as urban.[12] In the Straits Settlements, moreover, 56.9 per cent of all residents lived in the towns (settlements with more than 1,000 people), and the proportion was 22.4 per cent in the Federated Malay States. In comparative terms, the western parts of the Malay Peninsula were very heavily urbanized at a time when well under 10 per cent of the total population in other Southeast Asian countries and only about 10 per cent of the Asian population as a whole lived in towns or cities.[13]

Most Malayan towns were tiny, having fewer than 5,000 residents. In 1921, each state had one city whose population exceeded 10,000 people, and virtually all other urban places had no more than 5,000

---

[10] John H. Drabble, *An Economic History of Malaysia, c. 1800–1990: the Transition to Modern Economic Growth* (London: Macmillan Press, 2000), p. 83

[11] Ahmat Sharon, *Tradition and Change in a Malay State: a Study of the Economic and Political Development of Kedah, 1878–1923* (Kuala Lumpur: Malaysian Branch of the Royal Asiatic Society, 1984), p. 149; Barbara Watson Andaya and Leonard Y. Andaya, *A History of Malaysia*, 2nd ed. (London: Palgrave, 2001), p. 201

[12] J. E. Nathan, *The Census of British Malaya, 1921* (London: Waterlow and Sons, 1922), p. 38

[13] Greg Huff and Luis Angeles, "Globalization, Industrialization, and Urbanization in Pre-World War II Southeast Asia," *Explorations in Economic History*, 48 (2011) pp. 20–36; Paul Bairoch, *De Jéricho á Mexico: villes et économie dans l'histoire* (Paris: Gallimard, 1985), pp. 531, 551, 587

Table 3.2 *Distribution of Town Sizes in the Straits Settlements and the Federated Malay States, 1921*

District/state	Pop. 50,000+	25,000–50,000	10,000–25,000	5,000–10,000	1,000–5,000
Singapore	1				1
Penang	1			0	8
Melaka			1	0	2
Straits Settlements Total	2	1	0	0	11
Perak		1	3	2	19
Selangor	1	0	0	0	11
Negeri Sembilan	0	0	1	0	4
Pahang	0	0	0	0	4
Federated Malay States Total	1	1	5	2	38

Source: J. E. Nathan, *The Census of British Malaya, 1921* (London: Waterlow and Sons, 1922), p. 37

inhabitants (see Table 3.2). In fact, many of these places resembled overgrown villages rather than true cities. Only in Perak had towns of intermediate size developed before World War II. In that state, the early development of mining permitted Taiping and Kampar to become sizable settlements, while the growth of rubber cultivation and British administration brought Ipoh and Teluk Anson well above the 10,000 mark. But with these exceptions, the typical town on the Malay Peninsula before the British were chased out by the Japanese was very small in size.

The ethnic composition of towns in British Malaya also differed according to the size of settlements (see Table 3.3). Immigrants from South China (chiefly Teochews, Hakka, and Hokkien) were the largest group of town residents, and most of the rest of the urban population was South Asian and Malay, some of whom were immigrants from Sumatra. Europeans clustered in the cities of Singapore, Penang, and Melaka, as well as in the larger ports and administrative centres. Europeans not only constituted a minute proportion of the whole (0.4 per cent), but their absolute numbers were also so small that Europeans formed a critical mass for the creation and maintenance of social institutions only in a few places. Over half (52 per cent) of the European population of the

Table 3.3 *Ethnic Composition of Towns in Province Wellesley and Perak, 1921*

Town	Total pop.	Europeans	Eurasians	Malays	Chinese	South Asians	Other
Bukit Mertajam	3,873	4	34	540	2,676	606	13
Gopeng	3,624	10	8	211	2,856	519	20
Nibong Tebal	2,902	2	2	258	1,608	1,026	6
Batu Gajah	5,093	76	55	996	2,357	1,590	19
Papan	1,285	3	1	116	959	205	1
Taiping	21,111	285	232	1,839	12,193	6,349	213
Kuala Kangsar	3,369	41	24	941	1,378	968	17
Teluk Anson	10,859	42	44	2,251	5,859	2,587	76

Source: Nathan, *Census of 1921*, tables X and XI, pp. 170–171

Federated Malay States lived in rural areas in 1921, mostly on plantations, whereas in the Straits Settlements, most Europeans settled in the cities of Singapore, Penang, and Melaka, working in professional and commercial offices. Very few Malayan towns with fewer than 5,000 people in 1921 had more than ten European residents, and these small numbers were employed by the colonial government. The 1921 census counted four Europeans in the small town of Bukit Mertajam, two in Nibong Tebal, and three in Papan. In Perak, Bagan Serai had ten Europeans, while Port Weld, Trong, and Chenderaing had none. Only in the medium-sized towns of more than 10,000 could sizable European communities be found and those that did had unusual economic or political functions.[14] Kuala Kangsar, for example, had been the residence of the Perak sultan since the eighteenth century and became the administrative centre for an entire state after the British began to supervise his rule through a resident advisor. Butterworth and Prai were ports, where European agency houses and shipping firms maintained offices. The small towns were not only settled by, but also normally run by, Chinese, South Asians, Malays, and Muslims from Sumatra. They formed a distinctive colonial space where British authority was delegated to Asian populations and where Chinese, Malays, and South Asians dominated civil society as it developed. How authority was divided and exercised needs to be explored.

[14] For example, in Ipoh, 427 of 36,860; Taiping, 285 of 21,111; and Telok Anson, 42 of 10,859. There were fewer than 100 Europeans in the administrative centre of Batu Gajah (76 out of 5,093) in 1921.

Townscapes

The Malay Peninsula was a frontier district in the mid-1870s, and its settlements bore little resemblance to the bustling, well-built streets of central Penang, Melaka, or Singapore. In 1879, Isabella Bird dismissed the royal Malay town of Kuala Kangsar as a "village," whose trade was in the hands of the Chinese and a few Indians. To get there, Bird travelled by elephant and on foot for several hours, and after arrival, she found little to do or .to praise. Shops consisted of palm-roofed sheds with open fronts where men sold a few goods from rough tables. Its mosque served as a meeting place, as did the riverbanks where worshippers washed before prayers.[15] Although the British located their Residency at Kuala Kangsar to be near the Sultan of Perak and his court, the town remained in their eyes a rather sleepy Malay settlement.

Improved transportation proved to be the easiest first step in the British transformation of Malayan space. Straits Settlements' annual reports for the 1860s proudly tally several new bridges spanning the major rivers and cart roads linking ferries to the larger villages. Although in 1875 there were only 18 miles of roadways in the entire state of Perak, British officials soon supported the cutting of bridle paths and cart roads between mining centres and the larger settlements.[16] In 1884, a trunk road from Melaka to Province Wellesley was begun, its progress permitting the installation of inland telegraph lines and the expansion of postal service. Soon two-wheeled, pony-drawn carts and their Indian drivers carried letters regularly from village to village in the Kinta valley. Rickshaws, pony buses, and bullock carts abounded, creating "traffic" on town streets well before the era of the motorcar. At the century's end, travellers moving from town to town no longer depended on muddy cart tracks or elephant paths, but they could enjoy the relative luxury of well-drained, gravel surfaced roads. In 1901, a grid of roads spanned the land from the Kedah border south through Perak into Selangor and Negeri Sembilan, allowing plantations and mining sites relatively easy access to riverine ports, market towns, and the coast. Bridges spanned the larger rivers, some designed to handle even train traffic. The larger towns were linked to the north-south railway, which stretched by 1909

---

[15] Isabella Bird, *The Golden Chersonese* (Singapore: Monsoon Books, 2010) pp. 95–96
[16] "Annual Report of the Administration of the Straits Settlements for the year 1861–1862," in Robert L. Jarman, *Annual Reports of the Straits Settlements, 1855–1941* (London: Archive Editions, 1998), Vol. 1, pp. 24–25; "Annual Report for 1882," in Jarman, *Annual Reports*, Vol. 2, p. 170

from Penang to Singapore.[17] This expanding network of transport and communication can be called an "urban circuit" for its dependence on towns as the gathering points for people and products that flowed through British Malaya.[18]

The British were avid builders. The Public Works Departments in the Straits Settlements and Perak handled construction projects large and small all over the colony. European engineers and their assistants worked out of town offices, where they had storehouses, mid-level staff, and overseers to superintend convicts and hired labourers. In 1875, a European engineer headed the Province Wellesley Public Works, assisted by overseers, clerks, surveyors, and draftsmen of multiple ethnicities. Ah Chang and Zenodin worked as measurers, helping the two surveyors, T. Krishnasawmy and Mohamed Zein. The evidence of a growing colonial presence increased on urban streets, where police stations, post and land offices took central sites.

Along with making heavy investments in transportation, British administrators invested early in law and order. Police stations, barracks, courts, and jails were erected at many sites. Around 1860, crews built police stations at Ayer Itam, Batu Kawan, and Tanjong Tokong as well as new housing and a hospital for soldiers in Penang. They added a second storey to the Bukit Tambun Court House and the Butterworth Police Hospital. In 1881, a year when the Straits Settlements continued to build police stations, they allocated 14 per cent of their budgets to jails, to the military, and to police salaries. By the late nineteenth century, almost a third of the annual budget of the Straits Settlements went to support law and order and associated infrastructures. By 1885, 47 police stations dotted Penang Island and Province Wellesley, and more were planned for the next decade to house a large police force of over almost 700 men.[19] After the British set up their indirect rule of Perak in the mid-1870s, there were small police stations in 20 different settlements in the state employing about 423 constables, most of whom

---

[17] Map of Perak, 1901, Sir Frank A. Swettenham and W. Hood Treacher (Kuala Lumpur 1901) (Library of Congress, Washington, DC); Khoo, *Kinta Valley*, pp. 48–50
[18] H. D. Evers, "On the Evolution of Urban Society in Malaysia," in Kenial Sandhu and Paul Wheatley, *Melaka: the Transformation of a Malay Capital, c. 1400–1980*, 2 Vols. (Kuala Lumpur: Oxford University Press, 1983), Vol. 2, pp. 324–331; H. Dick and Peter J. Rimmer, *Cities, Transport, and Communications: the Integration of South East Asia Since 1850* (London: Palgrave Macmillan, 2003)
[19] "Annual Report for 1861–1862," in Jarman, *Annual Reports*, Vol. 1, p. 334; "Report on the Straits Settlements Blue Book for the year 1882," Jarman, *Annual Reports*, Vol. 2, p. 569; "Annual Report for 1885," in Jarman, *Annual Reports*, Vol. 3, p. 123

Figure 3.2 Police station in the town of Janing, Perak, 1890

were Sikhs and Malays (see Figure 3.2). By the end of the century, the towns of Perak all had police stations with their multi-ethnic contingent of constables led by European Commissioners and Inspectors, and there were jails in larger settlements, such as Taiping, Ipoh, Matang, and Batu Gajah. In 1900, the police force of the Federated Malay States had expanded to 2,146, at least 1,000 of whom were in Perak.[20]

The police cultivated high visibility in Malayan towns by placing their offices in central spaces. Built in 1881, the first Taiping police station lay along the town's central street near the market and the Chinese theatre. Visitors to Papan had to pass its station when walking into town along Main Street. In Teluk Anson, the police station stood near the town's central square and clock tower, and in Muar, Straits Settlements, the police bungalow dominated a central intersection. From its steps, vigilant constables scanned traffic along the flat, dusty streets in three directions.

---

[20] W. H. Treacher, *Annual Report for the Year 1901 of the Federated Malay States* (Kuala Lumpur: Selangor Government Printing Office, 1900), p. 12; "Return of the Perak Police Force on 23 February 1877," CO 273, Vol. 148, No. 11438 (National Archives, London); Oliver Marks, *Perak Administration Report for the year 1911*, Federated Malay States (Kuala Lumpur: Government Printing Office, 1912), p. 27

But how much attention did local residents pay to the few uniformed police? Contemporary descriptions of central streets concentrate on consumption, not on the local cops. Town streets also were crowded with colourful, tasty delights. Consider Papan, which in 1900 had around 2,000 inhabitants (see Map 3.1). In the eyes of the farm boy Pak Foo, the town supplied "almost everything that a person needed." On Main Street in the early morning, vendors served steaming bowls of rice porridge or noodle soup to hungry, hurrying workers. In the two-storey market, women stood by tables piled high with cabbages and cucumbers, radishes and bitter gourds. Sacks of white rice, yellow wheat, red beans, and green peas leaned against one another along the aisles. Tubs of grey, slippery eels stood next to piles of wriggling crabs and rows of freshly caught river fish. Hens and geese cackled from inside their stacked cages, while already-slaughtered haunches of beef, pork, and lamb hung from butchers' hooks. Puffs of smoke from the tin smelter announced its operations as children walked to the local schools. Men crowded into the local coffee shops or stopped to buy fried yams or rice cakes from the hawkers, while tailors, barbers, mechanics, and bakers opened their doors. Calls to prayer echoed from the Mandailing mosque just east of Main Street. Muslim and Chinese burial grounds stood close to the Daoist temple. Pleasure dominated the north end of town, where brothels, wine shops with sing-song girls, and a shooting gallery competed for attention near club and clan houses. Kerosene lanterns on slender, cast iron poles kept night at bay. When a Cantonese opera troupe was in town, the theatre stage at the end of the road was ablaze with lanterns and swirling silk costumes. Chinese and Malay miners crowded into town after work, as did Punjabi watchmen and drivers. Festivals, such as the celebration of the Hungry Ghosts, brought even bigger crowds and more business for the street hawkers and gambling shops.[21] Surveillance constituted only a minor part of the urban environment.

While cities like Singapore or George Town had suburban districts for wealthy residents, in small towns like Papan or Gopeng, the multi-ethnic Asian population lived cheek-by-jowl in compact districts. E. H. Dobby, who studied the geography of Malayan towns in the 1930s, described them as "overgrown villages," where small shops and warehouses clustered along a single road or a grid of streets. Within ten or fifteen minutes, a fast walker could move from one end to another. Temporary timber and thatch houses often sprawled around the central area and its few public buildings. Because Malay and Chinese architectural preferences differed, it is tempting to assign each group to structures with the proper ethnic

[21] Ho Thean Fook, *God of the Earth* (Ipoh: Perak Academy, 2003), pp. 76–78; Khoo and Lubis, *Kinta Valley*, pp. 162–167

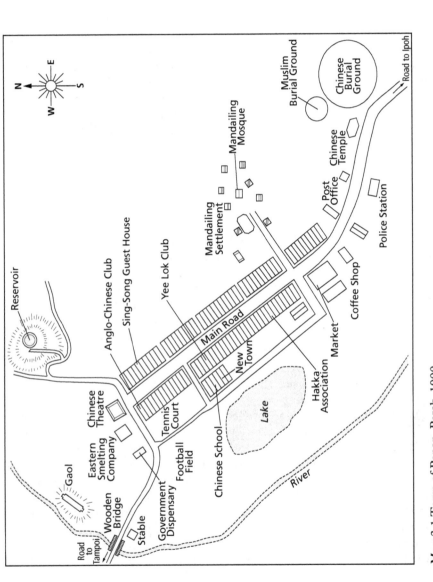

Map 3.1 Town of Papan, Perak, 1900

style.[22] Yet Chinese merchants often financed and Chinese builders constructed the core areas, so that they were responsible for stylistic choices, not later owners or renters. The few extant descriptions that I have discovered of small towns make it clear that Chinese, Malays, and Indians did business in the same areas, crossed paths in the streets, and met in the markets. Walter Skeat, when visiting Setul, Kedah in 1883, found Malay stores on the main street near the better-built, brick Chinese shophouses. On a trip to Kuala Terengganu in 1889, Skeat met a variety of Malay craftsmen at work and saw Malay women selling in the markets. He admired the extensive supply of Chinese and Indian goods available in the shops along the main street, which were probably imported by merchants of those ethnicities. Pedestrians could not avoid encountering cultural differences, and some were surely tempted to cross cultural boundaries. Local laws against inter-racial sex brought heavy penalties to all who transgressed them, a sure sign that at least some such relationships existed.[23] Katherine Lim offers the most explicit description of the central area of a small town, Parit Buntar, Perak in the later 1930s: "The town ... consisted of three short streets of semi-Chinese style two-storied houses, washed azure, viridian green, and cream. The shops below were just open rooms or tunnels under the dark arches of the five-foot way: Japanese photographers, Chinese carpenters, a tinsmith and a rattan basket maker, several Indian silk and cotton stores, goldsmiths and a pawnbroker, and a Japanese hairdresser, Chinese and Indian food shops and petrol stores and Malay coffee shops. There was an open market near the river with food stalls and portable kitchens."[24] Shopping meant mingling with others unlike oneself and lowering the barriers among communities.

Towns with thriving economies quickly acquired a range of civic institutions and public places open to residents, whatever their ethnicity. Around 1880 in Taiping, Chinese mine owners built the Yeng Wah Hospital for the poor, and they helped to finance a theatre. A public library opened in 1882, shortly followed by a British-run museum housing a collection of archaeological finds and natural history specimens. An

[22] See Hans-Dieter Evers, "The Culture of Malaysian Urbanization: Malay and Chinese Conceptions of Space," in Peter S. J. Chen and Hans-Dieter Evers, eds., *Studies in ASEAS Sociology: Urban Society and Social Change* (Singapore: Chapman Enterprises, 1978), pp. 333–342

[23] James Augustine, "Alor Setar 1883," in *Alor Setar 250 Tahun, 1735–1985* (Kerajaan Negeri Kedah Darulaman, 1990), pp. 98–99; Walter Skeat, "Kuala Trengganu in 1889," in J. M. Gullick, editor, *They Came to Malaya: a Traveller's Anthology* (Singapore: Oxford University Press, 1993), pp. 144–145

[24] Katherine Sim, *Malayan Landscape* (Singapore: Asia Pacific Press, 1969), pp. 28–29. Parit Buntar had around 2,400 residents in 1920.

abandoned mining site was converted by Col. Walker into the Lake
Gardens, and by the mid-1880s, the Central School (later the King
Edward VII School) offered English language instruction to boys from
ambitious Asian families. The Treacher Girl's School followed in 1889.
While the private Perak Club and the golf course were restricted to
Europeans, other sites were not: the Lake Gardens became a public
park in the 1880s, and both the Central Market and the Esplanade parade
ground constituted public space within the core of the town. Worshippers
could visit the Ling Nam Temple, the Kota Mosque (1897), or the All
Saints' Anglican Church (1886). By 1900, Taiping had a robust array of
institutions and public spaces funded by Asian citizens as well as by the
colonial state.[25] By the century's end, colonial towns had become complex, hybridized societies where several ethnic groups mixed in public
spaces and activities.

The Colonial State in the Towns: Layered Sovereignty

British movement into Malaya was not by conquest, but by invitation
shadowed by intimidation. Gunboats and Indian regiments kept a
low profile, although their military conquests in India, Burma, and
Ceylon were widely publicized and could stand as warnings to others.
Soon after their arrival, colonial authorities in Penang subcontracted
to powerful Chinese the task of keeping order in their community,
implicitly recognizing their authority and comparative British weakness. Following Dutch practice, Francis Light appointed in 1787
Koh Lay Huan, a Hokkien from Changchou, to be the Kapitan
China of Penang, giving him authority over security, welfare, and
disputes among the Chinese. In Singapore, Tan Tock Seng, a rich
merchant, became the informal leader of the Hokkien as that town
grew. But neither his nor Koh's influence extended to other dialect
groups, such as the Hakka, Teochew, or Cantonese, who had their
own leaders and networks, visible through multiple dialect associations, temples, and brotherhoods. These groups not only offered
welfare and religious services, but also mediated disputes and offered
protection. To bring such associations at least partially within the
compass of imperial governance, the British appointed some of the

[25] Federal Department of Town and Country Planning, Peninsular Malaysia, *Taiping, Life and Soul: a Town Planning Perspective* (Kuala Lumpur: Ministry of Housing and Local Government, Malaysia, 2005); Ho, *Returning Taiping*

headmen as justices of the peace or members of legislative councils. Soon after the Hakka mine owner, landlord, and revenue farmer Chung Keng Kwee was appointed the first Kapitan China of Perak, he was given a seat on the Perak State Council in 1877.[26] A privileged group of wealthy Chinese, some of whom were bilingual, moved quickly into positions of political power and influence that bridged Chinese and British communities.

When the British Empire expanded in Malaya and brought in its laws and governing institutions, the region's pre-existing political structures remained active. Carl Trocki and Craig Lockard argue that early colonial governance was handled jointly with a variety of communal power brokers. Malay chiefs commanded the loyalty of their subjects, while immigrant Muslim groups – Mandailing, Rawa, and Bugis – recognized their own headmen. Chinese newcomers joined their dialect groups, clan associations, and kongsi brotherhoods. Over time, the balance of power shifted more heavily to the British, but parallel structures of authority remained vital throughout the nineteenth century in areas of direct rule, as well as the indirectly controlled Malay states.[27]

Agreements negotiated in the 1870s between the Governor of the Straits Settlements and local sultans recognized the formal sovereignty of the rulers of Perak, Selangor, Pahang, and the units of the future state of Negeri Sembilan. These local rajas pledged, however, to make decisions with the "advice" of a British resident or advisor. A model of indirect rule had been used since the late eighteenth century in British relations with princely states in India, and it soon would become widely adopted in Britain's African and Southeast Asian colonies. The impact of the rebellions in India in 1857 and in Jamaica in 1865 convinced imperialists that "natives" could not be "civilized" and pushed them to the notion that subject populations were best ruled by their own customs. Using social theories that sharply differentiated "traditional" societies from modern ones, imperialists argued that "primitive" cultures required protection to survive, thereby legitimating British control. To avoid undermining those cultures, they also advocated the maintenance of existing local structures of authority. As the British took over the

[26] Lee Kam Hing and Chow Mun Seong, eds., *Biographical Dictionary of the Chinese in Malaysia* (Petaling Jaya: Pelanduk Publications, 1997), pp. 38–39
[27] Carl Trocki, *Singapore: Wealth, Power, and the Culture of Control* (London: Routledge, 2006), pp. 76–78; Craig A. Lockard, "Patterns of Social Development in Modern Southeast Asian Cities," *Journal of Urban History*, Vol. 5: 1 (1978), pp. 44–68; Yen Ching-hwang, *A Social History of the Chinese in Singapore and Malaya 1800–1911* (Singapore: Oxford University Press, 1986), pp. 37–43

Malaya Peninsula, they substituted the model of indirect rule for that of direct governance, which existed in the Straits Settlements.[28]

The form of indirect rule that evolved in Malaya was intrusive, however, and quickly moved well beyond the customs and structures of the Malay states. After the Pangkor Treaty of 1874, the administrative forms, laws, and technologies at work in the Straits Settlements, many of which had been borrowed from British India, were introduced in Perak. Hugh Low, soon after he joined the Malayan civil service in the mid-1870s, commented: "We must first create the Government to be advised."[29] The British promised progress and "civilization" in return for allegiance and the commitment not to weaken Malay culture or religion. Modern ways had to be fostered; yet Malay tradition had to be preserved. This contradictory imperative led to the permanent alliance of British rulers and local sultans. Together they invented a Malay "traditionalism," which used Malay forms to exalt royalty while accepting and legitimating British authority. Wilfully ignoring the transformative impact of capitalist investments, land markets, immigration, and urbanization, royal ceremonies and festivals enacted the preservation of old habits and hierarchies under the watchful eye of colonial masters. Together, British and Malay rulers cemented local Malay allegiances through the fiction that nothing had changed and the sultan was still in charge.[30]

An arrangement that began with acknowledgement of the British Queen as a protective overlord with personal authority gradually shifted to one in which British-style institutions became locally installed and accepted. Sultans were manipulated into adopting new legal systems and using taxes to pay for newly organized institutions. Pensions and grants flowed to the friendly, while the recalcitrant found their positions removed and their allowances stopped. By the end of the century, sultans presided over states with defined borders and centrally organized administrations which resembled one another and those in the Straits Settlements and British India. Malay chiefs, who had earlier raised rebellions and extorted tribute, sent sons to school to fit them for service in the colonial bureaucracy and to give their family's high status a dual

---

[28] The initial proposals to introduce indirect rule in Malaya came from men who cited Indian examples and who had worked either in the India Office or in Indian army; Michael H. Fisher, *Indirect Rule in India: Residents and the Residency System 1764–1858* (Delhi: Oxford University Press, 1998), pp. 464–465; Karuna Mantena, *Alibis of Empire: Henry Maine and the Ends of Liberal Imperialism* (Princeton: Princeton University Press, 2010)

[29] CO 882/4; quoted in Donna J. Amoroso, *Traditionalism and the Ascendancy of the Malay Ruling Class in Colonial Malaya* (Petaling Jaya, Malaysia: Strategic Information and Research Development Centre and National University of Singapore Press, 2014), p. 53

[30] Hendrik M. J. Maier, *The Center of Authority: The Malay Hikayat Merong Mahawangsa* (Ithaca, NY: Cornell Southeast Asia Program, 1988); Amoroso, *Traditionalism*

legitimacy. The influence of the English-speaking, Anglophile Abu Bakar, who ruled in Johore between 1885 and 1895, demonstrated how a modernizing Malay monarch could retain political power by introducing British-style reforms on his own.[31] The way forward was clear: rulers cast their lot with the British to ensure political survival and economic success. In practice, this meant that government in what became the Federated Malay States had three faces: that of the colonial bureaucracy, which policed, judged, built, and vaccinated; that of the Sultans, whose ceremonial presence proclaimed the continuance of Malay power and tradition; and that of the Chinese headmen, kongsis, and brotherhoods, who controlled local labourers and parts of urban economies. Although power was divided, each of the three structures of governance recognized the others and depended on them for help in maintaining order. Whether seen as "layered sovereignty" or another example of "divide and rule," British management of Malaya depended upon this arrangement of delegated control. Towns were the public spaces where this balancing act was performed.

British colonial administration in Malaya, which developed alongside Chinese structures of power, slowly expanded its reach and extended its services to local populations. The growth of government in Province Wellesley illustrates the process. Around 1830, a single official, who combined the roles of coroner, tax collector, police and convict superintendent, and magistrate, was based in Bukkah in the northern part of Province Wellesley, but the colonial establishment quickly expanded to include police stations in Batu Kawan and three other villages scattered throughout the colony.[32] By 1865, a public works department, a general hospital, and a land office had opened, probably in the new coastal town of Butterworth, just north of the mouth of the Juru River. The settlements of Bukit Mertajam, Teluk Ayer Tawar, Penanga, and Bukit Tambun became sites of police stations, dispensaries, and court buildings. Decade by decade, the number of employees and administrative offices multiplied in central places. Multi-lingual clerks, process servers, and translators assisted the growing army of inspectors, magistrates, surveyors, and postmasters who had offices in town centres. By 1900, A. W. O'Sullivan, the Butterworth-based Senior District Officer of Province Wellesley, employed a staff of twenty-seven, only two of

---

[31] Carl A. Trocki, *Prince of Pirates: the Temenggong and the Development of Johor and Singapore, 1784–1885* (Singapore: Singapore University Press, 1979)

[32] James Low, *The British Settlement of Penang* (Kuala Lumpur: Oxford University Press, 1972), pp. 235–236, 243; T. J. Newbold, *Political and Statistical Account of the British Settlements in the Straits of Malacca*, 2 Vols. (Kuala Lumpur: Oxford University Press, 1971) Vol. 1, pp. 105–106

whom – S. W. MacIntyre, Bailiff in the Court of Requests and Registrar of Hackney Carriages, and the Third Clerk, H. B. Sledge – were European. Others in his office run by the Chief Clerk Chee Kok Peng were a mixed group of Chinese, Eurasian, Malay, and South Asians. In Butterworth, Nibong Tebal, Bukit Mertajam, and Sungei Bacup, dozens of Asian employees worked for the state as apothecaries, clerks, interpreters, forest rangers, bailiffs, and shroffs. By that date the British colonial bureaucracy in Perak was even more elaborate. The British resident, W. H. Treacher, worked out of a secretariat in Taiping, aided by separate offices for Land, Audit, Post and Telegraph, Public Works, State Railways, the Trigonometrical Survey, Police, and Government Printing, each run by Europeans with largely Asian staffs of assistants and clerks. A small, multi-ethnic army of colonial employees had moved into towns from Selama in the north to Teluk Anson in the south to staff district offices, hospitals, jails, railway stations, and courts.[33] The long arms of the Malayan Civil Service with its extensive network of local Malay, Chinese, Tamil, and Sinhalese employees reached from colonial capitals down into the new settlements of Upper and Lower Perak, making the notion of indirect rule in the Federated Malay States a fiction. Similar patterns of governance existed in Selangor.[34]

Some parts of town life were carefully controlled by an expanding colonial bureaucracy, guided by a vast body of case law and municipal ordinances borrowed from the Straits Settlements. Similar institutions spread throughout the states of western Malaya, staffed by men with comparable training and powers. When Governors created municipalities, they also established new institutions and appointed English-speaking, educated men to govern them. Aspirations for control were vast: the regulated public sphere extended to baths, burial grounds, and back lanes, and it encompassed canals, carts, carriages, animals, markets, streets, and sanitation. Authority to curb unspecified "nuisances" and "obstructions" cast the official net still wider. Dogs, pawnshops, and

---

[33] *The Straits Times Almanac, Calendar, and Directory for 1846* (Singapore: Straits Times Press, 1846), pp. 29–33; *Straits Calendar and Directory for the Year 1865* (Singapore: Commercial Press, 1865), p. 3; *Singapore and Straits Directory for 1896* (Singapore: Fraser & Neave, Ltd., 1896), pp. 172–173; *The Singapore and Straits Directory for 1900* (Singapore: Fraser & Neave Ltd., 1900), pp. 199, 233–248

[34] Although Singapore and Penang were legally Municipal Corporations where during the nineteenth century citizens elected a committee of amateur administrators, this right was withdrawn in 1913, after official complaints about the "small interest taken in municipal matters by the general body of voters." Thereafter appointed committees in Singapore and Penang could comment on policies and review the budget, but they were advisory only and not intended to meet frequently; "Report to His Excellency Sir John Anderson from the Municipal Enquiry Commission," Colonial Office, *Straits Settlements Sessional Papers*, Legislative Council, Vol. II, 1910. CO 275/83 (National Archives, London)

rickshaws had to be licensed, lodging houses inspected, and festivals permitted.[35] British case law and sanitary regulations provided the model to be followed, and those with questions about procedures and ambiguities were directed to British legislation and legal decisions. In theory, colonial administrators aimed to bring Nibong Tebal and Newcastle-upon-Tyne up to the same standards of environmental health and safety. But they were not starting from an identical position, nor did they have voters' support to mandate and pay for changes. Raja Bilah, the leader of the Mandailing community in the state of Perak, also served as the penghulu or colonial administrator of the town of Papan. When a cholera epidemic broke out in the spring of 1885, Bilah received a shipment of medicine from a British magistrate and was instructed to give it to anyone with cholera and also to report the number of fatalities. He also tasked Bilah with recording births and death, disputes, and crimes.[36] Municipal administration was imposed from outside and from above, even if it was largely carried out by local men embedded in their communities.

Sanitizing the Towns

Urban governance and sanitary reform were intertwined in Britain and the Empire at least since the era of Edwin Chadwick in the 1840s, when cleanliness became a favoured weapon against death and disorder in towns. In South and Southeast Asia, doctors linked diseases such as cholera and dysentery to "filth," which arose from "Asiatic habits," justifying interference in the interest of public safety.[37] Sanitary reform both justified British rule and helped expand it in Malaya, where town inspectors and vaccinators brought the culture of the colonial power into people's homes. Towns showcased technologies that were designed to modernize the country and also to govern populations through control of their demography and epidemiology.

---

[35] D. K. Walters, *The Municipal Ordinance of the Straits Settlements, Annotated* (Singapore: Government Printing Office, 1937), pp. xi–xx, 20–23, 467–469

[36] Abdur-Razzaq Lubis and Khoo Salma Nasution, *Raja Bilah and the Mandailings in Perak: 1875–1911* (Kuala Lumpur: Malaysian Branch of the Royal Asiatic Society, 2003), pp. 49–52

[37] Edwin Chadwick, *Report on the Sanitary Condition of the Labouring Population of Great Britain* (Edinburgh: Edinburgh University Press, 1965); Brenda S. A. Yeoh, *Contesting Space: Power Relations and the Urban Built Environment in Colonial Singapore* (Kuala Lumpur: Oxford University Press, 1996), pp. 90–91, 312; Christopher Hamlin, *Public Health and Social Justice in the Age of Chadwick, 1800–1854* (Cambridge: Cambridge University Press, 1998)

The task of safeguarding public health gave the colonial state lofty goals and heavy responsibilities well beyond its power in the eighteenth and nineteenth centuries. Soon after its arrival in Penang, the East India Company set up hospitals in settlements under its jurisdiction, and in 1826, a medical department was set up with branches in George Town, Singapore, and Melaka. While soldiers and administrators received most of its care, the poor could apply to pauper hospitals for rudimentary treatment.[38] By the 1840s, the lessons learned from cholera epidemics in Europe were transferred directly to the tropics, where efforts to purify water and improve sanitation began haltingly in European districts. When a Municipal Board was set up in Singapore in 1856, its major jobs were to improve lighting, water supply, and drainage, while eliminating "nuisances" and tumble-down houses. From 1893, town governance in the Federated Malay States was vested in Sanitary Boards consisting of colonial officials (usually European civil servants, engineers, and doctors) and a few men representing local ethnic "communities."[39] Sanitary imperatives moulded the administration of small settlements too. Governors could create Rural Boards, whose supervisory powers over small towns and villages borrowed language from the Straits Settlements Municipal Ordinances. The chief difference between the Malayan and English styles of urban government, of course, was the lack of responsibility to a colonial electorate. The governor or resident appointed board members, and the right to appeal board decisions was limited.

The Colonial Office in 1911 identified sanitary control as "the main-spring of municipal action" in the Straits Settlements.[40] In the twentieth century, urban governance was primarily defined in terms of public health, not law and order. Sanitation brought with it a broad mandate over the built environment and over public behaviour. A stream of enabling laws in the Straits Settlements and the Federated Malay States, modelled upon the English Public Health Act of 1875, the Municipal Corporations Act of 1882, and the Local Government Act of 1894, as interpreted within the framework of English case law, gave Municipal Boards sweeping powers over public space, public behaviour,

---

[38] Leonore Manderson, *Sickness and the State: Health and Illness in Colonial Malaya, 1870–1940* (Cambridge: Cambridge University Press, 1996), p. 17

[39] Lim, *Urban System*, p. 47

[40] "Further Correspondence relative to the Sanitary Condition of Singapore," *Straits Times*, 17 August 1872, p. 4; Lim, *Urban System*, pp. 46–47; Yeoh, *Contesting Space*, pp. 32, 82. See also Lynn Hollen Lees, "Discipline and Delegation: Colonial Governance in Malayan Towns, 1880–1930," *Urban History* 38, 1 (2011), pp. 48–64

and private property.[41] Officials inspected, licensed, taxed, and regulated inhabitants in the interest of health and safety, as they defined those terms. Inspectors had the authority to cleanse, demolish, and remove, even to design improvement schemes for entire areas. In theory, the watchful eyes of town government extended everywhere – from rats in houses to spoiled meat in the markets to traffic on the streets. Legal codes in the Federated Malay States borrowed this model of the sanitary regulated town as it had developed in the Straits Settlements. Officials then restricted and regulated street hawkers, slaughter houses, and rickshaws. Night inspections, fines, and fees were used to control commerce and public behaviour.[42] In its meetings in 1911, North Kinta Sanitary Board, responsible for Ipoh and several nearby towns, used its substantial powers to shape the local housing market. Not only did it set lot sizes and approve designs, it voted to level the "huts" built by vegetable gardeners on the edge of Ipoh. Hotel owners were given occupancy limits, and houses suspected of overcrowding were inspected and fined.[43] The imperative that cities be clean led directly to the exercise of power over urban space and people.

By the late nineteenth century, sanitary services were considered municipal necessities by colonial officials, and they spread in the first half of the twentieth century to even small settlements of 1,000 people that had virtually no European residents. Tiny Papan employed labourers to empty latrines, and a reservoir was built to supply water.[44] But how did ordinary people respond to the array of sanitary regulations? Did they identify their welfare with public health practices? In Singapore, there was much resistance within Chinese communities to colonial designs for the built environment. Brenda Yeoh argues for a "constant contest over meaning and usage" of spaces within cities.[45] Ordinary people in their everyday practices could challenge colonial regulations and bend rules to their own purposes, but negotiation does not necessarily mean rejection.

Sanitary reform can be seen as a social technology, a form of discipline, designed to control individuals and to mould behaviour into a desired form, one tactic of many through which states exercised power.[46] Michel

---

[41] D. K. Walters, *The Municipal Ordinance of the Straits Settlements, Annotated* (Singapore: Government Printing Office, 1937)

[42] R. L. German, *Handbook to British Malaya, 1926* (London: 1926), pp. 51–52, 54, 165; Federated Malay States, *Chronological Lists of State and Federal Laws, 1877–1932 with Rules* (Kuala Lumpur, 1933), pp. 514–516; "Annual Report for 1896," in Jarman, *Annual Reports*, Vol. 4, 1892–1900 p. 270

[43] Kinta Sanitary Board North, "Minutes 21 March 1906," "Minutes 21 April 1906," "Minutes 19 May 1906," SBKN 1906 (Arkib Negara, Malaysia)

[44] Ho, *God of the Earth*, pp. 78–79   [45] Yeoh, *Contesting Space*, pp. 313–315

[46] Hamlin, *Public Health*

Foucault distinguished among the different methods of governance used by imperial states in the nineteenth century, some of which were directly repressive of individual behaviour and others of which manipulated behaviour indirectly.[47] The sanitary regimes in Malayan towns had two faces: surveillance combined with sanctions, but also the provision of services which populations came to expect and to desire. Judging the impact of these sanitary regimes requires, however, an estimate of their effectiveness. The fact that elaborate municipal regulations existed says more about political goals than about the ability of a tiny colonial bureaucracy to deliver high-quality services, and we know little about the reception of those regulations. In the small towns, no information exists to indicate the extent to which laws were ignored, but available sources cast doubt on the efficacy of enforcement. Lenore Manderson points to widespread use of streets as garbage dumps and inadequate urban services in Kuala Lumpur. In 1896, the Annual Report for the Straits Settlements complained of the unhealthy state of town streets, as well as the lack of funds for proper lighting and scavenging in the villages. The *Perak Pioneer* complained repeatedly in 1911 about the incompetent work of the Kinta Sanitary Board, citing broken, clogged drains, filthy public toilets and "nauseating" stenches. In Alor Star in Kedah, the Sanitary Board complained that it was "powerless to remove the masses of rubbish and filth that had accumulated ... behind the compact and impenetrable brick buildings," or to clean their latrines. These complaints could signal rising public standards, of course, but they also point to the inability of public authorities to deliver on their promise of sanitary cities. In any case, unlike the Chinese in Singapore, Alor Star's citizens seem not to have mobilized against government control of public spaces and public behaviour. In the surviving records for Perak, there is no evidence of mass objections via the press or public meetings to rulings of sanitary boards. In contrast, residents sometimes demanded more, rather than fewer, services. They asked that drains near their businesses be cleaned or that water supplies and street lighting be increased. Some asked for state aid to build schools or recreation grounds. In public meetings to discuss board regulations, audiences demanded and got postponements and concessions.[48] Sanitary rule in the towns included elements of negotiation and

---

[47] Michel Foucault, *Sécurité, territoire, population* (Paris, 2004), pp. 7, 321–322, 345–346; Hamlin, *Public Health*; D. Arnold, *Imperial Medicine and Indigenous Societies* (Manchester, 1988)

[48] Kinta Sanitary Board North, "Minutes 19 January 1907," "Minutes 21 December 1907," "Minutes 27 May 2010," "The Complaints re Board Notices, 27 May 1910," KSBN 1907–1910 (Arkib Negara, Malaysia); Sanitary Board, Sitiawan, "Complaint of filthy drains near their [Chin Tong & Co.] premises," 12 January 1932, SB Sitiawan 12/32 (Arkib Negara, Malaysia); W. George Maxwell, *The Annual Report of the Adviser to the*

compromise, as well as imposition and avoidance. The administrative weaknesses of municipal colonial governments opened the door for complaints by residents, who sometimes turned the demand for better public health and sanitation against the British. Sanitary and health reforms, rather than disciplining British subjects, brought their voices into a local political process, albeit a non-representative one.

Neither the costs nor the benefits of an English-style sanitary code were equally distributed. Colonial patronage had gifts to dispense: service contracts, building permits, and market and vehicle licences. Board employees – the inspectors, clerks, and sanitation workers – gained most directly from British governance, but those with appropriate permissions – local contractors, food sellers, and transportation workers – could function freely. Those who earned the board's approval moved on to the right side of the law, an advantage in small places where people were known and easily visible in public spaces. The losers came, for the most part, from among the poor, who lacked resources for self-protection and whose pleasures were taxed and frowned upon. As colonial rulers draped themselves in the shining robes of cleanliness, law, and order, the dirty and dishevelled struggled to comply with the terms of the sanitary state.

Divide and Rule: Who Controlled the Workers?

The practical meaning of colonial rule in British Malaya is best approached by looking at ordinary people, those with few resources and little power. Every year, thousands of young, male workers arrived in the larger ports and then moved on to the frontier towns of Malaya.[49] When hard times shut down tin mines in the Kinta Valley, laid-off workers wandered into Ipoh, Gopeng, and Taiping. Even small inland towns sheltered runaway contract labourers and offered opportunities for the unemployed. Men with muscles were in demand to build urban streets and clean stables, to pull a rickshaw or hawk second-hand goods. The need for labourers in expanding towns gave workers some options, even if

---

Kedah Government for the Year 1327 A.H. (23 January 1909–12 January 1910) (Kuala Lumpur: F. M. S. Government Printing Office, 1910), p. 46

[49] In 1911, 785 of every 1,000 Chinese residents and 680 of every 1,000 South Asian residents of British Malaya were male. This produced male-dominated populations in the towns. In Nibong Tebal, where men outnumbered women by a ratio of 2:1, the ratio stood at 6:1 among the Chinese. See John H. Drabble, *An Economic History of Malaysia, c. 1800–1990: The Transition to Modern Economic Growth* (London: MacMillan Press, 2000), p. 91; Hays Marriott, *Report on the Census of the Straits Settlements, Taken on 10 March, 1911* (Singapore: Government Printing Office, 1911), pp. 2, 79–84

wages were low. When Wong Ah Fook arrived in Singapore in 1854, he contracted himself for a year to pay off his passage and then became an apprentice carpenter to learn a trade. A few years later, he began building houses on his own account and soon had a thriving business.[50] Others, who were less lucky and resourceful, ended up as rickshaw pullers or street hawkers, trapped by an exploitative, low-wage economy in heavy chains of dependence.[51]

Relatively few female workers travelled on their own to Malayan towns. In 1892, Kwok Soo Kha, a young widow in Guangdong, decided to move with her two children to Taiping after a female friend bragged about the good wages and housing there. A strong and determined woman, she set off with her children to become a servant for a British family, hoarding her earnings so she could send her son, Ho Yuk Phooi, to an English-language school. While she began her life in Malaya as a household drudge, she later opened a successful Chinese herbal medicine shop, bought multiple houses, and, her family recounts, even ran a gambling house for a time before her death in 1917.[52] Kwok Soo Kha rebuilt her life in urban Malaya, taking advantage of the relatively open economy and the choices open to those with some cash. Few were that lucky.

Immigrants entered complex labour markets that mixed free access and local patronage networks only indirectly regulated by the British. The lucky ones got practical help through ethnic or religious ties. Relatives took in newcomers and introduced them to possible employers. Arriving Sikhs could lodge at local gurdwaras, while temples offered Tamils help and information.[53] Chinese brotherhoods like the Ghee Hin pressured immigrants to join, offering them protection and help finding work. In the highly subdivided urban labour markets, most employers were Asians, unconnected to the colonial elite. In comparison to plantations, colonial towns were areas of economic and social competition among Asians for low-wage work in which multiple patrons and employers jockeyed for position. While the colonial state kept strict watch on public behaviour, its role in the urban economy was limited for the most part to issuing licences, planning town spaces, adjudicating disputes, and worrying about sanitation. Town labourers, who lived largely outside the gaze of

---

[50] Patricia Pui Huen Lim, *Wong Ah Fook: Immigrant, Builder, and Entrepreneur* (Singapore: Times Editions, 2002), pp. 34–35

[51] James Warren, *Rickshaw Coolie: A People's History of Singapore, 1880–1940* (Singapore: Singapore University Press, 2003)

[52] Ho Tak Ming, *Phoenix Rising: Pioneering Chinese Women of Malaysia* (Ipoh: Perak Academy, 2015), pp. 1–2, 4–5

[53] See Malkiat Singh Lopo, *The Enchanting Prison: Punjabi Pioneers in Malaya* (Sebarang Jaya: Lopo-Ghar, 2006); S. Muthiah, et al., *The Chettiar Heritage* (Chennai: Madras Editorial Services, 2006)

colonial officials, depended far more on local Asian bosses than on their British overlords.

Indebtedness limited the options of many immigrants, tying them to local jobs and employers. Newly arrived Chinese labourers usually had to repay passage costs through a period of indenture, during which time they might have to borrow more money. Chinese and Japanese prostitutes, even if not sold into the trade for a sum they were expected to repay, often owed debts to brothel keepers and local shops for clothes and makeup.[54] Competition kept rickshaw pullers' earnings low, and they owed rent to the rickshaw owners and the lodging houses, where they slept when not out on the streets. Would they bring in enough each day for food and shelter? Few records exist to document labourers' debts and informal obligations, but they must have cast a long shadow over the daily lives of urban workers. After Iyem Perumal died in jail in Tapah in 1891, his brother Mudyah worked with a local magistrate to probate his estate. Perumal, a toddy tapper, also operated a small-scale savings and loan business among his Tamil neighbours. A few people with surplus income deposited money with him for safekeeping, but many others took out tiny loans to tide themselves over during a bad week. His debtors included dozens of mail carriers, carters, gardeners, and barbers, as well as a lot of men linked to no specific trade. Narayanasamy, a messenger, owed 22 cents, while Vengadalem, a labour recruiter and foreman, had borrowed over $16.[55] Local Tamils were divided into those with a surplus and those who owed money to local bosses and brokers, drifting into deeper dependence and restricted options. A similar pattern of alliance and obligation linked Chinese urban workers.

Any plan to keep rowdies segregated from respectable citizens in the early colonial towns was doomed to failure because of their small size and shared open space. Well-fed merchants and scrawny rickshaw pullers depended on one another, and the colonial state profited from both. In Nibong Tebal, the Chinese population ranged from rich merchants to outlaws, and they no doubt knew one another. The wooden bungalow of Khaw Boo Aun, the wealthy Teochew sugar planter and Kapitan China of Perak in the late nineteenth century, was among the largest wooden bungalows in central Nibong Tebal, and he was one of the most important men in town. With multiple ties both to Straits Settlements' authorities and to a range of Chinese associations, he gave added legitimacy to

---

[54] James Warren, *Ah Ku and Karayuki-San; Prostitution in Singapore, 1870–1940* (Singapore: Singapore University Press, 2003), pp. 52–53, 362
[55] Inspector of Police, Tapah, "Estate of Iyem Perumal, a convicted prisoner at Tapah, 4 March 1891" BP 149/91 (Arkib Negara, Kuala Lumpur)

the public face of the colonial government in the area. Leader of the Krian area Ghee Hin brotherhood, he commanded the loyalty of thousands of local plantation workers, and as a member of the Perak State Council and the Penang Chinese Advisory Board (1890–1904), he had the ear of British officials who consulted him on labour questions as well as administrative policies.[56] Nibong Tebal was one of his home bases, where he ran a sugar factory and hobnobbed with other Teochew.

The largest secret society in the southern part of Province Wellesley, the Ghee Hin, sometimes used Nibong Tebal as a central place for their activities, probably operating under Khaw's protection. Wanting to hold a communal feast in August of 1878, Tswa Tsoo Seng, a local Ghee Hin headman and a plantation labour recruiter, asked district officials for a permit for tables along a town street and for a show by a conjuror who would "stick pins into his body." The District Officer, who branded Tswa Tsoo Seng a "bad character," refused to issue the permit, blaming him for a minor riot in 1877 between plantation labourers belonging to the Ghee Hin and its rival society, the Ghee Hok. Unafraid of the local cops, Tswa Tsoo Seng and his men went ahead with the feast, which turned violent late in the evening. With most of their local Ghee Hok enemies out of town, the Ghee Hin crowd attacked their rivals' shops. Soon bricks flew through the air, and more Ghee Hok joined the fray. Eventually both sides turned on the heavily outnumbered police. Caught in the middle of a barrage of stones, Mr Pilfert, a former Inspector of Police, grabbed a rifle and killed one of the Ghee Hin. Shocked rioters fled down side streets and into the fields, while police arrested the leaders and then ordered society headmen in Penang to keep their provincial allies in line. When the Governor and the Legislative Council approved the banishment of Tswa Tsoo Seng and his Ghee Hok counterpart, Khaw Boo Ahn seems not to have interfered. Keeping the peace in Nibong Tebal required more than constables on the beat, and Khaw had a long-term interest in maintaining his control of local labourers.[57] The Ghee Hin and Ghee Hok lived on to fight another day, testing one another in the towns and on the sugar estates.

The respectable and the rough confronted one another in the frontier towns of the British Empire and slowly worked out rules of public behaviour. British visions of colonial law and order had to be learned before they could be enforced, and they clashed with the strategies of the Chinese

---

[56] Lee and Chow, *Biographical Dictionary*, p. 57
[57] "Minute by the Acting Superintendent of Police, C. E. Ommanney, to the Lieutenant Governor of Penang, 29 August, 1878," CO273, Vol. IXVI, No. 14049, pp. 53–68, 72–74 (National Archive, London)

brotherhoods. How ought town populations be organized and kept in line? Inconsistencies abounded. A free-trade economy clashed with a regime of licences and monopolies against a background of smuggling and protection rackets. Toddy shops and bars, where all were welcome, stood a few feet away from members-only clubs limited to particular ethnic groups or clans. Towns were open societies, where tight racial hierarchies blurred and where individuals could participate in competing social worlds according to opportunity and inclination, but they were also heavily regulated spaces with multiple sets of conventions. Most importantly, they offered a social environment that contrasted sharply with that of nearby plantations, which were organized around strict racial hierarchies, segregated spaces, and closely controlled work gangs.

Living in a town offered much more than dependence and heavy debt. Towns presented seductive pleasures to the poor as well as the wealthy. Vendors produced tasty noodles and snacks on demand, and lodging houses offered cheap beds, albeit in dark, badly ventilated rooms. Taverns, smoking shops, and gambling halls could distract customers at least temporarily from aching muscles and isolation. When in 1879 Isabella Bird arrived in Kamunting, a Perak mining settlement with around 4,000 people, she saw its gambling saloon filled with Chinese coolies, each of whom "takes his pipe of opium after his day's work."[58] In Singapore during the late nineteenth century, rows of Chinese brothels, where customers could smoke alongside prostitutes, lined back streets next to New Bridge and North Bridge Roads, near the tenements where the rickshaw pullers lived.[59] Each town had its places for pleasure, tucked into narrow shop houses or corner hotels, which formed an important part of the local economy. Yet these risky recreations could come at a high cost.

Entertainment in Malaya was not a free trade. Rather it was tightly regulated by the colonial state and run by Chinese contractors who became important local patrons and powerbrokers. Anyone in British Malaya who wished to buy opium or liquor or to gamble had to go to licensed shops. Their managers worked for the consortium of wealthy men who had bought monopoly rights over those commodities or activities from the colonial government for huge sums. Local police and the Protector of Chinese regularly raided unlicensed shops, brothels, and gaming tables and monitored the legal outlets. There was no shortage of places of supply: In 1895 in Penang and Province Wellesley alone the police licensed 145 opium farm shops or opium smoking shops, 166

---

[58] Bird, *Golden Chersonese*, pp. 261, 268
[59] Warren, *Ah Ku*, pp. 43, 293; Warren, *Rickshaw Coolie*, p. 239

retail liquor or spirit farm shops, 76 public houses, and 59 toddy farm shops, and they kept a close eye on brothels where prostitutes served processed opium or chandu to their customers.[60] Every town had its entertainment district where men went for a pipe, alcohol, games of chance, and sex.

The cash extracted from the Chinese and Tamil poor supported Malayan free-trade towns and the continued informal dominance of the Chinese. Colonial administration had to be paid for, and the Treasury did not expect British taxpayers to foot the bill.[61] Revenue farming proved an ingenious solution to the need for resources during the early decades of British colonial rule when the ability of government institutions to collect taxes was small but the need for capital investment large. The British merely followed local precedent: Well before they moved into the area, rulers throughout Southeast Asia had granted monopoly rights to favoured subjects to provide a particular service or to produce, sell, or tax certain goods in return for a set fee. The ruler got a steady income while the middleman had a strong incentive to increase the demand for the service or product. The British and the Dutch continued this practice, working with Chinese middlemen at the expense of Chinese immigrants, who provided a ready market for opium, alcohol, women, and games of chance. The effective extraction of a surplus went hand in hand, therefore, with economic development and with the existence of a large group of consumers who had some ready cash but no alternative sources of supply. After looking around Penang in the 1790s, Francis Light allegedly remarked that the Chinese "were the only people in the east from whom a revenue may be raised without expense and extraordinary efforts of government."[62] He was quite right; subcontracting tax collection saved the British the work of producing and delivering products or services of which they disapproved in theory, while guaranteeing a share for colonial coffers of the increasing profits of these "necessary evils."[63]

The system rested on the astute choice of men to run the farms and their commercial outlets. The early contractors were wealthy Chinese

[60] "Annual Report for 1895," in Jarman, *Annual Reports*, Vol. 4, p. 230
[61] Lance E. Davis and Robert A. Huttenback, *Mammon and the Pursuit of Empire: The Political Economy of British Imperialism, 1860–1912* (Cambridge: Cambridge University Press, 1987)
[62] John Butcher, "Revenue Farming and the Changing State in Southeast Asia," in John Butcher and Howard Dick, eds., *The Rise and Fall of Revenue Farming* (London: Macmillan, 1993), pp. 19–24, 31–32
[63] Trocki, *Singapore*, pp. 80–81

men who also controlled the brotherhoods or secret societies, for example the Hakka leader and mine owner Yap Ah Loy, who was also the Kapitan China of Kuala Lumpur, Chung Keng Kwee, the Hai San leader and Kapitan China of Perak, and Khaw Boo Aun from Nibong Tebal, who had supplied men and guns to Raja Abdullah in the Larut War (1871–1873).[64] Granting them and their allies revenue farms not only reinforced their control over local clansmen, but brought them under the umbrella of the colonial state. By the 1880s the leading farmers had appointments as justices of the peace and municipal commissioners. They were formally part of the colonial government, adding British authority to their already considerable social and economic power.[65] By the late nineteenth century, large syndicates of the most important Chinese financiers, industrialists, and planters, based primarily in Singapore and Penang, took over the farms, bidding up the concessions while driving down their profits and increasing state revenues. Risk was spread among powerful family clans with international connections, each of whom made tax farming one of their many businesses until the colonial rulers brought the system to an end in the early twentieth century.[66] The opium concession was by far the most profitable, accounting for between 40 and 60 per cent of the total revenue of the Straits Settlements during the nineteenth century. Virtually the entire income of the state of Kedah came from revenue farms, the opium farm being by far the largest. Carl Trocki argues that "opium was at the heart of British Malaya," where the "opium-smoking coolies financed free trade, paid for the accumulation of Chinese and European capital, and financed the state that oversaw their exploitation."[67]

Prostitution was another moneymaking business that linked the colonial state and local Asian power brokers. The Chinese Protectorate, established in 1869, was given the task of overseeing both the coolie trade and the welfare of immigrant Chinese women. They also registered and oversaw Chinese brotherhoods, which they considered secret societies.[68] Their mandate, therefore, lay exactly in the nexus between

---

[64] Lee and Chow, *Biographical Dictionary*, pp. 38–39, 57, 184–185

[65] Carl A. Trocki, *Opium and Empire: Chinese Society in Colonial Singapore, 1800–1910* (Ithaca: Cornell University Press, 1990), p. 231. See also Trocki, *Prince of Pirates*

[66] Michael R. Godley, "Chinese Revenue Farm Networks: The Penang Connection," in Butcher and Dick, *Rise*, pp. 89–99

[67] Trocki, *Opium*, pp. 2, 237; Sharom Ahmat, *Tradition and Change in a Malay State: A Study of the Economic and Political Development of Kedah 1878–1923* (Kuala Lumpur: Malaysian Branch of the Royal Asiatic Society, 1984), p. 51

[68] Wilfred Blythe, *The Impact of Chinese Secret Societies in Malaya: A Historical Study* (London: Oxford University Press, 1969), pp. 5–8, 206–207

the customers, the enforcers, and the workers in the sex trade. Because most of the prostitutes in British Malaya were Chinese, the Protector of Chinese and the police shared the job of oversight, occasionally asking the women to swear that they did their jobs willingly. Between 1870 and 1887, prostitutes in the Straits Settlements had to be registered, periodically inspected for venereal diseases by a doctor, and confined in lock hospitals if found to be infected. Licensed brothels were well known to town police, and their owners paid a head tax on inmates. Even after the British Parliament repealed the Contagious Diseases Act in 1887, colonial authorities in Malaya resisted giving up their control of the sex trade, and continued registration, expanding it into the Federated Malay States.[69] An 1895 Act tasked the Protector of Chinese with inspecting brothels and counting the prostitutes who lived within them. The Protector of Chinese, G. T. Hare, found 632 women in brothels in Perak towns, and he questioned them on their history. Some said they had been kidnapped from homes in China; others had been sold by their families or given to procuresses to settle family debts, but all had been officially certified as consenting participants in the Malayan sex industry.[70] Prostitution was an international migratory occupation for immigrant women, which operated through urban networks. Women moved from place to place as they aged and as employers dictated. Cantonese women came to Singapore from Hong Kong; Japanese peasant girls, essentially debt slaves, were sent via Osaka and Nagasaki to Hong Kong and Singapore, ending up in towns around the peninsula and throughout Southeast Asia. Kuala Lumpur's brothels employed several hundred Chinese females, although the more expensive establishments employed Japanese women.[71]

These female workers were literally in the care of the colonial state, which tracked their movements and captured their faces. J. Powell, the Assistant Protector of Chinese in 1887, notified police and the resident in Klang of the impending arrival from Penang of Wong Chau Kok, identified as an 18-year-old prostitute heading for the Tong Seng brothel. She was travelling with two other women to the same destination: Thong A. Sam, wife of the brothel's cook, and their daughter Wong Lin Ho, age 16, whom the Protector suspected would join the local

[69] Philippa Levine, *Prostitution, Race and Politics: Policing Venereal Disease in the British Empire* (New York: Routledge, 2003)

[70] G. T. Hare, *Annual Report on the Chinese Protectorate in Perak for the year 1895*, 1342/1899 (Arkib Negara, Malaysia)

[71] "Report from the Resident Surgeon, Selangor on the Brothels of Kuala Lumpur, 7.2.1893," Selangor Secretariat, 1055/1893 (Arkib Negara, Kuala Lumpur); Warren, *Ah Ku*, pp. 68–74, 82–83

workforce. Their photos were sent ahead so they could be recognized. Prostitutes had to be visible, but brothels had to be discrete. In 1900 in Kuala Lumpur, several Malay and South Asian merchants living on Java Street found the local bawdy houses and "immoral women" intolerable. They begged the government to demand that the house owners evict the prostitutes, but nothing was done. They attracted "ruffians and rowdies" who made "most filthy and indecent jokes." Moreover, the sounds of "accordions, tom-toms" and the singing of "most dirty Malay songs" kept them awake at night. The Protector of Chinese, however, worried that it was "impossible for Europeans and others to go in and out by Petaling Street and High Street to the open country ... or to pass from the west side of the river to the east to the Golf Links and chapels on that side without passing through rows of Brothel houses." He proposed that all the brothels in Kuala Lumpur, Taiping, and Ipoh be relocated out of sight of any major thoroughfare and concentrated in one place for easier control by the police and his office.[72] In practical terms, the Protector worked hand in hand with brothel keepers to keep both customers and the general public happy. The women, however, had been imported by Chinese brokers and were much more under their power than that of the colonial state. What on paper looked like British control could be more accurately described as a system of layered jurisdictions, where Chinese revenue farmers managed state finances and where Chinese headmen controlled much of the local labour market. Prostitutes were only one of many groups over which the colonial state had formal jurisdiction but little effective power.

British colonial rule in Malaya rested on a system of layered sovereignty. Malay rajas had formal authority over the Muslim religion and ritual and over Malay headmen. In the towns, state offices provided legal, administrative, and sanitation services for the multi-ethnic population, while police watched over the streets. In the background, however, grew up a network of Chinese clan and dialect groups, brotherhoods, secret societies, and labour brokers with effective control of the Chinese labouring population. South Asians founded their own organizations, according to their birthplaces, languages, and religions. These ethnic and political divisions did not map easily onto urban spaces because town businesses drew their clientele from multiple

---

[72] "Petition for the Removal of Immoral Women from Java Street, Kuala Lumpur, 19 February 1900," Selangor Secretariat, 1046/1900; "Women and Girls Enactment, FMS; Suppression of Brothels and Confinement of Brothel Houses to one Definite Locality," Selangor Secretariat, 4903/1902 (Arkib Negara, Kuala Lumpur)

communities. Most importantly, small towns were neither walled nor formally segregated. Visitors from local plantations, mines, and villages crossed their boundaries daily, blurring the lines between urban and rural worlds. The relatively open world of the small towns contrasted sharply with the regimented, ethnically segmented plantations. The expansion of British colonial rule in Malaya required both environments, which balanced one another and permitted both to survive.

4   Urban Civil Society

In 1893, Leong Fee, a Hakka who emigrated to Malaya from a small village in South China as a poor teenager in 1876, founded and funded the Han Chin Pet Soo, a club for rich Hakka-speaking tin miners in the town of Ipoh (see Figure 4.1). After working his way up from hawker to clerk to shopkeeper to successful mine owner, he relished the role of patron and host. Leong Fee's framed picture continues to look down on the tiled floor, bentwood chairs, and gleaming wooden tables of the club's dining room, which became a welcoming space for other Hakka men.[1] Mine owners came to eat, drink, and play mah-jong in the company of sing-song girls, as well as to do deals. It drew Hakka men with money together, and gave them an upscale alternative to the brothels, gambling halls, and opium shops in the neighbourhood. Leong's club functioned as a community centre for those men who shared the same language, industry, and social status. The mixture of business and pleasure bonded them together. Clubs like the Han Chin Pet Soo spread new styles of male sociability within town populations.

As he aged, Leong Fee reached out well beyond his male Hakka compatriots. His activities as a philanthropist and political advisor to the British show the extent of his connections to other cultural groups. A member of the Ipoh and Penang elites, he funded the Chung Hwa School, which taught in Mandarin to bring together students who spoke various Chinese dialects. It also introduced them to a modern curriculum which included foreign languages, mathematics, geography, and history. He donated money to help build the Temple of Supreme Bliss (*Kek Lok Si*), an important pilgrimage site for Buddhists from all parts of East and Southeast Asia. Leong Fee not only travelled in Europe, but he was also elected to the Royal Society for the Encouragement of Arts, Manufactures, and Commerce while on a trip to England. Leong's ties were global and his tastes were cosmopolitan. Vice-

---

[1] The club has been beautifully restored by Ian Anderson and IpohWorld with much of its original furnishing maintained, recreating the early days of Han Chin Pet Soo; www.ipoh world.org/exhibition/

Figure 4.1 Entrance hall and dining room in the Han Chin Pet Soo Hakka miners' club in Ipoh, Perak. A picture of Leong Fee, its founder, hangs on the end wall.

Consul for the Qing government between 1901 and 1907, he organized celebrations of imperial birthdays and raised money for victims of famine in China. Leong also supported British colonial rule and served several terms on the Perak State Council and the Federal Council. Moreover, Leong gave his six sons, who were British subjects, a solidly bi-cultural identity by sending them to the best English schools in Penang. At least one, Leong Yin Khean, attended Cambridge. When photographed in 1918, all of his sons wore European dress.[2] Leong Fee served as a broker between the different cultural worlds of British Malaya and China.

Leong Fee became part of a culturally hybrid urban society which nudged individuals to cross cultural boundaries in their public and private lives. Urban schools, businesses, public rituals, and entertainments created places where individuals met and mixed with people unlike themselves. Towns introduced inhabitants to the unfamiliar, whether it be languages, religions, styles, technologies, or ideas, and gave them opportunities to sample what appealed. People of middling status, as well as

[2] Christine Wu Ramsay, *Days Gone By: Growing Up in Penang* (Penang: Areca Books, 2007), pp. 11–16, 23–24, 26, 29; Lee Kam Hing and Chow Mun Seong, eds., *Biographical Dictionary of the Chinese in Malaysia* (Petaling Jaya: Pelanduk Publications, 1997), p. 102

wealthy elites, formed the core of this group, but it extended to an unknown number of others who were exposed to cultural novelty on town streets and in shops. This chapter traces the growth of urban civil society as it developed slowly in the small towns of British Malaya and explores its social and political consequences during the nineteenth century. Clubs, schools, and public ceremonies take centre stage as spaces where individuals learned new vocabularies of action and self-expression.

Social Class and Social Life in Malayan Towns

While stark contrasts in wealth and social status were easily visible on Malayan streets, it is inaccurate to portray colonial towns as divided by social class into only two groups – the rich and the poor or the elite and the masses. As the Malayan economy developed, occupational structures became more differentiated among all ethnicities, and towns were central places for new jobs in administration, commerce, and the professions. Several scholars of Southeast Asia point to the existence of a group of middling status, whose members were drawn from multiple ethnic groups. Although their incomes and social prestige were inferior to landlords of high rank or to hereditary elites, this middling group became increasingly important in colonial towns during the nineteenth century. In their analyses of Chinese immigrants in Malaya, Wang Gungwu and Yen Ching-hwang point to three clusters of occupations, which they label businessmen (shang), educated professionals, teachers, and clerks (shih), and workers, both urban and rural (kung).[3] In his studies of the Malay population, J. M. Gullick identifies a middle group of Malay businessmen in the towns and larger villages who stood between the ruling elite (orang kaya) and the ordinary people (rakyat).[4] In South Asian immigrant communities, a middling group of shopkeepers and professionals grew in the towns, remaining separate from the plantation workers and town labourers. Demand for English-educated clerks and office workers led thousands of young Tamils from Ceylon and South India into urban settlements in Malaya.[5] At issue are the size, cohesiveness, and the importance of this population of many ethnicities and occupational titles,

[3] Wang Gungwu, *Community and Nation: Essays on Southeast Asia and the Chinese* (Singapore: 1981), p. 426; Yen Ching-hwang, *A Social History of the Chinese in Singapore and Malaya 1800–1911* (Singapore: Oxford University Press, 1986), pp. 141–143
[4] J. M. Gullick, *Malay Society in the Late Nineteenth Century* (Singapore: Oxford University Press, 1987) pp. 210, 225
[5] David West Rudner, *Caste and Capitalism in Colonial India: The Nattukottai Chettiars* (Berkeley: University of California Press, 1994); Kernial Singh Sandhu, *Indians in Malaya: Immigration and Settlement 1786–1957* (Cambridge: Cambridge University Press, 1969), p. 69

not its presence in cities and towns. By the late nineteenth century, members of this middle group, while certainly not self-conscious or united as a "class," became recognizable in British Malaya as they built institutions and added more modern commitments to loyalties they had inherited. They unsettled older social hierarchies and blurred communal lines of division. The presence of a middle group of upwardly mobile men who worked alongside one another in businesses and government offices created the possibility of widespread cultural learning and new cultural alliances among ethnic groups.

The way in which distinctions according to race operated in British Malaya requires re-examination. In that colony, discussions of racial difference meant distinctions among what today would, by many, be called ethnicities. Colonial censuses reveal the categories imposed by British administrators on the enumerated population. The earliest tallies in 1881 and 1891 divided people into "nationalities"; tabulated results designated Europeans and Americans as category 1 and assigned lower numbers to Eurasians, Chinese, Malays, South Asians, and Others. By 1911, the term "race" became the standard label for all the groups classified. The 1911 census used alphabetical order to rank the dozens of different categories it surveyed. Census takers asked informants to identify themselves by choosing among eight different classes of Chinese (e.g. Cantonese, Hokkien, Teochew), nine varieties of Malay, four types of South Asians, seventeen categories of European or American residents, and ten "other races" (e.g. Africans, Arabs, Egyptians, Singhalese). Group designations shifted somewhat from census to census, and they were not equivalent even within one survey. Some identified a nationality (Japanese, Italian) and others used religion (Jews). Although the colonial administration used the language of race to divide the residents of Malaya, the categories it employed were unstable and based on different criteria.

At a time when scientific racism became more dominant in Britain, it was exported to colonies by administrators and settlers. In Malaya, it became particularly powerful on plantations. An ideology of racial difference and racial hierarchy hardened among many British in Malaya, who worked to maintain colour bars in the colonial service, the railways, and social clubs.[6] Yet Asians repeatedly challenged such colour bars. Chinese, Malays, or South Asians had little reason to accept the racial stereotypes

---

[6] Charles Hirschman, "The Meaning and Measurement of Ethnicity in Malaysia: An Analysis of Census Classifications," *The Journal of Asian Studies*, Vol. 46, No. 3 (1987), pp. 555–582; John Butcher, *The British in Malaya 1880–1941: The Social History of a European Community in Colonial South-East Asia* (Kuala Lumpur: Oxford University Press, 1979), pp. 97–120

that circulated about them in colonial circles. Moreover, the extent to which those categories were used by Asians themselves is difficult to determine. Charles Hirschman, who argues that European racial ideology "permeated deeply into the consciousness of most Asians," bases his analysis on the geographical, economic, and social segregation of immigrant populations from one another and from Malays.[7] He moves from observed behaviour in rural areas to a generalized argument about ideology among multiple Asian populations. His reasoning does not describe accurately social and cultural life in Malayan towns among the educated population of middling status who developed cosmopolitan tastes and friendships.

The society of British Malaya was built around much more than distinctions among ethnicities and incomes. Other publicly proclaimed divisions – political, linguistic, occupational, and religious – cut across one another. Multiple vocabularies of difference shaped everyday life, making impossible any simple partition of the population into binary categories of colonizer versus colonized or European versus Asian. John Furnivall, who characterized "tropical dependencies" as "a medley of peoples" who "mix but do not combine," recognized the ethnic complexity of Asian plural societies, but he underestimated the permeability of boundaries and the capacity of urban institutions to create new networks and allegiances.[8] Similarly, arguments that stress a British policy of "divide and rule" ignore the ways in which institutions and policies produced multi-cultural alliances and overlapping social worlds.[9] Colonial states energetically classified their populations, but as Ulbe Bosma has argued, those divisions were "porous."[10] "Class, profession, geographic origin, religion, and education as well as skin colour" influenced where individuals stood in local social hierarchies and how they related to their neighbours.[11] Just as in the

---

[7] Charles Hirschman, "The Making of Race in Colonial Malaya: Political Economy and Racial Ideology," *Sociological Forum*, Vol. 1, No. 2 (1986), pp. 356–357

[8] John Furnivall, *Colonial Policy and Practice: a Comparative Study of Burma and Netherlands India* (Cambridge: Cambridge University Press, 1948), p. 304

[9] A. J. Christopher, "'Divide and Rule': The Impress of British Separation Policies," *Area* 20 (1988), pp. 233–240

[10] Much historiography of the 1990s identified race as the most important perceived division among the populations of Southeast Asia. See Ann Laura Stoler, *Carnal Knowledge and Imperial Power: Race and the Intimate in Colonial Rule* (Berkeley: University of California Press, 2002); Jan Bremen, in *Taming the Coolie Beast: Plantation Society and the Colonial Order in Southeast Asia* (Delhi: Oxford University Press, 1989), also stresses the weight of racial divisions on Sumatran plantations.

[11] Hirschmann, "The Making of Race," pp. 330–362; David Theo Goldberg, *The Racial State* (Oxford: Blackwell, 2002); Ulbe Bosma and Remco Raben, *Being "Dutch" in the Indies: A History of Creolisation and Empire, 1500–1920* (Athens: Ohio University Press, 2008) pp. 21, 24

cities of the United States, rapid economic growth and urbanization forced migrants of multiple ethnicities into common social spaces where they learned from one another.

During the nineteenth century, Asian men of middle status (but few women) in British Malaya were drawn into an emerging urban civil society created by economic development and the growth of the colonial state. This civil society, which had ties both to Asia and to Europe, can be described as "cosmopolitan," or having a "relationship to a plurality of cultures," within which individuals had "competence."[12] The sorts of cultural fluidity and multiple allegiances that characterize contemporary world cities can be glimpsed in the later nineteenth century among educated urban immigrants who helped establish civil society in British Malaya. Yap Ah Loy, whose roots were in a Hakka farming community in South China, learned other cultural styles and appreciations when he became the kapitan, or head, of the Chinese community in Kuala Lumpur. At his installation, he dressed as a Malay raja, and he sponsored Malay plays to entertain the population. The Daoist temple that he founded and led brought several Chinese communities, as well as Tamils and Japanese, together through its ritual life. After the British became advisors to the Selangor raja, Yap requested naturalization as a British subject! He recognized different cultural styles and manipulated them as needed to bolster his political power.[13] As early as the 1870s, the active cultural hybridity of Penang and Singapore residents existed in smaller towns.[14] Colonial towns, even the small ones, fostered socially mobile, multilingual, culturally sophisticated groups of people with complex loyalties that crossed standard racial, ethnic, and religious boundaries. This phenomenon spread widely in cities and towns throughout the Federated Malay States and the Straits Settlements among men of elite and middle status, blurring categories of difference and widening a common social, imperial space.

Two scholarly generations ago, such Asian men were labelled "collaborators" because their help for their colonial masters was thought to

---

[12] Steven Vertovec and Robin Cohen, eds., *Conceiving Cosmopolitanism: Theory, Context, and Practice* (Oxford: Oxford University Press, 2002), p. 13; Ulf Hannerz, "Cosmopolitans and Locals in World Culture," *Theory, Culture and Society* 7 (1990), pp. 237–251

[13] Sharon A. Carstens, *Histories, Cultures, Identities: Studies in Malaysian Chinese Worlds* (Singapore: Singapore University Press, 2005), pp. 18–20, 32–34

[14] Timothy Norman Harper, "Empire, Diaspora, and the Language of Globalism, 1850–1914," in Anthony G. Hopkins, ed., *Globalization in World History* (London: Pimlico, 2002), pp. 142, 146, 152, 156; Su Lin Lewis, "Cosmopolitanism and the Modern Girl: A Cross-Cultural Discourse in 1930s Penang," *Modern Asian Studies* 43 (2009), pp. 1385–1419

have undermined the growth of nationalism. Using a language inherited from the 1940s and 1950s, Ronald Robinson identified such figures with traditional Asian and African elites who bargained to retain power and gain patronage for their mediating functions.[15] More recently, they have been called "brokers," or "go-betweens" to signal their culture-crossing skills. Their education and resources permitted exchanges among those who could not communicate on their own. In Southeast Asia, Chinese compradors ran the day-to-day operations of European banks and businesses with local clients; Malay munshis taught languages to British officials; Tamil vakils served as attorneys or agents; Banyāns and chettiars acted as bankers and money changers. Their multilingualism eased the flow of information between groups and institutions, as did their knowledge of different cultural traditions.[16] Although most of these men have left only the lightest traces in colonial archives, a few had a direct impact on colonial society and are remembered. Abdullah bin Abdul Kadi, a Malay of Yemeni and Tamil ancestry, worked as a scribe, language teacher, translator, and diplomat in Melaka and Singapore during the first half of the nineteenth century. Sir Stamford Raffles employed him as a secretary and copier because of his expertise in English, Dutch, Tamil, Arabic, and Malay, and he worked for the London Missionary Society translating parts of the Bible. Both an ardent Anglophile and a Malay reformer, Abdullah helped to modernize the Malay language through his writing, and used liberal principles to criticize rule by the Malay sultans.[17] Less famous is Malaiperumal Pillay from the Vellalar caste of farmers who migrated from Pondicherry to Perak in 1888 to help relatives run a construction business. Malaiperumal got rich helping to build the town of Batu Gajah and became a locally important temple patron and a labour boss. Convinced that knowledge of English was necessary for his sons and daughters, Malaiperumal financed an English-language school, which he opened to neighbourhood children. The school then produced several generations of Tamils, Chinese, and Malays, who absorbed British history and literature along with the English language; it also drew these

[15] Ronald Robinson, "Non-European Foundations of European Imperialism: Sketch for a Theory of Collaboration," in Roger Owen and Bob Sutcliffe, eds., *Studies in the Theory of Imperialism* (London: Longman, 1972), pp. 117–140

[16] Simon Schaffer, et al., eds., *The Brokered World: Go-Betweens and Global Intelligence, 1770–1820* (Sagamore Beach, MA: Science History Publications, 2009); C. A. Bayly, *Empire and Information: Intelligence Gathering and Social Communication in India, 1780– 1870* (Cambridge: Cambridge University Press, 1996), pp. 229–234

[17] Abdullah bin Abdul Kadir, *The Hikayat Abdullah*, A. H. Hill, trans. (Kuala Lumpur: Oxford University Press, 1970); Anthony Milner, *The Invention of Politics in Colonial Malaya: Contesting Nationalism and the Expansion of the Public Sphere* (Cambridge: Cambridge University Press, 1995), pp. 12–13, 31–32

young people into cross-cultural activities and friendships.[18] Not only was he personally a "go-between," but Malaiperumal institutionalized in Batu Gajah the training of hundreds more like himself. His school opened up a modern space where students learned competence in a second culture while they learned about one another.

By the early twentieth century, walls separating ethnic groups had become lower in urban society for educated males, as colonial institutions and print culture spread. Clubs, religious institutions, and schools multiplied, presenting individuals with alternative societies and allegiances, thereby unsettling inherited hierarchies. In towns but not plantations, social place was not identical with race, and individuals had greater freedom of movement among social worlds.

Middle Groups and the Growth of Urban Civil Society

Immigrants crowding into town streets and shop houses brought with them the habits and expectations of past lives. Chinese looked forward to celebrations of the New Year and Tamil Hindus to Thaipusam and Muslims to Hari Raya. Christians waited eagerly for Christmas. At the same time an aching need for sociability and protection, which neither employers nor governments could satisfy, pushed migrants together into wider networks and groups that could stand in for absent kin and natal communities. In the *Philosophy of Right*, Hegel posited a social realm between the family and the state, in which voluntary associations brought their members individual dignity and rank and directed individual self-seeking into common pursuits. He used the phrase "civil society" [*burgerliche Gesellschaft*] to express this organization of citizens acting collectively in pursuit of common interests and welfare. In the German language, this term locates the membership of civil society in the middle class or urban groups of citizens with property. Hegel also stresses the educational role that these new institutions played in transforming members into fictive kin.[19] As frontier towns in Malaya became better organized, a range of associations developed outside the state, which drew immigrants into new social forms, some of which included more than one ethnic group. Together they created a local civil society.

---

[18] The school was taken over by the state in 1911, becoming the Government English School, Batu Gajah. Rokiah Talib, *Selvamany: More Than a Teacher* (Bangi Selangor: Penerbit Universiti Kebangsaan Malaysia, 2012), pp. 16–21

[19] G. W. F. Hegel, *Hegel's Philosophy of Right*, T. M. Knox, trans. (London: Oxford University Press, 1967); Gareth Stedman Jones, "Hegel and the Economics of Civil Society," in Sudipta Kaviraj and Sunil Khilnani, eds., *Civil Society: History and Possibilities* (Cambridge: Cambridge University Press, 2001), pp. 105–130

Religious institutions seem to have been the first sort to be established, and they served far more than those of middle status. In George Town, the Kwang Fu Kung Temple dedicated to Kwan Yin, the goddess of Mercy, was founded in 1799 by Hu Shih Ming, the appointed Kapitan China. Several dialect groups came together in Singapore in 1838 to establish the T'ien Fu Kung, dedicated to the seafaring goddess T'ien Hou. The early Chinese temples in the key cities of the Straits Settlements acted as welfare and community centres, in addition to being places of worship. Some served all the dialect groups, with Chinese headmen using them as administrative centres and places for mediation of disputes. As Malaya urbanized, each new town had at least one Chinese temple that served as a cultural hub, and the larger places had several. Over time in the larger towns, the major dialect groups founded their own temples in honour of regional deities, separating their ritual life from that of other Chinese communities.[20] Tamil Muslims, called Chulia, built a simple mosque in their George Town neighbourhood as early as 1791. Rebuilt in brick with contributions from wealthy Tamil merchants, the Kapitan Kling mosque, its burial ground, and an adjacent Sufi shrine, the Nagore Dargah, became the centre of Tamil Muslim community life in Penang.[21] The George Town Sri Muthu Mariamman temple began as a simple shrine on land granted in 1801 to Betty Lingam Chetty, who was probably the headman of the Tamil Hindu community. The oldest Hindu temple in Malaya, it celebrates the mother goddess, who offers protection from disease and other calamities, and it served as a community centre for the Tamil stevedores and labourers who worked at the port. Sikh soldiers founded Gurdwaras in Penang and other Malayan towns, where they were hired as policemen or soldiers. Nattukkottai Chettiars, merchants from Tamil Nadu who moved into Straits Settlement towns around 1824, put down roots in their new communities by establishing temples in towns such as Teluk Anson (now Teluk Intan).[22] Tamil labourers created their own worship spaces. As workers walked from the Penang Sugar Estates into Nibong Tebal along Jalan Victoria and Jalan Byram, they stopped at a small, dark-garlanded statue of Ganesh, whose shrine later became the site of the elaborate Sri Sithi Vinayagar Devasthanam

---

[20] Yen, *Social History of the Chinese*, pp. 111–115

[21] Khoo Salma Nasution, *The Chulia in Penang: Patronage and Place-Making around the Kapitan Kling Mosque 1786–1957* (Penang: Areca Books, 2014), pp. 57–59, 68–71

[22] Himashu Batt, *Little India of Georgetown* (Penang: Georgetown World Heritage Inc., 2015); Saran Singh Sidhu, *Sikh Gurdwaras in Malaysia and Singapore* (Kuala Lumpur: Sikh Naujawan Sabha Malaysia, 2003), p. 158; S. Muthiah, Meenakshi Meyappan, and Visalakshi Ramaswamy, *The Chettiar Heritage*, rev. ed. (Chennai: The Chettiar Heritage, 2006), p. 58

Temple, built in the 1920s. Large urban temples, built with support from Chettiar communities and Ceylon Tamils, served as regional sites for celebration.[23]

Christian churches serving Asian as well as European parishioners multiplied in the Straits Settlements and, later, in the Malay states. Eurasian Catholics fleeing persecution in Thailand and Kedah began to worship in Penang soon after 1786, and the East India Company built an elegant, white-pillared Palladian church there for Anglicans in central George Town in 1816, several years after the congregation had formed. Towns served as central places for the religious life of Province Wellesley too, as Anglicans and Roman Catholics built mission churches to draw in plantation labourers. French Roman Catholic priests based in Penang moved into Nibong Tebal in the late nineteenth century, preaching in the open air to cart drivers and estate labourers. Monseigneur Gasnier, after visiting workers on the Caledonia estate in the summer of 1883, passed through Nibong Tebal as he continued south.[24] In 1891, Father Fée, a French priest, established there the congregation of St Anthony, which continues today to draw hundreds of South Asians to its masses and meetings. In 1911, Holy Trinity, a small, austere wooden building with four gothic-style windows and a gold cross on its pitched roof, opened on land donated by the Penang Sugar Estate to serve a fledgling congregation of Tamil Anglicans.[25] A range of needs, sacred and profane, brought plantation populations regularly into Malayan towns, where they rebuilt their social lives.

These religious communities did not aim to unsettle social hierarchies. While churches might offer food and shelter to the poor, their primary mission was not that of social mobility. Instead, they provided places and times for prayer, spiritual expression, patronage, and recognition. Yet they also offered opportunities to those with energy and talent, inevitably disturbing the status quo. Temples had governing boards and welfare committees. Churches organized Sunday Schools and youth organizations, and they appointed teachers and directors. Faith communities representing all major religions and ethnic groups created leaders who swelled the ranks of the towns' middling groups and gave them added status and visibility.

[23] Sinnappah Arasaratnam, *Indians in Malayasia and Singapore*, rev. ed. (Kuala Lumpur: Oxford University Press, 1979), p. 162
[24] "Lettre de Mgr. Gasnier á le Directeur au Seminaire des Missions Étrangéres, 24 Aôut 1883," #306, p. 45, Malaisie-Lettres 1873–1891 (Archives des missions étrangéres, Paris)
[25] Penang Sugar Estates, "Letter from E. Underdown to William Duncan, 29 April 1910," D/Pen/Malaya/2/18/1910 (Cumbria Record Office, Whitehaven)

In the towns, schools contributed even more effectively than churches and temples to the growing numbers of those of middling status. Ho Thean Foo recounts his grandfather's move into Papan in the early twentieth century, after his family was ousted from their Perak farm to make way for a rubber plantation. His parents sent Pak Foo to the Papan Hwa Chiao, or Overseas Chinese School, which was funded by the richer town residents and run by a public committee. It offered both boys and girls a modern form of Chinese education, which included math, geography, Mandarin, and English, and it taught writing using simplified Chinese characters. If students passed annual examinations and continued through the secondary level, they could qualify for a university.[26] In any case, its modern style of secondary education fitted students for white-collar occupations and for positions in offices and businesses throughout the colony.

When there were enough families and children to create a demand, Chinese communities in Malaya commonly set up primary and secondary schools. Initially they used a group's home dialect as the language of instruction, but by 1900, some opted for Mandarin or English to broaden opportunities for pupils. In 1904, Foochow settlers in the Sitiawan area set up a village school, partly funded by the Methodist Church and by Chinese and European well-wishers in the nearby town of Teluk Anson. It soon became an English-language institution, whose teachers were a Tamil pastor and Rev. and Mrs C. E. Draper, Methodist missionaries active in Sitiawan.[27] By 1912, the Methodist Episcopal Mission supported and staffed nineteen boys' and six girls' schools in the towns of Perak and Selangor and Singapore, several of which taught in English. The Penang Anglo-Chinese School had 938 students on the books in 1905. Although it was run by the Methodist Church, wealthy Chinese tin miners such as Leong Fee and Foo Choo Choon became patrons, funding its library and scholarships for poor boys.[28] Protestant missionaries, rich towkays, and local communities combined forces to support English-

---

[26] Ho Thean Fook, who wrote about his grandfather's experiences, used education to escape manual labour. Ho parlayed his English-language schooling in Ipoh into a job teaching English at the Khai Meng Chinese School Sungkai, and later joined the Kinta Sanitary Board and the Perak Secretariat. Ho Thean Fook, *God of the Earth* (Ipoh: Perak Academy, 2003), pp. 75, 84, 205

[27] Shih Toong Siong, *The Foochows of Sitiawan* (Sitiawan: Persatuan Kutien Daerah Manjung, c. 2004), pp. 128, 142

[28] Ted T. Goh, "Challenged by the Spirit," *90 Methodism: A Brief History of the 90 years of Methodism in Singapore and Malaysia* (Singapore: Hoong Fatt Press, 1975), p. 7; "Death of Rev. W. E. Horley, M. B. E.," in *The Straits Budget*, 9 April 1931, p. 15; Methodist Episcopal Church, *Minutes of the Thirteenth Session of the Malaysia Conference of the Methodist Episcopal Church* (Kuala Lumpur, FMS, 15–20 February 1905), p. 23

language education for local children, who were provided with the tools for jobs in business, the colonial civil service, or the professions.

Schools multiplied in George Town and in Province Wellesley from the early nineteenth century, educating children drawn from all the major language communities. English-language schools in British Malaya date from 1816, when the Penang Free School, funded by public subscription, opened for a small number of boys. The school drew primarily Chinese, Tamil, and Eurasian boys intending to be "native merchants, ... clerks and subordinate employees," but it grew into what has remained one of the premier schools in Western Malaysia.[29] Christian missionaries became the prime movers of English education in Malaya for families who could afford the fees and were comfortable with the religious framework of the institutions. In 1824, the parish priest of the Assumption Church in Penang began a small English-language school to keep Catholic boys away from the Protestant-directed Free School, and it grew into St Xavier's Institution, run by the Lasalle Brothers, who also directed prestigious English-language schools in Singapore, Ipoh, Melaka, and Kuala Lumpur. Sisters of the Holy Infant Jesus founded Convent Light Street and opened the first girls' school in 1852 in George Town, and the Anglicans added St George's School for Girls in 1885. Singapore supported an even larger collection of English-language schools by the end of the century.[30] Missionaries spread English-language education to smaller towns too. Around 1900, Methodists, led by the energetic Rev. W. E. Horley, organized Anglo-Chinese schools in Ipoh, Teluk Anson, Kuala Lumpur, and Kampar, all of which taught children in English (see Figure 4.2). With some government and some church funding, Horley recruited Chinese teachers, dunned local merchants and miners for donations, and persuaded the colonial government to grant land and subsidies in return for inspection rights. The Ipoh school, which charged each of its Tamil, Chinese, Malay, and English students a fee of $1 per month, soon educated about 200 pupils. With the aid of aggressive headmasters and much community support, one-room schoolhouses expanded into major establishments teaching through the secondary

[29] "Annual Report for 1872," in Robert L. Jarman, ed., *Annual Reports of the Straits Settlements 1855–1941* (London: Archive Editions, 1998), Vol. 2, p. 169

[30] Keith Tan, *Mission Schools of Malaya* (Subang Jaya: Taylor's Press, 2011); Ian Ward, Norma Miraflor, and David Webb, *De la Salle: The Tradition, The Legacy, the Future* (Ipoh: Media Masters Publishing Sdn. Bhd, 2009); Khoo Salma Nasution, Alison Hayes, and Sehra Yeap Zimbulis, *Giving Our Best: The Story of St George's Girls' School Penang 1885–2010* (Penang: Areca Books, 2010); Tan Yap Kwang, Chow Hong Kheng, and Christine Goh, *Examinations in Singapore: Change and Continuity (1891–2007)* (Singapore: World Scientific Publishing Co., 2008), p. 8

Figure 4.2 Anglo-Chinese School in Ipoh, 1938. Staff and students line up to receive a visitor.

level.[31] A growing demand for English-language education among Chinese, South Asians, and high-status Malays sustained these schools as they expanded into well-equipped, large campuses and multi-story buildings.

The study of English spread quickly in the Straits Settlements and Federated Malay States, defining a group of higher status who could take on jobs within the colonial administration or work more effectively in European-owned businesses. English-language schools for both boys and girls were organized early in Singapore, Penang, and Melaka and educated a significant fraction of all the enrolled students in those towns by the later nineteenth century. The 24 English-only schools enrolled 53 per cent of the 8773 children attending school in those areas in 1886, and several hundred more students attended bilingual schools run by the Methodists in smaller towns, where they learned to read simple English.[32] By 1900, English-language education had spread significantly in the Federated Malay States, too. In 1888, English medium schools could be found in Taiping, and government-inspected, bilingual schools

[31] E. C. Hicks, *History of English Schools in Perak* (Ipoh: The Perak Library, 1958); Ho Tak Ming, *Ipoh: When Tin Was King* (Ipoh: Perak Academy, 2009), pp. 108–109
[32] "Annual Report for 1886," in Jarman, *Annual Reports*, Vol. 3, pp. 175–176

existed in Matang, Kamunting, Kuala Kangsar, and Teluk Anson. Government inspectors counted 714 children studying in 11 English-medium schools throughout Perak (16 per cent of the total number of pupils) in 1897, and the numbers rose steadily into the 1920s. While most of their pupils were Chinese or Tamil boys, they claimed 70 Malay boys and 46 girls from different groups.[33] Interest in learning English was not limited to Europeans, Eurasians, and Malays of high status. Muthamal Palanisamy tells of her father, Ayyan, who as a teenager ran away from South India to Malaya around 1912 to work on a rubber plantation. He quickly became an overseer and enrolled himself in a night school English class taught in a Methodist-run, Anglo-Chinese school. Ayyan sent both his daughters and his sons to English-language schools.[34] The Anderson School in Ipoh, founded in 1909, had from its founding students and teachers drawn from all of the colony's major ethnic groups.[35]

Soon there were sizeable numbers of English speakers and readers in British Malaya. The census of 1921 reported that 8.7 per cent of the total urban population and 10.3 per cent of adult urban men in British Malaya could speak English. While there is no independent measure of what this meant in terms of proficiency, it signalled at least acquaintance with spoken English and some level of aspiration, if not skill. Over 42,000 Asians in the Straits cities and over 17,000 in the Federated Malay States' larger towns claimed to be bilingual. While this number is a minority of the urban population, it represents a significant share of urban residents. Most importantly, the census identified English as the preferred second language of not only Malays, but also Chinese and South Asians.[36] Knowledge of English opened up a common cultural space among educated Asian immigrants, one in which all were newcomers and non-native speakers. English was not only the language of the colonial masters; it also became the preferred choice of middle groups because of their common education and cultural aspirations. Bazaar Malay, while a lingua franca of trade and production, remained for them a language of commerce and

---

[33] "Comparative Return of Average Enrolment and Attendance at All the Schools in the State during the Years 1888 and 1889," *Perak Government Gazette*, 25 July 1890, p. 493; "Report of the Education Department for the Year 1897," *Perak Government Gazette*, 23 March 1898, pp. 175–176

[34] Muthammal Palanisamy, *From Shore to Shore* (Kajang Selangor: VGV Management Consultant, 2002), pp. 26, 39

[35] Malim Ghozali, *Images 1909–2009: Centennial Anniversary Anderson School, Ipoh Malaysia* (Ipoh: Seladang Ventures, 2009)

[36] J. E. Nathan, *The Census of British Malaya for 1921* (London: Waterlow & Sons, 1922), tables XL–XLVII, pp. 322–332. Relatively few Chinese and Tamils claimed literacy in Malay (although they probably had some speaking skills) and almost no Malays learned either Chinese or Tamil.

command. English, in contrast, opened areas of sociability and cosmopolitanism. English became a local language.

In several respects, the fact of education mattered more than the
language in which it was conducted. Those who were literate, whatever
the language, had access to the written tradition of their community and
access to information about a world beyond village and family. Print
culture surrounded urban populations – on street signs, wall posters,
newspapers, and books. Just as in the United States in the nineteenth
century, urban cultures in Malaya expressed themselves through written
words.[37] To find out about railway timetables, the visit of the town
vaccinator, or the arrival of a Chinese circus troupe it helped generally
to be literate, and people had increasing opportunities to learn to read and
write. Partly in response to family demand and partly through colonial
support for basic education for Malays, schools multiplied in British
Malaya. Madrasas taught boys the rudiments of Arabic, which gave
them access to Islamic texts, as well as publications in Jawi. Then, during
the later 1870s and early 1880s, the colonial government opened free,
secular schools teaching Malay to pupils in Perak and Selangor, and by
1900 over 169 such schools with 6,500 pupils operated in the Federated
Malay States. Malay interest in literacy went hand in hand with the
appearance of newspapers and government jobs that demanded it.[38] In
1890, the Inspector of Perak Schools reported that a small but significant
number of students from the Malay vernacular schools had gone on to
jobs as teachers, clerks, police constables, and village headmen (*penghulu*), moving into a different world as a result of literacy.[39] Chinese
communities operated their own schools, while Tamils relied on what
plantation managers would provide, in addition to those run for them by
religious groups. In 1921, when the census first inquired about literacy, it
recorded that about half of the male inhabitants of the larger towns of the
Straits Settlements and the Federated Malay States could read and write.
Literacy among females was significantly lower, ranging from 11 per cent

---

[37] David M. Henkin, *City Reading: Written Words and Public Spaces in Antebellum New York*
(New York: Columbia University Press, 1980)

[38] The first newspaper in Malay, *Jawi Peranakan*, appeared in 1876. Published in Singapore
especially for the culturally hybrid group of the same name (the offspring of South Indian
Muslims and Malays), it circulated widely among those able to read Jawi (Malay written
in Arabic script). William Roff, *The Origins of Malay Nationalism*, 2nd ed. (Kuala
Lumpur: Oxford University Press, 1994), pp. 26–27, 48–49, 128–129

[39] Straits Settlements, *Blue Book for the Year 1890* (Singapore: Government Printing Office,
1891), pp. 8–17; *Perak Government Gazette, 1897*, Volume X, 24 September 1897, pp.
624–625; While most students from Malay schools took up agricultural or labouring jobs,
the return counted 59 teachers, 57 clerks, 43 constables, and 2 penghulus and an
unknown number of shopkeepers in a group of 5,200 for which there was information.

in Penang to 25 per cent in Taiping.[40] By the end of the nineteenth century, paths to literacy were widening among the Asian population in British Malaya, opening up their access to what Jurgen Habermas referred to as a "public sphere," a space for the exchange of information and political views through the written word.[41] In British Malaya, however, the multitude of languages and information networks raises the question of how a public sphere or spheres operated in a world of diasporic populations. Translation from one language to another was necessary, and educated Asian men had the skills and the interest to do most of this work. Expanding cultural literacy came along with education; it was part of the cultural life of middling groups in British Malaya.

Clubs and Urban Civil Society

In Malayan towns, literate people of middling status not only read about a wider world, they also created a flourishing civil society built around clubs and committees. When Europeans set up empires in South and Southeast Asia, clubs where they could drink and relax soon followed. Men of property, both European and those of mixed ancestry, formed *Harmonie* clubs in Batavia and Surakarta, where they debated political questions and gossiped. In Bombay in the later eighteenth and early nineteenth centuries, Europeans and Anglophone Indians organized multiple literary and scientific societies. John Butcher judged that "club life was nearly synonymous with social life" in Malaya, where such institutions existed even in small towns by the later nineteenth century.[42] Europeans gathered regularly to gorge themselves on imported food and drink and to toast Queen Victoria. Soon after its founding in 1884 in Kuala Lumpur, the Selangor Club ran pot-luck dinners and fielded a cricket team At the Perak Club in Taiping, smartly dressed Chinese boys served members roast goose, boiled beef, and iced asparagus while Sikh soldiers stood at attention.[43] Such clubs symbolized a social politics of exclusion, where non-Europeans were normally welcome only as servants. But it was

[40] Nathans, *Census*, p. 109
[41] Jürgen Habermas, *The Structural Transformation of the Public Sphere: an Inquiry into a Category of Bourgeois Society*, Thomas Burger (trans.) (Cambridge, MA: The MIT Press, 1991)
[42] Bosma and Raben, *Being "Dutch"*, pp. 133, 196; Prashant Kidambi, *The Making of an Indian Metropolis: Colonial Governance and Public Culture in Bombay 1890–1920* (Aldershot: Ashgate, 2007), pp. 159–161; John Butcher, *The British in Malaya, 1880–1941* (Kuala Lumpur: Oxford University Press, 1979), pp. 59, 147
[43] See the account of a banquet at the Perak Club in Taiping to honour Colonel R. S. F. Walker, commander of the Perak Sikh regiment, on the occasion of his departure for leave in England; *Perak Pioneer*, 16 November 1895, p. 3

difficult to maintain strict segregation in a world where Chinese dominated the economy and Malays had a titular right to rule. Not only were
exceptions made, but imitation soon followed.

A model of club sociability spread widely among Asians in Malaya,
perhaps through the handful of rich Tamils, Chinese, or Malays who
were invited to join European clubs. The first social club in Kuala
Lumpur had a few Eurasian, Malay, Tamil, and Chinese members. To
be a club member signalled an Asian's arrival in the colonial elite, although
the Selangor Club's nickname, "The Spotted Dog," certainly indicates
European ambivalence toward their presence.[44] Social clubs on the
British model multiplied in Malaya as Asian immigrants with cash and
connections settled into the larger towns, although the written record of
their existence is sparse before 1910. Considering his compatriots in
Singapore, Song Ong Siang mentions the Straits Chinese Recreation
Club, the Weekly Entertainment Club, and the Straits Chinese Social
Club. Some groups, such as the Straits Chinese Literary Association,
had a more intellectual purpose. The Straits Confucian Association was
open to all, "irrespective of race or creed" as long as they behaved like
gentlemen. Meetings aimed to spread "scientific and useful knowledge," as did the Straits Philosophical Society, a multi-ethnic debating
club that functioned in English, attracting civil servants as well as
soldiers, doctors, and lawyers. Such societies closely resembled their
counterparts in London, Manchester, and Edinburgh.[45] The newspaper
Bintang Timor commented in 1894 that Singaporean Malays were taking
up the Chinese habit of forming clubs, and Penang, too, housed multiple clubs by the later nineteenth century.[46] These associations created
far more than just places to meet. Most of them had lending libraries,
many with books in English, as well as newspapers and periodicals. The
clubs encouraged literate men to read about others like them and to
move into a public sphere of discussion.[47]

In small towns, clubs provided a new style of social life. In Papan,
Europeans and the wealthier mine owners founded an Anglo-Chinese
Club in a two-story shophouse not far from the hall where the Hakka clan

---

[44] Butcher, *British in Malaya*, pp. 61–62. George Orwell has immortalized the racial
exclusiveness of a Europeans Only club in *Burmese Days* (New York: Harcourt Brace
& World, Inc., 1950), p. 17, calling them "the spiritual nirvana, the real seat of British
power."

[45] Peter Clark, *British Clubs and Societies c. 1580–1800: The Origins of an Associational World*
(New York: Oxford University Press, 2000)

[46] Song Ong Siang, *One Hundred Years' History of the Chinese in Singapore* (Singapore:
Oxford University Press, 1984; orig. ed. 1902), pp. 216, 319, 343, 501; T. N. Harper,
"Globalism," pp. 276–277

[47] "Malaya's Reading Public," *The Straits Times*, 3 September 1932, p. 14

association, the Tsen Lung Fui Kuon, met.[48] Clubs that grouped immigrants according to ethnicity multiplied in Taiping in the later nineteenth and early twentieth centuries. According to the Taiping Municipal Council, Europeans founded the Taiping Club (1885), the Freemason's Lodge (1889), and a Cricket Club (1881). Leading Cantonese men set up the Kwantung Hui Kwan in 1887, and the Hokkien Khoo clan set up a branch of the Khoo Kongsi. Chung Keng Kwee, the first Kapitan China, founded a group for Hakkas from Guangzhou, in 1887 or 1888. A group of South Asians, which included a Muslim apothecary, several Tamils, and at least one Sikh, organized an Indian Association in 1896. In addition, Sikhs living in Taiping had their own society, and a Taiping Recreation Club opened in 1900. Then in 1901, the Ceylon Association, primarily for Tamils working for the government or the railroads, appeared, to be followed in 1910 by the Eurasian Association and in 1920 by an Indian Muslim Association. So many Jaffna Tamils subscribed to their new club in 1901 that it immediately rented space and opened a reading room for members. Under the Sultan's patronage, around 30 leading Malays joined together in the Muslim Club and elected a slate of officers.[49] Similar associations were begun in George Town and Singapore at earlier dates. Ethnicity obviously shaped sociability, but clubs pushed men into broader identifications – Indian and Chinese for example, rather than narrower classifications. Moreover, men belonged to multiple clubs which had different memberships and interests; the groups also worked together sometimes on public events and ritual occasions. Sociability widened social worlds and broadened identifications. In the twentieth century, the mingling of ethnic groups in urban civil society became much more extensive.

These clubs, most of which concentrated on recreation and welfare, were not perceived as politically threatening. If they registered with the government and stayed out of trouble, they could operate freely. In contrast, many of the older, more inclusive kongsi brotherhoods headquartered in the towns were rebranded as "secret societies" and banned in 1890, their lower-ranking leaders being jailed or exiled.[50] As politically neutral groups multiplied among educated men, the labour protection societies that had embraced immigrant labourers were driven underground and outside the legal economy. Urban social life became more deeply divided along lines of class and education as the colonial state drew

---

[48] Ho, p. 117
[49] www.malaysiacentral.com/information-directory/cities-and-towns/state-perak/taiping-the-historically-rich-town-in-perak-malaysia/ (site viewed on 25/3/2014); Khoo Khay Kim, *Taiping: the Vibrant Years* (Taiping: OFA Desyne, 2003), pp. 75–77
[50] Wilfred Blythe, *The Impact of Chinese Secret Societies in Malaya* (London: Oxford University Press, 1969)

a line between banned associations and permitted forms of sociability that attracted men of middling status.

By the later nineteenth century, forming a club based upon interest or ancestry had become an accepted style of urban sociability for Asian men in the professions, commercial occupations, and colonial administration. A few organizations crossed ethnic lines, usually when a particular group had too few people to support activities on its own. Sport offered the most important middle ground, bridging different communities. Skill, not identity, mattered for the cricket and football teams organized in the many missionary-run secondary schools. During the 1890s, several Perak and Selangor towns had football teams of mixed ethnicity, and matches did not pit one "race" against another. Institutions such as the YMCA, private companies, and government departments fielded multi-ethnic teams too. By 1906, when the Selangor Association Football League was founded, most local teams in that state were racially defined, but Asian and Europeans still competed as equals on the field. Competition for the colony-wide Malay Cup was fierce, and the best teams tended to be the multi-racial state contenders.[51] Although some local sports groups were communally based, others had more porous boundaries. The Taiping Recreation Club was dominated by Chinese members. Nevertheless, its football and cricket captains and its vice president were Eurasians. In the 1890s, wealthy Malays, Chinese, and Europeans ran their horses at yearly meetings hosted by sporting associations in the larger towns. The Kinta Gymkhana Club in Batu Gajah publicized the high stakes available for winners months in advance and proudly announced that competitions were "open to all comers" who would pay the fees.[52] Even if the world of sports did not operate with strict race neutrality, skill and interest could trump skin colour.

Freemasonry was another group whose members crossed communal lines. Begun early in Singapore (1845) and Penang (1867), it spread to Taiping and Kuala Lumpur in the 1880s, and then into Ipoh and Teluk Anson in the early twentieth century. An imperial secret society that spread around the globe with the British army in the eighteenth century, its ideology was that of a race-blind brotherhood, whose members entered into a sort of global family. During the nineteenth century, however, its rhetoric of brotherhood clashed with rampant imperialist enthusiasms and Anglo-Saxon pride, which produced exclusively European lodges in some colonial settings. Nevertheless, British Masons in India and in

[51] Butcher, *British*, pp. 117–120, 169–170
[52] *Perak Pioneer*, 11 September 1895, p. 5; 24 July 1895, p. 3; 30 July 1901, p. 3; 3 October 1901, p. 3; 10 October 1901, p. 2a

Burma initiated Muslims and Parsis, and created a few interracial lodges there. In Singapore and the state of Johore, several elite Malay Muslims supported and belonged to Masonic lodges, although Europeans certainly predominated. A Eurasian man, H. C. E. Zacharias, served as the first secretary of the Teluk Anson chapter, formed from planters and other businessmen from the southern part of Perak.[53] Educated male English-speakers found in Freemasonry another cultural space that lowered religious and ethnic boundaries.

Before 1900, multi-ethnic associations that spread beyond communal groups could be found in Malayan towns. The small scale of places like Papan certainly encouraged social mingling among propertied Chinese and Europeans in its Anglo-Chinese Club. Yet the need for a wider clientele was not the only pressure decreasing ethnic boundaries. Similarity of occupations and individual skills became increasingly important criteria shaping sociability. In Kuala Kangsar, Haji Abdul Majid bin Zainuddin, whose Minangkabau father immigrated to Kuala Lumpur from Sumatra, belonged to both a club for elite Malays and the Ellerton Club for Asian clerks and lower-ranking colonial officials. He also played football in various mixed-race leagues. His English-language education and later career as a teacher of English and of Malay in government-funded schools drew him into a cosmopolitan multilingual world, where friendships, diets, and social life crossed racial lines.[54] Over time, the groups and the occasions drawing together men of middling status multiplied in the towns. Educated Asian men learned to mix, talk, and play with people unlike themselves.

Public events also made it possible to cross not only ethnic lines, but also those of gender and class. State fairs drew thousands of people annually into urban public spaces to admire the best local flora and fauna and to watch team sports. Admission was free, and when the attractions included Malay football, the fairs became a popular addition to public culture. Since "native ladies" had the grounds to themselves between noon and 2 PM, not even conservative Malay families could object to visits by mothers and daughters. To encourage farming, colonial administrators in Perak mounted the first statewide agricultural show in Taiping in 1894, and it was such a success that they sponsored a growing number of fairs around the state during the mid-1890s. Newspapers and

---

[53] *Napier Lodge No. 3418 E. C. Centenary Celebration 1910–2010* (Ipoh: Dewan Freemason, 2010), p. 7; Jessica L. Harland-Jacobs, *Builders of Empire: Freemasonry and British Imperialism, 1717–1927* (Chapel Hill: University of North Carolina Press, 2007), pp. 216–217, 238, 283–297; T. N. Harper, "Globalism," pp. 273–274

[54] Haji Abdul Majid bin Zainuddin, *The Wandering Thoughts of a Dying Man* (Kuala Lumpur: Oxford University Press, 1978), pp. ix, 43, 68–69, 102

placards in three languages publicized the events, promising money prizes to winners in more than 150 competitions. Initially, few Malays or Chinese were interested, but District Officers spread the word and got local farmers to send in samples of products ranging from rice to rattan. Soon, estate owners vied for supremacy in coffee beans, sugar cane, and peppercorns; Malay and British judges inspected horses and buffalos, poultry and pigeons, to crown a champion. Even if Mrs Swettenham, the resident's wife, dominated the competition for orchids and ferns, Aregasam from Lower Perak carried off the pomegranate prize and Taiping resident Fam Ah Fook's bricks beat out the competition in 1894. Prize winners ranged from European, Malay, and Chinese elites to ordinary artisans and farmers, whose headmen had prodded them to send goods to the fair.[55] While the state fair demonstrated the dominance of the British government, it also communicated more subversive messages. Although British administrators determined the categories for competition and supplied most of the judges, the fair ratified a level playing field. Anyone could visit and wander freely around the grounds. All products were equal in terms of prize money and emphasis: wood carvings did not outrank tapioca flour or turnips. Let the best cabbage win, whoever had produced it! The fair helped to meld British, Chinese, Malay, and Tamil into a viewing public that applauded merit in multiple forms. Fairs, despite their agricultural enthusiasms, were fundamentally modernist, urban institutions that nudged communal groups into a hybridized civil society that crossed linguistic and ethnic lines.

Learning to Be British

During the later nineteenth and early twentieth centuries, the multi-ethnic town populations of Malaya gradually learned the forms and rhetoric of British colonial subjecthood, which spread well beyond the small British-born population. Pageants, colonial honours, and royal birthdays drew rich and poor into public expressions of loyalty. David Cannadine's term, "ornamentalism" captures this identification of the British Empire with a "cult of imperial royalty ... carried along ... by unrivalled and interlocking displays of regular ritual and occasional spectacle." Over time, the enthusiasm for and participation in these performances grew substantially. It is worth exploring which people participated and how these events represented relationships to the British crown. Cannadine emphasizes a vision of the British Empire as a

---

[55] *Perak Government Gazette*, 9 June 1894, Vol. 7, 468–471; 10 July 1894, Vol. 7, pp. 544–547; 4 August 1894, Vol. 7, pp. 630–634; *Perak Pioneer*, 19 June 1895, p. 2

"layered, rural, traditional, and organic society," assumed to be similar to a conservative version of Britain itself.[56] In other words, imperial ritual equalized colonial and domestic populations by representing them all as stratified, traditional societies governed by elites, who were themselves subjects of the British monarch. This concept describes accurately the formal relationship of an indirectly ruled colony such as the Federated Malay States, whose sultans and their subordinates owed allegiance to the British queen. Nevertheless, the homogenization of Chinese, Malays, South Asians, and British into the same position as subjects had radical implications, which were noticed by the Asians in British Malaya. What if equivalent rights were claimed as a consequence of fealty?

Queen Victoria's Golden Jubilee, which celebrated her fifty years on the throne, introduced many residents of British Malaya to a new language of imperial loyalty. The governor of the Straits Settlements proclaimed the date of London celebrations, 27 and 28 June in 1887, to be public holidays, when there would be Thanksgiving services, parades, cannon salutes, and fireworks. Proclamation of a holiday, however, does not guarantee participation or signify acceptance. The Jubilee offers a way to test the limit and nature of local people's identification with the British Empire in 1887. In Singapore, a Jubilee Committee, which included high status Europeans, Chinese, South Asians, Arabs, and Malays, planned local events, which featured a state ball to which elite Chinese, Malay, and Arab-Malay men were invited. Celebrations seem to have been limited outside Singapore, and the formal expressions of loyalty indicated at best a distant and coerced embrace of a British identity by non-Europeans. William Evans, newly appointed as Collector of Land Revenue in Melaka and Second Assistant Protector of Chinese in the Straits Settlements, wrote to his brother in Bradford in 1887 about the Jubilee of "the great, good, and glorious Queen and Empress." He complained that local people had been badly informed about the occasion and that "they" had refused to write and sign a congratulatory address because "there was no knowing what the government would do with [it]." Evans adds that "his spirit rose in anger," and he claims to have denounced them as foolish, "rebellious children" with ridiculous suspicions. After his tirade, he claimed that his audience agreed to produce a statement of congratulation, as Evans required, which was formally transmitted to the government to be sent on to London. Given Evans's job, the reluctant local worthies were most likely Straits Chinese, British subjects by birth, men of wealth and relative sophistication who benefited directly from British

[56] David Cannadine, *Ornamentalism: How the British Saw Their Empire* (Oxford: Oxford University Press, 2001), pp. xix, 122

rule in the region.[57] At this first royal Jubilee, whose rituals had to be invented before they could be learned, it is not surprising that the Straits Chinese seemed unfamiliar with the role assigned to them.

The Jubilee of 1887 was also observed in the state of Perak, where three addresses from Malay commoners and tradesmen written in Jawi script were sent to Queen Victoria. Using flowery, ritualized expressions of loyalty similar to those directed to Malay rajas, they offered prayers to the "incomparable" Queen and her family, praised her fairness and wise administration adding that her "brightness shone all over the world." Chinese merchants from Perak sent finely calligraphed scrolls to Queen Victoria, presented in the name of the Chinese Emperor, their "August Master." They announced their gratitude for the "friendly relations" existing between the two empires and for the "well-being of that very large proportion of the human race which it has pleased Heaven to confide to the High Keeping of Your Majesties."[58] Although they affirmed admiration for the Queen and her rule, they did not claim a British identity. The form and content of Perak participation in the Jubilee linked residents more closely to their Malay and their Chinese roots than to their new colonial home. It seems reasonable to conclude that in 1887 most Asian urban residents did not identify strongly with the British Empire.

By 1897, public loyalties had evolved. A larger group of people were drawn into the celebrations of Victoria's Diamond Jubilee than had participated a decade earlier. Multiple events took place, not only in Singapore and Penang, but also in several Perak towns (see Figure 4.3). Local committees planned church services, parades, sports days, illuminations, fireworks, and treats, giving residents several days of public celebrations using the model of the 1887 events. The Diamond Jubilee brought subjects of all nationalities together at local recreation grounds to see the ceremonies, to acquire official Jubilee trinkets, and to sing "God Save the Queen." A parade in Kuala Lumpur included representations of St George and the Dragon, and the See Yeh temple flew the royal standard. Exactly how spectators interpreted these images is unclear, but local English-language newspapers mentioned large, happy crowds and buildings draped with Union Jacks. At the very least, observers were

---

[57] *Straits Times*, 22 May 1887, p. 2; 27 May 1887, p. 2; 8 June 1887, p. 3; 24 June 1887, p. 2; 30 June 1887, p. 3; "Letter W. Evans to Samuel Evans, 20 June, 1887," Box 2, PPMS 11 (SOAS Archive, London)

[58] I would like to thank Mohammed Taib bin Mohammed for his translation of the Jawi text, "Jubilee Addresses to Queen Victoria," *Journal of the Straits Branch of the Royal Asiatic Society*, No. 18 (1887), pp. 366–371; "Jubilee Addresses of the Tradesmen of Perak to Queen Victoria, 1887," PP 1/222/3 (National Archive, London); a translation of the Chinese text is included in the original wrappings of the scrolls.

Figure 4.3 Street decorations in Penang in honour of Queen Victoria's Jubilee, 1897

exposed to representations and symbols of Britishness, and they learned some of the rituals of public patriotism.[59]

Local town committees worked out the details of the late-June celebrations, most of which seemed quite similar. Each of the major ethnic groups in the larger settlements helped to plan local events for their own community and for a general audience. European clubs sponsored formal dances and dinners, flower shows, and horse races, which drew large crowds of mixed ethnicity. The Chinese mounted evening lantern parades and fireworks; Malays organized theatre performances, processions, and sports events. Food for all palates overflowed tables and street stalls. In Ipoh, children who attended such events received Chinese cakes, Malay kabobs, and lemonade. The celebrations added British ceremony and rhetoric to local cuisine and entertainments, giving everyone a chance to taste the unfamiliar. The audience for the Jubilee was far wider than just Europeans. In the small town of Kampar, which had only one resident British man, several thousand people from the district came into the town for fireworks and various evening shows "arranged gratis

---

[59] *Perak Pioneer*, 26 June 1897, p. 3; 3 July 1897, pp. 2–3; see also Lynn Hollen Lees, "Being British in Malaya, 1890–1940," *Journal of British Studies*, Vol. 48 (January 2009), pp. 76–101

to suit the tastes of the native population." The District Officer, Mr Nutt, was identified as the person responsible for the events and decoration of the town, although he got help from Lam Yen, a wealthy Chinese resident who invited his male Chinese friends to dinner and who offered a toast to Queen Victoria. The Jubilee produced widespread expressions of British patriotism, although it is hard to judge its depth and its enthusiasm.[60]

During the events of 1897, multiple symbols of the British state surrounded residents who came to see the parades and festivities. Crowds saw countless Union Jacks flying from ceremonial gateways, while military bands played "God Save the Queen" in the background. In Ipoh, Chinese, Malays, South Asians, and "nearly every one of the European community" showed up for the school sports day arranged by the Rev. W. E. Horley, a leading Methodist cleric. The Jubilee gave both colonial officials and the resident population the chance to agree on appropriate patriotic messages and forms, which proclaimed joint devotion to Empire and Queen. One staple of these imperial celebrations was the congratulatory address. Groups of local citizens self-defined by religion, place of origin, and sometimes occupation, produced formal statements of allegiance which were read by their authors to colonial officials and assembled crowds. Simultaneous translations of key statements into English and into Malay were offered, and written copies went to London. Authors of every ethnicity identified themselves as humble or loyal subjects of the Queen. These same phrases were used by the Governor of the Straits Settlements, by European, Eurasian, and Chinese residents in Singapore, by the Chinese and the Hindus of Penang, and by the Eurasians, Europeans, Ceylon Tamils, Bengalis, and South Indians of Perak. These men of property and public status represented their ethnic communities as part of a greater Britain. They vied to outdo one another in singing royal praises: "The whole of Your Majesty's Empire, which is ever watched by the sun, is celebrating today with one heart this unique and auspicious occasion and we [the Bengalis of Taiping, Perak] join them from this remote part of the national chorus."[61] Taiping Bengalis praised the crown's "impartiality . . . uniformly indistinctive of caste, creed, colour, and religion." South Indians in Perak and Singapore Chettiars mentioned "equity of justice," and the former group applauded the use of competitive exams for Crown Colony

[60] *Perak Pioneer*, 26 June 1897, p. 3; 30 June 1897, p. 3; 3 July 1897, p. 3
[61] In Penang, foreign consuls, Europeans, Muslims, the Chinese Town Hall, the Chinese Literary Association, the Chinese Club, Tamil Hindus, Chettiars, and Indians from the N. W. Province wrote such tributes. See *Straits Observer*, 25 June 1897, p. 5; *Singapore Free Press*, 23 June 1897, p. 3; *Pinang Gazette*, 22 June 1897, p. 3; *Perak Pioneer*, 26 June 1897, p. 3

civil services so that they could compete on an equal footing for positions. Singapore Chinese said that "We, as [Her] Majesty's Chinese subjects, . . ." were "given the very same privilege as those enjoyed by Englishmen." Singapore Jews thanked Victoria for "the removal of the political disabilities of our race and their admission on terms of equality to social privileges." Praise for imperial rule came in tandem with claims of rights, as well as duties. Willingness to be called a British subject meant far more than expression of loyalty to the British crown.

In the space of one decade, educated males in the towns of the Straits Settlements and the Federated Malay States had learned the rhetoric of imperial subjecthood. Schools, newspapers, and clubs had done their work, spreading the language and forms of British allegiance. Moreover, as towns grew and the economy prospered, so did obvious opportunities for those in the middle and upper ranks of the colony, which included far more than those born in the United Kingdom. In any case, belonging to the world's largest empire in a place and time where nationalism had yet to develop meant that most individuals did not have to choose among their multiple loyalties and networks. The British colonial state demanded little of them: taxes were low and they did not owe labour or military service to their rulers. As British subjects, they could travel freely within Britain, South Asia, and much of Africa, as well as be protected on trips to China. As urban residents, they had access to town services, water supplies, hospitals, communication, and transportation networks. Unlike workers on the plantations, their daily lives were neither regimented nor organized tightly around racial hierarchies. Expressing British loyalties brought benefits and had little cost, but self-government was not on offer.

When Queen Victoria died in January of 1901, memorial meetings and church services attended by Asians as well as Europeans were held in many Malayan towns. While British administrators and clergy normally led such gatherings, the press reported large audiences. In Taiping, Chung Thye Phin, revenue farmer and mine owner, presented condolences from the "Chinese community of Perak," and Leong Fee added his sincere sympathies. Sikh soldiers representing the Indians of Perak announced their "deep sorrow for the sad calamity that has befallen the nation and the Royal Family by the death of Her Most Gracious Majesty the late Queen Victoria and desire to convey to the Throne their sense of continued loyalty and devotion," while bells tolled.[62] This open mourning spread beyond the European community, at least among local elites and middling groups. The Sultan of Perak and his ministers lowered the State flag to half-mast and sent statements of sympathy to the Secretary of

---

[62] *Perak Pioneer*, 29 January 1901, pp. 2–3; 31 January 1901, p. 2; 25 April 1901, p. 2

State for the Colonies. A group of middle-class Chinese in Taiping held their own condolence service, as did the "leading Towkays" of the Larut district, who proclaimed that her death was a "very great loss" to the British Empire. They also closed all the Chinese shops and businesses in the area during her funeral as a mark of respect. Prominent Singapore Chinese were said to be wearing black armbands, and a "Chinese Citizen" wrote to the *Perak Pioneer* urging a public subscription among the Chinese to fund a statue of Victoria as a testimonial to her and to mark their recognition of "the advantage of British laws." Yet on the same weekend, crowds of Taiping Tamils celebrated with parades, music, and devotional dances the holiday of Thaipusam, an annual festival of devotion to the Hindu god Murugan. There were clearly limits to the numbers mourning and the attention given to the British at a time of competing attractions.[63] These British subjects maintained cultural ties other than allegiance to Victoria, and they did not hesitate to celebrate them. Multiple allegiances remained compatible with empire.

Ceremonial and rhetorical loyalty to Queen Victoria was only one way to display Britishness in colonial Malaya. Those who participated in urban civil society picked up the methods and discourses of Liberalism, which were then used to challenge the colonial state on issues of social reform. Clubs served as miniature democracies, where members learned the methods of active citizenship, rather than just the rhetoric of subject-hood. One of the first social issues to mobilize educated men in Malaya was the question of drug use, which drew both Chinese and British into an international crusade to block opium sales. The Anti-Opium Movement, active in the larger towns between 1906 and 1908, followed the inter-nationally familiar format of a middle-class social crusade: meetings, societies, and resolutions for action, all publicized in the local press.[64] Local societies had presidents, officers, general committees, and annual dues. They collected funds and published pamphlets. Their demand for a war on drugs came into direct conflict, however, with the governments of the Straits Settlements and the Federated Malay States, both of which depended heavily on revenue from opium taxes gathered by tax farmers to finance state administrations.

By the early twentieth century, urban civil society in Malaya as well as in Europe was divided over the use of opium. Hakka tin mine owners smoked opium at the Han Chin Pet Soo in Ipoh only a block away from

---

[63] *Perak Pioneer*, 31 January 1901, p. 2; 5 February 1901, p. 2

[64] Brian Howard Harrison, *Drink and the Victorians: The Temperance Question in England, 1815–1872* (Keele: Keele University Press, 1994); Judith R. Walkowitz, *Prostitution and Victorian Society: Women, Class, and the State* (Cambridge: Cambridge University Press, 1982)

the Perak Miners Hall, where other Chinese met to discuss how to combat addiction. Just as in Britain, Malayan towns offered spaces where educated men could organize and take positions on questions of public policy. Newspaper accounts of opposition to the opium trade in China and in Britain sparked local debates. The press in Singapore reported London meetings of the Society for the Suppression of the Opium Trade. Readers of the *Straits Times* learned that Australia and New Zealand had restricted the sale of opium, and that the United States government had banned its use in the Philippines.[65] In 1898, Dr Lim Boon Keng, a medical doctor and editor of the *Straits Chinese Magazine*, published a long analysis of opium abuse in Singapore and the dangers of addiction. He called on adult Chinese to organize to combat the habit. Public health was more important than public revenue, he said. Lim's recommendations were those of a Liberal reformer who thought that voluntary efforts were the key to solving the opium problem. To discourage use of the narcotic, he advocated outdoor sports, education, and better housing. In his opinion, rehabilitation clinics would be more effective than banning the drug.

Lim got relatively little public support until 1906, when the British Parliament branded the opium trade as "morally indefensible," and the newly elected Liberal government in Britain stated its willingness to work with China and with India to suppress the opium traffic.[66] This empowered Chinese and European medical doctors in the Straits Settlements and the Federated Malay States to publically oppose opium farming and opium use. As the Anti-Opium Movement expanded in British Malaya, they organized a convention of delegates in Ipoh in 1907. Foreign-educated Chinese doctors, such as Dr Wu Lien-Teh in Penang and Dr Chen So Lan in Kuala Lumpur, led the mobilization, organizing mass rallies to spread the news of Parliamentary resolutions. They called on the colonial government to end opium farming and to register users. The visit to Malaya of J. G. Alexander, the Honorary Secretary of the Society for the Suppression of the Opium Trade provided an occasion for meetings in several Malayan towns, which were said to include "practically every Chinese of any note." The assemblies claimed they were inclusive: the Penang Chinese who greeted Mr Alexander described themselves as

[65] "The Royal Commission on Opium," *Straits Times Weekly Issue*, 17 October 1893, p. 1; "The Opium Commission," *Daily Advertiser*, 21 March 1894, p. 2; "The Opium Trade," *Mid-day Herald*, 15 June 1896, p. 2; "The Opium Trade," *Straits Times*, 26 March 1901, p. 2; J. G. Alexander, "The Opium Traffic," *Straits Chinese Magazine*, Vol. 10 (1906), pp. 186–190
[66] Lim Boon Keng, "The Attitude of the State towards the Opium Habit," *Straits Chinese Magazine*, No. 2 (1898), pp. 47–54; J. G. Alexander, "The Opium Traffic," *Straits Chinese Magazine*, Vol. 10 (1906), pp. 186–190

"merchants, doctors, lawyers, ministers, teachers, journalists, small traders, coolies, and other residents."[67] Nevertheless, most were professional men of middling status, the sort who joined urban clubs. European missionaries and doctors joined the campaign too. Soon there were chapters of the Anti-Opium Movement in Ipoh, Kampar, and other Kinta mining centres, as well as Selangor towns. Speakers denounced the evil opium trade and demanded that the colonial government abolish the opium farms. Local clubs, which had earlier tolerated or encouraged members' smoking, also joined the campaign. The Penang Mutual Improvement Association decided to destroy all the opium pipes and other drug equipment in their meeting hall, while the Penang Chinese Cycling Club voted unanimously to prohibit any opium smoking on their premises. Encouraged by the Consul General for China, donors in Singapore funded an opium refuge where addicts could go for rehabilitation as well as "cold-turkey" treatment. Widespread rumours that a local plant could cure addiction produced mass efforts to gather, brew, and bottle the infusion, which clinics distributed for free. The efforts of the anti-opium activists had, for a time, the tenor of a religious revival and an abolitionist crusade that reached out into their communities.[68] The cause mobilized members of a growing civil society for the purpose of social reform, placing them in dialogue with similar groups in Britain, India, and China.

For a short time, a public campaign outflanked the colonial government, which then changed its strategy to retain its opium revenues.[69] Rather than opting to curb consumption as requested, the state decided that a government monopoly would be a more effective source of revenue than dependence on the opium farmers. It took over the monopoly of opium sale itself in 1910. The message of the Anti-Opium Movement in Malaya was officially ignored. Nevertheless the campaign against opium marks an important political moment in the Straits Settlements and the Federated Malay States. It drew both Chinese and British men of

---

[67] Carl A. Trocki, *Opium and Empire: Chinese Society in Colonial Singapore, 1800–1910* (Ithaca and London: Cornell University Press, 1990), pp. 209–213; Wen Li, "The Anti-Opium Movement in Malaya," *Straits Chinese Magazine*, No. 11 (1907), pp. 3–8; J. G. Alexander, "The Opium Traffic," *Straits Chinese Magazine*, No. 10 (1906), 186–190

[68] Within a few months, faith in an easy cure seems to have waned. "Penang Anti-Opium Association," *Eastern Daily Mail and Straits Morning Advertiser*, 14 November 1906, p. 1; "Anti-Opium Work in Ipoh," *Straits Times*, 6 December 1906, p. 8; U Wen Cheng, "Opium in the Straits Settlements, 1867–1910," *Journal of Southeast Asian History* 2 (1961), pp. 52–75; Harper, "Globalism," p. 281

[69] Carl Trocki calculates that the opium revenue contributed between 46 and 70 per cent of Singapore's yearly revenue between 1883 and 1914; Trocki, *Opium*, pp. 188, 214–215. In the Straits Settlements, as a whole its contribution ranged from 45 to 52 per cent between 1875 and 1905. After a short period of decline, revenues rose again when the state took over the monopoly of sales in 1910; Cheng, "Opium," p. 52

middling status into political activism, and they mobilized against state policies. Leaders tried to capture "public opinion" as they petitioned for changes, copying previous international campaigns against slavery, alcohol use, and prostitution. Rather than timidly asking the colonial government to solve the problem, members called for self-help and social action to curb a practice that threatened the wellbeing of the population. This activism in the interest of public health was of a type widespread in British towns, better seen as civic engagement than anti-colonial politics. The failure of the Anti-Opium Movement demonstrates, however, the limited resonance and public power of liberal reform campaigns in British Malaya in the early twentieth century. Although members of urban civil society had gained in numbers and resources, they generally accepted their inferior political status under colonial rule. Their public engagement brought them into a transnational world of liberal reformers; yet their power to influence the colonial state remained limited.

These same town residents also saw the repressive side of the colonial rule. The warm glow of veneration for the great and distant queen did not last when it confronted the inevitable violence of colonial policing and resentment of non-representative government. Although there were no open rebellions in Malaya in the later nineteenth century and fights among rival Chinese brotherhoods declined, continuing fear of Chinese secret societies led colonial administrations to regularly deport and prosecute those suspected of hostility to British rule. In a letter to the *Malay Mail* in April of 1901, a Kuala Lumpur resident complained of "gloom" and "unrest" in the Chinese community, spread by fear of the Banishment Act which had given British authorities summary power to arrest and exile immigrants suspected of crimes. J. C. Pasqual complained of the Act's "secret and inquisitorial methods," which had spread "terror" among the wealthy Chinese and encouraged "many well-known towkays" to leave the country. One allegedly told him, "If any man can be arrested by the Chinese Protector and deported without a public trial, nobody feels any longer that it is safe to remain." While Pasqual was happy to have highway robbers deported without a fuss, he drew the line at the reputable Chinese who were withdrawing their investments and closing down businesses. He asserted that distrust of the state was rampant, triggered by fears of the census and by the corrupt informers and detectives who would flaunt a secret "black list" and demand a payoff.[70] Treatment of the "respectable" Chinese in the colony remained a central issue for the colonial government. How were these influential men of high status to be incorporated into the colonial polity? What rights should they have?

[70] *Perak Pioneer*, 2 April 1901, p. 3

The practice of layered sovereignty through which administrators in the Straits Settlements and, later, the Federated Malay States delegated control of ethnic communities to their leaders began to break down in the twentieth century. As the colonial state expanded its reach along with its police force, it took over more of the disciplinary functions that it had earlier assigned to others. The contradictions inherent in colonial indirect rule intensified over time in Malaya as urbanization and education created a civil society among middling groups, who absorbed liberal ideas which clashed with the practices of autocratic government.

Part II

The Twentieth Century

The name "British Malaya" refers to a highly decentralized array of disparate places. Culturally Malay areas adjoined Chinese-dominated towns and European-run estates filled with South Asian labourers. The Straits Settlements boasted modern, multi-cultural port cities with paved streets and large administrative buildings, while the eastern, predominantly Malay areas of the peninsula showed few signs of economic development. In Kedah, Kelantan, and Terengganu, largely rural populations of farmers and fishermen lived in small villages, and their rulers worked to preserve local customs and an Islamic heritage. The challenges of administering this oddly constructed colony led in the twentieth century to greater but incomplete centralization of all of its parts. Governors of the Straits Settlements, who also served as High Commissioners of the Federated Malay States, effectively asserted their control of state residents and sultans. In 1910, the post of Resident General, the top-ranking official in the Federated Malay States, was re-named Chief Secretary to make clear his subordination to the leader of the Straits Settlements. Whoever served as the High Commissioner and Governor of the Straits Settlements also ran the Federal Council, which was launched in 1909. It had the power to legislate on projects that touched all the states, and it supervised state budgets. The Federated Malay States also set up overarching departments of Education, Agriculture, Mining, and Public Works. Predominant political and economic power was clearly lodged in British hands. The High Commissioner could decide which subjects were "within his competency" and then take charge of them. The same situation obtained at the state level: British residents administered their kingdoms with occasional advice from the sultans, but both had to listen to the High Commissioner.

British control of the Malay Peninsula widened and deepened during the early twentieth century. The northern state of Kedah, which was formally subservient to Thailand, was slowly drawn into the British imperial sphere as roads and canals linking it to British territories multiplied, and plantation agriculture grew. Continuing financial problems and rising debts that bedevilled Kedah and the other independent

167

Malay kingdoms forced their sultans to accept British economic advisors. In 1909, British officials negotiated a treaty with the Thai state that made the British king the new overlord of Kedah, Perlis, Kelantan, and Terengganu. By 1914, the state of Johore also had a General Advisor who was legally responsible to the British Governor and High Commissioner, rather than to its Malay ruler.[1] Together, this group of kingdoms formed the Unfederated Malay States, each a British protectorate with slightly different constitutional arrangements. One of the most influential and experienced men in the Malayan Civil Service, Sir Frank Swettenham, who served as Resident General of the Federated Malay States (1896–1901) and Governor of the Straits Settlements (1901–1904) consistently and effectively pushed for the extension of British sovereignty in the area. In his book titled *British Malaya*, he exalted the "expansion and progress" brought by British rule which would "continue to make rough places smooth and to attract strangers of all colours and nationalities to a country big with possibilities of great development."[2]

Sir John Anderson, one of the strongest of the early Governors, hoped to create a pan-Malayan federation that would cover the entire peninsula and rationalize its government under British control, but he had little success in getting others to adopt this idea. The idea of combining all of the Malay states and the Straits Settlements into a unified Malaya remained alive through the interwar period under the governorships of Sir Cecil Clementi (1930–1934) and Sir Shenton Thomas (1934–1942). The opposition of elite Malays, in particular the leaders of the Unfederated Malay States, blocked their efforts. Sultans made clear their hostility to additional British interference and worked to maintain as much of their independence as they could manage.[3] The inability of officials to create a unified colony under direct British control made it much more difficult at the time of independence for them to defend the political rights of non-Malays who had moved into the peninsula.

Despite a strong drift of power to the centre of the colony, colonial officials remained committed to indirect rule. It was cheaper than direct administration, and the sultans provided political cover for intrusive and unpopular colonial actions. Moreover, some of the most influential residents in the Malay states, such as Sir Frank Swettenham and Hugh Clifford who had spent most of their careers in the Malayan Civil Service, were great admirers of Malay culture and traditions. Their vision of

[1] Barbara Watson Andaya and Leonard Y. Andaya, *A History of Malaysia*, 2nd ed. (Houndsmill: Palgrave Macmillan, 2001), pp. 194–203
[2] Sir Frank Swettenham, *British Malaya* (London: John Lane, 1907), p. 345
[3] M. C. Ricklefs, ed., *A New History of Southeast Asia* (Houndsmill: Palgrave Macmillan, 2010), pp. 267–269

Malaya centred on remote courts reachable by canoe and by elephant, where they met brave warriors and were entertained by dancing girls and shadow plays. Their writing popularized across the British Empire archaic notions of the colony.[4] Swettenham and Clifford saw in indirect rule the best way to safeguard the primary position of the Malays in a land that the British had transformed. Despite regular administrative infringement of rulers' sovereignty, the British state officially maintained that the sultans were independent and had legal immunity. Ratifying this interest in maintaining Malay primacy, Sir Samuel Wilson, Undersecretary of State for the Colonies, argued in 1932 that "the maintenance of the position, authority, and prestige of the Malaya Rulers must always be a cardinal point in British policy."[5] Such a position not only identified the country with a single ethnic group – purposefully neglecting several million Chinese, South Asians, Arabs, Eurasians, and other non-Malays – but it also ratified a quasi-feudal social order based upon hereditary rulers, rather than representative government. Officials self-consciously placed the political development of their Malayan colonies on a completely different track from that of Britain itself. This defence of indirect rule continued through the interwar period and resurfaced powerfully in the 1950s, when it became a political tool in the hands of conservative Malays who sought to exclude rivals with more democratic policies from gaining power. British colonial policies built a multi-ethnic state and at the same time undermined its ability to function fairly and effectively.

The international context for British rule in Southeast Asia changed dramatically in the new century. The American state occupied the Philippines in 1899, bringing another imperial power into the region. With the collapse of the Qing Empire in China, the balance of power in East Asia shifted rapidly toward the expansionist state of Japan. Nevertheless, after 1919 imperialism moved into a defensive mode. The Russian, Austro-Hungarian, and Ottoman empires ended as a result of World War I, and the victors took over the losers' colonies, now re-baptized as mandates. Oversight by the League of Nations permitted new anti-imperial constituencies to be given a voice via petitions and public debates.[6] Moreover, attacks on colonial rule mounted in India, Burma,

---

[4] J. de V. Allen, "Two Imperialists: A Study of Sir Frank Swettenham and Sir Hugh Clifford," *JMBRAS*, Vol. 37, No. 1 (1964), pp. 41–73; Frank Athelstane Swettenham, *The Real Malay: Pen Pictures* (London: J. Lane, 1900); Hugh Charles Clifford, *Saleh, a Prince of Malaya* (Oxford: Oxford University Press, 1989)

[5] Quoted in Andaya and Andaya, *History of Malaysia*, p. 249; Simon C. Smith, *British Relations with the Malay Rulers from Decentralization to Malayan Independence 1930–1957* (Kuala Lumpur: Oxford University Press, 1995)

[6] Susan Pedersen, *The Guardians: the League of Nations and the Crisis of Empire* (New York: Oxford University Press, 2015)

Vietnam, and the Netherlands Indies. Those living in British Malaya, whatever their ethnicity, found it harder and harder to ignore international issues and networks. Newspapers and radios brought news of wars and civil conflicts. Politicians from China and India toured the peninsula looking for money and support. Not only foreign nationalists, but also international communist groups sent organizers to Malaya to proselytize. As minorities in former Ottoman lands clamoured for independence from European rule, the question of colonial legitimacy was hard to ignore. Although World War I had stimulated a strong patriotic response in the Straits Settlements, it had also demonstrated the fragility of some empires and highlighted an array of alternative arrangements. Maintaining the status quo in British Malaya became more and more difficult as transnational pressures mounted. The political and economic instability of the early twentieth century led some residents of British Malaya to question what it meant to be a British subject or a British-protected person.

5   Rubber Reconstructs Malaya

Rubber production transformed the Malayan economy, and with it the lives of all of its residents and its rulers. Not only was every major ethnic group in the colony involved in its cultivation, production, and sale, but every state had large plantations and small rubber farms (see Map 5.1). Within a few decades, a colony that had been built around trade with China and the export of tin, forest, and sea products moved decisively into export agriculture, becoming the world's leading source of rubber. Thousands of immigrants rushed in annually, changing local demographic patterns and shifting balances of power. As land was stripped and replanted, workers adapted to the routines of an industrialized agriculture, and the new product replaced sugar, coffee, pepper, and rice. Tiny Malaya quickly became Britain's most profitable colony because of the high volume of its exports and huge purchases of British goods.[1] Rubber quickly outran the boundaries of the plantations. Malay farmers added rubber trees to their family's fields, while thousands of small landholders shifted from producing food to collecting latex. Rubber meant rising incomes and changing opportunities for their families too. In 1929, before the Great Depression began, Gross Domestic Product (GDP) per head in British Malaya was higher than that of any other Asian country, including Japan.[2] Rubber's impacts were psychological and social, as well as economic. Its profits financed social mobility and investments in modernity, but its gains easily vanished in depression years, when debts mounted. For some individuals, rubber brought adventure and self-discovery, along with independence.

[1] John H. Drabble, *An Economic History of Malaysia, c. 1800–1990* (London: Macmillan, 2000) p. 54; Michael Havinden and David Meredith, *Colonialism and Development: Britain and Its Tropical Colonies, 1850–1960* (London: Routledge, 1993), p. 94

[2] W. G. Huff, "Monetization and Financial Development before the Second World War," *Economic History Review*, Vol. 56, No. 3 (2003), p. 310

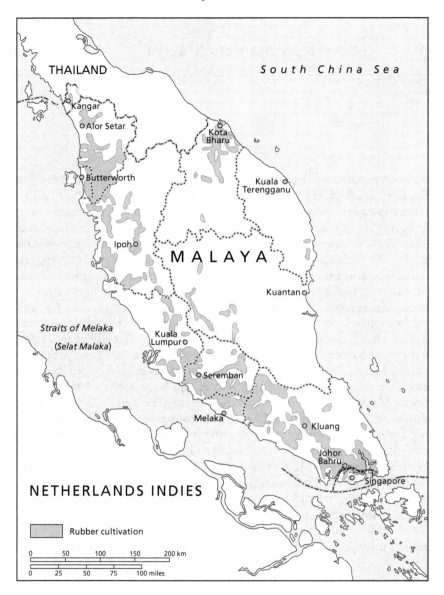

Map 5.1 Rubber Production in British Malaya, c. 1940

Others experienced plantation life as "slavery" imposed by harsh managers and factory-like work routines.[3]

A creation of the British Empire, the industry's economic health depended on international trade and price levels. The exploding global demand for rubber tied Malaya into the world economy during a period of boom-and-bust trade and price fluctuations. When the bicycle and automobile industries expanded, demand for rubber outstripped supply, and prices rose sharply. In the early twentieth century, thousands rushed to plant rubber, and the pioneers reaped windfall profits. After 1910, however, supplies expanded faster than demand, and prices fell steadily for a decade. During much of the period between World War I and World War II, producers held more rubber than the market would absorb. When international trade contracted and firms in Western Europe and North America made fewer tyres, boots, belts, and bands, rubber growers suffered. Prices dropped to or below the level of production costs. Companies cut wages and jobs. Only on the eve of World War II did rising prices and profits signal recovery.[4]

The colonial state not only planted the industry in Malaya, but it shaped its expansion and policed its operations. Rubber as a colonial creation exemplified the contradictory values and inconsistent actions of officials with multiple constituencies and limited power. In good times from the standpoint of the United Kingdom, British Malaya was the model colony, a showpiece for successful, progressive colonial rule. It demonstrated how an alliance of planters and civil servants could modernize a territory and make many residents rich. But times were not always good, and interests were not identical in an inegalitarian, non-democratic, ethnically divided society. Rubber reinforced these inequalities: while the average size of European-owned plantations was 1,431 acres, it was only 356 acres for Chinese properties, and 3 or 4 acres for Malay farms.[5] Rubber represented and tested British colonial rule. What did British "protection" signify in a time of prosperity? What did it mean when times turned bad? The ability and commitment of the British state to support the welfare of its most vulnerable subjects rose and fell with the rubber industry.

---

[3] The word is used to describe plantation labour by scholars, such as Hugh Tinker in *A New System of Slavery: the Export of Indian Labour Overseas, 1830–1920* (London: Hansib Publishing Company, 1993), but also by doctors and plantation managers; see Henri Fauconnier, *The Soul of Malaya* (Paris: Didier Millet, 2007)

[4] W. G. Huff, "Boom-or-Bust Commodities and Industrialization in Pre-World War II Malaya," *Journal of Economic History*, Vol. 62, No. 4 (2002), pp. 1074–1115; D. J. M. Tate, *The RGA History of the Plantation Industry in the Malay Peninsula* (Kuala Lumpur: Oxford University Press, 1996), p. 321

[5] John H. Drabble, *Malayan Rubber: The Interwar Years* (Houndsmill and London: MacMillan, 1991), p. 2

Industrial Agriculture Expands

Between 1900 and 1940, rubber cultivation exploded in the states of western Malaya. Starting from zero, the British government counted 2.3 million acres planted in rubber by 1922 and 3.5 million acres by 1940. By 1930, over half of the cultivated land and about 30 per cent of the agricultural workers in British Malaya had turned to rubber production.[6] Moreover, these statistics missed many smallholders and their plots. There was indeed a rush into rubber, a frenzy of clearing, planting, and cultivating that extended from the old sugar plantation districts in Province Wellesley and Perak to the entire region from Thailand south through Johore to Singapore, touching all the Malay states (see Map 5.1). Not only was the local equatorial climate ideal for rubber cultivation, but there was ample uncultivated land for expansion of the industry. Moreover, the colonial government had already built good networks of roads, rails, and telegraph lines, which permitted easy communication and marketing. Although estates in the Netherlands Indies, French Indo-China, and Ceylon also grew rubber, Malaya was the largest supplier, producing 56 per cent of the world's rubber crop in 1930.[7]

The rubber industry in Malaya grew directly out of the structures of British rule and imperial interest in economic development. During the 1860s, Sir Clements Markham of the India Office hoped to transfer rubber cultivation from Brazil into British colonies in Asia. An agent in Brazil sent *Hevea* seeds to Kew Gardens in 1873, where they were successfully germinated and then sent to British botanic gardens in Southeast Asia. Early efforts by Singapore botanists to encourage farmers to grow *Hevea* sparked little interest or enthusiasm. Nevertheless, H. N. Ridley, appointed in 1888 as director of the Singapore Botanic Gardens, cultivated seedlings and did research on young *Hevea* trees. "Rubber Ridley," who was said to stuff rubber seeds into the pockets of uninterested planters, proselytized his product effectively during the 1890s, building up a seed bank of older trees on the lands of his contacts. Meanwhile, *The Agricultural Bulletin of the Malay Peninsula*, edited by Ridley, spread information on best tapping and planting practices. Anyone interested could get free advice and seedlings, and the time was

---

[6] Drabble, *Malayan Rubber*, p. 308; L. B. Beale, *A Review of the Trade of British Malaya in 1928* (London: His Majesty's Stationery Office, 1929), p. 18. The figures include the colonies of the Straits Settlements, the Federated and Unfederated Malay States. See also Labour Research Department, *British Imperialism in Malaya, Colonial Series No. 2* (London: Labour Research Department, 1926), p. 31

[7] P. T. Bauer, *The Rubber Industry: A Study in Competition and Monopoly* (Cambridge MA: Harvard University Press, 1948), p. 8

ripe for agricultural innovation, given the dismal state of sugar and coffee markets.[8] World demand for rubber exceeded its supply from the late 1890s, and its market price doubled and then doubled again by 1910, enticing thousands of new people into its production.[9]

Malayan rubber quickly developed into a plantation crop, monocultural production for export undertaken on a large scale. Rubber plantations sprang up on land formerly used for sugar and coffee cultivation. Workers on the Penang Sugar Estates continued to hoe the same fields, substituting rubber seedlings for cane tops. Male managers continued to be recruited from Scotland and Demerara from the same sorts of families and firms as had staffed the sugar estates. Foremen returned to their home villages in Tamil Nadu to recruit new field hands, as they had for years. Gangs of Chinese labourers cleared fields, and indentured workers continued to arrive from Java. In an essentially seamless transition, habits and hierarchies established as canes were planted and cut persisted as workers turned to tapping. Estate housing and work gangs remained ethnically segregated and socially stratified. Although corporate ownership and the ever-present issue of dividends added layers of oversight and interest to the operation of Malayan plantations, they did not change the local organization of properties, their hierarchies, and their heavy dependence on the colonial state. A "plantation complex" with roots in Caribbean estates operated with slave labour survived into the rubber era.[10] It brought with it a culture of command and assumptions about European supremacy that permeated everyday life in rural areas.

The Malayan rubber industry was a creature of the imperial state. The eyes of aspiring planters were caught by the favourable regulations in the Federated Malay States introduced to lure them into the new industry. After 1897, the colonial government taxed land granted for rubber cultivation for ten years at only 10 cents per acre, and 50 cents per acre thereafter. Export duties on output were to be limited to 2.5 per cent for fifteen years. At a time when an acre of rubber trees could produce about 300 pounds of rubber a year, which around 1900 would sell for about $250, these taxes were negligible. In addition, managers could keep their concessions through modest amounts of annual clearing and

---

[8] Coffee prices collapsed during the 1890s, and yields fell because of blight and insect infections. Sugar growers faced increasing competition from lower-cost producers in Java and Cuba, while increasing production periodically dampened prices. D. J. M. Tate, *The RGA History of the Plantation Industry in the Malay Peninsula* (Kuala Lumpur: Oxford University Press, 1996), pp. 140, 194–195; John H. Drabble, *Rubber in Malaya, 1876–1922* (Kuala Lumpur: Oxford University Press, 1973), pp. 3–9

[9] Tate, *RGA History*, pp. 206–212; Drabble, *Rubber*, pp. 2–3, 6–8

[10] Philip D. Curtin, *The Rise and Fall of the Plantation Complex: Essays in Atlantic History* (Cambridge: Cambridge University Press, 1990)

transplanting. Approved in 1904, a "Loans to Planters" scheme provided money at a low interest rate to aspiring agriculturalists, and all the available funds were soon allocated to the mostly European applicants. Neither incomes nor profits were taxed, except as a temporary wartime measure between 1915 and 1918.[11] Moreover, state governments openly favoured European-style plantations over land granted to Asians, some of whom still practised shifting cultivation. Titles stipulated that "permanent" crops like rubber or coconuts had to be planted, rather than gambier or tapioca, which had been the crops of choice for Chinese farmers in Western Malaya. The best concessions near roads and rivers were usually reserved for large companies, which the government expected to spark local economic development.[12] The helping hand of the state continued its largesse through the 1920s. The Labour Research Department in London announced proudly that the government gave "British capitalists" land and an imported labour supply, and then worked to raise their profits by empowering the Colonial Office to oversee output restrictions.[13]

By 1920, rubber had become British Malaya's principal export crop, which it remained during the remaining decades of British colonial rule. Its cultivation expanded steadily until 1940, although the profitability of each pound of rubber declined sharply after 1910 as growing supplies flooded the market. Demand remained high through World War I, but then dipped as the world slid into recession during the early 1920s, rose again, and then fell sharply with the onset of deep depression in 1929. After rubber prices crashed, plantation owners in Malaya and Ceylon lobbied for restrictions on production to raise prices, and the British government agreed, despite the refusal of the Dutch and French governments to join them. Power struggles at the international level shaped the rubber market during the two decades before World War II. Since producers within the British Empire had sufficient clout to reshape the international rubber market on their own, British officials set up the Stevenson Scheme (in force from 1922 to 1928) under which appointed committees gave each grower in Malaya and Ceylon an annual quota of rubber for export. The large European-owned plantations fared better in the assignments than did small estates and small farmers, and the losers

---

[11] Drabble, *Rubber*, pp. 24, 105, 128–129

[12] Only one-twentieth of a concession of 1,000–2,000 acres had to be planted in rubber each year; James C. Jackson, *Planters and Speculators: Chinese and European Agricultural Enterprise in Malaya, 1786–1921* (Kuala Lumpur: University of Malaya Press, 1968), pp. 219–220, 223–224, 237–238

[13] Labour Research Department, *British Imperialism in Malaya, Colonial Series No. 2* (London: Labour Research Department, 1926), p. 31

were quick to notice inequities. The Stevenson Scheme soon produced rampant resentment, smuggling, corruption, and forgery among those who were not its direct beneficiaries. Chinese brokers and Malay ship captains moved thousands of pounds of illicit rubber into the world market through Singapore and Sumatra, where the agreement was not in force.[14] Rubber suppliers had to make political decisions: would one comply with the law or try to skirt its provisions? Rubber production involved power struggles on the international level, but also on estates and in Malay villages.

The Penang Sugar Estates, well supplied with land, capital, and ambition, moved into the rubber industry early and heavily. John Turner, the general manager, experimented with rubber seedlings on several hundred acres of abandoned Caledonia land in 1902. Then a sustained planting took place on the Rubana Estate in south Perak, which had been cleared for sugar cultivation in 1899. Managers' inability to stop rats from attacking early cane crops led them to plant rubber seedlings in 1903 on 94 acres, and then to continue adding young trees each year to other fields. Sugar cane quickly became a catch crop, to be harvested only until the trees began to yield latex. In 1914, Rubana produced over half a million pounds of rubber annually on over 3,000 acres of rubber trees; its high dividends and relatively low production costs set a pattern to be followed on the company's other estates. While sugar continued to be produced by Penang Sugar for another decade, its fields and those of its offshoot company, Straits Sugar, were quickly replanted with rubber. Savvy general managers, in particular William Duncan, who spent his adult life running sugar plantations, engineered the shift, retraining workers and mastering the requirements of the new industry.[15] They and their assistants also hired dozens of Chinese farmers to replant company land with rubber seedlings and to watch over them until maturity, while earning

---

[14] Tate, *The R. G. A. History*, pp. 336–348, 354–357, 367; Colin Barlow, *The Natural Rubber Industry: Its Development, Technology, and Economy in Malaysia* (Kuala Lumpur: Oxford University Press, 1978), pp. 58–69. For a detailed discussion of the Stephenson Plan (1922–1928) and the International Rubber Regulation Agreement (1934–1941), see Drabble, *Malayan Rubber*.

[15] William Duncan (1871–1931) left Scotland for British Guiana to work on a sugar plantation. He joined the staff of the Penang Sugar Estates in 1893 as an assistant manager and by 1910 he had become the general manager of the entire company with the job of shifting the Ramsden estates to rubber production. Duncan became a leader of the Malayan planting community, serving as chairman of the Planters' Association of Malaya and as an appointed member of the Federal Council of the Federated Malay States until his retirement to England in 1920. Thereafter he defended the rubber industry as chair of the Council of the Rubber Growers' Association and as a member of the Rubber Advisory Committee of the Secretary of State for the Colonies. "The Late Mr. William Duncan, 1871–1931," *British Malaya*, Vol. 5, No. 11 (1931), p. 300

money from catch crops such as sugar or tapioca, which were interplanted among the young trees. By May of 1911, John William Ramsden and his directors had decided to plant rubber "all over the Caledonia sugar fields," and they were on the track of seedlings from particularly productive rubber trees. Ramsden had the confidence and the capital to buy additional land in Perak, Johore, and Selangor, as adjoining properties came on the market and as good terms could be negotiated with colonial authorities. Directors floated new company after company on the London stock exchange, raising the money for continued expansion from investors eager to cash in on the rubber boom. By 1915, the Ramsden family held controlling interests in the Penang Rubber Estates, the Straits Rubber Company, and six other smaller incorporated rubber estates, which together controlled 55,000 acres and produced annually over 4 million pounds of rubber.[16] At that time, the Ramsden group of companies was one of the most important rubber producers in Malaya.

In 1914, the Ramsden companies were unusually large and unusually old, but taken together they illustrate important changes in Malayan plantations. Properties that Edward Horsman acquired as individually owned estates had been incorporated atypically early. But their transition from one proprietor to control by a joint stock company headquartered in London was typical of hundreds of other Malayan properties. By the twentieth century, Malayan export agriculture was highly capitalized and corporate in its organization, its health depending upon global markets and information flows from distant corners of the world and anchored in the empire. As British imperial control of the peninsula expanded, so did the scale and international ties of its companies. The Malayan variant of colonial capitalism extended throughout and beyond the British Empire, bringing together an international crew of investors and managers with their consumers in the Americas and Europe. In Malaya, the evidence of that far-flung network was easy to see: newspapers reported London commodity prices and steamship schedules. They wrote of production in Ceylon and Liberia and pictured

---

[16] The Penang Sugar Estates Company was liquidated in 1913 and reconstituted as the Penang Rubber Estates Company in that same year. The agency house of Boustead & Co. helped the Straits Sugar Co. make the transition to rubber planting, but the Ramsden family and their directors and managers masterminded the shift on most of the family's holdings. See "Straits Rubber and Allied Companies: Some Features of a Unique Plantation Group in the Northern Half of Malaya," *The Financier*, 29 June 1914, p. 15; The Rubana Rubber Estates, Ltd., "Report by the Directors for the Year ending April 30, 1914," RA Box 5 (West Yorkshire Archive Leeds); "Straits Sugar Company: Letters and Correspondence from and to Penang, 1898–1900," in PSE, "Letters and Papers," Vol. 24, 644 p. 19 (APS); "Letter J.W. Ramsden to E.L. Hamilton," 23 May 1911, D/RA/A/3E/28/2, and "Interview with Mr. Turner at Ardverikie on 31 October 1902," D/RA/A/3E/28/27 (Buckinghamshire Archive); Tate, *RGA History*, p. 242

the imported motorcars and machinery needed on the large estates. Editorials complained about inadequate and expensive supplies of labour from India and Java, and they gave readers the gory details of epidemics and wars, which could threaten the smooth operation of recruitment, shipping, and marketing. The isolation of individual estates was in many ways an illusion. Whatever the view from the bungalow veranda, just beyond the shadowy, silent acres of rubber trees lay a road to a town which had post and telegraph offices. Nearby rivers ran to ports connected to Singapore, London, and Tokyo. By the 1930s, estates had telephones, automobiles, and motorboats. Many managers could spend evenings in a town at their club. They read newspapers and received letters regularly. Technology linked plantations to an outside world which shaped their functioning.

Rubber brought riches to some and the dream of wealth to many more. The spectacular rise of rubber prices between 1902 and 1910 and the dizzying level of company dividends before 1920 unleashed a frenzy of speculation and spending, buoyed by rising wages and salaries. Investors, elated by dividend levels that could exceed 100 per cent per year, poured money into more stock purchases, while owners rushed to outbid one another for new land.[17] Managers demanded and got higher salaries, which they rushed to spend on themselves and their families. Plantation profits flowed into golf courses, tennis courts, bigger clubs, and huge bungalows. Gardens with herbaceous borders blossomed in front of shaded verandas. In 1917, the general manager of the newly re-named Penang Rubber Estates moved into the extravagant "House with the 99 Doors" built on the Caledonia plantation. Its neoclassical columns, elegant carved wooden staircase, and pale, stuccoed walls resembled an English country house more than the simple wooden bungalows built during the nineteenth century. Light and airy rooms with plastered walls and high ceilings opened onto a deep veranda, and balconies extended on all sides of the house.

In the mid-1920s, Werner Michael Iversen, manager of the Lima Belas estate, had his architect brother design for him a large, modern house which had running water, flush toilets, electric lighting, and telephone connections to all the plantation's buildings.[18] When rubber profits rose, even lowly assistants gained better quarters. A "suitable" house for an assistant manager in the 1920s boasted two large rooms and a broad

---

[17] Drabble, *Rubber*, pp. 213, 228

[18] Werner Michael Iversen, "Memories," translated by Ruth Iversen Pollitt (unpublished manuscript), pp. 29–30. I would like to thank Ruth Iversen Pollitt, his niece, for permission to read and to quote from this essay.

veranda, one end of which was carefully screened to keep out mosquitoes. All the household and gardening work was allocated to a cook, male servant, laundryman, and water carrier. The Incorporated Society of Planters told assistants they would need at least $250 a month to pay for servants, club expenses, food, and other bare necessities.[19]

Rubber draped the bare-bones existence of early planters with the soft tissues of a modern consumer culture. The ships that carried away sheet rubber and tin brought back motorcars and cycles, phonograph records, and radios. Gasoline-powered refrigerators permitted an endless supply of cold drinks. Planters could eat Australian lamb and Irish cheese, indulge in Cuban cigars and French cognac, and drink Scotch whisky. To be well equipped, a new assistant manager was advised to bring to Malaya two suits for evening wear and afternoon events, in addition to the multiple shirts, trousers, shorts and shoes needed for days on the estate. The Incorporated Society of Planters also recommended a tennis racquet, golf clubs, shotgun, and certainly a bicycle or good motorcycle.[20] Planters had active social lives in the towns and in their clubs away from the rigid order of the plantations, for which they were expected to be well outfitted and well dressed.

By the 1920s, the standards of European life on rubber estates had been transformed by the combination of new wealth and women. In 1927, a manager's wife wrote a description of her life on a Malayan plantation for *Blackwood's Magazine*. Although she lived in a simple, two bedroom, wooden, palm-roofed bungalow, her habits were set in Europe. Surrounded by dark walls of rubber trees on three sides, the house boasted a carefully cultivated flower garden, which brightened its grassy lawn. No gleaming kitchen or bathroom appliances made domestic chores easier in a house lacking electricity and running water, but servants aired bed linen daily and served meals. Although the estate lay several miles from the nearest village, it had at least two automobiles, permitting weekly shopping trips and excursions. Imported food, ice, and drinking water were brought in from Penang regularly.[21] Nights at the club were considered a "necessity," "the only means by which the lady, who has been shut in by dark and dank rubber trees for a week can meet congenial

[19] C. Ward-Jackson, *Rubber Planting: A Book for the Prospective Estate Assistant in British Malaya* (Kuala Lumpur: The Incorporated Society of Planters, 1920), pp. 38–39, 47–50; C. Mathieu, *Para Rubber Cultivation: Manual of the Planter in Malaysia* (Paris: Augustin Challamel, ed., 1909), p. 31. See also Peter and Waveney Jenkins, *The Planter's Bungalow: A Journey down the Malay Peninsula* (Singapore: Editions Didier Millet, 2007)
[20] Ward-Jackson, *Rubber Planting*, pp. 47–50
[21] A. B. H., "Housekeeping and Life in the Malayan Rubber," *Blackwood's Magazine* (May 1927), Vol. 221, pp. 598–613

friends and neighbouring Europeans of her own sex."[22] The Malayan Civil Service's handbook for newcomers observed, "the motor car has largely eliminated the factor of distance in social life. Few are now so isolated that they cannot conveniently come in to the local club at least once a week." When employed on a plantation a few miles outside Kuala Lumpur, Leopold Ainsworth began to follow the pattern of other Europeans in the district: he drove to town every day at 4 PM, spent two hours playing at tennis at the Spotted Dog – which he compared to an English country club – and then started drinking at its "famous" long bar.[23]

The money and technologies spawned by the rubber boom made it possible to interweave plantations and cities. Not only did buses and cars join estates to the larger towns, but by the 1920s and 1930s, links between rural and urban sectors in Malaya became deeper and more official. Dozens of managers and assistants served as jurors in town courts and justices of the peace. Leading rubber planters were appointed to town sanitary boards, becoming part of the urban elite who planned towns and distributed patronage. The group stretched well beyond European planters.[24] During the 1920s, Nagamuthu Ganapathipillay, who was a millionaire planter in the Sitiawan region, worked actively on the Sanitary Board there, as well as on local hospital and various licensing boards. Karthigesu Arumgan, who owned several rubber estates in Seremban, joined its Sanitary Board, as well as the Asian Estate Owners Association and the Rubber Restriction Committee in the 1930s. Salomon Ramanathan, a director of the Kuala Kangsar Plantation Group, served both as a justice of the peace and a nominated member of the Kuala Kangsar Sanitary Board.[25]

Rubber made an agricultural style of imperialism dominant in British Malaya. Leasing and selling land for rubber, inspecting the new estates, and licensing its export brought the state into negotiation with every ethnic group and into every part of the peninsula. Rubber brought most of the colony's people into contact with colonial administrators, and it

[22] These comments were written by a doctor in the Federated Malay States to would-be planters about the hardships and high cost of living for married couples in Malaya; Letter to the Editor, "Fever and Poverty, A Doctor and Life in the F. M. S.," *The Planter* (August 1923) Vol. IV, No. 1, p. 15

[23] Leopold Ainsworth, *The Confessions of a Planter in Malaysia: A Chronicle of Life and Adventure in the Jungle* (London: H. F. and G. Witherby, 1933), pp. 182–183

[24] For information on how this system worked in Kuching and Sarawak, see Craig A. Lockard, "The Evolution of Urban Government in Southeast Asian Cities: Kuching under the Brookes," *Modern Asian Studies*, Vol. 12, No. 2 (1978), pp. 245–267

[25] S. Durai Raja Singam, *A Hundred Years of Ceylonese in Malaysia and Singapore, 1867–1967* (Kuala Lumpur: S. Durai Raja Singam, n.d.), pp. 233–235

brought rubber managers and employees into the towns and into town politics. Rubber had two major voices: that of the growers who demanded protection of their profits and investments, and that of workers and employees concerned with their own benefits and health. The Great Depression undermined government attempts to satisfy both of these constituencies and undercut political support for the social welfare of colonial subjects. Despite the efforts of the colonial state to make rubber plantations showplaces for their efforts to secure workers' welfare, the industry's economic problems in the interwar period undermined investments in biomedicine and sanitation. Meanwhile, a harsh style of plantation discipline based on hierarchy and racial divisions remained in force from the days of sugar cultivation, setting the tone of colonial rule in the twentieth century.

Workers and Work

British Malaya was a frontier colony easily adapted to the demands of rubber. Its roads, rivers, and telegraphs provided the necessary infrastructure. Tree-covered areas crowded with wildlife and rich in native species were assigned by the state to new owners who had them clearcut. The sugar, coffee, and spice trades had created a large group of managers who could run the new plantations, and a growing group of European merchant firms had access to foreign stock markets for needed capital. The question of who would do the work of cultivation seemed straightforward as the industry expanded. Under the watchful eye of the state, the indenture system for decades had brought thousands of labourers annually from South India, arranged their transference to individual estates, and then supervised their compliance with multi-year contracts. From the point of view of Malaya's planters, the continuance of current arrangements seemed all that was needed.

International support for unfree labour in any form dropped off markedly, however, in the early twentieth century after the founding of the Congo Reform Association in 1904. The publications of the British journalist E.D. Morel and the Irish diplomat Roger Casement exposed the enslavement, torture, and mutilation of rubber workers in the Belgian Congo, which fuelled an international campaign in defence of the human rights of colonial subjects. Since the British government commissioned, published, and defended Casement's report, it was in a weak position to protect its own practice of indentured labour, which had come under attack, too. During the first decade of the twentieth century, Indian nationalists had mounted fierce assaults on indenture in South Asia as well as in South Africa, while local opposition to the practice grew in Natal, Mauritius, Assam, and

Table 5.1 *Rubber Estate Workers in the Federated Malay States,*
1906–1940

Year	Indian	Chinese	Malay	Total
1907	44,000	5,300	6,000	55,300
1910	99,000	46,000	34,000	179,000
1915	126,347	27,446	16,958	170,741
1920	161,000	41,000	15,000	217,000
1925	137,761	37,879	8,714	184,354
1930	154,000	42,000	9,000	205,000
1935	118,591	29,950	4,599	153,140
1940	218,000	77,000	45,000	351,000

Source: Parmer, *Colonial Labor Policy,* p. 273; Peter J. Rimmer and Lisa M. Allen,
The Underside of Malaysian History: Pullers, Prostitutes, and Plantation Workers
(Singapore: Singapore University Press, 1990), p. 26. The figures for Malays
include Javanese. The figures for 1930 and 1940 include the Straits Settlements,
and the figures for 1940 also include the Unfederated Malay States.

Trinidad. Workers' groups took to the streets, while colonial officials felt
free to point out abuses in the system. The Anti-Slavery and Aborigines'
Protection Society added its voice to an international anti-indenture
campaign, which helped to abolish the practice in British Malaya in
1910 and in remaining British colonies by 1920.[26] The end of indenture
did not mean the end of unfree labour in Malaya, however. Recruitment
of South Asians by estates' foremen sent back to their home villages
brought in thousands of workers on short-term contracts, which they
were pressured to renew. Unfree labour continued under a different
name and in a softer form.

The number of estate workers tripled in the five years between
1907 and 1912, and then quadrupled by 1921 and kept on rising (see
Table 5.1). Aided by an Indian Immigration Fund which paid the transport and subsistence costs for labourers from their recruitment until they
arrived on an estate, thousands of South Asians arrived annually in
Singapore and Penang debt free to take up plantation jobs. Thousands
of Chinese labourers poured each year into Malaya too, recruited by
agents in China and contractors who financed their transport costs,

[26] E. D. Morel, *The Congo Slave State: a Protest against the New African Slavery and an
Appeal to the Public of Great Britain, of the United States, and of the Continent of Europe*
(Liverpool: J. Richardson and Sons, Printers, 1903); Hugh Tinker, *A New System of
Slavery: the Export of Indian Labour Overseas 1830–1920,* 2nd ed. (London: Hansib
Publishing Ltd., 1993)

which workers had to repay from future earnings.[27] Although debts tied them to their foremen and employers, this mechanism to finance travel allowed even very poor Chinese to move to Malaya. Estates also hired growing numbers of assistants, clerks, foremen, factory workers, and drivers from local communities, and local hospitals hired doctors and medical personnel. Estates that had begun with managers and labourers quickly became complex communities of mixed skills, responsibilities, and places of origin.

Between 1911 and 1931, peninsular Malaya gained 1,428,000 people, and the proportion of women among the immigrants rose. After 1922, the Indian Immigration Fund required that 40 per cent of the workers sent to Malaya be females, who qualified for paid passage if they were married or accompanied by a relative.[28] As a result, Indian families multiplied on Malayan plantations among field workers and foremen. As the need for rubber workers swelled, so did officials' interest in their reproduction. Appalled by high infant mortality rates in the twentieth century, medical administrators in the Straits Settlements set up programmes to train Asian midwives and to fund infant welfare clinics. They distributed free powdered and condensed milk to families along with advice on "good mothering" to the Chinese, Indian, and Malay populations throughout the colony.[29] The colonial state embraced the notion that workers should reproduce themselves, not merely be imported.

European plantation managers grouped these thousands of workers into racial categories both literally and discursively. Leopold Ainsworth, who worked for years in Malaya as an estate manager and surveyor, divided local people into the childlike and lazy Malays, the hardworking, opium-smoking and gambling Chinese, the Tamils who, he believed,

---

[27] J. Norman Parmer, *Colonial Labor Policy and Administration: A History of Labor in the Rubber Plantation Industry in Malay, c. 1910–1941* (Locust Valley NY: Association for Asian Studies, 1960), pp. 38–39, 99–100

[28] The Indian government did not mandate or enforce a particular ratio of female and male emigrants to Malaya until the 1930s, although by the 1860s such ratios were written into regulations for emigrants to Mauritius, Natal, and various Caribbean islands. Thomas R. Metcalf, *Imperial Connections: India in the Indian Ocean Arena, 1860–1920* (Berkeley: University of California Press, 2007), p. 141; Marina Carter, *Voices from Indenture: Experiences of Indian Migrants in the British Empire* (London and New York: Leicester University Press, 1996), p. 138; Sinnappah Arasaratnam, *Indians in Malaysia and Singapore*, rev. ed. (Kuala Lumpur: Oxford University Press, 1979), pp. 67–69. See also J. E. Nathan, *The Census of British Malaya, 1921* (London: Waterlow & Sons, Ltd., 1922), pp. 347–348.

[29] V. S. Srinivasa Sastri, *Report on the Conditions of Indian Labour in Malaya* (New Delhi: Government of India Press, 1937), pp. 18–19. By 1931, there were 482 Indian women per 1,000 adult Indian men in Malaya; Lenore Manderson, *Sickness and the State: Health and Illness in Colonial Malaya, 1870–1940* (Cambridge: Cambridge University Press, 1996), pp. 206–218

"beat their womenfolk," and Europeans who ran things.[30] In his hand-book for rubber planters, C. Matieu explained the varieties of "Asiatic labourers." "Native workers" (meaning Malays) were suitable for "felling the forest" and simple construction jobs, but were either unwilling tem-peramentally or unable to take on regular plantation duties. Employers therefore needed to turn to Chinese, Javanese, or Tamil immigrants, each group working separately on its own tasks. The Chinese, as long as they had their "opium and . . . gambling, which is in the blood," could become "mule-like workers" if employed on specific tasks, such as road building or transplanting. But they were tricky and would cheat if not watched closely by a Chinese headman. Javanese were good field labourers and could also do the heavy jobs involved in building a new estate. "Docile and gentle, the Javanese is and [sic] ideal workman for the tropics. He has neither the strength nor the strenuousness of the Chinaman, but he is less turbulent and he is more easy to govern." He recommended Tamils – "garrulous . . . given to drink, but strong"– to do the permanent jobs on estates.[31] Such caricatures set the tone of work relations and complicated attempts to treat estates as machines, which only had to be switched on to function perfectly.

Between 50 and 75 per cent of those who went to work on European-owned rubber estates were Tamils, while Chinese employers tended to employ more Chinese. Smaller numbers of Javanese and Malays were added as needed. Between 1906 and 1940, the number of estate workers in the Federated Malay States increased by about 600 per cent, although the total decreased sharply in 1920 and 1921 and 1924, and again between 1930 and 1933[32] (see Table 5.1). These numbers would have been even larger if estates had not found ways to increase the productivity of their workers, despite a limited amount of technological change in the industry. If average land/labour ratios in force on rubber plantations are examined and compared with those of late-nineteenth-century sugar estates, it is clear that the number of field workers employed to run a plantation decreased sharply in the first half of the twentieth century. The Penang Sugar Estates management estimated that it needed approxi-mately one worker to cultivate and harvest each acre of land planted in sugar cane. Rubber needed far fewer workers, even during the early stages of land clearing and planting. During the first rubber boom, official returns calculated that estates used one worker for each 2.5 acres planted. This ratio increased to one worker per 6.25 acres in 1920

---

[30] Ainsworth, *Confessions*, pp. 47, 54–55
[31] C. Matieu, *Para Rubber*, pp. 38, 42–43, 47–49
[32] Parmer, *Colonial Labor Policy*, p. 273

and one per 9.25 acres in 1930, although there was little change in the processes of planting, tapping, or collecting latex. By the mid-1930s, European managers found that they had to supervise twice as large an area as that assigned to them a decade earlier, and workers were given many more trees to tap each day. Since rubber yields per acre did not decline, estates maintained output while lowering their cost of production.[33] Effectively, the plantation assembly line was speeded up.

The trade-off for harder pressed workers came in the form of sharply rising wages during the early years of the rubber boom. After 1884, the Straits Settlements' Immigration Ordinance mandated a daily wage of 12 to 14 cents for indentured Tamil men until the end of the indenture system in 1910. Thereafter, competition for workers intensified. After 1908, rubber growers had to offer as much as 50 cents per day to the non-indentured Tamil males and 40 cents per day for female workers brought to Malaya with minimal debts. These higher rates were cut by 1913 as rubber prices fell, but rose again around 1920 in response to increasing demand for male tappers to a daily rate of 65 cents or $17 per month. For the next two decades, planters' associations cut wages during depression years and worked aggressively to maintain the cuts when conditions improved, while the Government of India lobbied to return to rates of 50 cents for men and 40 cents for women. Tense negotiations among the Malayan Controller of Labour, the Government of India, and the Planter's Association of Malaya over what constituted a fair wage in the face of changing food and rubber prices continued throughout the 1930s.[34]

Although the Labour Code of 1923 mandated a minimum "standard" wage for Tamil estate workers, disputes over what it should be and a lack of enforcement made the requirement ineffective. Planters, who were struggling to sell rubber at a profit, embraced wage reduction as their major cost-cutting strategy. Moreover, they defined a fair wage as one that

---

[33] During the later 1930s, the average ratio of workers/acre declined to its level in 1920; Colin Barlow, "Changes in the Economic Position of Workers on Rubber Estates and Smallholdings in Peninsular Malaysia, 1910–1985," in Rimmer and Allen, *Underside of Malaysian History*, p. 33; Drabble estimates that annual "output per estate worker in the FMS rose from 0.7 to 1.1 tons (1929–1933)" and then remained at 1.0 tons until 1940; Drabble, *Malayan Rubber*, pp. 39, 51, 78

[34] Drabble, *Rubber*, p. 111; see also Parmer, *Colonial Labor*, p. 181. By 1937, the larger estates agreed to pay male tappers 45 cents per day and women a wage of 36 cents. Negotiators emphasized the changing rubber sale price, not costs of living, in their analyses. See V. S. Srinivasa Sastri, *Report on the Conditions of Indian Labour in Malaya* (New Delhi: Government of India Press, 1937), pp. 4–6

allowed Tamils to maintain an "accustomed" style of living, which they defined as a primarily rice and salt fish diet, a few bits of cotton clothing, one mat, one pillow, and a monthly visit to the barber. Yet the cost of even this Spartan existence for a single man in 1925 was calculated to be above the standard monthly wage of tappers when rice prices were high. Wives had to work for households to survive, and expenditures on children seem to have been kept to a minimum. The Government of India's demand that labourers be kept in "tolerable comfort" and be able to save money as well as provide for a family fell on deaf ears.[35] Planters knew that their major cost of production was labour, and when rubber prices fell as they did regularly after 1910, companies' primary tactic for decreasing costs was to cut wages and furlough labourers and assistants.[36] In the period between the two world wars, a continual struggle among rubber companies, the colonial state, and workers over wages and jobs underlay the day-to-day operation of rubber estates.

Rubber workers reconstructed the land, clearing its surface and flattening its contours. Plantations were born in the back-breaking labour of sweating, half-naked men who sawed down trees, burned off vegetation, and dug out charred stumps. Only at that point could the landscape be replanted with seedlings of the rubber tree, *Hevea brasiliensis*. Photos of the Henrietta plantation in Kedah at the time of its opening show nearly empty land, ringed by dark forest. Wooden barracks for the workers rose in the midst of acres of dull brown dirt, soon to be divided into numbered fields and rutted roads.

Just as sugar plantations had done, rubber plantations mimicked factory procedures as workers went into the fields. Despite the lack of time clocks, a work day began with a wake-up bell and communal muster at 5:40 or earlier. Assistants shouted out workers' names, recording attendance and assigning tasks. Set work gangs marched together before dawn to the assigned fields with their foremen, who watched and yelled at

---

[35] The Indian Immigration Committee calculated a cost of $7.19 as the monthly budget of an Indian labourer in September of 1925, using a rice price of 46 cents per gallon, allowing no expenditure for drink, fruit, and vegetables, and minimal expenditures on household goods, meat, and tobacco. See Parmer, *Colonial Labour*, pp. 179, 258, 278. Colin Barlow calculates that the average Tamil tapper earned $17 a month in 1920 and $9 a month in 1930, giving a more generous portrait of incomes, although he emphasizes the "miserable working and living conditions for early Malaysian estate labourers," and does not take into account the issue of un- or underemployment. Colin Barlow, "Changes in the Economic Position of Workers on Rubber Estates and Smallholdings in Peninsular Malaysia, 1910–1985," in Rimmer and Allen, *Underside*, p. 31

[36] Using figures supplied by C. Matieu in 1909, I calculate that 80 per cent of a plantation's cost of development during its first year went to pay its workers and managers. In the second year, the ratio rose to 94 per cent. Land rents were low, and little equipment other than shovels, hoes, seeds, and wood was required.

slackers to finish their jobs quickly. Tapping required skill, but it was physically much easier than the cultivation of sugar cane. Each tapper had a quota of trees to cut and on which to fasten a cup. A few hours later, latex was collected and taken to a weigh station. The job, begun in the pre-dawn light, involved careful slicing and endless repetitions. A successful cut of no more than ¼ inch wide would remove the top layer of bark, allowing latex to flow without injuring the tree's cambium. The season's tapping would mark a parallelogram of cuts no more than 3 inches in width, minimizing long-term damage to the tree. A tapper was expected to produce mathematically accurate, machine-like measurements as he worked. Rotational systems of tapping and alternative designs of bark removal ("fourth daily full spiral," "double cut tapping," or "alternative daily tapping on half circumference") were instituted to cut walking times between trees and to increase the yield of each tree. Release came to tappers only after a second muster to register completed tasks and to measure productivity, generally in the early afternoon.[37]

Assistants took on the job of quality control in multiple areas, as they moved from the core of the estate to the fields, to the office, and back (see Figure 5.1). They checked on tappers, weeders, and pest control gangs; they supervised the transfer of latex to the factory and its coagulation, and then compiled attendance records. Sometimes they did clerical work. Assistants found that between 1914 and 1932 the acres they had to supervise doubled and then doubled again, as the workers available for tasks decreased in number. The best-trained assistants could handle agronomy, accounting, and first aid, and they had to be adept with both angry supervisors and hostile labourers. Instruction manuals warned a new assistant that he "may feel that he is regarded and treated as if he were an automaton." Each had too many tasks and too little time. Just as he kept workers in line, so too did his manager ride herd on him.[38]

Estates disciplined their workers partly through division into groups according to race, gender, and status, which determined work assignments, housing, and wage levels. Continuing debates over wages, which pitted rubber companies and their lobbying groups against colonial officials but did not involve workers directly, testify to the imbalances of power on the plantations. There is little evidence of large strikes or effective labour organizations before 1940.[39] The rubber variant

---

[37] Sastri, *Report*, p. 7; Matieu, *Para Rubber Cultivation*, pp. 75, 111–112, 142, 146–147; Bauer, *Rubber*, pp. 226, 254–256

[38] Bauer, *Rubber*, p. 254; Ward-Jackson, *Rubber Planting*, p. 22

[39] Norman Parmer includes estate workers among the "restive" labourers who occasionally went on strike in 1937; Parmer, *Labor Policy*, pp. 77, 129. Michael Stenson dates the emergence of trade unions among estate workers as occurring around 1941, pointing to a

Figure 5.1 Manager and Chinese rubber tappers collecting latex on a
Perak plantation, 1901

of agricultural imperialism depended on a strategy of divide-and-rule,
which proved impossible to challenge in a sustained fashion before
World War II.

Severe and Softer Disciplines

The tone and style of plantation discipline were set by managers whose
assumptions and tactics shaped daily life on agricultural estates.
Furthermore, field workers' lack of freedom distorted all social relations.
Analyses of post-emancipation plantation labour regimes recall the world
of slave owners and their treatment of people they considered their
property. Unfree labour in its multiple forms was compatible with not
only colonial rule but also global capitalist enterprise. Jan Bremen

Malacca Rubber Estates' Employees Association; Michael R. Stenson, *Industrial Conflict
in Malaya: Prelude to the Communist Revolt of 1948* (London: Oxford University Press,
1970), pp. 28–31, 35

describes a "climate of violence" and a regime on Sumatran tobacco plantations in the twentieth century, where workers were subjugated to employers and lacked protections. Rana Behal and Prabhu Mohapatra identify the indenture system on Assam tea plantations as one that fostered physical abuse and kept birth rates low. Whether estates grew coffee, sugar, tea, cotton, or rubber, the verdict has been similar: they were sites of an exploitative capitalism characterized by punitive disciplines and severe inequalities.[40]

The British colonial administration claimed responsibility for the treatment of plantation labour, and their policies changed in Malaya after the early twentieth century. During the rubber boom, the colonial state slowly retreated from the harsh penal regime that it had enforced on sugar estates. A softer style of labour control that emphasized workers' welfare was put in place in years of relative prosperity, although its main elements – higher wages, improved housing and sanitation, and public health services – virtually collapsed along with the international economy during the early 1930s. Colonial rule on the plantations of British Malaya responded to three different forces: managerial attitudes and policies, state regulation and inspection, and the international economy. Together, they moulded the labour regime of rubber.

During the nineteenth century, penal systems of contract enforcement dominated colonial labour law. Labour codes covering indentured workers, which had been designed in the era of sugar with West Indian models in mind, set a pattern of rigid expectations and limited workers' rights. These norms transferred directly to rubber plantations. The Indian Immigration Ordinance of 1904 obligated labourers who had signed written and properly registered contracts and received free passage to Malaya to complete 600 days of work, which were defined in terms of tasks set by employers, not hours. Moreover, those convicted of not completing twenty days' work in a month "without a reasonable excuse" faced a penalty of seven days in jail. Anyone who disobeyed orders or neglected duties "necessary ... for the management, discipline, and good order of the place" could be jailed for up to two weeks for a second offence, and a month in jail was the penalty for anyone who fled from his or her estate. The threat of jail time hung over the heads of workers

[40] Jan Bremen, *Taming the Coolie Beast: Plantation Society and the Colonial Order in Southeast Asia* (Delhi: Oxford University Press, 1989), pp. 198, 216–218; Rana P. Behal and Prabhu P. Mohapatra, "Tea and Money versus Human Life: The Rise and Fall of the Indenture System in the Assam Tea Plantations 1840–1909," *Journal of Peasant Studies*, Vol. 19, Nos. 3 & 4 (1992), pp. 142–171; Vincent J. H. Houben, J. Thomas Lindblad, et al., *Coolie Labour in Colonial Indonesia: a Study of Labour Relations in the Outer Islands, c. 1900–1940* (Wiesbaden: Harrassowitz Verlag, 1999); Jayeeta Sharma, *Empire's Garden: Assam and the Making of India* (Durham: Duke University Press, 2011)

who sold food rations, ignored sanitary rules, or injured themselves "wil-fully." Penalties for planters were less harsh. While labourers could file complaints of "ill-usage" or defects in their housing or medical facilities, employers faced a fine, rather than jail, as the first penalty.[41] In a world where police chased runaways and where assistants and managers served on colonial juries, Sanitary Boards, and labour inquiries, planters clearly had the upper hand. Yet they did not have a completely free hand. In 1915, when state courts convicted 102 employers for infractions of the labour code, 13 were found guilty of molesting a labourer and 15 for failing to pay wages on time.[42] The majority of convictions, however, followed a complaint (probably from another planter) that someone had enticed workers away from their lawful employer. The weight of legal processes continued to fall much more heavily on workers than on their managers.

But by the outbreak of World War I, the British colonial state took two steps back from its aggressive support of planter interests and plantation discipline, probably because of continued labour shortages and dimin-ished coercive power. The indenture system, outlawed for Indians in 1910 and for Chinese in 1914, ended the long-term servitude of labourers to particular estates.[43] Although labour laws in the Straits Settlements and the Federated Malay States, which mirrored one another, continued to impose penalties of imprisonment on labourers for disobedience, desertion, and failure to work, the laws were not enforced strictly. The Singapore Supreme Court supported Sellappan Kavandan in his refusal to be sent back to the Braunston Estate in Selangor, after he was arrested in 1913. Kavandan had fled to Singapore rather than complete the terms of his thirty-day unwritten labour contract. Although the estate demanded his return rather than financial compensation, the court held that the offence was "of a trivial nature and that it would be too severe and oppressive to order the defendant's surrender."[44] Although, in 1915, courts in the Federated Malay States convicted 980 workers for desertion, only 72 labourers were jailed for disobedience, neglect, insolence, or

[41] *Indian Immigration Ordinance, 1904* (Medan: *Deli Courant*, 1904), pp. 12, 23–27
[42] N. E. Marjoribanks, and Ahmad Tambi Marakkayar, *Report on Indian Labour Emigration to Ceylon and Malaya, Part II, Malay Peninsula* (Madras,1917), Appendix XVI A, p. 92
[43] Objections to indenture from Indian nationalists and the Government of India, in combination with state subsidies for the transportation of kangany-recruited workers, led all parties in Malaya to retreat from long-term labour contracts. British administrators in Hong Kong also opposed its use for Chinese nationals. As a result, the Malayan government set dates in 1910 and 1914 beyond which indenture contracts would not be enforceable. See Parmer, *Labour Policy*, pp. 48–50, 83; Jackson, *Planters and Speculators*, pp. 238–239
[44] F. G. Stevens and M. J. Upcott, eds., *Straits Settlements Law Reports, 1915*, Vol. XIII (Singapore: Kelly and Walsh Ltd., 1915), pp. 11–14

usal to work. Even if the Labour Code of 1912 gave the colonial state
oad powers to support employers, the more subtle rejections of man-
gerial authority no longer led directly to prison. The colonial state, which
.egularly denied planters' petitions for additional controls over workers'
movements, seems to have retreated from interference in day-to-day
labour relations, except to investigate workers' complaints. Labour law
softened both in form and in enforcement after the end of indenture.
Workers were technically free labourers who could leave their posts after
giving one month's notice. Although over 40,000 estate workers simply
walked away from their jobs without giving notice in 1915, fewer than 3
per cent of this group were even charged for desertion and only 2.5 per
cent were convicted.[45] Actions that led to jail time in the 1880s were
tolerated thirty years later. The colony as a whole needed workers to settle
permanently, and it became counterproductive to alienate them with jail
time. Moreover, international outrage over the treatment of rubber workers in the Belgian Congo made it clear that imperial regimes could be held
accountable for abuses of unfree labour.[46]

In 1923, the Federated Malay States removed penal sanctions for all of
the common labour offences including desertion, and fines replaced jail as
penalties for the few that remained. By the mid-1920s, employers could
no longer use the state to throw workers in jail for work-related misde-
meanours, and new editions of planters' manuals omitted references to
labourers' offences, commenting instead that "to hinder or molest by
word, gesture or act any labourer in the performance of his agreement
or contract is punishable with a fine or imprisonment."[47] Moreover,
workers began to bring complaints in significant numbers to the Labour
Department of the Federated Malay States. In 1938, over 2,000 labourers
charged that they had been paid late or not at all; over 200 claimed they
had been assaulted by a manager or foreman; 635 protested against what
they considered "wrongful dismissal." In that year, one in every 80
employed workers on the estates brought forward a complaint, which
was heard by an investigating officer. If not settled, the complaints could
be taken to court, and fines could be imposed as sanctions.[48] It is not clear
how effective these protests were, but their numbers indicate that by the
late 1930s workers regarded the Labour Department as a potential ally in
their self-defence during a period when they were not unionized.

[45] Marjoribanks and Marakkayar, *Indian Labour Emigration, Part II, Malay Peninsula*, p. 33
and Appendix XVIA, p. 92.
[46] Adam Hochschild, *King Leopold's Ghost* (Boston: Houghton Mifflin, 1999)
[47] Parmer, *Labor Policy*, pp. 118, 122; C. W. H. Cochrane, *Law for Planters*, 2nd ed. (Kuala
Lumpur, Federated Malay States Printing Office, 1929), p. 20
[48] Parmer, *Labor Policy*, pp. 138–139, 276

Standing behind the Labour Department was the International Labour Organization (ILO), created in 1919 as an agency of the League of Nations to advocate for social reform and workers' rights. Member governments, which included Great Britain, pledged themselves to apply ILO conventions that they had ratified to their colonial territories, and the Colonial Office dutifully forwarded these documents throughout the empire. Unfortunately, colonial officials in Malaya declared most of the new rules inapplicable to the immigrant estate populations, who were classified as "aliens" and therefore permanent residents, but they did accept new limits on forced labour and night work by women and children. In 1929, imperial administrators mandated a system of workmen's compensation, although its enforcement was postponed indefinitely. Finally, on the eve of the Japanese invasion, new laws permitted the organization of industrial courts and legalized trades unions.[49] Albeit grudgingly, the colonial government of British Malaya moved its labour laws very slowly toward similarity with those of the United Kingdom. Inspections by the ILO and circulation of its reports brought international standards into play in Malaya, introducing a new destabilizing element into the negotiations between planters and colonial officers charged with "protecting" labour. The meaning of protection shifted from a limited inquiry into labourers' formal acceptance of their lot to a more aggressive setting of minimum standards whose levels rose over time.

A second destabilizing influence on conditions within plantations came from more determined efforts by government inspectors to protect the health of estate workers. After all, one of the official justifications for imperial rule was the British pledge to defend local populations and to improve their condition. The Labour Department, working together with the legislature of the Federated Malay States, moved to regulate working conditions in the rubber industry. Labour codes enacted in 1909 and 1910 set minimum wages, maximum hours, and health standards. Labourers had to have "proper" housing and sanitation, as well as "sufficient wholesome water." Hospitals, medical personnel, and medicines also had to be provided free of charge.[50] Niggling disputes over the meaning of "proper" and "sufficient" arose regularly, but Labour Department officials and health officers inspected the larger estates to ensure compliance, occasionally using their ability to block new hiring until problems were corrected. In addition, colonial officials were sufficiently invested in the issue of workers' welfare to mount periodic investigations into employment conditions. As interest in

[49] Parmer, *Labor Policy*, pp. 128–129
[50] "Treatment of Immigrants at Place of Employment," Part VI, *The Indian Immigration Ordinance of 1904*, pp. 18–19; Also see Cochrane, *Law for Planters*, 2nd ed., Part VIII, pp. 14–17; Parmer, *Labor Policy*, pp. 116–118

sanitation as a sign of progressive colonial rule spread throughout the peninsula and as general standards rose, state inspectors nudged plantation managers to improve their physical environments. They took on the role of protectors of imperial subjects, denying the need for unions or democratic processes to safeguard workers' welfare.[51]

Members of a committee charged in 1910 with investigating conditions on estates judged what they saw generously. Dominated by planters, the group thought that labourers were "fairly well-housed" in structures which were "satisfactory in type" and "fairly clean." Nevertheless, the Perak Health Officer held a different opinion. He thought that Chinese workers in the Krian area lived in "mere hovels" that lacked proper sanitation.[52] Conditions on estates varied from Spartan but clean to wretched and dirty, but all of the structures described lacked windows, screens, cross-ventilation, electricity, and running water. Photographs of early housing on larger, better-run estates show back-to-back, barracks-style buildings where light could enter only from the front facade. Made of wood and roofed with palm leaf, which leaked in the rain, or corrugated iron, which became baking hot in the sunshine, even the best of these apartments were crowded, noisy, and dark.[53] Cooking was done outside or on a veranda. Not until the mid-1930s, after the Labour Department condemned the older-style design and forbade any new housing to be built as back-to-back barracks, did housing standards improve significantly. The most generous employers tore down the old barracks and built cottages raised on stilts, giving families two rooms and greater privacy. Standpipes for water and cement drains helped labourers to stay clean and dry.[54] On the Lima Belas plantation in Selangor, the Danish manager Werner Michael Iversen ordered the building of three "garden villages," where each labourer's family had a separate two-roomed house with a veranda and a plot of land. Not only did each of these houses have running water, but each complex had its own schools, nursery, medical dispensary, and sports fields.[55] While much more elaborate facilities were built for managers and senior staff, the company decided by the later 1930s that its labourers deserved more than minimal accommodation and services. Multiple

---

[51] Rachel Sturman, "Indian Indentured Labor and the History of International Rights Regimes," *AHR*, Vol. 119, No. 5 (2014), p. 1457

[52] Federated Malaya States, *Report of the Commission Appointed to Enquire into the Conditions of Indentured Labour in the Federated Malay States, 1910* (Kuala Lumpur: Government Printing Office, 1910); also see Lenore Manderson, *Sickness and the State: Health and Illness in Colonial Malaya, 1870–1940* (Cambridge: Cambridge University Press, 1996), pp. 132–133

[53] C. N. Parkinson, *The Guthrie Flagship*, p. 137

[54] Sastri, *Report on the Conditions of Indian Labour*, pp. 7–8

[55] Iverson, "Memories," pp. 35–38

pressures combined to produce improved conditions. The rapid expansion of the industry increased the need to recruit and retain skilled tappers. Bringing in new workers who had to be trained remained expensive and risky. At the same time, the colonial state raised legal standards of treatment and increased its scrutiny of estates. During the first two decades of the twentieth century, high profits provided resources to fund rising wages and better housing. Employers who claimed paternalist responsibility for workers' welfare were able to invest in human capital. In good years, employers' self-interest and workers' welfare were compatible.

Public health concerns also led the colonial government to push rubber companies to invest more in their employees. In the early twentieth century, primitive sanitary conditions on some rubber estates horrified health inspectors, who complained of insufficient supplies of clean drinking water and of leaky, dirty latrines which contaminated wells. Nearby rivers and creeks of dubious purity supplied water for drinking, as well as cooking, bathing, and clothes-washing for hundreds of workers, as they did for the Malay rural population. Faeces-contaminated soil spread hookworm. At risk because of poor hygiene and sanitation, workers contracted infectious diseases at appallingly high rates. Crowded housing permitted the rapid spread of tuberculosis, smallpox, cholera, dysentery, diarrhoea, pneumonia, and measles. Moreover, estates were fertile breeding grounds for the malaria-carrying Anopheles mosquito. The felling of jungle and the cutting of drains intensified the danger to non-immune immigrants, as pools of stagnant water multiplied. Dr Malcolm Watson, a public health specialist who served as Chief Medical Officer of the Federated Malay States, insisted that around 1910 it was not uncommon for 20 per cent of an estate's labour force to die of malaria every year, and infection rates remained high until around 1920, when mosquito control programmes became much more effective.[56]

Mortality and morbidity rates reveal the initial ineffectiveness of colonial welfare standards early in the twentieth century. Estates were obligated to register deaths at local police stations, and the larger European-run plantations and the Rubber Growers' Association collected information, which they supplied to the government. Although state records of deaths and births remained seriously incomplete throughout the period of British rule, they show the direction and timing of changes. In the Straits Settlements in 1908, the general population died at an annual rate of around 43 per thousand, while more than a quarter of all infants died within their first year. Conditions were significantly worse among estate labourers in the Federated Malay States, where statisticians

---

[56] Manderson, *Sickness*, pp. 135–136

have calculated that the crude death rate among Tamils was 65 per thousand persons and 79.6 per thousand among all estate labourers in 1908. (At the same date in England and Wales, crude death rates were only 14.8 per thousand.)[57]

After 1910, strengthened labour laws, new medical knowledge, and pressure from the colonial state worked together to improve workers' health. The Institute for Medical Research, which specialized in tropical medicine, opened in Kuala Lumpur in 1901, and it quickly turned its attention to malaria control. The colonial government opened a medical school in Singapore. Public programmes, which supplied quinine for malaria, salvarsan for yaws, and carbon tetrachloride for hookworm, moved into high gear in the 1920s and 1930s. Not only were estate managers pressured to improve local conditions, but travelling dispensaries criss-crossed the colony, vaccinating and medicating local people while lecturing them about ways to prevent endemic diseases. Standing water was removed on estates or treated, and wells were lined with concrete to prevent pollution. On Lima Belas estate, malaria was virtually eliminated by spraying oil on all stagnant ponds or drains, and children received regular doses of cod liver oil at local dispensaries. The purchase of a fancy ambulance and the offer of free rides persuaded most mothers to give birth in the estate hospital's maternity ward. Progressive planters invested more in their workers, recognizing the link between productivity and improved health. As a result, crude death rates in the Straits Settlements dropped by 50 per cent for adults and around 40 per cent for infants between 1908 and 1937, and they declined sharply on rubber estates as well. By the late 1930s, sanitation on estates as well as the provision of clean water had improved. Then the collapse of rubber prices and markets in the 1930s undermined these improvements. The Malaria Action Board and local health boards stopped functioning in 1932, and inspections of estates declined. Some estates closed their hospitals, and during the late 1930s, infant mortality rates and adult morbidity both

---

[57] On a limited group of estates from which information was collected in 1911, the crude death rate was almost three times as high: 232 per thousand workers. Civil registration of births and deaths was legally mandated in the Straits Settlements after its governance was transferred to the Colonial Office in 1866, but massive under-registration persisted until at least 1931, when the last census was taken before World War II. State figures of varying accuracy are available for some of the Malay states from the late nineteenth century and can be supplemented with data from hospitals and censuses. See Manderson, *Sickness*, pp. 32–39, 53–58 for a discussion of the sources for birth and death rates, and pp. 43–44, 146 for data on crude death rates. For data on Britain, see B. R. Mitchell, *Abstract of British Historical Statistics* (Cambridge: Cambridge University Press, 1962), pp. 34–42

rose.[58] The colonial state's public commitment to workers' welfare
became increasingly hollow as the grim economics of the rubber market
depressed wages and investments in the estates.

While progressive managers accepted the need to improve conditions
on plantations and went beyond the letter of the law, planters' organizations such as the Rubber Growers' Association and the Planters'
Association of Malaya balked at changes in the colony's labour regime.
Many planters preferred harsh discipline to what they saw as the government's coddling of disobedient and feckless workers. In a letter to the
Perak Pioneer in 1910, one writer accused the colonial government of
"overzeal" in considering coolies' "petty complaints" and of "too much
protection" for workers, whom he charged that the law favoured over
employers.[59] In the 1920s, satires of lazy, stupid Tamils, who could not
be made to follow orders or complete tasks, regularly appeared in *The
Planter* magazine. By giving them too much freedom, the government
allegedly blocked employers from maintaining discipline and production
levels. The "S. D.'s [Superintendent of the Division] Nightmare"
described the possible results, fifty years hence, of the changing direction
of colonial labour laws:

> ... I took the book and read ...
> *"Each night each cooly shall be tucked up warm inside his bed."*
> I then read on: *"The task devolves upon the management"*
> (The idea being, I presume, to make them feel content)
> *"The penalty for non-compliance – instant banishment."*[60]

Planters wanted the ability to command and to have "fair and just"
orders obeyed, and they accused the government of subverting this process by "imposing upon Indian immigrants a freedom which they neither
like, wish, nor understand." They preferred – but also complained about –
in loco parentis as an effective style of control. Indeed, some argued that the
"cooly" looked upon his employer "as his 'father and mother,'" thereby
justifying their power to treat him as a child.[61] Managers relished what
they saw as their rightful paternal role, but they were unwilling to concede
this status to the state, which competed with them for oversight of dependent workers. During the colonial period, a European boss was a *"tuan
besar,"* or great master, who expected deference and obedience. On the
Sebereng estate in Perak, workers and assistants had to dismount from

[58] Manderson, *Sickness*, pp. 9, 15, 153, 164, 230–231, 237
[59] S. P. S., "Indian Labour," *Perak Pioneer*, 4 April 1911, p. 5
[60] "The S.D.'s Nightmare," *The Planter*, Vol. 4, No. 8 (March 1924), p. 240. See also
"Labour," *The Planter*, Vol. 7, No. 4, (November 1926), p. 420; G. L. O'Hara Hickson,
"Tamil Labour in Malaya," *The Planter*, Vol. 7, No. 2 (September 1926), pp. 38–42
[61] "Labour," *The Planter*, Vol. 7 (November 1926), p. 420

bicycles and take off hats or other headgear when the manager appeared. On Lima Belas plantation in Selangor, workers felt they had to lower their umbrellas and go bareheaded when a manager appeared, even in a heavy rain.[62] These daily dramas of power and dependence ratified the racial hierarchy that many planters were happy to maintain, even if it stoked anti-colonial critiques and workers' resentments.

In the inaugural issue of *The Planter* in 1920, Shakespeare Junior promised "THE LABOUR QUESTION SOLVED";[63]

> If a cooly gives you cheek, and you can catch the giver,
> To make him civil heave a brick, and dislocate his liver.
> When he refuses labour, or works in a manner airy,
> Just knock him down, and while he's there jump on his little Mary.
> And any time you find him do what he didn't oughter,
> Don't hesitate, but shove him in a pot of boiling water.

Even if offered as a joke, this manager's gleeful recommendation of serious injury in return for minor insubordination or disobedience is a chilling evocation of the continuing casual violence on plantations. The suggestion that it was fair game to maim a worker or to parboil him, as if he were dinner, raises the question of what limits on managers' abilities to punish were publicly asserted and accepted. On one Kedah plantation in the early twentieth century, assistants who found workers still asleep on their wooden platforms, rather than out at the morning muster, yanked them by their ankles onto the ground. Leopold Ainsworth, an assistant manager in training, commented that he "found the process comparatively simple, and, strange to say, actually enjoyed it as a new and rather amusing form of sport." Chinese foremen and Tamil supervisors carried heavy whips, which they felt free to use on workers who had slowed or stopped their digging and weeding.[64] Ainsworth accepted his own brutality uncritically as a game, a normal part of the morning muster. Those with power could freely boast about the small-scale cruelties that were interwoven in the daily routines of estates.

The question of discipline in the tropics was intertwined with those of inter-racial sex and violence. New assistants were explicitly warned against both: "Womenfolk on an estate should never be interfered with, and in no circumstance should an assistant strike or chastise an estate labourer."[65] Such transgressions were thought to undermine colonial authority because

---

[62] Interview of V. Renganathan, 5 October, 2009, p. 14 (Perak Oral History Project, Ipoh Perak); Iversen, "Memories," p. 39
[63] "The Labour Question Solved," *The Planter*, Vol. 1, No. 1 (August, 1920), p. 9
[64] Ainsworth, *Confessions*, pp. 34, 36, 45–46, 49, 54, 71, 102
[65] Ward-Jackson, *Rubber Planting*, p. 35

they breached the social distance necessary to preserve discipline. Nevertheless, such events were common enough to prompt regular warnings against them. Leopold Ainsworth described the sexual temptation he felt, when attending the "Ti-Vali" [sic] festival at the estate temple: "I found myself suddenly and unaccountably drawn toward these glamorous and voluptuous beings that in the course of the ordinary day's work were no more than drab, musty smelling human weeding machines." He frankly admitted that moonlight and "a few dusky maids" had upset his composure.[66] He clearly relished the "dangers and excitement" of his "new life" where familiar rules did not obtain. Tamil women for him had no individuality or social identity. They were either mechanical objects or targets of lust and fantasy. They were nameless and indistinguishable one from the other.

Even after the practice of indenture ended and workers were technically free to leave their contracts, the assumptions of hierarchy and dominance continued to condition Europeans' attitudes to their workers. William Shellabear, a British Methodist minister and small plantation owner, explained his treatment of plantation labourers and servants to his son, comparing it to those of his American assistant. "Draper began to pay the coolies, not as I used to do on the veranda outside, but had them all come one by one into the study... The Drapers allow the natives to do all sorts of things that I would never permit," and he felt that they got less respect from their coolies as a result than did he or his foreman, Joseph Dorai. "Americans have such an exaggerated idea of the liberty of the individual that they seem to think people ought to be allowed to do just what they like, though in so doing they make themselves a positive nuisance to others. Americans generally spoil their servants by allowing them unlimited familiarity."[67] When men's bodies and behaviour, rather than their souls, were at issue, Shellabear believed in inequality and deference, and he privileged racial categories over religious ones.[68]

Ideas of racial difference merged into defences of racial hierarchy and European privilege, which, some acknowledged, had dangerous consequences. Plantation manuals warned assistants to beware of "the feeling of authority that seems so little limited over peoples of other races and colour... The remoteness from Western civilization and the lack of

[66] Ainsworth, *Confessions*, pp. 83–84
[67] "Letter W. Shellabear to Hugh Shellabear, 26 March 1912," Missionary Files, 1107-5-3.33, 78233 (Methodist Archive, Drew University)
[68] Shellabear commonly wrote of Tamil and Chinese although he also referred to Christian Tamils or Christian Chinese. Missionary Files 1107-5-3.33, 78233, 78222, 78154 (Methodist Archive, Drew University)

restraint upon a man's movements are apt to throw him off his balance." They criticized not the principles of difference and inequality, but possible psychological and behavioural results for Europeans of applying those principles. The Danish manager Werner Michael Iversen and his wife, who lived on Lima Belas plantation in Selangor during the 1930s, noticed that their eight-year-old son was beginning to give orders to servants and house staff. Worried that he was putting "on the airs of Master," they decided that he had to leave Malaya for boarding school in England "in order to not get the wrong ideas." Iversen, who described effective management as "working together" under conditions of "mutual trust" and respect, seems to have been atypical in his willingness to negotiate with estate labourers and to give them areas of self-governance and representation.[69]

Work relations, when seen from labourers' points of view, take on quite a different shape. Labourers did not write memoirs, but they left traces in colonial archives when they ran away, complained, sued, or went on strike. The legal system of British Malaya combined with its multi-state structure offered various opportunities to those struggling to survive the poverty and relentless discipline of plantation life. Although conflicts rarely erupted into large-scale violence, workers had ways to demonstrate hostility and to push back against the overarching authority of plantation masters.

Running away was one of the easiest ways to escape disliked discipline or the abuse of power. Long before the British arrived in Malaya, peasants unhappy with the rule of their raja would disappear, moving out of his territory, and the pattern continued through and beyond the era of indenture. Desertion or "absconding" from an estate remained by far the most frequently reported plantation "crime," even in the early twentieth century.[70] Mydeen Kutty Mydeen, who was born on a rubber estate in 1919, described his family's flight from a plantation in Pahang. His parents, who had emigrated from South India to work as tappers, were not happy on the plantation. Hearing about Singapore, they talked with other labourers about how to get there. Even after four years when their initial contract had long expired and they could give notice, the family felt they had to sneak away at night because the owners "would not approve," and "the estate owned their work contract" [*Dia tak benarkan; estet punya*

---

[69] Iversen, "Memories," pp. 31–42

[70] Michael Adas has written of "avoidance protest." See his article, "From Footdragging to Flight: the Evasive History of Peasant Avoidance Protest in South and Southeast Asia," *Journal of Peasant Studies*, Vol. 13 (1986), pp. 64–86; See also James C. Scott, *Weapons of the Weak: Everyday Forms of Peasant Resistance* (New Haven: Yale University Press, 2008); Marjoribanks and Marakkayar, *Indian Labour*, Appendix XVIA, p. 92

contract kerja situ]. The parents made their way one evening from the estate to a main road, where they and their two young children hitchhiked to Johore and then went on to Singapore to build a new life.[71] Thousands followed the same path from plantation to town, where they could find better-paying work and schools for their children. Thousands of others returned to India when contracts expired, whether or not they had saved much money to help and impress their families.

Workers also complained. The chance to vent dissatisfactions, whether to a visiting health inspector or to magistrates, probably brought satisfaction even if not redress. Colonial officials recorded formal charges and investigated, forcing managers and foremen to answer accusations in the District Office or local court. After running away from the Ayer Tawar Estate in Perak in the summer of 1914, seven labourers wrote to the local magistrate and to the Indian Immigration Agent in Madras, complaining of "brutal treatment." One man, Gopal, charged that he had been thrashed and kicked by his tindal and then caned by his manager, after he said he was feverish and too ill to work. Others complained of passports retained and illegal detention.[72] In the fall of 1917, Gopalasamy complained to Raja Omar in the Sitawan District Office that one month's wages had not been paid to him, after he and his wife gave notice to leave the Selene estate. His suit led nowhere because his manager claimed that he had not worked the requisite number of days in October, and Gopalasamy ceded the point, agreeing to work off the remainder of the contract, but his claim for wages had been recognized by the court. A legal case could be a call for help or a tactical move as individuals manoeuvred for advantage. By the mid-1920s, large numbers of plantation labourers went to court every year to charge that they had been assaulted or refused permission to quit their jobs. During the lean years of the late 1920s and 1930s, hundreds protested wrongful dismissal, and thousands objected that pay had been given late or withheld.[73] Complaints to the Labour

---

[71] Mydeen became a telephone operator and supervisor at the Singapore Naval Base. The official family memory of the estate concentrated on their escape from it and their difficulty learning how to leave and where to go. Mydeen Kutty Mydeen, 7 February 1990, Oral History Interviews, "Communities of Singapore," #A001117/05 (National Archive, Singapore)

[72] "Complaint against J. R. Harrod, Ayer Tawar Estate," 21 July 1914, Pejabat Daerah Sitiawan, 31/14; "Complaint of Gopalasamy, Selene Estate," 7 November 1917, Pejabat Daerah Sitiawan, 107/17; "Complaint against Munasamy, Kangany, of Mikal Rubber Estate," 17 February 1919; Pejabat Daerah Sitiawan 74/1919 (National Archives, Kuala Lumpur)

[73] Between 1925 and 1938, the total number of complaints registered with the Labour Department in the Federated Malay States increased from 1 for every 123 estate workers to 1 for every 72 workers. Parmer, *Labor Policy*, p. 276

Department against employers increased far more than the size of the plantation work force, indicating an increasing willingness to challenge managerial decisions. By the 1930s, the colonial state had retreated from a penal regime of plantation governance to one that actively recognized workers' legal rights and welfare commitments. Even if they had not yet established trade unions, labourers had begun to be more assertive in their efforts to protect themselves.

Attacks on employers could be masked as jokes or deflected by smiles. When questioned about her work digging drains on the Caledonia plantation in the mid-1940s, Muniammah remembered the hardness of the soil and the way her body ached. Dressed in immaculate white clothing, John St Maur Ramsden, who was the manager and heir to the Penang Rubber Estates as well as the family baronetcy, one day strode by her work gang. He stopped to talk, and the girls began to play, soon pelting him with mud from the drainage ditch. She claims that he laughed along with them, but no record of his response has survived. The incident still glowed in her memory more than sixty years later. Looking backward in time, she described him to me as a "nice man," who gave local children rides to school in his car and fed them breakfast, but her recollections contained hard nuggets, as well as the soft feelings she reported to an outsider.[74]

Attacks, of course, could be real fights with fists and sticks and rocks that drew blood. Planters liked to remember times when they deflected the blows of hostile tappers and forced them to back down, restoring proper hierarchy and discipline.[75] Plantation workers clearly had both the will and the capacity to fight back well before labour unions multiplied on estates during the late 1930s. William Shellabear, who employed an Indian foreman and sometimes a European missionary to oversee his small rubber estate and one owned by the Methodist church in Perak, reported a series of labour conflicts in his letters to family members. In 1910, Chinese work gangs employed to cultivate new land went on strike until he threatened them with jail and loss of wages, and in 1912, a group of Chinese tappers struck, demanding a lighter work load. Shellabear immediately hired some Tamils as strike breakers. In 1911 a Chinese tapper attacked a Chinese minister who was acting as an assistant manager of the Methodist plantation while they were out in the fields. This attack led to his arrest and prosecution. Shellabear's letters convey a sense of intermittent, but simmering contestation: rubber seedlings disappeared from the nursery; Tamil workers harassed him as he bicycled

---

[74] Interview with Muniammah, Caledonia Plantation, Perak, Malaysia, 4 January 2009. She spoke in Tamil, which was translated by her great-great nephew, Vithubalan, who was with her during my visit.

[75] Ainsworth, *Confessions*, pp. 45–46, 183–189

around Sitiawan. His desire for conflict-free cultivation and ample rubber profits never materialized.[76] As entry into rubber cultivation expanded, so too did the willingness of workers to stand up for themselves. Even without trades unions, labourers started to explore strategies of self-defence that challenged the power of managers.

The low-level power struggles on estates and rural roads had an important outside participant: the colonial state. Across British Malaya, an array of district officers, magistrates, interpreters, and police were regularly drawn into conflicts. They not only enforced the law, but had the chance to interpret it, shaping local labour relations. As laws softened in the early twentieth century, British officials sometimes preferred conciliation to threats, even in the case of strikes. In February of 1911, three Bengali watchmen on the Gading estate near Melaka "ill-treated" two Chinese estate workers, provoking them and about 150 of their compatriots to run the watchmen off the property and into the jungle. The manager vanished too, unwilling to deal with them. The next day, the workers went on strike and marched to the town of Jasim, demanding justice, but two Malay police blocked the road and tried to force them to return to work. Obviously outnumbered, a policeman panicked and fired his gun, wounding a striker. As a fight began, more police arrived and rushed the two constables away into a waiting car. The police then retreated and allowed the strikers to march down the muddy road to Jasim, where they camped out and waited to be heard. A young officer from the Malayan Civil Service, Alan Baker, was told to "settle the trouble if he could" and call for Sikh reinforcements if he could not. Baker drove up with an interpreter the next morning and ordered breakfast for all. Big buckets of rice and pork and pots of coffee soon simmered over a wood fire. While Baker questioned the strikers, police moved out to find the Bengali watchmen who had started the trouble. Later in the day, Baker presided over a short trial in the packed hall of the local courthouse. To the great delight of the Chinese workers, Baker convicted the watchmen and "had them chained and taken through the coolies and placed in the lock-up." Baker then walked with the strikers part of the way back to their estate, talking with the foremen and ordering the police escort to stay in the background. As far as he was concerned, the matter was settled, and the workers seemed to be satisfied too.[77] Twenty

[76] "Letter of William Shellabear to Emma Shellabear, 29 June 1909," 78016, "Letter W. S. to Emma Shellabear, 27 January 1910," 78070, "Letter of W. S. to Emma Shellabear, 2 June 1910," 78100, "Letter of W.S. to Margaret and Fanny Shellabear," 10 January 1911, 78165, "Letter of W.S. to Emma Shellabear, 22 January 1912," 78223, "Letter of W.S. to Hugh Shellabear, 31 January 1912," 78225, in Missionary Files, 1107-5-3.3 (Methodist Archive, Drew University)

[77] "Letter Alan Baker to Constance Baker, February 8, 1911," PP MS 11, box 3, file 13 (SOAS archive)

years earlier, this confrontation would probably have ended differently, with jail terms for the leading strikers. In the rubber era, however, when the need for both workers and what they produced rose, British colonial courts became more willing to enforce workers' contractual rights, and state officials sometimes responded sympathetically to workers' complaints.

Plantation colonialism, born in Malaya out of the collapse of slavery in the West Indies, moved slowly away from the penal regime of the sugar era and more toward industrial models of negotiation, which the state reinforced with limited welfare legislation. While imbalances in power remained extreme, short-term contracts, higher wages, and free passage to Malaya gave estate workers by the 1920s greater autonomy and bargaining power. Without large debts to repay, they could and did leave their jobs and look for better ones. While their political rights were limited, their rights under labour law increased, and many pushed to exercise those rights. Even if heavy disciplines and racial hierarchies dominated daily routines, estates were becoming healthier and less-harsh places to live. After World War I, the growing power of discourses and organizations supporting human rights and social welfare policies added pressure on the British government to move away from its strong collaboration with rubber companies. The League of Nations and the International Labour Organization added a degree of international publicity and investigation of local conditions, which governments could find uncomfortable.[78] Nationalists, humanitarian reformers, and Marxist internationalists raised their anti-colonial voices and prodded the British government to live up to public commitments to protect its colonial subjects. The production of rubber not only changed the land and the demographics of British Malaya; it also adjusted upward the aspirations and opportunities for the entire colonial population.

Alternative Worlds of Rubber

The social world of rubber encompassed far more than rich managers and impoverished labourers. A focus on stark oppositions, whether of race, money, property, or power, misses the growing numbers of those who lived between the extremes. Rubber production helped to create a multi-ethnic group of literate male employees and independent contractors who became the core of the Malaysian middle classes in the post-war period. As the industry expanded, its impact extended well beyond plantation boundaries. Aspiring Chinese set up shops near estates to sell rice,

---

[78] Susan Pedersen, *The Guardians: The League of Nations and the Crisis of Empire* (Oxford: Oxford University Press, 2015)

clothing, toddy, and provisions, while others started bus and cart services or worked with steamship companies transporting labourers. A penumbra of suppliers surrounded estates, building small businesses around their needs. Plantations needed clerks, assistants, and bookkeepers. They employed teachers, doctors, dressers, and, later, midwives, whose incomes, attitudes, and education separated them from the labourers. European estates and agency houses needed staff literate in English who could communicate with managers and owners, and they also desired employees who could speak one or more Chinese dialects to the Chinese labourers and foremen who cleared the land and watched over the seedlings. The urban Anglo-Chinese and English-language schools were obvious recruiting grounds because their graduates were multi-lingual and had training in math and science. Because families had invested heavily in education so that their sons would not become labourers, rubber estate offices offered a visible pathway into management jobs and middle-income work (see Figure 5.2). Town schools taught rural

1. Charles Elliot. Manager of Henrietta Estate later on the board of Plantation Holdings.   2. C S Wah. Chief Clerk
3. Assistants   4. Conductors.

Figure 5.2 Managers and staff of the Henrietta plantation in Kedah in front of the estate's office, 1927

boys urban ways. Estate staff were geographically and socially mobile. Rubber helped to finance their rise while grounding them in the structures of colonial rule and the global economy. They were men in the middle who had to function within the hierarchical world of plantation colonialism but who had learned the ways of urban cosmopolitanism and internalized some of its values.

Such employees came of age learning the rules of plantation colonialism, which mandated separation by ethnicity and by status. Joseph Chopard, a Eurasian man educated at St Joseph's Institution in Singapore, spent childhood summers on a rubber estate managed by his uncle, who lived in a large bungalow. His friends were the doctor's children, not those of the tappers, whose religion and language marked them as different.[79] Natesan Panevelu described his social isolation when he worked as a clerk and Tamil teacher between 1928 and 1930 on the relatively small Bajan Pasir Estate near Teluk Anson. He earned $55 per month, a "very big salary in those days" which set him apart from the "very simple ... very poor" Tamil labourers. In his eyes, estate life was "boring" because he had no friends: "I cannot go to the labourers, it is very difficult." Differences of status weighed more heavily than similarity of language and religion. But he was not really alone. One of his uncles managed the estate and another kinsman, whom he called a "brother," served as chief clerk. Another uncle, who had left India much earlier, had prospered and owned shops in the Klang area, as well as several small estates. This family, originally farmers in South India, found the rubber industry a road into the Malayan middle classes.[80] Following a similar pattern, Chinese clerks and accountants who normally lived with their families separate from the labourers found they could save money and then invest it in rubber land, opening their own small plantations with the aid of kin.

The availability of cheap land from the government or private buyers provided what seemed an easy path to wealth and higher status. During the rubber boom, those who could save a bit invested in land, which could be turned into an estate with tappers and field hands under one's command or farmed with family labour. Managers, office clerks, preachers,

---

[79] Joseph Chopard, born in 1912, was a Roman Catholic who became a draughtsman for the Public Works Department and later the Air Ministry in Singapore. Joseph Henry Chopard, 12 August 1985, Oral History Interviews, "The Communities of Singapore," # 000561 (National Archives Singapore)

[80] Palanivelu, who had finished secondary education in India, soon left the plantation for Singapore where he became a writer of Tamil plays and poetry and eventually worked for Radio Singapore; Interview of Natesan Palanivelu, 2 August 1985, Oral History Interviews, "The Communities of Singapore," # 000588113 (National Archive Singapore)

and teachers of all nationalities leapt to the bait. Leopold Ainsworth shifted from assistant to "man of property" by buying 10 acres already planted in rubber trees from a Malay. He immediately hired tappers and began sending smoked sheets to the Penang market. A few months later, a Chinese merchant bought the property from him for a much higher price and took over the estate. Several of the Penang Sugar Estate managers and assistants bought land around 1900, relishing the leap from employee to owner.[81] Malays planted rubber trees too, and then sold off the fields to others at a high profit. Land and trees were commodities, which enriched their purchasers.

A shift into middling status in Malaya via rubber could occur over an individual's life cycle as well as between generations. In contrast to the vast numbers of labourers who died young or returned to their homeland, the successful were survivors, and some left an archival trail or have descendants who remember them. Chin Teik Boon, a Teochew who emigrated to Malaya around 1936 at the age of 16, began working as a tapper on the Byram estate, but he was soon promoted to be a supervisor. Literate in Mandarin, he gained a reputation as hardworking and trustworthy. By 1941, Chin had saved some money, married, and started a family in Nibong Tebal. By pooling resources with his wife's father and brother, he later bought land from the Penang Rubber Estates and started his own small plantation. Chin's aspirations became those of an urban property owner. A son-in-law, Tang Juay Chai, went to a local Methodist school where he learned English and made friends from other ethnic groups.[82] For him, the Byram rubber estate was a place where he and his Malay, Chinese, and Indian companions went to collect fighting fish, not a site where he experienced ethnic segregation and heavy discipline. Tang Juay Chai had moved into a more cosmopolitan world of mixed ethnicities and wider horizons. Education, knowledge of English, and capital moved the Tang family into the middle ranks of Malayan society.

Golden hopes and dividend cheques tied a growing circle of investors to Malaysian plantations. While the Ramsden family controlled a majority of shares in their joint stock companies, they allocated shares to their clerks, as well as directors and friends in Malaya. Estate managers also demanded and received shares, making them part owners of the lands on which they lived. Asians soon rushed to invest in the Ramsden companies too. Tam King Keng and Averba Subgaran Pillay, both planters based in

[81] Ainsworth, *Confessions*, pp. 86–88; Straits Sugar Company, "Letter J. Turner to J. Arnold, 4 April 1899," in PSE, "Letters and Papers," Vol. 24, part 2, n.p. MSS. 644.1 p19 (APS)
[82] Interview with Tang Tsen Tsen, Nibong Tebal 1/11/2009. Three generations of the family have remained in Nibong Tebal, living next door to the grandfather's two-storey house.

Penang, bought Straits Rubber stocks, as did several Chinese merchants from Singapore. O. J. M. Meyappa Chitty, a South Asian moneylender from Nibong Tebal, owned over 200 shares in 1910. In Malaya, skilled workers and civil servants, miners and nurses – all aspiring rentiers – purchased a few shares of Straits Rubber stock.[83] The Ramsden companies bound together Europeans, Eurasians, Chinese, and Indians not only in their operation but also in the hopes of good fortune and social mobility through rubber. Individuals drawn from multiple ethnicities, colonies, and countries acquired indirectly a stake in plantation colonialism, admittedly of different strengths and degrees of advantage.

The climbing price of rubber in comparison to the market values of coffee, gambier, sugar, and rice tempted farmers throughout the colony to substitute *Hevea* trees for their other crops early in the century. In the state of Johore, groups of Chinese farmers who had cleared the jungle for the planting of pepper and gambier lived in self-governing communities (*kang*) which were run by their headmen (*kangchu*), generally kinsmen from their home villages. The Sultan of Johore, Abu Bakar, who was eager to develop his state, encouraged immigrants by giving their headmen rights to occupy land as well as to collect taxes. By the early twentieth century, farmers had begun to plant rubber trees, shifting their fields as soon as they could to a more profitable product, which was also easier to grow. Yap Ah Bai, who had immigrated to Malaya as a teenager, was taken in by his extended family and offered work first as a stable boy and later as the manager of a prosperous *kang* in the interior of Johore. Soon rubber was the community's chief export, and Yap Ah Bai was persuaded by a visiting Christian missionary to give his son, Yap Pheng Geck, a western-style education. Yap Pheng Geck and the son of another kang staff member left the jungle for Singapore to be enrolled in the Anglo-Chinese School, although they returned regularly during vacations. Pheng Geck later earned a doctorate at the University of Hong Kong and eventually became a banker in Singapore.[84] Rubber profits supported his family's aspirations for their son; transportation networks permitted movement between inland settlements and the larger towns; the English-language schools were well enough known and trusted to be used by Chinese families with resources. Pheng Geck's education made him fluent in different cultural languages and eased his way into the Malayan middle classes.

Missionaries in Malaya, as well as in Sarawak on the island of Borneo, were active partners of the colonial state and its support for

---

[83] Straits Rubber Company, "Summary of Share Capital and Shares of Straits Rubber, 31 Dec. 1910," #22, BT 31/19144/106542 (National Archive, London)

[84] Yap Pheng Geck, *Scholar, Banker, Gentleman Soldier* (Singapore: Times Books International, 1982)

economic development. Not only did Roman Catholics and Methodists settle Indian and Chinese Christians on land bought or granted by British authorities, but priests and pastors, as well as schools and churches, were important middlemen between Christian immigrant communities and the colonial administration.[85] In September 1903, 363 Chinese farmers arrived in Sitiawan, Perak in the company of Dr H. L. E. Leuring and Reverend Ling Ching Mi, two Methodist missionaries, to set up an agricultural colony on undeveloped land. G. T. Hare, the Secretary of Chinese Affairs in the Federated Malay States, had brokered a deal between the American Methodist Episcopal Mission and the Perak government for subsidized immigration from Fujian province in China for farmers who would promise to grow rice. Then missionaries collected a large group of Foochow-speaking Christian converts eager to emigrate in return for land, free passage, and low-interest loans. The initial group – much depleted by a cholera epidemic as well as defections sparked by rumours of marauding Malayan tigers and giant ants – had to trek several miles inland across swampy marshes. Unfortunately, they found that colonial authorities had reneged on important promises. Their plots had been neither surveyed nor drained, and families received only 3, rather than 10, acres of land. Crammed into a few palm-leaf longhouses, the settlers had to build their own homes and clear trees before any crops could be planted. Soon the idea of rice growing evaporated in the tropical heat; sweet potatoes and pigs initially seemed smarter choices.[86]

But the Foochow group's arrival coincided with the beginning of the rubber boom, and nearby landowners had already begun to try the new crop. When Reverend B. F. Van Dyke arrived in 1904 to take charge of a Methodist mission school and a planned orphanage, he noticed local Malays tapping their own rubber trees and began to boost its cultivation. Both Rev. W. E. Horley, who led the Methodist Mission to Perak, and William Cowan, the Perak Protector of Chinese (Chinese Affairs Officer), became early enthusiasts of rubber planting, as did Foo Choo Choon, the millionaire Hakka tin miner and industrialist who had supported the original Foochow immigration scheme. These three men brought the Foochow farmers together and lectured them, effectively it seems, on the virtues of rubber

---

[85] Father Fee, "Kampong Padre: A Tamil Settlement near Bagan Serai Perak," *JMBRAS*, Vol. 36, Pt. 1 (1963), pp. 153–181; Craig Alan Lockard, *From Kampung to City: A Social History of Kuching, Malaysia, 1820–1870* (Athens, Ohio: Ohio University Center for International Studies, 1987), pp. 97–103

[86] Shih Toong Siong, *The Foochows of Sitiawan* (Sitiawan: Persatuan Kutien Daerah Manjung, c. 2005), pp. 46–53, 62–66. The text of the agreement between A. R. Venning, Acting Resident of Perak, H. L. E. Leuring, and W. Cowan, dated 7 May 1903 is reproduced on pp. 306–312.

planting. To lead the shift, the Methodist Church ordered its 10-acre plot to be given over to *Hevea* trees, and it purchased an additional 203 acres for rubber growing under the supervision of their resident missionary. Soon the Foochows' plots and those of the mission's plantation were covered by rubber seedlings, and both settlers and pastors learned the intricacies of rubber tapping and cultivation, intertwining the fates of the mission and the Christian immigrants.[87]

Between 1905 and 1930, smallholdings and tiny plantations multiplied in western Malaya like woodland mushrooms after a rain. Thousands of people had cast their lot with rubber. The 1931 census report estimated that approximately one-third of the working population of British Malaya engaged in rubber cultivation. A generous deduction for those employed by large plantations (over 100 acres) yields a figure of 356,000 people who worked on or owned a small rubber holding, most of which were under 20 acres and used family labour. This group constituted 18 per cent of all those employed in agriculture throughout the peninsula.[88]

By 1930, smallholdings of under 100 acres produced at least 47 per cent of the total crop and accounted for 39 per cent of total acreage (see Table 5.2). The smallest holdings of less than 10 acres produced roughly a third of all planted rubber. Their Malay and Chinese owners combined rubber growing with a mixture of other crops and family businesses.[89] It was a good strategy that brought added protection during depression years. Although European planters belittled these smallholding operations as uneconomic and technologically backward, smallholders sustained their production. Moreover, their yields per acre remained higher than those of their European competitors. Malay smallholdings had on average between 210 and 400 trees per acre, in comparison to only 150 on a large European estate. Despite charges from British agricultural officers that smallholders used destructive tapping methods, evidence from the 1930s suggested that smallholders produced more rubber per acre at less cost with simpler methods.[90]

---

[87] Foo Choo Choon bought 3,000 acres adjoining the Methodist concession and set up his own rubber estate in 1905. Shih, *Foochows*, pp. 103, 204–205. The Christian roots of the settlement ran deep, and the number of Christian churches in the area grew through the 1930s, financed by parishioners; Shih, *Foochows*, pp. 65, 83–84, 88, 94, 128–129

[88] C. A. Vlieland, *British Malaya: a Report on the 1931 Census* (London: Crown Agents for the Colonies, 1932), p. 96

[89] By 1922, over 2,200,000 acres in British Malaya were planted in rubber, 40.6 per cent of which were in estates of fewer than 100 acres and smallholdings of under 10 acres; Drabble, *Rubber*, pp. 216–217

[90] Yields per acre on smallholdings during a period of unrestricted tapping were probably around 500 lb per acre, while on estates yields have been calculated as averaging 284 lbs. per acre in the 1920s and 409 lbs. in the early 1930s; Drabble, *Malayan Rubber*, pp. 54, 87, 92–93, 98

Table 5.2 *Rubber Production in Peninsular Malaya, 1910–1940*

	Estates			Smallholders						
Year	Output	Area	Yield	Output	Area	Yield	Total output	Os/Ot	Total area	As/At
1910	?	173	?	?	46	?		?	219	21%
1920	?	539	365	?	344	496		?	883	39%
1930	238	763	424	218	483	562	456	47%	1,246	39%
1940	382	843	463	216	543	426	598	36%	1,386	39%

Source: This data is taken from Colin Barlow, "Changes in the Economic Position of Workers on Rubber Estates and Smallholdings in Peninsular Malaysia, 1910–1985," in Peter J. Rimmer and Lisa M. Allen, eds., *The Underside of Malaysian History: Pullers, Prostitutes, Plantation Workers* (Singapore: National University of Singapore Press, 1990), pp. 26–27. The figures for output are in thousands of tons, the area planted is measured in thousands of planted hectares, and the yield is measured as kilograms per hectare of planted mature rubber. Os/Ot calculates the percentage of total output constituted by smallholders' output; As/At calculates the percentage of total acreage constituted by smallholdings planted in rubber.

Rubber soon became a major source of family income among Asian farmers in British Malaya, who combined its cultivation with other crops and wage-earning activities. It bankrolled the educations of their children while increasing standards of living in rural areas. In the 1920s, Sitiawan children came to their school anniversaries dressed in immaculate white shirts and shorts, their hair carefully cut. The Uk Ing School in Kampong China even financed a drum corps whose members sported military style caps and jackets (see Figure 5.3). Shops multiplied in the commercial centres of Sitiawan, where families could buy textiles, tobacco, shoes, tools, and books. Some of the families had religious pictures and texts on their walls, and a small library of books was set up by the mission, using Sunday school donations.[91] Rubber income brought the Foochows to urban patterns of consumption and financed children's education.

When the price of rubber rose, so did the resources of local settlers, some of which were poured back into Methodist institutions via Sunday offerings and "first fruit" donations of early tapping profits. Together, Foochow families funded schools, pastors' salaries, and new church buildings. Some of the pastors helped to tap mission land and increased church income. The core of the Sitiawan settlement was the Pioneer Methodist Church, whose simple but elegant neo-Gothic structure still

[91] Drabble, *Malayan Rubber*, pp. 85, 138–139; Shih, *Foochows*, pp. 84–85, 132–133

Figure 5.3 Uk Ing School teachers, pupils, and band, 1920

serves as the centre of the local Christian community. Its clergy acted as communal leaders (*Ketua Pastor*). They settled disputes, maintained order, and handled the complexities of loan repayments and quit rents for the Perak government. The community church leadership pledged to keep the settlement free from gambling, opium, and spirit shops, substituting its own brand of recreation centred on saints' days and parish festivals. Settlers drank literally from the well of the church, a source not only of drinking water but also the moral and spiritual underpinning of daily life.[92]

Although both types of rubber production were enterprises subsidized and partially set up by the colonial state, the Foochow smallholdings had little in common with the European-owned plantations. The Chinese smallholdings were relatively egalitarian: Foochow family units all began with the same amount of land and loans. Each had its own small house with a palm leaf roof near others of their dialect group, sited in clusters along the primitive roads that settlers had hacked out of the surrounding jungle. Relative equality of work and income existed during the early decades of the settlement. Even Chinese pastors raised rubber and spent much of their time tapping and weeding. Family labour was

[92] Shih, *Foochows*, pp. 65, 85, 128–129

used as much as possible, with households making the decisions about how densely to plant the trees, when and how often to tap, and how to divide and schedule tasks. No doubt children helped with multiple chores, but they were expected to learn to read and write at one of the many small, dialect-specific Chinese schools organized soon after arrival. While they came to depend on rubber for most of their income, local families raised pigs and probably vegetables too, which women took into the town market on Sundays. They were a community of peasant proprietors, who eventually moved many of their children into positions of middling status in British Malaya. Their Chinese and Methodist identities provided the Foochows with a layer of local institutions largely under their own control, which shielded them from the British colonial government and the rigid hierarchies of plantation life.[93]

A similar independence marked the Johore smallholding settlement where Yap Pheng Geck spent much of his childhood. He described a largely self-governing community of about 700 people, which managed its temples, schools, and burial grounds and organized local ritual life. Yet the settlement was neither a staid garden city nor a proto-democracy. Evening entertainment centred on the gambling hall, the opium shop, and the bars, all of which were supplied and run by rich "farmers" who had paid handsomely for the privilege of earning money from a state monopoly. Inhabitants also had access to communal wells, public bathing spots, and a central public space. The community offered aid to poor and elderly neighbours by paying wages for simple service jobs, like cleaning streets. The Johore state administration kept out of day-to-day governance. Although he referred violent crimes to a local Malay headman who could turn offenders over to the police, the settlement's leader dealt with most disputes and offences. Yap defined the community's participatory government as "self-help and mutual help," a style diametrically opposed to that of the standard rubber plantation. The rubber industry therefore supported at least two different styles of governance: a hierarchical and authoritarian form on the large estates and more egalitarian, participatory structures that grew up among smallholders, who used neighbourhood and religious institutions to learn about leadership and to practice local control. At the same time, it introduced plantation staff and the more affluent smallholders to modern styles of consumption and financed

---

[93] "Letter William Shellabear to Emma Shellabear, 20 June 1909," 78013, Missionary Files 1107-5-3.3 (Methodist Archive, Drew University); Shih, *Foochows*, p. 172; virtually all of the early pastors were Chinese, as were school governing committees and most of the teachers. The Christian Foochows remain today in the Sitiawan area, clustered around their Methodist churches and the Anglo-Chinese School, outliving the rubber industry in Perak.

children's educations. The rubber industry taught both political and cultural lessons to those of middling status who depended on it for their disposable income. The contradictions in rubber's messages were inherent in the British colonial enterprise in Malaya.

Surviving the Slump

Wherever one worked in Malaya, the economic instability of the interwar years brought hard times. When the demand for automobile tyres collapsed in the United States after the stock market crashed in 1929, so did the major market for Malayan rubber. Exports of that product from Singapore shrank in value by 84 per cent between 1929 and 1932.[94] During the worst years, the larger plantations kept tapping at full capacity to maximize sales, retreating to selective production only when markets became flooded. Malayan estates plunged into frenzied cutting of costs, trying to maintain profitability. Managers fired labourers and staff, while increasing workloads of those who remained. Half the Indian estate workers in both the Straits Settlements and the Federated Malay States lost their jobs between 1929 and 1932. Over 75,000 Chinese and 190,000 Indians left Malaya at government expense between 1930 and 1932, and thousands more paid for their own passage back to India or China. Most of the remaining workers had their state-mandated wage rates cut substantially from 50 to 30 cents a day for men and from 40 to 25 cents for women, which was considered to cover subsistence needs in 1932. The Controller of Labour agreed to the cuts, even though he admitted that the more unscrupulous planters and agency house employees pushed wages even lower than the cost of subsistence. His efforts to challenge these cuts had little success.[95] Although companies forced each worker to become more productive, the human toll was considerable. Draconian methods helped the estates to survive and even to pay low dividends during most of the interwar period. Although there were no new methods introduced to lower costs, managers muddled through the depression by restricting workers' incomes and increasing their workloads.

Smallholders and the owners of the smaller estates survived using strategies different from those of the plantations. Anyone with cultivatable land had some protection against the collapse of rubber prices. Since many Malay farmers already raised vegetables and fruits, they could expand their attention to food crops and cut back on tapping, thereby

---

[94] For the impact of World War I on the Malayan rubber industry, see Drabble, *Rubber*, pp. 123–150, 213, 227

[95] Parmer, *Labor Policy*, pp. 185, 202–203, 242, 272; Drabble, *Malayan Rubber*, pp. 18–24, 81–83

lowering their dependence on rubber revenues. Alternatively, they could expand output and devise ways to market it even during times of restriction. Even during the worst years of the slump, peasant smallholders found that rubber production continued to be profitable. Because the colonial state had little information on what and how much they produced, effective control of their output was difficult if not impossible to maintain. Chinese entrepreneurs adopted a different way of lowering their risk when building a rubber estate in a time of extreme price fluctuations. With limited capital at their disposal, they invested far less in their plantations than did European owners. They negotiated sharecropping agreements with small farmers who worked the land for free in return for the right to plant cash crops – normally pineapples – amid the rubber trees. The owners and the labourers then split the profits of the seasonal crops. Even after trees grew to maturity, cash crops could be used to compensate for low rubber prices.[96] Since the colonial government treated both of these groups less well than they did European companies when allocating production quotas, the owners of small farms or estates had little incentive to be grateful to their rulers. Fighting for more marketing coupons cannot have deepened their loyalty to the British Empire.

The economic troubles of the rubber industry between the two world wars revealed not only vulnerability produced by heavy dependence on international trade but also the limited power of the colonial government to protect workers and smallholders, who primarily had to fend for themselves. Although the smallholding half of the rubber industry remained normally outside the gaze of colonial officials, their problems came into view through colonial courts, whose judges regularly dealt with debt cases. In a time and place of weak local financial institutions, South Asian chettiar banking firms were major sources of capital for Chinese, Indian, and Malay landowners turned away by the larger European banks. Short-term loans at high interest rates led all too often, however, to default and foreclosures, at which point the colonial state ratified the claims of the despised moneylenders.[97] During decades when hundreds of thousands of people flocked into rubber production and deepened their contacts with the colonial state, the responses of the British government

[96] Lim Teck Ghee, *Peasants and their Agricultural Economy in Colonial Malaya 1874–1941* (Kuala Lumpur: Oxford University Press, 1977), pp. 187, 191–192; W. G. Huff, "Sharecroppers, Risk, Management, and Chinese Estate Rubber Development in Interwar British Malaya," *Economic Development and Cultural Change*, Vol. 40, No. 4 (1992), pp. 743–773
[97] District Office Files, Sitiawan 74/18; Sitiawan 667–76/25 (Arkib Negara, Kuala Lumpur); Ho Tak Ming, *Ipoh: When Tin Was King* (Ipoh: Perak Academy, 2009), pp. 91–94

to the economic needs of its subjects were relatively weak. Unhappiness simmered in a world of open inequalities and colonial privilege.

Unemployment brought the problems of the rubber industry into the towns. When jobs vanished on the plantations, housing rights disappeared too. Thousands found themselves adrift and in search of work. Singapore and Penang, whose ports offered labouring jobs as well as the possibility of passage home, were obvious targets, but so were the other larger settlements, where there was demand for servants, rickshaw pullers, and hawkers of food. In 1930, homeless workers settled under the bridges in Ipoh, and others built a shantytown in an outlying field near a rubber estate. In Kuala Lumpur, a government-run home for elderly and decrepit labourers sheltered a few of the needy, but most had to fend for themselves in a colony that lacked welfare entitlements. The government considered poor Indian, Chinese, and Javanese to be foreigners whose rights to remain were contingent upon employment; therefore repatriation was considered the most appropriate response to their distress. Between 1930 and 1933 about one-third of Malaya's Indian residents (243,000) left the country, and there was a net outflow of 443,000 Chinese from Singapore from 1931 to 1933. While mass emigration eased the unemployment problem, many were caught in a poverty trap – too poor to afford a return fare and not entitled to free passage at government expense. Towns were their best refuge, where they could at least scavenge food from market cast-offs and build mud huts on empty land.[98] Colonial authorities turned neither to public works nor to welfare payments, but expected the unemployed to shape up or ship out. It is difficult to exaggerate the importance of rubber cultivation to British Malaya. For decades the dominant business in the Federated Malay States, rubber reshaped the peninsula's population, its social organization, and its consumption patterns. Moreover, rubber was a truly global industry. Seeds originally from Brazil grew in soil cleared and cultivated by Malays, Chinese, and Tamils. British chemists and machinery processed rubber latex, which Chinese and European merchants then marketed and sent to factories in Europe and North America. Profits circulated to shareholders and owners throughout Eurasia and the Americas. The politics of rubber spread outward from day-to-day power struggles on the plantations to company headquarters in cities throughout the British Empire and to government offices in Kuala Lumpur, Singapore, Delhi, and London. The Rubber Growers' Association aggressively lobbied for planters'

---

[98] W. G. Huff, "Entitlements, Destitution, and Emigration in the 1930s Singapore Great Depression," *Economic History Review*, Vol. 54, No. 2 (2001), pp. 290–323; Ho, *Ipoh*, pp. 563, 572–573, 579

interests, while the leading merchant houses happily added retired colonial officials to their boards of directors. Plantation managers, such as William Duncan of the Penang Rubber Estates, helped mould immigration and labour policies through their service on government committees and the Federal Council of the Federated Malay States.[99] Eventually workers widened political conversations about rubber as they learned to strike and to use the courts to their advantage. The politics of rubber involved every ethnic group in British Malaya, extending to those living in urban as well as those in rural areas.

Rubber politics comprised far more than struggles over resources and power. The industry represented the colonial state in British Malaya – its technological expertise, its global markets, and its commitment to rising, international standards of workers' welfare, as guaranteed by inspection and contract. When that framework cracked, so did the attraction of British control. The paternalist pledges of the colonial government outran its capacity for their enforcement. In the Federated Malay States, not only were jurisdictions divided, but planters' lobbies often resisted state policies, and the economic slumps of the interwar years were ruinous. What remained constant were the ethnic divisions, and inequalities embedded in plantation work regimes. If sugar planted a harsh, hierarchical empire in rural Malaya, plantation rubber cultivated its growth by identifying colonial rule with unfree labour, endemic violence, and racial separation. Independent smallholders saw this pattern of production from the outside, but they had to have absorbed its messages. Moreover, during the depression they experienced the colonial state primarily as an impediment that limited production and collected fees while giving little in return. Rubber both sustained and undermined British colonial rule in Malaya.

---

[99] Tate, *RGA History*, pp. 248–250; "Planters Past and Present," *The Planter*, Vol. 1, No. 2 (September 1920), p. 1

6   Cosmopolitan Modernity

In December 1936, hundreds of people crowded into the coffee shops and open-air restaurants of central Taiping to celebrate Race Day. Music and alcohol lured many young people into the Palladium Dance Hall, a popular spot owned by a syndicate of Chinese and Eurasians. Hostesses, available as dance partners, smiled to signal availability, while waiters wove through the room with rounds of beer, whisky, and lemonade. European couples sat near tables of Chinese and South Asian men. Jal Manecksha, a merchant who was probably a South Asian Muslim, came that evening with several Chinese friends: Lim Eng Hong, a teacher in a government English school; Tan Cheng Leng, a medical doctor; and Lye Kan Chow, a local businessman. Well-dressed in suits and ties, they wanted to have a good time. After several hours of drinking and dancing, Lim Eng Hong wished to waltz, so he hopped up on the stage to request a piece from the orchestra, but the annoyed manager asked him to get down and leave the hall. Lim refused, supposedly shouting "Eurasian bastard, swine, and dog." In the next few minutes, fighting broke out. Ashtrays were smashed and chairs lifted into the air before Chinese bouncers escorted Lim and Manecksha outside. They made the situation worse by calling the bartender, Mervyn Lessler, the bastard "son of a Malay prostitute." Accounts of who started punching first differ, but a nasty brawl between Manecksha and Lessler ended in arrests. Police charged and fined Manecksha for assault. This particular dispute then disappeared from the historical record, although multi-ethnic crowds continued to flock to the Palladium.

Most accounts of cosmopolitan friendships stress harmony and cross-cultural understanding, but such relationships also included conflict. These men who fought were schoolmates and friends. Some had moved into the professions and others had ordinary service jobs, but they stayed in contact with one another. Sexual and racial insults were hurled within a long-standing network of multi-ethnic sociability. The Chinese and South Asian men who appeared in court described their relationship as "one for all and all for one." Lessler, probably a Christian of mixed

218

ancestry, was a former pupil of Lim Eng Hong. His and Manecksha's families were close enough for their mothers to call one another "kaca" and "achi-achi" – the Tamil terms for elder sister and mother or grand-mother. Although the major witnesses spoke English to the court, they were multilingual, able to function in at least two languages. One of the witnesses was a young Sikh landowner who said he knew Manecksha "quite well." Tan Thye Thong, a local insurance agent, said he had been acquainted with Manecksha since their school days. Musa bin Junus, the manager's chauffeur, who supported his employer's story, said he had known Manecksha for almost ten years. This group of immigrant Chinese, Punjabis, Bengalis, Malays, Tamils, and Eurasians in Taiping had a long local history of friendly encounters and conversations. They banded together to play, not to denounce the colonial state.[1] By the 1930s, many educated males functioned easily in multicultural, multi-lingual urban environments. Commercial culture, not nationalism, drew them outside their ethnic groups. Nevertheless, their cosmopolitanism fractured during a night of shared drinking and dancing, when racist taunts trumped friendship. Colonial cosmopolitanism coexisted along-side persistent divisions and disputes over power and belonging. Empires ruled over divided populations; they did not homogenize them into citizens with equal rights and statuses. Towns brought together immi-grants of various ethnicities and religions who learned to deal with one another, but alliances sometimes collapsed and led to violence, as will become clear in Chapter 8.

This chapter explores social life in multicultural Malayan towns in the 1920s and 1930s. It uses literacy, language, education, entertainment, and associations as windows into a cosmopolitan, civil society open to people from multiple ethnic groups. Print culture combined with modern forms of sociability drew educated townspeople into a new, engaged style of subjecthood, which straddled the line between loyalism and challenges to the colonial state. As civil society trained its members in social inter-actions, they debated its meaning, along with the forms of its practice.[2] How should British subjects and local citizens define their public

---

[1] "Jal Manecksha vs. Public Prosecutor," Magistrate's Court, Taiping; Summons Case, 207/1937, DPP No. 172/1937 (Arkib Negara, Kuala Lumpur)

[2] I define civil society as a realm distinct from the state and from the family, a third domain where modern liberal freedoms were developed. A public sphere is the arena where people come together to develop concepts of moral and political life; Sudipta Kaviraj and Sunil Khilnani, *Civil Society: History and Possibilities* (Cambridge: Cambridge University Press, 2001); Rajeev Bhargava and Helmut Reifeld, *Civil Society, Public Sphere, and Citizenship: Dialogues and Perceptions* (New Delhi, Thousand Oaks, and London: Sage Publications, 2005); Jürgen Habermas, *The Structural Transformation of the Public Sphere: An Inquiry into a Category of Bourgeois Society* (Cambridge, MA: MIT Press, 1991).

identities? Could cosmopolitan ties override the divisions among ethnic groups? The modern sectors of town life drew members into civic engagement, which led in this time and place to a redefinition of subjecthood and languages of belonging.

Urban Language Domains and the Impact of Literacy

People in the towns of British Malaya communicated through multilinguality and translation. Street signs in multiple scripts attracted the eyes, and the sounds of unfamiliar tongues flowed past in the air, forcing acknowledgement and tempting curiosity. While customers could point to a desired purchase, a few words of Malay would aid bargaining and diminish distance. Even immigrant rickshaw drivers had to be able to understand destinations when not spoken in Hokkien or Cantonese. A simplified spoken Malay served as a *lingua franca* for many day-to-day encounters, and enterprising Chinese traders learned Malay and possibly some English. Newcomers had to insert themselves in this linguistic pot pourri as best they could, but both the state and the international businesses invested in language training and services to serve their culturally diverse clients. Young British cadet civil servants had to pass exams in Malay to secure their positions, and a few were sent to various towns in China to become literate in a regional language, as well as in classical Chinese. Roman Catholic priests and Protestant missionaries learned the languages of those they wished to convert, running multilingual congregations and bilingual services. Government courts employed multiple translators, and business offices hired multilingual clerks and compradors.

Towns were multicultural mosaics of different language domains. In international business, mass entertainment, and civic ceremony, English linked its speakers into global networks and drew them into a transnational culture. At the same time, English became and has remained a local language in British Malaya – just as in India, Kenya, Jamaica, Puerto Rico, and the Philippines.[3] Particular spaces in Malaya had dominant languages: government offices and law courts functioned primarily in English and in Malay; ordinary shops and shopkeepers stuck to varieties of Chinese with different amounts of Malay or English added; Tamil and Punjabi were useful in the many toddy shops and transport services run by

[3] Robert Phillipson, *Linguistic Imperialism* (Oxford: Oxford University Press, 1992); Shefali Chandra, *The Sexual Life of English: Languages of Caste and Desire in Colonial India* (Durham, NC: Duke University Press, 2012); Christina Higgins, *English as a Local Language: Post-Colonial Identities and Multi-Lingual Practices* (Bristol: Multilingual Matters, 2009)

South Asians. Scattered around the towns were madrasas and vernacular schools, which functioned in Arabic, Malay, Tamil, and different forms of Chinese, although the most prestigious institutions either were Anglophone or functioned bilingually in English and Chinese. Calls to prayer in Arabic rang out from the mosques. Meanwhile, worshippers heard the languages of their faith in religious spaces: Gurmukhi in Sikh gurdwaras; Sanskrit or Tamil in Hindu sacred places; Cantonese or Teochew or Hokkien in each dialect group's temples. Cinemas and theatres tended to specialize in a particular culture's productions and languages, but they advertised multi-lingually. Coffee shops and bars drew in a polyglot set of customers who leaped language barriers to drink together. Pawnshops announced their services in multiple scripts, while brokers, if they wanted to draw in business, had to deal with customers who used various dialects and vernaculars. In Malaya, linguistic pluralism was part of the cultural landscape, which town dwellers confronted as best they could. Communication required good ears, a nimble tongue, and the flexibility to shift among the different vocabularies according to audience and setting.

Literacy was the easiest key to unlocking these multiple cultural doors, and by the 1930s, while literacy in British Malaya remained relatively low in comparison to western European countries, it was relatively high in comparison to India and China.[4] In the census of 1931, about 48 per cent of the adult male population of the Straits Settlements and the Federated Malay States claimed to be able to read and write at least one language. Among females over 15, the proportions in those two areas were much smaller – respectively, only 12 and 10 per cent – but the proportions were rising as schools expanded. Although virtually all Europeans and Eurasians were literate, the proportions dropped off sharply among Chinese, South Asians, and Malays (see Table 6.1). Nevertheless, the few figures available for the larger towns indicate that literacy was widespread among urban males of all ethnic groups, even though the drive to provide schooling for the mass of the population had begun in the Federated Malay States only in the twentieth century. Chinese parents wanted their sons to be literate, so

---

[4] A UNESCO analysis of census data estimated literacy rates in India in 1931 of 15 per cent among males and 2 per cent among females at a time when literacy rates in Britain exceeded 90 per cent; UNESCO, *Progress of Literacy in Various Countries: a Preliminary Study of Available Census Data since 1900* (Paris: UNESCO, 1953), Table 96, p. 110. In China, the Ministry of Education estimated a literacy rate in 1950 of between 15 and 25 per cent; Ted Plafker, "China's Long but Uneven March to Literacy," *New York Times*, 12 February 2001. Using a broader definition of literacy, Evelyn Rawski presents a much higher figure, estimating that 30–45 per cent of males were literate in 1900; Evelyn Sakakida Rawski, *Education and Popular Literacy in Ch'ing China* (Ann Arbor: University of Michigan Press, 1979), pp. 17–20.

Table 6.1 *Literacy in Selected Towns, 1931 (Percentage of Males over 15 Able to Read and Write)*

Town	Chinese	Indians	Malays	Europeans
Singapore	43	52	40	99
Penang	59	58	50	100
Kuala Lumpur	52	47	63	100
Kuala Kangsar	52	38	61	100
Seremban	54	30	58	100
Raub	60	43	50	100

Source: C. A. Vrieland, *A Report on the 1931 Census of British Malaya* (London: Crown Agents for the Colonies, 1931), Tables 146–156, pp. 329–339.
The proportions should be considered as approximate guides to the literacy proportions rather than precise statistics. We have no information on the levels of language expertise represented by these numbers, nor any estimate of the consistency with which census takers used this definition.

they privately funded local primary schools. By the 1930s, an increasing number of primary schools educated Chinese, Tamil, and Malay children in the villages and towns of the Straits Settlements and Federated Malay States.[5]

About half of the urban male population and a small proportion of urban women in British Malaya could participate in print culture. The literate could write letters, check contracts, and read the terms of a recorded loan payment. Advertisements dangled the delights of an international consumer culture before the eyes of the interested reader, who could see images of modern amenities such as automobiles and electric fans. Moreover, multilingual street signs and posters gave clues to the alternate language worlds that interpenetrated that of the reader's mother tongue. In bookshops, lending libraries, and newspapers, literate urbanites read Gandhi's words and learned of Japanese incursions into China. They entered worlds far beyond those of family or neighbourhood. Print culture not only broke through the boundaries of time and space but also brought access to multiple and even distant imagined communities.[6] Packages of newspapers from the larger towns went by railway and bus to bookshops scattered around the Federated Malay States. By the early

[5] Barbara Watson Andaya and Leonard Y. Andaya, *A History of Malaysia*, 2nd ed. (Houndsmill: Palgrave, 2001), pp. 226–235
[6] Benedict Anderson, *Imagined Communities: Reflections on the Origin and Spread of Nationalism*, rev. ed. (London: Verso Books, 2006)

1930s, it was possible to buy popular London periodicals and weekly papers in bookstores in the Straits Settlements, and even street hawkers carried them about. Chinese-run reading rooms in Malayan cities stocked Chinese literature and classics for their members.[7]

The wealth of resources available to the literate is signalled by the dozens of newspapers printed in British Malaya. William Roff located over 100 different Malay-language periodicals and newspapers printed between 1910 and 1940 in Singapore, Penang, Kuala Lumpur, Johore Baru, Ipoh, and other towns on the peninsula. Daily papers, such as *Utusan Melayu*, *Majlis*, and *Warta Malaya* had Malay Muslim editors, and they circulated widely among educated Malays who could read the Jawi script in which they were printed.[8] Several Tamil-language papers circulated from presses in Penang and Kuala Lumpur, while issues of 31 different Chinese papers, mostly published in Penang and Kuala Lumpur between 1910 and 1940, have survived. Dozens more were published in Singapore.[9] *Lat Pau* (Straits Newspaper) ran from 1882 until 1931, reproducing stories from Hong Kong and Shanghai papers to give readers a running account of Chinese politics, along with editorial commentaries. Its advertisements for cigarettes, alcohol, opera, and cures for venereal disease appealed to a conservative, well-educated male audience whose members could afford the 10-cent daily price.[10] When added to the many local and imported English-language periodicals, they offered urban readers a wealth of information about commerce, culture, and consumption, as well as political events both local and international. The Malay journalist Za'ba said that "Of an evening, one sees at the wayside Chinese shop some lettered man, perhaps an old guru of the local school or perhaps the local penghulu reading one or other of these papers, and a little crowd of elderly people less literate than he eagerly listening, questioning, and commenting around him."[11] Print culture, to which almost half of the urban population had direct access, spread its cosmopolitan messages to non-readers too. Its impact extended far beyond the elites of the colony.

---

[7] "Malaya's Reading Public," *Straits Times*, 3 September 1932, p. 14

[8] William R. Roff, *Guide to Malay Periodicals, 1876–1941* (Singapore: Eastern Universities Press, 1961), pp. 5–35. See also P. Lim Pui Huen, *Singapore, Malaysian and Brunei Newspapers: an International Union List* (Singapore: Institute of Southeast Asian Studies, 1992), pp. 59–74

[9] Lim Pui Huen, *Newspapers*, pp. 97–118

[10] I would like to thank Dr Leander Seah for pointing me to *Lat Pau* and outlining its importance.

[11] Zainal Abidin b. Ahmad (Za'ba), "Malay Journalism in Malaya," *Journal of the Malaysian Branch of the Royal Asiatic Society*, 19 (February 1941), p. 249; quoted in William R. Roff, *The Origins of Malay Nationalism*, 2nd ed. (Kuala Lumpur: Oxford University Press, 1994) p. 167

During the nineteenth century, Singapore became a publishing centre for the Malay Muslim world, as well as a British imperial city. Works in law, religion, literature, and current events circulated widely in several languages. Missionaries brought in printing presses and hired editors and translators. By late in the century, Penang, Ipoh, Taiping, and Kuala Lumpur also had printers and publications. In the absence of formal censorship, a vernacular press operating in Chinese, Malay, and Tamil turned out journals, pamphlets, and local newspapers for the growing numbers of literate persons.[12] Anyone who could read could find discussions of trade, foreign events, religion, and at least some local politics. Language domains were not, however, walled off from one another; instead, they mixed and borrowed, contributing to a growing intellectual hybridity in the many "information regimes" that coexisted in British Malaya.[13] Local newspapers fostered hybridity as they collected their stories and staff. Syed Abdul Hassan Burhan established the *Perak Pioneer*, which was published in English in Taiping between 1894 and 1912. A Muslim of Arab descent, he migrated from India to teach Hindustani to British officers in the Perak Sikh regiment. Later he moved into publishing. Lim Seng Hooi, a Penang-born Hokkien who was educated in English and Chinese, established a Chinese daily newspaper (*Sin Poe*) and a Malay weekly (*Chahaya Pulao Penang*) before he founded the English daily, the *Straits Echo*, in 1903. He and some of his Straits Chinese friends felt the need for an English-language paper that expressed "the Chinese point of view," which would counterbalance the European-owned *Pinang Gazette*. To that end, Lim hired a British journalist from Hong Kong, Chesney Duncan, to be the *Echo*'s editor while Lim worked as its managing director.[14] Both papers reported not only on local political and economic news, but also on team sports and lurid crimes. English-language papers also covered the activities of leading Chinese in the colony. While most of the social reporting in the *Perak Pioneer* in its early years focused on Europeans, it also announced the planned trip to China of Khew Ah Ngo, the "well-known towkay of Papan," and told readers of his plans to lease his tin mines on favourable terms. The paper also advertised teaching jobs at the Anglo-Chinese

---

[12] E. W. Birch, "Vernacular Press in the Straits," *Journal of the Straits Branch of the Royal Asiatic Society*, 4 (December 1879), pp. 51–55; Roff, *Nationalism*, pp. 43–49

[13] Tim Harper uses the apt phrase "information regimes" to describe "overlapping diasporic worlds" in Singapore, and I would apply the term to other towns in British Malaya. T. N. Harper, "Globalism and the Pursuit of Authenticity: The Making of a Diasporic Public Sphere in Singapore," *Sojourn: Journal of Social Issues in Southeast Asia*, 12 (1997), 261–262

[14] Ho Tak Ming, *Ipoh: When Tin Was King* (Ipoh: Perak Academy 2009), p. 476; Manicasothy Saravanamuttu, *The Sara Saga* (Penang: Areca Books, 2010), pp. xvi, 55

School and published announcements of tax farming opportunities. Educated Chinese and Indians not only got gossip and commercial news from the paper, but also learned that Celestine Chong had won the arithmetic prize for Standard IV in 1895 at the Taiping Girls' School. If they wanted to buy some town land in Gopeng, which had been mortgaged to Subramanian Chetty, they could contact Mohamed Saeid, licensed auctioneer, for details.[15] The English-language press drew Anglophone readers into a cosmopolitan space that assumed common interests and spread information among cultural groups.

The early Malay-language periodicals were heavily influenced by the English-language papers from which they drew articles. Running from 1894 to 1895, *Bintang Timor*, the first Malay-language daily paper in the Straits Settlements, was sponsored by the Chinese Christian Association and edited by Song Ong Siang, who had studied law at Cambridge and Middle Temple in London. He had the financial backing of an English-educated Malay, Dato Bintara Luar, from Johore. Designed to appeal both to Jawi Peranakans (Muslims of mixed South Asian and Malay ancestry) and the Baba Chinese, the paper used Rumi script (Romanized Malay) for an audience of Malay speakers who could not read Arabic characters. The paper borrowed freely from the *Straits Times* and other English-language papers, and it encouraged its readers to support English-language education and Western medical care.[16]

Utusan Melayu, which appeared first in 1907, translated into Malay stories from the English-language *Free Press*. Its owner was the Englishman William Makepeace and its first editor was the reformist intellectual Mohd. Eunos bin Abdullah, who was born in Singapore to a family of Minangkabau Muslims from Sumatra. Although his primary education was in Malay, he later attended the prestigious Raffles School, which taught in English, and then entered the colonial government service. Characterized as a "loyalist Malay," Eunos gave his readers translated versions of local and international news drawn from British papers, as well as football scores and tips on rubber planting. Nevertheless, his editorials tackled important topics of the day – educational policy, welfare issues, or taxation, for example – from a reformer's point of view. He aimed, declared one editorial, to help Malays "understand matters taking place each day just as they are understood by races which live in a modern way." The paper circulated widely, being read aloud in town coffee houses, and served as a teaching tool in Malay vernacular schools and training colleges. That paper and *Lembaga Melayu* (the

---

[15] *Perak Pioneer*, 9 February 1895, p. 2; 21 February 1895, p. 4; 6 March 1895, p. 6; 27 March 1895, p. 27; 21 December 1895, p. 4; 25 December 1895, p. 2
[16] See "Derihal Queen's Scholarship," *Bintang Timor*, Singapore, 4 July 1894, pp. 11–12. See also, Roff, *Nationalism*, pp. 49, 51.

Malay-language arm of the *Malaya Tribune*, also edited by Eunos) were intended to draw readers into an international world of secular learning and to lessen the cultural distance between Malays and their neighbours. William Roff describes both papers as "the voice of moderate, progressive Malay opinion" which spoke to urban middle-class Malays.[17] Information regimes in British Malaya borrowed freely from one another and helped to draw readers, whatever their ethnicity, into an imperial public sphere where information flowed across communal lines. The communicative power of even the most local and ephemeral of such publications ought not to be underestimated, for they wove together speech communities through a hybridized print culture. Print culture in British Malaya was solidly transnational and intercommunal.

The press in British Malaya was not regulated in advance of printing, although publishers could be sued for libel in government courts. In Ipoh in 1931, a Chinese newspaper called the *Thunder News* printed a third-rate novel called "A 'Big' Master's Five Whiskers" that described the clumsy efforts of the Headmaster of an Anglo-Chinese school and President of a local Chinese maternity home to seduce a young and pretty pupil midwife, who eventually outwitted him and extorted several thousand dollars in hush money. Alerted by friends about the story, an enraged Cheong Tsun Kong, who coincidentally headed the Anglo-Chinese School and the Maternity Home in the town of Kampar and shared various other characteristics of the Big Master, sued the publisher of the *Thunder News* for slander. Although he easily won his suit, the case and trial aggravated his humiliation and no doubt boosted circulation of the juicy story. Reading "only a little Chinese," Cheong had paid no attention to the *Thunder News* until Cantonese and Hokkien friends literate in Chinese who subscribed to the paper translated it for him. Whether they smirked or scowled as they read to him can only be imagined, but they spent time and effort to spread the story among the affluent Kampar and Ipoh Chinese. By the time the publisher's trial and appeal were finished, not only had the novel been translated into English and introduced into the court record for newspapers to pick up, but several English-speaking prosecutors and solicitors of different ethnicities had also surveyed the evidence. The Protector of the Chinese joined in the

---

[17] Roff, *Nationalism*, pp. 159–161; Anthony Milner, *The Invention of Politics in Colonial Malaya* (Cambridge: Cambridge University Press, 1994), pp. 90–98. Milner sees Eunos's writings as arguing for a race-based sense of community, but the writings also advocated loyalty to the British Empire and admiration for its policies. See also, E. W. Birch, "The Vernacular Press in the Straits," *Journal of the Straits Branch of the Royal Asiatic Society*, 4 (December 1879), pp. 51–55.

fray to attack the unrepentant publisher. Colonial courts and the press – both English-language and Chinese – magnified the power of a flimsy story and the rumour mill to make Cheong look ridiculous. In the process, the prestige of the Chinese Anglophone elite was wounded. Although colonial courts could defend British subjects from attack, they also spread contradictory cultural messages and undermined local hierarchies.[18] English-, Chinese-, and Malay-language domains had by the 1930s become deeply intertwined. The literate, whatever their ethnicity, got information from a broad range of sources from outside their communities of birth. They operated in a world of networked knowledge and multiple meanings.

The Spread of English

In 1931, approximately 130,000 Asians in British Malaya claimed literacy in English, and approximately the same number said they could carry out a conversation in that language. Since census takers asked about competency in both reading and writing, the bar was set relatively high, discouraging a positive answer among those uneasy about their level of comprehension. Although census data is only a rough guide to language abilities, it indicates that a sizeable number of English speakers lived in the region. English-language skills seem to have been more widespread in the Straits Settlements than in the Federated Malay States, and Chinese and Indians were much more likely to know English than were Malays.[19]

The numbers of English speakers in British Malaya rose in the early twentieth century among Asians as English-medium schools spread throughout the peninsula and their enrolments increased. The Federated Malaya States, which counted 31 English-language schools in 1913 with 5,788 pupils, reported 44 in 1938. The number of pupils enrolled in English-language schools grew by 266 per cent between 1913 and 1929 in the state of Perak alone. In the Straits Settlements, enrolment in

---

[18] "Lee Say Long vs. Public Prosecutor," Magistrate's Court of Appeals, Ipoh, 2 February 1932, DPP No. 33/32 (Arkib Negara, Kuala Lumpur)

[19] The census depended upon self-reporting of competence. Instructions were given in English and Malay, and literate enumerators distributed the forms, and translated and filled in the schedule as needed. Literacy was defined as the ability to read AND to write. Respondents were asked if they were literate, if they were literate in English, and if they could speak English. Among the Chinese, 90 per thousand were recorded as literate in English in the Straits Settlements and 38 per thousand in the Federated Malay States. Among Indians, the comparable rates were 79 and 42 per thousand, while among Malays, the rates were 23 and 13 per thousand. Chinese and Indians in the Federated Malay States were about three times as likely to be Anglophones as Malays. See Vlieland, *Census of 1931*, pp. 26–27, 95, 370–372.

English-language schools reached more than 39,000 children by 1940.[20] Although the number of people who claimed to be literate in English amounted to only 4.8 per cent of the total population of the Straits Settlements and Federated Malay States in 1931, this group's absolute size provided a critical mass in the towns of people who had direct access to British colonial messages. Moreover, this group served as a conduit of such messages to their families and neighbourhoods.[21] Even if those literate in English were a small fraction of the total population of British Malaya, English-educated Chinese, Indians, Malays, and Eurasians dominated the professions, schools, and businesses in the larger towns. They and their children connected the cultural world of the British Empire to the Asian networks within which they moved.

By late in the nineteenth century, the practice of offering higher education primarily in English had been firmly established in India and in Hong Kong, influencing imperial administrators throughout Asia.[22] Proficiency in English was the major aim of secondary education in British Malaya, which expanded its reach during the 1920s and 1930s. Both the commercial and the scholarship tracks in schools emphasized grammar, composition, and speaking skills. Students learned idiomatic British English, read sophisticated books, and studied how to write correctly. Malayan secondary schools calibrated their curriculum to exams given by the University of Cambridge Local Examinations Syndicate, which wrote and graded tests administered throughout the Empire. From 1892, students in the scholarship stream studied set texts to win a precious "pass," qualifying them for advanced education in the United Kingdom or Singapore. The very best could win a Queen's Scholarship, which paid for study at Oxford or Cambridge. Schools and families waited for weeks to learn examination results, which the local press reported, measuring one school's successes against its rivals and listing the names of the triumphant.[23]

[20] J. B. Elcum, "Annual Report on Education in the Federated Malay States in the Year 1913," *Supplement to the F. M. S. Government Gazette*, 31 July 1914 (Kuala Lumpur: F. M. S. Government Printing Office, 1914), p. 2; "Perak Administrative Report, 1913," *Supplement to the F. M. S. Government Gazette*, 1914 (Kuala Lumpur: F. M. S. Government Printing Office, 1914), 20; "Annual Report for 1940," in Robert. L. Jarman, ed., *Annual Reports of the Straits Settlements 1855–1941*, Vol. 11: 1936–1941 (London: Archive Editions, 1998), p. 509
[21] Vlieland, *Census of 1931*, pp. 32, 91, 370–372
[22] The major universities founded in India during the 1850s used English in their classrooms, and the group of officials and educators who reassessed the status of education in Hong Kong in 1882 concluded that "the primary object to be borne in view by the Government should be the teaching of English." Alistair Pennycook, *English and the Discourses of Colonialism* (London: Routledge, 1998), pp. 91, 109, 114
[23] The University of Cambridge Local Examinations Syndicate began certifying exam results for overseas students at the secondary level in 1864. Tan Yap Kwang, Chow Hong Kheng, and Christine Goh, *Examinations in Singapore: Change and Continuity,*

English-language education in Malaya included far more than grammar and punctuation. Designed to produce bilingual cosmopolitan people who were politically loyal, schools radiated British culture and patriotism. The Junior and Senior Cambridge exams demanded that students use their English to demonstrate mastery of English and imperial history, geography, poetry, and literary classics. They read Tennyson and Shakespeare and learned about British victories at Plassey and Trafalgar. The Roman Catholic Sisters of the Holy Infant Jesus ran the Ipoh Convent School, which educated girls through the secondary level. Girls in the Senior Cambridge class impressed the visiting school inspector in 1926 with their knowledge of *As You Like It*. At other Ipoh secondary schools in the 1920s and 1930s, students acted in plays drawn from the Cambridge syllabus and entered essays in Empire-wide competitions. Choirs sang and orchestras played British music. Empire Day and royal coronations were festivals with parades and treats. At the 1927 dedication of new buildings at the Ipoh Anglo-Chinese School, Bishop Titus Lowe identified the school's education with "all that is good, true, and beautiful," stressing its duty to "helping to create a fruitful fealty to King and Country and for the teaching of Christian patriotism." The audience, which included Sir Hugh Clifford, High Commissioner of the Federated Malay States, as well as the Sultan of Perak, teachers, school inspectors, and parents, stood to sing "God Save the Queen" before departing.[24] Schools sponsored Boy Scout troops that learned imperial loyalty (see Figure 6.1). T. B. Macaulay's well-known recommendation that education in English could, and should, create persons, whatever their "blood or colour," who would be "English in tastes, in opinions, in morals and in intellect," may not have reflected reality either in India or in Malaya, but it animated teachers and shaped curricula throughout the Empire in the early twentieth century.[25] When English language teachers met in 1926 to organize a Teachers' Association of Malaya, they listened to Rev. W. E. Horley, prime mover of the Methodist-run schools, laud their work as forming "character as well as brains, intellect as well as muscles, good citizens as well as traders."[26] These schools preached not

1891–2007 (Singapore: World Scientific Publishing Co., 2008), pp. 9–10, 12, 16–18; *Malaya Tribune*, 5 March 1936, p. 3

[24] *Our Argosy: Anglo-Chinese Girl's School* (Ipoh: Charles Grenier, 1950), pp. 4–5; SMK Convent, *Ulang Tahun Ke-90, 90th Anniversary* (Ipoh: SMK Convent, 1997), p. 18; Khoo Salma Nasution, et al., *Giving Our Best: the Story of St George's Girls' School, Penang, 1885–2010* (Penang: Areca Press, 2010) p. 70

[25] Thomas Babington Macaulay, "Minute on Education in India, 1835," in Antoinette Burton, ed., *Politics and Empire in Victorian Britain: a Reader* (New York: Macmillan, 2001) p. 20; Andaya and Andaya, *Malaysia*, pp. 226, 232

[26] W. E. Horley, "Inaugural Address," *The Pedagogue*, Vol. 1, No. 1 (June 1926), p. 25

Figure 6.1 Boy Scout troop, Anglo-Chinese School, Kampar, 1928

only a gospel of British cultural hegemony, but also a liberal political discourse that privileged progress, justice, liberty, and representation – even if the precise meanings of these terms were left undefined. Students learned about politics through an increasingly international liberal vocabulary and through the rituals of imperial loyalty. They came of age within a framework that both valorized British subjecthood and gave them the tools to redefine it.[27] As immigrants to a frontier society, they had to develop roots in new communities which had been created by colonial rule and not by the indigenous Malay culture. Education in English not only brought access to imperial circuits of knowledge, but opened avenues of communication with their Asian counterparts. All were struggling to establish themselves in a new polity, where English opened avenues to empowerment.

The secondary schools of British Malaya, which spread British culture along with a discourse of British exceptionalism and patriotism, drew pupils from all ethnic groups on the peninsula and streamed them into professional life in the colony. The Anderson School gave leadership awards in the mid-1930s to R. Vivekananda, Yeop Mahidin Bin Md Shariff, Liew Why Hone,

[27] Douglas E. Haynes, *Rhetoric and Ritual in Colonial India: The Shaping of a Public Culture in Surat City, 1852–1928* (Berkeley: University of California Press, 1991); C. A. Bayly, *Recovering Liberties: Indian Thought in the Age of Liberalism and Empire* (Cambridge: Cambridge University Press, 2012)

and Ooi Eu Tee, all of whom served as school captains, or head boys. After further study in Singapore, Hong Kong, Oxford, or London, this early group all returned to Perak, settling into careers as barristers, engineers, medical doctors, and teachers, eventually moving into careers in local and national politics. The Old Boys of St Michaels earned similar professional credentials.[28] The English-language schools nurtured the men who helped run British Malaya before and after the war and who helped shape the post-colonial Malayan settlement. Moreover, the social ties they created bridged the major language communities and gave future leaders a *lingua franca* to use internationally, as well as locally. The question of how deeply students absorbed the imperial patriotism of the schools and the colonialist English-language domain is difficult to answer, but post-1945 nationalist and post-colonial opinions ought not to be automatically imposed upon the students and parents of the years before 1941. English was an imperial and an imperialist language whose vocabulary and official use spread the values and prejudices embedded in British culture as it echoed the messages of colonial governments. Working from the ideas of Antonio Gramsci, many scholars have argued that discourses shape minds, and there is ample evidence of the continuing influence of British cultural and political messages among English-educated Asians.[29] As long as higher education in British Malaya remained largely education in English, the urban middle classes were drawn into a cosmopolitan, global Anglophone world that privileged the British state and its culture, and simultaneously created social networks that crossed barriers among ethnic communities.

Defining Modernity

What did it mean to be modern in British Malaya? Educated Asian men debated this question in print, staking out some common ground. Reformers in Malaya, whether Malay, Chinese, or South Asian, agreed on the centrality of education: to be modern, one had to be literate, whatever one's age or gender. "Malays of this Generation" (*Orang-orang Melayu Zaman Ini*) were praised for educating all their children in

[28] Malim Ghozali, ed., *Centennial Anniversary Anderson School, Ipoh Malaysia: Images 1909–2009* (Ipoh: Seladang Ventures and Old Andersonians' Club, 2009), pp. 70, 71, 136; "Footprints on the Sands of Time: Who's Who among Old Lasallians," *The Michaelian*, Vol. 1, No. 1 (December 1948), pp. 16–26; Eric Hobsbawm and Terence Ranger, eds., *The Invention of Tradition* (Cambridge: Cambridge University Press, 1983 and 2012).

[29] Ashis Nandy, *The Intimate Enemy: Loss and Recovery of Self under Colonialism* (Delhi: Oxford University Press, 1983); Alastair Pennycook, *English and the Discourses of Colonialism* (London: Routledge, 1998); Robert Phillipson, *Linguistic Imperialism* (Oxford: Oxford University Press, 1992)

English as well as in Malay. Educated women were needed to run house-holds properly, using new knowledge about hygiene and disease. Literate mothers could help children with schoolwork. Educated women could be granted more freedom and be treated as friends (*sahabat*), not household slaves (*bukannya hamba kita*).[30] Using similar arguments, Straits Chinese and Indian authors emphasized the importance of women's education, which would benefit communities as well as individuals. Exactly what should be taught was a more complicated matter, and although answers reflected cultural priorities, there were common denominators. Being modern meant being literate and studying history and science. Modern people were educated cosmopolitans who knew how to function within a transnational empire.

Educated Malays worried about their modernity – but in relation to the group, rather than as individuals. The word *moden* had come into use in Malay by the early twentieth century and was used both as an adjective to mean modern and as a noun (*kemodenan*) signifying modernity. The newspaper *Utusan Melayu* argued in a Social Darwinian fashion that Malays had to compete with other, more energetic peoples who had progressed more rapidly over time and who had already become modern. In order not to be left behind, Malays had to change their ways, become educated, and, like the Turks, reject the absolute control of their sultans in favour of representative institutions.[31] The editor of *Utusan Melayu*, Mohd. Eunos bin Abdullah, an English-educated journalist, introduced Enlightenment-style political vocabulary into Malay as he pushed his readers toward political liberalism. Eunos framed his arguments for change in terms of the Malay race (*bangsa*), which he wanted his compa-triots to love and to uplift to bring it greater power and prosperity. Although racial separation from and cutthroat competition with the Chinese underlay the march to modernity that Eunos advocated, it also necessitated acceptance of a cosmopolitan, urban world. How both could be achieved simultaneously was not made clear.[32] Through *Utusan Melayu* and other reformist Malay newspapers such as *Saudara* and *Majlis*, a powerful plea for a prosperous, modern community entered into Malay discourse. Editorials professed loyalty to sultans and to the

---

[30] "Orang-orang Melayu Zaman Ini," *Saudara*, 28 February 1931, p. 6; "Plelajaran Inggeris di Sekolah Melayu," *Saudara*, 7 March 1931, p. 8

[31] *Utusan Melayu* was published between 1907 and 1921 and was succeeded by the ideo-logically similar *Lembaga Melayu*, which appeared through the 1920s. Roff, *Nationalism*, pp. 159–161. Anthony Milner, *The Invention of Politics in Colonial Malaya* (Cambridge: Cambridge University Press, 1994), pp. 120, 198

[32] Milner, *Invention*, pp. 90, 109; "Melayu Dengan Cina: Pertandingam Hidup Disemenanjung," *Saudara*, 8 August 1931, p. 1

British, framing political questions in terms of jobs in the colonial state.[33] These reformers located the modern Malay squarely within the British Empire and its institutions.

Students at the Sultan Idris Training College, a boarding school for future teachers in the small town of Tanjong Malim, can be seen as products of a Eunos-style modernism. Drawn from villages around the Federated Malay States, they were given a liberal education centred on Malay history and literature along with secular subjects. After returning home to teach in local schools, graduates wrote of the social changes needed in Malaya. During the 1930s, they expressed a growing self-consciousness of themselves as Malays and of the need to work for the improvement of their community, which they conceptualized in terms of race and religion. Few at the time actively defended political independence or conventional nationalism.[34]

Eunos's liberal construction of a modernist Malay politics was opposed by Muslim conservatives comfortable with top-down reforms led by royal courts, but he gained support from Muslim intellectuals linked to reformers and schools in Egypt. Men educated in Cairo brought back to Singapore the ideas of Muhammad Abduh, who argued for the compatibility of Islam with modern science and liberal constitutionalism. The influential journal *Al-Imam*, published in Singapore between 1906 and 1908, defended religious education which included English and other secular subjects in addition to Arabic and the Qu'uran. One of its founders, Sayyid Shaykh, opened a modernised madrasa in Melaka around 1916, which served as a centre for advancing a progressive form of Islam. Referred to as *Kaum Muda* (Young Group), reformist Muslims in the Straits Settlements circulated a vision of a modernized Pan-Islamic world ruled by shari'ah law, which would bring prosperity and greater power to their community.[35] *Kaum Muda's* political targets were the religious establishment and the royal courts that supported them, rather than colonial authorities. The most overt and widely circulated messages about needed changes in Malaya were compatible with continued British rule. A conventional anti-colonial nationalism of the sort that had exploded in India and in China, unifying reformers of many different language and ethnic groups into a political movement, did not exist in British Malaya in the 1930s.

---

[33] "Orang-orang Melayu Zaman Ini," *Saudara*, 28 February 1931, p. 6
[34] Roff, *Nationalism*, pp. 142–157
[35] Roff, *Nationalism*, pp. 56, 59, 75–78; Ibrahim Bin Abu Bakar, *Islamic Modernism in Malaya: the Life and Thought of Sayid Syekh al-Hadi* (Kuala Lumpur: University of Malaya Press, 1994), pp. 45–77

The most aggressively modern Asians in British Malaya were the Straits Chinese, descendants of immigrants to Melaka, Penang, and Singapore, who found the cheap land and free trade economies of those prosperous ports congenial and who tied their fortunes early to those of their colonial rulers. Their children and grandchildren normally spoke Baba Malay (a dialect that mixed Hokkien and Malay), but many used the missionary-run English-language schools, which expanded the Anglophone population.[36] Leading Straits Chinese articulated modernist, liberal interests early. Modelling themselves on London literary societies, members of the Chinese Christian Association in Singapore founded a journal in 1896. Known as the *Straits Chinese Magazine*, it circulated broadly for a decade. Its editors, Dr Lim Boon Kheng and Song Ong Siang, who had both studied in England as Queen's Scholars, helped to create a public voice for the Straits Chinese and define its values.[37] The *Straits Chinese Magazine* recommended the use of European medicine and the broader education of women in the interest of progress. The magazine's strongest enthusiasms were reserved for the British Empire and loyalist politics, which it defended using a liberal vocabulary. The Straits Chinese "have long ago learnt to venerate and to love the British constitution," the paper claimed, and the Straits Settlements were for them "a paradise," where they found "justice and liberty."[38] At the time of the Boer War, over 800 men, including Dr Lim and Mr Song, founded the Straits Chinese British Association in Singapore. Promoting familiar liberal values and identifying itself as "the party of progress," the group also pledged to "promote . . . an intelligent interest in the affairs of the British Empire and to encourage and maintain their loyalty as subjects of the Queen." During World War I, Straits Chinese men volunteered for local service, and their wives and daughters collected money to buy a fighter plane. The Straits Chinese British Association spearheaded their efforts.[39] Their rhetoric remained loyalist and deferential even after the Qing emperor was ousted and their ties to the new political leaders of China deepened.

---

[36] A free English-language school for Chinese and other Asian boys opened in 1864 in Singapore and a second in 1875. At the same time, wealthy Chinese merchants were funding scholarships for Chinese boys at the Raffles Institute, the earliest and most prestigious secondary school in the colony. In the early twentieth century, teaching in Mandarin expanded in the Chinese vernacular schools, pushed by reformers to unify the emigrant population; Song Ong Siang, *One Hundred Years' History of the Chinese in Singapore* (Singapore: Oxford University Press, 1984), pp. 127, 139, 178, 252

[37] Song, *Hundred Years*, pp. 295–296   .

[38] Lim Boon Keng, "Straits Chinese Reform, I. The Queue Question," *The Straits Chinese Magazine*, Vol. 3, No. 9 (March 1899), pp. 22–25; "The Chinese Abroad," *The Straits Chinese Magazine*, Vol. I, No. 4 (October 1897), pp. 154–155

[39] Song, *Hundred Years*, pp. 319–320, 526, 534

The leading Straits Chinese remained supporters of the British Empire through the 1930s, although these ties were compatible with growing transnational commitments. Kinship and family memory linked them to particular villages and clans in South China, and newspapers kept them well informed about Chinese politics. Nationalist sentiments and political energies were directed toward China, where reformers and republicans who replaced the Qing dynasty in 1912 were working toward a broader modernization of that country. After the revolution, Dr Lim Boon Keng left his medical practice in Singapore and his seat on the Legislative Council to serve as the president of Xiamen (Amoy) University in China between 1921 and 1937, where he insisted that the curriculum must include English as a second language. Through his adult life, Dr Lim combined an active enthusiasm for British culture and institutions with commitments to Chinese political causes and schools. His world was transnational, and he functioned effectively in multiple societies. The British Empire offered him a home and a base from which he could move freely: to the University of Edinburgh, to London, to the Federated Malay States, to Hong Kong, and to China – on a British passport. He and other Singaporean Chinese, such as Tan Kah Kee, agitated for liberal reforms – more education for women in both the Straits Settlements and in China – while expressing both allegiance to Britain and ardent Chinese nationalism.[40] Similar multilingual men could be found in towns throughout the Federated Malay States. They were transnational in their interests and habits, belonging simultaneously to several cultural worlds and disparate polities. As part of a self-conscious Chinese diaspora with international economic interests and kinship networks, they had active ties stretching from London to Canton and Shanghai. No one identity defined them, and they cultivated flexibility in their political, as well as their cultural commitments. For them, British subjecthood and Chinese citizenship were overlapping, fluid categories.[41] The British Empire not only permitted, but also fostered such multiple loyalties.

Urban South Asians had similar choices to make and questions of self-definition to answer. The numbers of merchants, moneylenders, clerks, interpreters, surveyors, and teachers grew along with the colonial

---

[40] Jürgen Rudolph, *Reconstructing Identities: a Social History of the Babas in Singapore* (Aldershot: Ashgate, 1998), pp. 380–390; C. F. Yong, *Chinese Leadership and Power in Colonial Singapore* (Singapore: Times Academic Press, 1992), pp. 136–147. See also Tan Liok Ee, "Descent and Identity: the Different Paths of Tan Cheng Lock, Tan Kah Kee and Lim Lian Giok," *Journal of the Malaysian Branch of the Royal Asiatic Society*, Vol. 68: 1, No. 268 (1995), pp. 1–28

[41] For a discussion of transnational citizenship, see Aihwa Ong and Donald M. Nonini, eds., *Ungrounded Empires: The Cultural Politics of Modern Chinese Transnationalism* (New York and London: Routledge, 1997)

administration in Malaya. By the twentieth century, Indian lawyers, medical men, and railway officials abounded. These were people whose education and migration histories anchored them in the transnational networks of the British Empire.[42] A Ceylonese Tamil educated at Oxford, "Sara" Saravanamuttu arrived in Penang in 1930 to help edit the *Straits Echo*. At the time, his greatest pleasures seem to have been cricket and hobnobbing with influential men of all nationalities. His children described him as a "global soul" on the strength of his cosmopolitan tastes, travels, and social activism.[43] Although South Asians of middling status came late to the towns of the peninsula, they helped to define cosmopolitan modernity through their careers and writings. They anchored their children firmly through education into an Anglophone colonial world. George T. James, who began his career in 1936 in government service in Singapore, described his childhood in the small towns of British Malaya. His parents, who were Tamil Christians, enrolled him and his sisters in English-language schools, where they had Chinese, Malay, and South Asian teachers as well as friends. He recalled lessons in grammar, writing, history, and mathematics, as well as religion. He and his sisters competed for the best grades and victory on the playing fields. Piety was a part of their definition of progress, as was a rough sort of gender equality. The James family crossed communal lines at work, worship, and play.[44] They were part of a growing Anglophone public sphere which touched South Asians of middling status across the peninsula.

The Indian, which began publication in Kuala Lumpur in 1936 and could be found in railway stations and town bookstores all over Malaya, embraced cosmopolitan modernity. Its pages advertised "modern Hindu hotels," "Tamil talkies," and Tiger beer, tempting its readers with the delights of consumer culture. Its editors, who attacked a "superstitious regard for tradition," clearly cast their lot with modernizers and reformers. The column "Our Women's Corner" took a stand in favour of "the really well-educated modern girl of the middle-class today," who could discuss Ibsen and Shakespeare as well as prepare dinner. But the mission of the paper was a larger one: its announced purpose was "to let the Indian sun break in on the cobwebbed windows of the souls of the local Indian Community" and "to consolidate this feeling [of Indianness] among the

[42] R. B. Krishnan, *Indians in Malaya: A Pageant of Greater India* (Singapore: Malayan Publishers, 1936). See also David West Rudner, *Caste and Capitalism in Colonial India: The Nattukottai Chettiars* (Berkeley: University of California Press, 1994); Interview with M. Singaram, 22 August 2014 (Perak Oral History Project, Ipoh Malaysia)

[43] Manicasothy Saravanamuttu, *The Sara Saga* (Penang: Areca Books, 2010)

[44] Interview of Mr George T. James, 20 October 1983, Oral History Interviews: "Communities of Singapore," No. 000352 (National Archives of Singapore)

compatriots that bear its name." Its columns and letters to the editor communicated, and worked to create, an "Indian" public opinion undivided by the retrograde divisions of religion, caste, languages and politics. The paper privileged sports and political news from British India, giving laudatory coverage to nationalists such as Nehru and Gandhi, while steering clear of topics such as plague or poverty. Seeing the world through rose-coloured glasses, it presented Malayan Indians as imperial loyalists. Royal jubilees and birthdays were celebrated events, not reminders of subjection. Filling its pages with accounts of energetic Indian associations and uplifting social events, the paper depicted a clearly middle-class "Indian Community" enjoying itself while engaging selectively with issues of the day.[45] South Asian expatriates in Malaya did not bring with them the hard-edged, nationalist politics of British India, where in the 1930s mass rallies and strident protests challenged the British right to rule. Even Tamil reformers did not challenge the legitimacy of imperial governance, but focused instead on issues of religious ritual and temple access. Purifying Hinduism by conducting worship in Sanskrit rather than Tamil and by opening temples to untouchables mobilized Tamil-speakers in Penang and Singapore.[46] Although an interest in modernity was not uniformly spread among middle-class South Asians, it had taken hold in the towns of the peninsula, where it was nurtured by print culture.

Being modern in Malaya during the 1930s, whether one was Malay, Chinese, or South Asian, meant calling for social and cultural reforms that appealed to families of middle status. Activists directed their energies toward social and religious targets, rather than political or economic ones. Nationalist sentiments were projected away from the peninsula to India and to China, while imperial loyalties dominated local political discourse.

Marketplace Modernities

Anyone who picked up a newspaper or went to the cinema could get a taste of new technologies and tastes. Pictures of aeroplanes and automobiles

---

[45] "Looking Forward," *The Indian*, 28 December 1935, p. 8; "Modern Ways of Indian Marriages," *The Indian*, 28 March 1936, p. 14; "The King-Emperor's 42nd Birthday," *The Indian*, 20 June 1936, p. 20; See also *The Indian*, 28 February 1936, p. 12; 25 April 1936, p. 6; 16 May 1936, p. 10
[46] S. Arasaratnam, "Social Reform and Reformist Pressure Groups among the Indians of Malaya and Singapore, 1930–1955," *Journal of the Malaysian Branch of the Royal Asiatic Society*, Vol. 39, No. 2 (December 1966), pp. 54–67

trumpeted the attractions of speed and travel. Advertisements for radios and programme listings showed how to find modern sounds and world news beamed into Malaya by the British Broadcasting Corporation's Empire Service, by Netherland Indies Radio, and by Germany's Berlin Station. By the mid-1930s, shortwave radios allowed voices from Tokyo, Johannesburg, Buenos Aires, and even Pittsburgh into appropriately equipped homes and shops.[47] Jazz, big-band swing, or *kayou-kyoku* (Japanese pop music) could be found with turns of a dial, and town shops sold gramophone records of local hits, as well as songs imported from Europe or from India.

Even more accessible were images from Bollywood, Hollywood, and their competitors. By 1929, when talkies began to replace silent films, Japanese, Chinese, Indonesian, and Malay productions appeared in urban cinemas. The larger towns had multiple movie theatres, which advertised in several languages (see Figure 6.2). Tickets were relatively cheap. *Alli Arjuna*, a Tamil "Magnificent Love Drama," played at the Sapphire Theatre in Seremban in 1936, while Joan Blondell could be seen nearby in *Kansas City Princess*, a Warner Brothers "Laugh Hit." Kuala Lumpur audiences watched beauties with permed, bobbed hair singing with Bing Crosby as they danced their way out of trouble.[48] Schoolboys flocked to see Tarzan or American cowboys on the screen, and anyone walking past a cinema could see posters of liberated American women flaunting "modern" hairstyles and short skirts. Advertisements for local stores reinforced the signals given by the film stars in less dramatic fashion. Town tailors could produce tuxedos and lounge suits, as well as more traditional styles. Embracing European definitions of fashion and beauty, some city shops sold European-style hats, shoes, face powder, and lipstick. Refrigerators, radios, and fans could be purchased to furnish a "proper" home. The New China Optical Company urged its customers to "Be Up To Date!" in their choice of eyewear, and Bata Shoes bragged of "NEW DESIGNS, coming MONTHLY."[49] The marketplace shaped the tastes and aspirations of those exposed to international styles. In Malaya, just as in India, Burma, and Nepal in the 1930s, consumer capitalism allowed city dwellers with

[47] The British Broadcasting Corporation's Empire Service began as short-wave transmissions in 1932, but relay stations soon multiplied, permitting a broader audience via medium-wave broadcasts. Dozens of stations could be tuned in by listeners in Kuala Lumpur by 1936; *Malaya Tribune*, 5 March 1936, pp. 5, 8

[48] *Malaya Tribune*, 1 January 1936, p. 2; 4 March 1936, p. 2; Tan Sooi Beng, *Bangsawan: A Social and Stylistic History of Popular Malay Opera* (Singapore: Oxford University Press, 1993), pp. 9–10

[49] *Malaya Tribune*, 4 January 1936, p. 6; 3 March 1936, p. 4

Figure 6.2 Poster for film, "The Lost Jungle," Nanyang Theatre, Menglembu, 1930

some extra cash to sample the wares of an international modernity and to adopt a different look.[50]

The taste for modern objects and clothing crossed ethnic boundaries. A newspaper sketch of Rao Sahib K. A. Mukundan, Agent of the Government of India in Malaya, depicted him in a European style living room proudly displaying his stuffed armchairs, sofas, coffee table, and electric lamp to Tamil immigrants so that they would see his high standard of living to which they should aspire![51] Educated Indians photographed in the 1930s made British-style choices about their public images: short hair, European style suits, collared shirts with neckties. Even the socially conservative Nattukottai Chettiars, whose life in Malaya revolved around family temples, dressed in jackets, ties, and boots on public occasions.[52] By the early twentieth century, Straits Chinese men had adopted several types of European styles of dress and defended publicly their preference for "European books, undershirts, hats, tweeds, handkerchiefs, collars, and what not"; even office workers wore trousers and collared cotton shirts. In the 1930s, middle-class (or aspiring middle-class) men in international businesses and government departments in Malaya normally wore collared shirts, jackets, ties, and leather shoes. Younger Chinese, Eurasian, and Sinhalese women bobbed their hair and sometimes wore European-style frocks. Modern Chinese brides wore long, white, frilly dresses during part of their elaborate wedding ceremonies. Schoolteachers, railway officers, and professionals of all sorts adopted western-style clothes in the workplace, signalling their similarity to colonial rulers and difference from the rickshaw pullers, labourers, and vendors whose simple wardrobes confirmed poverty along with their ethnic identifications.[53] While the new consumer culture

---

[50] See Chie Ikeya, *Refiguring Women, Colonialism, and Modernity in Burma* (Honolulu: University of Hawai'i Press, 2011), p. 119; Mark Liechty, *Suitably Modern: Making Middle-Class Culture in a New Consumer Society* (Princeton: Princeton University Press, 2003), pp. 45–46

[51] *The Indian*, 22 February 1936, p. 5

[52] S. Muthia, Meenakshi Meyappan, and Visalakshi Ramaswamy, *The Chettiar Heritage* (Chennai: The Chettiar Heritage, 2006), p. 273; Rudner, *Caste and Capitalism*

[53] Lim Boon Keng, "Straits Chinese Reform, II: Dress and Costume," *Straits Chinese Magazine*, Vol. 3, No. 10 (June 1899), 57; Khoo Joo Ee, *The Straits Chinese: a Cultural History* (Amsterdam and Kuala Lumpur: The Pepin Press, 1996), p. 214; Christin Wu Ramsay, *Days Gone By: Growing Up in Penang* (Penang: Areca Books, 2007), pp. 40–41; James Francis Warren, *Rickshaw Coolie: A People's History of Singapore 1880–1940* (Singapore: Singapore University Press, 2003), p. 199. Picture postcards of street scenes from the early twentieth century show Asian workers in sarongs, dhotis, loose shirts, floppy trousers, and shorts. They wore sandals or went barefoot. See Khoo Salma Nasution and Malcolm Wade, *Penang Postcard Collection 1899–1930s* (Penang: Janus Print and Resources, 2003), pp. 90–106. See also Ho Tak Ming, *Doctors Extraordinaire* (Ipoh: Perak Academy, 2000), pp. 112–113

levelled ethnic differences, it re-emphasized those of class. Those moving into the middle ranks of colonial society used dress to signal their separation from the urban poor.

Mass entertainment provided a profusion of international delights, for those who could pay. Patrons of the town amusement parks could watch a Hollywood film or Malay ronggeng dancers, listen to Chinese opera or a European-style orchestra. Street hawkers sold steamed dumplings, Indian roti, grilled satay, and Malay cakes to whoever had enough cash. Not only was sampling encouraged, but no one needed to be consistent. During the course of a year, town dwellers could attend a Chinese circus, Malay bangsawan theatre, Indian dance, or British vaudeville with no conflict of interest implied. Commercial entertainment found ways to please many tastes, drawing in customers without reference to religion or ethnicity.

One popular strategy was to borrow and mix, to woo audiences with aggressively hybridized styles of music, dance, and comedy. Bangsawan theatre, which reached the peak of its popularity in the 1920s and 1930s, modernized traditional Malay, Arab, Chinese, Indian, and European fantasy tales and then added dancers, clowns, magicians, and even fireworks. In successive performances in Penang in 1936, the aptly named Dardanella Company promised audiences a tragedy about Tibet, a Burmese romance, and provocative plays titled "Bombay Scandal" and "Shanghai Nights." Wayang Kassim, which toured towns from Thailand east through Java, added to its ever-changing roster of plays dances from Hawaii to Hungary, as well as racist "coon songs" from the American South. Virtually any sort of foreign music and lyrics, especially those popularized on the wireless or available on gramophone, filled gaps between scenes and novelty acts. Bangsawan orchestras were as hybrid as their repertoires, mixing Western and Asian musical instruments and swapping musicians as needed for the performance at hand. Despite its rich borrowings from imagined Asian pasts, bangsawan was a modern form of commercial theatre whose models were urban music hall entertainments adapted to local taste. Differently priced tickets separated middling groups from workers; women and children could buy seats in the balcony. Dialogue was in Malay, but much of its appeal rested on action and music. Bangsawan attracted both genders, all ethnic groups, and even the respectable and the rough. Colonial governors and sultans sometimes appeared, testifying to the wide popularity of the bangsawan brand of multicultural fun.[54]

[54] Tan, *Bangsawan*, pp. 35–56

Urban entertainments and town public spaces were not cut by ethnicity and class into air-tight compartments in Malaya, although divisions and self-segregation certainly persisted. The pluralism of Malayan colonial society, which had solidified on the plantations into rigid ethnic hierarchies and compartmentalized worlds, took on new shapes in the towns, where commercial entertainment and mass culture worked to bridge and, consequently, to lower the boundaries of ethnic differentness. By the 1930s, the towns of British Malaya had drawn many of their inhabitants into a culturally hybridized, transnational commercial culture. The impact was greatest on elites and those of middle status, but all could see the advertisements in shop windows or on town walls.

Sociability and Urban Civil Society in the 1930s

By 1930, urban civil society in Malaya had broadened and deepened. Just as in Britain, Western Europe, India, China, and the Netherlands Indies, townspeople met regularly in temples, churches, schools, associations, and clubs, creating social worlds outside the control of the colonial state.[55] They worshipped, studied, and socialized in groups of their own choice where they learned the practices of democratic governance and social engagement. Civil society not only fostered sociability and connections among individuals; it also nurtured and widened the sphere of collective action.[56]

Towns gave residents multiple ways to define their public identities, choices which reflected not only inherited loyalties but also newly discovered possibilities. While many still chose clubs according to their ethnicities, religions, or birthplaces, by the 1920s individuals could also emphasize their occupations, hobbies, or political commitments. An enthusiasm for cricket, for chess, or for reading drew people together

---

[55] Ulbe Bosma and Remco Raben, *Being Dutch in the Indies: A History of Creolisation and Empire 1500–1920* (Athens: Ohio University Press, 2008); Peter Clark, *British Clubs and Societies 1580–1800: The Origins of an Associational World* (Oxford, 2000); Douglas E. Haynes, *Rhetoric and Ritual in Colonial India: The Shaping of a Public Culture in Surat City, 1852–1928* (Berkeley: University of California Press, 1991); Prashant Kidambi, *The Making of an Indian Metropolis: Colonial Governance and Public Culture in Bombay, 1890–1920* (Aldershot Hampshire: Ashgate, 2007); Robert J. Morris, "Voluntary Societies and British Urban Elites, 1780–1850: An Analysis," *The Historical Journal*, Vol. 26, No. 1 (1983), pp. 95–118; Susan Naquin, *Peking: Temples and City Life, 1400–1900* (Berkeley: University of California Press, 2000)

[56] Sudipta Kaviraj and Sunil Khilnani, eds., *Civil Society: History and Possibilities* (Cambridge: Cambridge University Press, 2001); Rajeev Bhargava and Helmut Reifeld, *Civil Society, Public Sphere and Citizenship: Dialogues and Perceptions* (New Delhi: Sage, 2005); See also William T. Rowe, "The Public Sphere in Modern China," *Modern China*, Vol. 16, No. 3 (1990), pp. 309–329

across ethnic lines. Other voluntary associations brought together people from a single community who worked for a particular social reform or political cause.[57] These groups often cooperated with other associations with similar aims. Campaigns against opium use or in support of the British military during World War I appealed to multiple groups. Urban sociability provided, therefore, mechanisms for overcoming communal division and segmentation.

It is clear that many society members mixed and matched their memberships and did not remain within one ethnic compartment. Individuals could belong to multiple clubs, creating cosmopolitan social worlds for themselves. In the mid-1930s, Chan Kang Swi, a Melaka merchant and owner of local rubber estates, served as President of the Hokkien Community and head trustee of the Cheong Hoon Teng Temple. But at the same time he was a member of the Straits Chinese British Association and served as a justice of the Peace. P. C. Pamdasa founded and headed the Indo-Ceylonese Association in Melaka for several years, and he also belonged to the alumni association of his Melaka secondary school, St Francis. Most of his volunteer activity was given to multi-ethnic sport clubs and the Boy Scouts.[58] Each of these men had a wide circle of friends and interests not limited to one religious or ethnic affiliation. Urbanization in Malaya fostered a cosmopolitan civil society shaped by its location in a global empire and adoption of global discourses of liberalism and modernity. What needs to be determined is how powerful these cosmopolitan affiliations and interests were, and for whom they outweighed communal ties.

By the 1930s, civil society incorporated women too. Educated women in Southeast Asia had stepped out of domestic spaces and tested gender norms in the realms of both discourse and practice. Across Asia, advanced education correlated to European-style clothing, public activities, and changing aspirations. Sometimes seen as progressive and sometimes viewed as threatening, young women in Burma, India, and China joined nationalist, anti-colonial groups and became politically active.[59] In less politicized Malaya, the reconfiguring of women's traditional roles was most visible within the Straits Chinese community, although even there it did not take an overtly nationalist turn. Helen Song, wife of the Singapore

[57] Sudipta Kaviraj, "In Search of Civil Society," in Kaviraj and Khilnani, eds., Civil Society, p. 311

[58] P. V. Gopalan, Coronation Souvenir of the Settlement of Malacca (Kuala Lumpur: Commercial Press, 1937), pp. 105–106, 149

[59] Ikeya, Refiguring Women, pp. 46–48; Barbara Hamill Sato, The New Japanese Woman: Modernity, Media, and Women in Interwar Japan, Asia-Pacific (Durham, NC: Duke University Press, 2003); Louise Edwards, "Policing the Modern Woman in Republican China," Modern China, Vol. 26, No. 2 (2000), pp. 115–147

barrister Song Ong Siang, tried to stay out of the public eye, but press reports of her activities show how a wealthy, "modern-minded" Straits Chinese woman spent time in the 1930s. An active Christian, Lady Song served as organist for the Prinsep Street Presbyterian Church in Singapore and worked with the Girl's Friendly Band. She wore Chinese-style clothes, but she bobbed and waved her hair, rode horseback, and liked the cinema. She helped organize flower shows, served on school boards, and distributed trophies. Song remained a stalwart of the Singapore charity and social scene, where she appeared with her husband.[60] Most South Asian and Malay women were much less likely to participate as actively in civil society as did Helen Song, but as the number of professional Asian women mounted, so did the range of socially sanctioned activities.[61] Mrs E. V. Davies, who had earned a Master of Arts degree and had immigrated to Singapore from India in 1925, organized the Indian and Ceylonese Ladies Club to bring the women of several South Asian communities together to work for "women's welfare." By the mid-1930s, it re-baptized itself as the Lotus Club in an effort to attract Malays, Persians, and others to the organization. It claimed members from all of the subcontinent's larger language and religious groups and boasted of attendance by women "who never before attended any public function [and] those who go out only in veiled cars." The Kuala Lumpur Indian Association opened a Ladies Section in 1935, signing up thirty-four women for meetings and social welfare projects.[62]

The naming of associations signals how members saw themselves, and in Malaya naming patterns changed over time. Early gatherings of South Asian immigrants developed around temples whose names had a narrow reference. Founded in 1801, the Kapitan Kling Mosque was built just south of Chulia Street in Penang by Tamil Muslims; its name referred to the Chulia community's headman, who was appointed by the East India Company. Over time, however, the labels adopted by urban clubs and temples became broader, picking up terms that circulated internationally and were used by both Britons and Asians. Near the Kapitan Kling mosque were the Bengali Mosque (1855) and the United Muslim Association (1929). W. E. Perera, a Sinhalese teacher in Teluk Anson, organized a Cosmopolitan Club for his friends in the early 1920s. It

---

[60] "Lady Helen Song," *Straits Times Supplement*, 23 January 1936, p. 1; *Morning Tribune*, 7 April 1936, p. 22; *Straits Times*, 24 July 1936, p. 1; Blythe Collection, box 3, folder 15, PP MS 31 (SOAS Archive, London)

[61] The 1931 Census counted 6,013 Chinese, Indian, and Malay women who had professional jobs in the Straits Settlements, the Federated and Unfederated Malay States; C. A. Vlieland, *Census for 1931*, p. 99

[62] R. B. Krishnan, *Indians in Malaya: A Pageant of Greater India* (Singapore: The Malayan Publishers, 1936), p. 31; "Selangor Indian Association," *The Indian*, 30 May 1935, p. 6

included not only men from Ceylon but also Malays and Indians.[63] *Kelab Truna* (Youth Club) was launched in 1921 in Batu Gajah in Perak, its name making a general appeal, rather than one dependent on birthplace or religion. Located on the edge of a Malay neighbourhood, it sponsored sports, drama, and music for its male members, following the pattern of similar clubs opened by Chinese, Indian, or Ceylonese immigrants.[64]

Around 1800, when Chinese settlers in Penang organized societies, they identified themselves with relatively small units, but they broadened their labels and recruitment in the twentieth century. Hakka immigrants from eastern Guangdong in 1801 organized the earliest dialect group in Penang (the Chia Ying Association) and named it after the prefecture of their five districts. Shortly thereafter, Cantonese speakers labelled themselves the Chung Shan Association for the Hsiang Shan district from which they had immigrated.[65] After 1900, however, some Chinese dialect and lineage societies widened their list of eligible groups and changed their names to encompass larger regions. Surname associations for the Sin, Quah, and Chuah families amalgamated their separate associations around 1920.[66] The Chinese Chamber of Commerce in Singapore gave itself a broad title and was a quasi-democratic structure based on a constitution and staffed via annual elections. In it, power was exercised by members of several dialect groups: the presidency rotated between Hokkien and Cantonese representatives, who were assisted by a council that included Teochew, Hakka, Cantonese, and Hainanese members.[67] The most powerful public organization of Chinese in Singapore, it had broad political and economic functions as well as influence as a mediator and fund-raiser. Over time, educated Chinese in the towns learned not only to speak to one another but also to work together in broader groups for communal purposes. They used constitutions and written rules to ensure fair representation and the sharing of power.

By the 1930s, associations in Malayan towns became wider in their recruitment and more oriented toward personal development and social

---

[63] S. N. Arseculeratne, *Sinhalese Immigrants in Malaysia and Singapore, 1860–1990: History through Recollections* (Colombo: K. V. G. De Silva & Sons, 1991), p. 144

[64] I would like to thank Mohammed Taib bin Mohammed and Law Siak Hong of the Perak Heritage Society for their information on Kelab Truna; see also Khoo Salma Nasution and Abdur-Razzaq Lubis, *Kinta Valley: Pioneering Malaysia's Modern Development* (Ipoh: Perak Academy, 2005), p. 12

[65] Yen Ching-hwang, *A Social History of the Chinese in Singapore and Malaya, 1800–1911* (Singapore: Oxford University Press, 1986) pp. 37–39; Tan Kim Hong, *The Penang Chinese* (Penang: Areca Press, 2007) pp. 53–56

[66] Khoo Salma Nasution *The Chulia in Penang: Patronage and Place-Making around the Kapitan Kling Mosque, 1786–1957* (Penang: Areca Books, 2014), pp. xxviii–xxix; Tan Kim Hong, *The Penang Chinese* (Penang: Areca Press, 2007), pp. 59, 66, 69

[67] Song, *Hundred Years*, pp. 387–389

reform, as had happened earlier in Bombay, Calcutta, and Surat. Various short-lived groups identifying themselves as Indian or Hindu Associations appeared in Penang and Singapore, first in the 1890s and then again around 1906. Aiming to bring together Ceylonese immigrants as well as Tamils, they sponsored football games, public lectures, and reading rooms to foster sociability along with solidarity and social improvement. In the next few years, similar groups spread to Kuala Lumpur and Klang, and they banded together in 1936 as the Congress of Indian Associations of Malaya. The Tamils Reform Association of Singapore, which had a library and sports facilities, claimed 1,109 members in 1935.[68] Many of these societies followed models made familiar by British expatriates: they had officers, dues, regular meetings, and reading rooms. Members debated, voted, and petitioned on public issues, such as the registration of Hindu marriages or the appointment of Indian representatives to Malayan state councils. Through participation in civil society in Malaya, South Asians learned the forms of representative, liberal democracy even in the absence of its practice in Malaya at the state level. Just as in India, educated urban men participated in a public culture which borrowed key principles and strategies from colonial rulers in their efforts to achieve social recognition and to improve their situation. They claimed a share of civic space while accepting colonial authority.[69]

Alongside these local communal associations grew imported societies linking Malayan urban public culture to that of cities throughout the English-speaking world. Branches of the Young Men's Christian Association opened in Singapore in 1902 and in Penang in 1905, led by the head of the Anglo-Chinese School.[70] The Penang YMCA added a Boy Scout troop in 1910, at the same time as similar groups organized in Kuala Lumpur and Singapore, drawing members from middle status and elite families. By the mid-1930s, scouting spread to Muslim boys and less affluent families, as Malay vernacular schools sponsored their own troops. This movement spread well beyond boys drawn from the urban middle classes. In 1935, organizers in the state of Perak boasted that they were training 1,160 boys in character, handicrafts, public

[68] Khoo Kay Kim, "The 'Indian Association Movement' in Peninsular Malaysia: The Early Years," *Journal of the Malaysian Branch of the Royal Asiatic Society*, Vol. 65, No. 2 (1992), pp. 3–24; "The Tamils Reform Association," *The Indian*, 9 May 1936, p. 6

[69] Douglas E. Haynes, *Rhetoric and Ritual in Colonial India: The Shaping of a Public Culture in Surat City, 1852–1928* (Berkeley: University of California Press, 1991), pp. 142–143; S. Arasaratnam, "Social Reform and Reformist Pressure Groups among the Indians of Malaya and Singapore, 1930–1955," *Journal of the Malaysian Branch of the Royal Asiatic Society*, Vol. 39, No. 2 (1966), pp. 54–67

[70] www.ymcapg.com/index.php?Cat=about; www.ymca.org.sg/enews/appeal/A%20brief%20history%20of%20YMCA.pdf; cited 9 December 2014.

status and affiliation which cut across social classes and ethnic groups and permitted multiple loyalties.

Enthusiastic Rotarians had hybrid, international ties. Datoh Dr Haji Mohamed Eusoff bin Mohd. Eusoff worked during the 1930s in the Malayan Civil Service as a Land Registrar and Assistant Registrar of Cooperative Societies. Although his father was a rich Malay territorial chief and major landlord, Eusoff was one of many sons and the child of a secondary, estranged wife, so he was expected to work for a living. Sent to an English-language school in Ipoh, he grew up alongside the sons of wealthy Europeans and Chinese. In photos he wore three-piece British-style suits, tight collars, and neckties. His daughter described him as "very English," an enthusiastic Rotarian, and an avid international traveller. But he had a strong sense of himself as a Malay too, and during the 1930s he gave several well-publicized speeches to Rotarians on the need for them to sympathize with the problems of Malay farmers and villagers. His oblique references to the injustices of colonial rule and the not endless patience of Malays expressed a moderate anti-colonialism laced with Malay nationalism.[76] Dr Wu Lien Teh, who joined the Ipoh Rotary Club in 1939, studied at the Penang Free School, Cambridge University, the Liverpool Institute of Tropical Medicine, and the Pasteur Institute in Paris before opening a medical practice in Penang. An enthusiastic debater at Cambridge, he helped to found the Selangor Literary and Debating Society, which drew a large group of English-educated Chinese, British, and European men interested in spreading "a better knowledge of and sympathy between Eastern and Western civilizations." To that end, Dr Wu was active in the World Chinese Student Federation, the Chinese Recreation Club, the Penang Anti-Opium Association, and the Confucian Revival Movement, as well as London's Royal Medical Society and the Straits Chinese British Association. During the middle years of his career, he moved to China, where he founded a national quarantine service and multiple hospitals, ending his career there as Surgeon-General to Chiang Kai Shek before returning to the Federated Malay States.[77] Neither Datoh

---

[76] Datoh Hami Mohamed Eusoff, "The Charm of Malay Life," *The Roda*, Vol. 8, No. 71 (May 1937), pp. 236–237; "The Malay Peasant," *Roda*, Vol. 11, No. 86 (October 1938), pp. 121–124. Haji Mohamed Eusoff spoke Malay at home, had two wives in separate households, and in adulthood took on the duties of a Malay territorial chief; Datin Ragayah Eusoff, *Lord of Kinta: The Biography of Dato Panglima Kinta Eusoff* (Petayling Jaya, 1995).

[77] Ho Tak Ming, *Ipoh, When Tin Was King* (Perak: Perak Academy, 2009), pp. 221–224; Rotary Club of Ipoh, "Membership list, 1929–1958"

Eusoff nor Dr Wu was a typical Rotarian, but they illustrate well the reformist interests of the group and the international friendships which the group encouraged. Men such as Eusoff and Wu had flexible notions of subjecthood and diverse identities. Their loyalties were fluid, not fixed, fitting well into the transnational networks of the British Empire.

Even if the British colonial government formally divided the subjects of British Malaya into separate racial groups, educated town dwellers had become increasingly cosmopolitan and interconnected by the 1930s. They had absorbed and adapted the forms of British sociability, which rested on political liberalism as well as imperial patriotism. Civil society, fed by new forms of association, entertainment, consumption, and print culture, became increasingly hybridized and international, breaking down rigid political and social boundaries. In the 1930s, the language of civil society still functioned as a discourse that accepted British control of Malaya as legitimate. Commitments to equal status under the law, to international brotherhood, and to political participation were embedded in the contemporary idea of British subjecthood. These ideals, however, were undercut by the daily habits of colonial urban governance and by the harsh realities of contract labour on the plantations. The two conflicting styles of colonial rule in Malaya sent contrary messages to the people who moved between the two spheres. The benign face of cosmopolitan modernity in the towns only partially masked the racial inequalities of plantation production, on which it depended. The fundamental contradictions between colonial practices and the political values practised in civil society ultimately destabilized colonial rule in the colony.

During the Great Depression, hundreds of unemployed tin miners and rubber tappers arrived in the town of Ipoh looking for work. Some settled on the riverbanks, sleeping under the bridges; others built flimsy huts on vacant state-owned land, where they grew vegetables and raised chickens and pigs. The town provided them no services, but it levied a water rate, a school tax, and an annual Temporary Occupation License Fee of 10 per cent of an assessed value of land and homes. In the spring of 1931, about a hundred Chinese squatters in the district of Pasir Pinji decided to protest the charges. They petitioned the Chair of the Kinta Sanitary Board, Major G. M. Kidd, to cancel, postpone, or lower the tax, which they said they were too poor to pay. The group cleverly sent a copy of their petition to Jack Jennings, Managing Editor of the *Times of Malaya*, who also served on the Kinta Sanitary Board. He not only printed their statement, but later described the squatters' settlement for his readers: "No Lights, Roads, or Water, Huts Made Out of Packing Cases and Patched with Pieces of Tin." Unmoved, Major Kidd insisted that the taxes be paid, despite the recommendation of a majority of the Sanitary Board's members that the taxes be waived. Jennings resigned from the board in disgust and continued to publicize the case. Eventually enough public pressure was brought to bear on colonial officials in Perak that the British Resident, Andrew Caldecott, postponed collection of the tax for a year, a respite which was extended through 1932.[1]

Urban government in British Malaya brought into dialogue several groups with contradictory assumptions and disparate powers. Appointed boards dominated by colonial officials ran the towns in both the Straits Settlements and the Federated Malay States. District officers, engineers, police chiefs, public health officers, Protectors of the Chinese, and Malay headmen, who all belonged because of their administrative jobs, ran the boards with the aid of the "Unofficial Members," influential local leaders

---

[1] *The Times of Malaya*, 18 April and 29 April 1931, quoted by Ho Tak Ming, *Ipoh: When Tin Was King* (Ipoh: Perak Academy, 2009), pp. 568–576

appointed by the British residents of the individual states. Normally they selected at least one man from each "community" – the Chinese, the South Asians, and the Malays – to represent others like themselves. The number of Asian appointees and British businessmen was always kept smaller than the total of the "Official Members," to safeguard administrators' control of decisions. The fight over the taxation of the squatters in Pasir Pinji revealed dissent in the ideologies of colonial governance and representation that existed around 1930. A member of the Malayan Civil Service as well as chair of the Sanitary Board, Major Kidd spoke in terms of the law and of power. He asserted his legal right to control all matters put before the board, which he said was merely an advisory body. In other words, British Malaya was not a democracy, and leading planters, merchants, and doctors need not even be consulted if the colonial administration did not wish to do so. In contrast, the squatters of Pasir Pinji – or whoever wrote their petition – used moral and emotional language to defend their much weaker position. They labelled the taxes as "unjust" and unfairly calculated. They added an emotive appeal asking for "kind and sympathetic consideration" of their request. Their deferential petition neither claimed rights nor threatened consequences. It merely asked for mercy. The elite men appointed to the Sanitary Board, even if formally powerless, were not nearly so submissive. Jennings defended free speech and refused to participate in local administration if the unofficial members had no rights or standing. He and his friends pointed out that board decisions were normally respected, and overruled only in exceptional cases. In practice, he maintained, urban elites had standing and deserved consideration. The resident disagreed. Sanitary boards merely gave an illusion of openness to a closed system of control quite out of step with practices in Britain and with liberal notions of progressive government.

The case of Pasir Pinji reveals not only the anti-democratic assumptions of British colonial officials but also the narrowness of their conception of good government, which focused on two areas: policing and sanitation. Constables kept order on the streets, while town services were intended to regulate the health and safety of human bodies. But a major gap existed between aims and execution. Modern infrastructures – paved roads, drains, water, electricity, bus services – did not reach outlying areas, and little information exists on the quality of service and usage. The municipality felt free to levy taxes for schools and water, even if it provided neither. Moreover, social welfare services were almost completely lacking, except where charities provided them. A regime of licences and intrusive inspections gave the state great power over property and economic activities. Yet the results seem to have fallen far short of official claims. Both the Federated and the Unfederated Malay States were in theory indirectly ruled, sovereignty being layered and divided. Whatever the inflated claims of colonial administrators, they operated in a political arena where power was shared and decentralized.

In the 1930s, municipal councils and sanitary boards found themselves tasked to a high British standard to license, regulate, and cleanse, but with diminished resources and bigger problems to solve than in more prosperous times. In the township of Sitiawan in the state of Perak, the Sanitary Board found that owners could not afford either to repair their property or to bring rental housing up to code. Moreover, tearing down squalid houses and squatters' settlements only increased the ranks of the homeless. In response, town planning efforts slowed down as did enforcement of sanitary regulations.[2] In 1931 in Sitiawan, Malay sanitary inspectors responsible for over 4,000 people brought a total of only 114 cases before local courts; over three-quarters of them concerned cleanliness in the food market, eateries, or street stalls. Only ten householders were prosecuted for infringing sanitary codes, and fines were less than $2 per offence. The rate of prosecution seems low and the extent of intervention narrow, suggesting that colonial authorities were not aggressively working to turn towns into sanitary showplaces during depression years.[3] Many rules and few inspectors set the system up for failure, particularly during hard times.

The little surviving evidence in colonial records from the 1920s and 1930s paints Malayan towns as being dirty and sorely in need of better infrastructure. Singapore's water supplies were too limited to support a sewage system, which in any case had been constructed only in a small part of the city. Householders and tenants regularly dumped human waste in public drains to avoid paying removal fees from private companies. Horses and bullocks defecated on public streets and moved on. Poor drainage, limited street cleaning, and overcrowding magnified public health challenges throughout the colony's towns. In Sultan Street in Kuala Lumpur in 1927, an average of thirty people lived in each of the two- or three-storey shop houses. In the lodging houses, tenants shared windowless cubicles, eight feet square, in which seven or eight individuals could be packed. Inspectors estimated that twenty-four people shared each (certainly filthy) latrine.[4] Smaller towns lacked sewage

---

[2] Sanitary Board Sitiawan, *Annual Report for 1931*, 22/1932, pp. 8–9 (Arkib Negara, Kuala Lumpur)

[3] Sanitary Board Sitiawan, *Annual Report for 1931*, 22/1932, pp. 6–7

[4] Brendah S. A. Yeoh, *Contesting Space: Power Relations and the Urban Built Environment in Colonial Singapore* (Kuala Lumpur: Oxford University Press, 1996), pp. 200–203; Deaths from tuberculosis, a disease spread by over-crowding, remained high in Singapore and rose markedly in the Federated Malay States during the mid-1930s; Leonore Manderson, *Sickness and the State: Health and Illness in Colonial Malaya, 1870–1940* (Cambridge:

systems during this period and relied on a bucket system and employed collectors to rid towns of human waste. Yet how effective could such a system be?

At the same time, colonial claims of achievement remained high. The semi-official *Handbook to British Malaya* bragged to prospective visitors of "rapid progress" in the colony as shown by its railways, roads, hospitals, dispensaries, and schools. "Comprehensive" sets of laws covered "housing, drainage, scavenging, conservancy," while inspectors "controlled" dairies and slaughterhouses and "prevented" nuisances, such as mosquito breeding. Visitors were promised "sand-filtered" water supplies in most towns, and house-to-house collection of refuse. Food supplies were to be monitored for cleanliness and purity. Pictures of gleaming town halls, water towers, and courthouses made urban Malaya look very good (see Figure 7.1).[5]

Residents could easily juxtapose inflated public promises against obvious underperformance, but they had almost no latitude for making improvements without official permission. Property owners had to consult sanitary boards to repair a roof or to build a house; those wanting to open a coffee shop or stable horses had to get approval. Owners did not have absolute control over their property, for a sanitary board could order them to make changes or block their proposals. Private property was not as sacred in British Malaya as it was in Britain at the time. Town governments had wide legal authority to interfere and to mandate, as well as aspirations to do so effectively. Nevertheless, townspeople had some voice in the outcomes of municipal decisions: they could and did object to, as well as obstruct, the enforcement of ordinances. Brenda Yeoh has shown how Chinese inhabitants of Singapore successfully negotiated accommodations in town policies that they opposed. In her opinion, the asymmetries of power in a colonial setting produced a "constant contest" over the "meaning and usage" of the colonial urban built environment.[6] This struggle can also be seen as citizens demanding a voice in local governance – a shift from passive subjecthood to active participation. Inhabitants of smaller towns seemed less well organized and contentious, but they too found themselves drawn into a public arena where they challenged administrative decisions and petitioned for better services. Key issues were water and drains, not political representation or

Cambridge University Press, 1996), pp. 113–114; see also James Warren, *Rickshaw Coolie: A People's History of Singapore, 1880–1940* (Singapore: Singapore University Press, 2003), pp. 258–272

[5] R. L. German, *Handbook to British Malaya, 1929* (London: Malayan Information Agency, 1929), pp. 42, 161–163, 171–172

[6] Yeoh, *Contesting Space*, pp. 314–315

THE WATER TOWER, TELUK ANSON,
FEDERATED MALAY STATES.

Figure 7.1 Water tower in Teluk Anson, Perak, built in 1885.
The contractor, Leong Choon Chong, modelled it on a Chinese pagoda.
The structure stored water in case of fire or drought.

nationalist claims. Towns offered inhabitants training in civic duties
through conflicts over sanitation and colonial control. Despite public
challenges, towns remained both filthy and highly regulated, governed
by men who competed for local support and who had different views of
good administration. None mounted effective opposition to the British
right to rule in Malay before 1941, although they sometimes objected to
specific decisions.

Middle-Class Urban Government

In the early twentieth century, municipal government in the Straits Settlements became less rather than more participatory, increasing the effective power of colonial officials. Support for the principle of elections declined over time, as few bothered to vote. Colonial officers claimed that Asian taxpayers were ignorant and apathetic, and political conservatives feared elections might one day permit Asians to control the councils. When both the powerful Chinese Advisory Board and the Chinese Chamber of Commerce accepted a shift from elected to nominated representatives, a deal between the Straits administration and Chinese elites was struck. The Straits Legislative Council in 1913 passed a new Municipal Ordinance, which ended the right of a very small, rich primarily Chinese and European electorate to choose a few members for the Municipal Commission and gave the governor the duty of nominating representatives of his choice. Then, in the mid-1920s, Governor Laurence Guillemard allowed powerful interest groups to recommend candidates for the council, probably to conciliate them and to gain their support for the limited political consultation that took place. In effect, this gave automatic seats to the European and Chinese Chambers of Commerce, to the Straits Settlements Association, the Straits Chinese British Association, the Eurasian Association, the Mohammedan Advisory Board, and the Hindu Advisory Board. Fair representation was defined in terms of ethnic and religious affiliation, not political position. In practice, nominations went to educated men of proven loyalty, most of whom could function in English.[7]

In the Federated Malay States before World War II, municipal government was handled through sanitary boards. Governors selected board members using an informal quota system which recognized ethnicity, political loyalty, and local standing. Majority representation on these local boards, however, went to members of the Malayan Civil Service, which in the 1920s and 1930s was restricted to "natural born British subjects of pure British descent on both sides," who had passed exams given annually in London. Elite Malays "of good education and character" were very slowly promoted to higher posts in local administration

---

[7] Much of the support for elections in Singapore came from European taxpayers, who wanted more control over city finances. The opinion that an electoral experiment undertaken between 1887 and 1913 had failed was widespread. Critics, including the *Straits Times* newspaper, cited voter apathy, low election turnouts, and unwillingness to serve on the Commission. Brenda Yeoh argues that neither the form nor the objectives of the Municipal Commission responded to the needs of the Asian electorate. Brenda Yeoh, *Contesting Space*, pp. 31–34, 53–58; German, *Handbook to British Malaya*, pp. 51–52, 54

starting in 1921, but the same privilege was denied to Chinese and South Asians.[8] Normally, a district officer chaired a local sanitary board, assisted by a health officer, the chief of police, the senior engineer, assistant district officers, and several justices of the peace. In Kuala Kangsar in 1936, Malays had four representatives. Three of them had middle-ranking posts in the Malay Administrative Service. One of them, a nobleman, Enche Osman, held the local title of Dato Shahbandar. Two Chinese were also on the Board. Europeans outnumbered Asians, eight to six. In the predominantly Chinese district of Sitiawan, the European members of the Malayan Civil Service dominated the Board, assisted by two Malay administrators, two wealthy Chinese, and one Tamil from the Pillai caste of landowners.[9] Meetings were conducted and proceedings recorded in English, giving an advantage to British members and well-educated Anglophones, who were the voices most easily heard in municipal debates.[10] Their power enhanced by detailed newspaper coverage and by a language of public interest and public opinion, such men could pressure sanitary boards for changes in policies. In Kuala Lumpur in 1936, John Hand agitated successfully for the publication of all town planning schemes so that ratepayers could review them. He was supported by all the unofficial members of the Board, and they persuaded the rest of the group to open development plans to public scrutiny.[11]

Individuals and groups sometimes opposed town decisions or the quality of services offered. The Sitiawan Sanitary Board regularly received letters from property owners contesting a tax assessment or objecting to a ruling. Ong Jong Kwang wrote to the Assistant District Officer in Simpang Ampat in 1932, complaining that the open drain in front of Chin Tong & Co. stank and bred mosquitoes. Moreover, customers were "endangered" by the rickety bridge over it, and he wanted a proper, concrete drain constructed. Ong Jong Kwang, a Chinese justice of the peace, pointed out that inhabitants of Kampong Koh were drinking water from polluted wells and asked that the board extend the public water supply from a nearby town. Both of these men used the language of

---

[8] Khasnor Johan, *The Emergence of the Modern Malaya Administrative Elite* (Singapore: Oxford University Press, 1984)

[9] "Kuala Kangsar Sanitary Board," *Malay Tribune*, 4 March 1936, p. 4; Sanitary Board, Sitiawan, "Annual Report for 1931," No. 22/1932, p. 1 (Arkib Negara, Kuala Lumpur). The Tamil member was from the Pillai caste, who had become moneylenders and landowners in Malaya; the Muslim members served as local administrators: a penghulu and an assistant district officer.

[10] In Singapore, the Asians nominated to the Municipal Commission were virtually all English-speaking, Anglophile merchants and professionals. Virtually no leaders of clan groups or dialect associations were selected as spokesmen for the Chinese population, who dominated the city; Yeoh, *Contesting Space*, pp. 63–64

[11] "Future Development of Kuala Lumpur," *Malaya Tribune*, 5 March 1938, pp. 1, 2, 19

public health and public safety to shame the sanitary board to act.[12] Even ordinary citizens petitioned the board, paying multi-lingual writers to translate their complaints into English. In 1931, groups of Chinese and Malay vendors in Sitiawan objected to their transference from one market to another and to competition from unlicensed street hawkers. In each case, they tried to stake out the moral high ground, pointing out what they saw as improper enforcement of rules or "illegal" actions. At least when self-interest was involved, some residents in the towns contested official decisions, and they got some results: the Sitiawan Sanitary Board ordered the police to check on and restrict the hawkers.[13]

The precedent of organizing to gain influence was established early in the colony. Prominent merchants in Penang and Singapore set up branches of the Straits Settlements Association in 1868. They lobbied the British government to defend their commercial interests, and they weighed in on questions of local governance. In 1921, wealthy Chinese and European members agitated successfully against the imposition of an income tax. Described as "rapidly becoming the most important unofficial body in the Straits Settlements," the Straits Settlements Association combined with the Straits Chinese British Association in 1927 to agitate for direct election by British subjects of all the currently appointed members of the Straits Legislative and Executive Councils. They also demanded that there be equal numbers of elected members and government officials, who held seats because of their political positions and who dominated the councils at that time. The campaign was continued through the 1930s by Tan Cheng Lock, an Anglophone, Anglophile Melaka-born plantation owner and banker, who served for years on the Melaka Municipal Council as well as the Straits Settlements Legislative Council. While the proposal to set up elections for the Singapore Municipal Council got little support either locally or from the Colonial Office, both associations pushed liberal arguments for representative local government among their members and in meetings with colonial governors.[14] Even in the absence of active local political parties, proposals

---

[12] Sanitary Board, Sitiawan, "Letter from Chin Tong & Co.,12 January 1921," 12/1932; "Letter from Ling Ti Kong, December 9, 1934," SB 140/1934 (Arkib Negara, Kuala Lumpur). In both cases the Sanitary Board said the requests were reasonable but they did not have the money to make the desired change.

[13] Sanitary Board, Sitiawan, "Petition against unauthorized persons selling fish in Ayer Tawar Village," 18 October 1931, 192/1931; "Complaint of street stalls carrying on the trade of selling coffee and food," 12 August 1931, SB Sitiawan 147/1931 (Arkib Negara, Malaysia)

[14] Chinese made up 20 per cent of the initial founding group; Song Ong Siang, *One Hundred Years' History of the Chinese in Singapore* (Singapore: Oxford University Press, 1984), p. 242. The Straits Settlements Association (Singapore) had 700 members in 1927. C. M. Turnbull argues that the "wealthy and well educated had voice in government," although she downplays their influence and considers the vast majority of Singapore

that would add some of the rights of active citizenship to British subject-hood had surfaced among educated Anglophones.

The demand for greater representativeness in municipal and local governance grew in the 1930s, reinforced by the practices of voluntary associations themselves. When the Straits Settlements Association discussed their new plan for direct election to the Municipal Commission, its members voted on all proposals for reform, and the results were tallied and publicly reported. Under the rules current in 1930, the association regularly elected its own representative, whom the Governor would then appoint to the Municipal Commission.[15] Members of the Straits Settlements Association learned the processes of political democracy in their clubs and decided to push them beyond the boundaries of the group. In Singapore in 1936, a majority of the members went a step farther and attacked recent votes and opinions of the Straits Settlements Association's representative on the Municipal Commission, and they pushed for a resolution that would bind him to follow assembly-set policies. When the Colonial Secretary replied that the appointed representatives were not delegates but free agents chosen because they were "men of standing" willing to serve the public, the Association's ruling committee took offence and threatened to stop electing anyone. Nothing came of the threat, but the question of the responsibility of nominees to the Municipal Commission was debated in the local press and in meetings for some months, with voices weighing in from multiple positions. A rhetoric of public service and democratic representation was spreading in British Malaya. In the mid-1930s, the Singapore Ratepayers' Association, which comprised property owners from all ethnic groups, asked for representation on the Municipal Commission, describing themselves as "a real mouthpiece of the public." Mr Vethavanam, one of the nominees to the Kuala Lumpur Sanitary Board, asked in 1937 that the minutes of meetings be published to "enable an expression of public opinion before the Board came to a decision on [a] matter." Educated urbanites were learning a language of democracy, even if they were not able to practice it through elections and political parties.[16] In the colonies

residents to be apathetic about local politics. C. M. Turnbull, *A History of Singapore, 1819–1988*, 2nd ed. (Singapore: Oxford University Press, 1998), pp. 152–154

[15] "The Straits Settlements Association and Nominees," *Malaya Tribune*, 6 May 1936, p. 11

[16] "Letters to the Editor," *Malaya Tribune*, 3 December, 1936, p. 7; "The SSA and Its Nominees," *Malaya Tribune*, 3 December 1936, p. 10; "The Ratepayers' Association & Municipal Commissioners," *Malaya Tribune* 5 October 1936, p. 12; "S. S. Association Decides to Retain Nomination Privilege," *Malaya Tribune*, 2 June 1937, p. 11; "Kuala Lumpur Sanitary Board," *Malaya Tribune*, 4 February 1937, pp. 1, 20

as in Britain, voluntary organizations introduced their members to democratic processes and drew them into civil society.[17]

Social service organizations also helped to spread the practice of active participation in Malayan towns without arousing the opposition of the colonial state. The global movement toward civic engagement by middle-class populations that developed in the early twentieth century throughout the British Empire, Western and Central Europe, Russia, Japan, and North America also took place in Malaya. In Ipoh and Kuala Lumpur, as well as Manchester, Boston, and Tokyo, associations moved into civic space through the practice of philanthropy and social service. As they raised funds for hospitals, charities, and schools, groups helped to shape civil society, gaining a voice in its administration.[18] Freemasons in Malaya, who interpreted the ideal of brotherhood as including active charity for themselves as well as others, joined together into a district-wide benevolent society in 1902.[19] Wealthy Chinese funded and supervised asylums for former prostitutes and runaway girls in Penang, Kuala Lumpur, and Singapore. Their boards discussed ways to combat sex trafficking and to integrate inmates back into local society, working closely with Protectors of the Chinese in the Straits Settlements.[20] Clan associations and temple societies organized relief efforts and ran local charities, compensating for the weakness of state welfare functions. In 1921, several wealthy Chinese businessmen and medical doctors formed the Perak Chinese Maternity Association to run the Ipoh Maternity Hospital, which provided free care for the town's poor. The Ipoh chapter of Rotary, which had members from all the colony's major ethnic

[17] See for example Leonore Davidoff and Catherine Hall, *Family Fortunes: Men and Women of the English Middle Class, 1780–1850* (London: Hutchinson, 1987); Seth Koven, "Borderlands: Women, Voluntary Action, and Child Welfare in Britain, 1840–1914," in Seth Koven and Sonya Michel, eds., *Mothers of a New World: Maternalist Politics and the Origins of Welfare States* (New York: Routledge, 1993), pp. 94–135

[18] José Harris, *Private Lives, Public Spirit: a Social History of Britain 1870–1914* (Oxford: Oxford University Press, 1993); Colette Bec, et al., *Philanthropies et politiques sociales en Europe (XVIIIe–XXe siècles)* (Paris: Anthropos, 1994); Adele Lindenmeyr, *Poverty Is not a Vice: Charity, Society, and the State in Imperial Russia* (Princeton: Princeton University Press, 1996); Olive Checkland, *Humanitarianism and the Emperor's Japan, 1877–1977* (London: Macmillan, 1994); Jerry Israel, ed., *Building the Organizational Society: Essays on Associational Activities in Modern America* (New York: Free Press, 1972)

[19] Jessica L. Harland-Jacobs, *Builders of Empire: Freemasons and British Imperialism, 1717–1927* (Chapel Hill: University of North Carolina Press, 2007), pp. 70–71; District Grand Lodge of the Eastern Archipelago, *Freemasons in Southeast Asia, Sesquicentenary 1858–2008, The Pentagram*, Volume LV (2008) (Singapore: District Grand Lodge of the Eastern Archipelago, 2008), p. 702

[20] Neil Khor Jin Keong and Khoo Keat Siew, *The Penang Po Leung Kuk: Chinese Women, Prostitution and a Welfare Organization* (Kuala Lumpur: Malaysian Branch of the Royal Asiatic Society, c. 2004); Philippa Levine, *Prostitution, Race, & Politics: Policing Venereal Disease in the British Empire* (New York: Routledge, 2003), pp. 213–217

groups, founded the Destitute Boys' Home for abandoned children.[21] Throughout British Malaya, Rotary members sponsored and volunteered in local boys clubs and hostels, which operated on the same cosmopolitan principles that animated their clubs. In the process, members learned not only how to organize themselves and others, but also how to perform the "duty" of social service through civic engagement, defining "public good" on their own terms, not those of the colonial state.

The Selangor Indian Society, whose major activities seem to have been sport and sociability, also cared enough about local unemployment to send representatives to a Selangor Asiatic Unemployment Committee. In 1936, the Tamils Reform Association in Singapore joined with other groups to request changes in the government's Hindu Marriage Bill, and they pressured the British India Steam Navigation Company through its local agents to improve treatment of poor passengers.[22] Throughout Malaya, social service groups debated temperance, opium smoking, and education for women, criticizing current behaviour and official policies. Looking at colonial towns in India, Carey Watt argues that service associations bred a loyalist style of citizenship that could co-exist with colonial rule, although it ultimately turned toward nationalism.[23] Similarly, activists in a growing civil society in British Malaya took stands on public policies and took on various local welfare tasks, just as their counterparts did throughout the Empire. In the early twentieth century, associations drew educated, middle-class males in Malaya into active participation in urban civil society. Such groups usually prioritized sanitation and social reform over issues of political power and direct representation.

A taste for more active government also grew in the towns of Perak during depression years. In 1930, a large open meeting in Ipoh brought together Chinese, Europeans, Malays, and South Asians from all the larger towns. The *Times of Malaya* claimed that virtually every important community leader in the state was present. Planters, merchants, mine owners, and businessmen joined with unofficial members from the Kinta Sanitary Board and the Perak State Council to ask that the Federated Malay States take aggressive action to revive the local economy, which had been hit hard by the slump. The meeting called for government spending to provide jobs and relieve distress. The meeting reminded the resident that in 1928 the administration had promised to make Ipoh the state capital of Perak, which would require the construction of new

---

[21] Ho, *Ipoh*, pp. 519, 523

[22] "Selangor Indian Association," *The Indian*, 30 May 1936, p. 6; "Tamils Reform Association," *The Indian*, 9 May 1936, p. 6

[23] Carey Anthony Watt, *Serving the Nation: Cultures of Service, Association, and Citizenship in Colonial India* (New Delhi: Oxford University Press, 2005)

office buildings. Speakers argued that extraordinary needs and times required state intervention in the "public interest." Nevertheless, the government believed in balanced budgets. Since no money had been allocated for Ipoh construction, the suggestions were tabled. Years passed and nothing happened, despite widespread unemployment in the town.[24] While journalists and community leaders saw themselves as representing a broadly defined public with the right to be heard, the colonial government felt free to ignore community pressure. After all, British Malaya was not a democracy. It had the trappings of a consultative government – councils, boards, petitions, public meetings – but its government was under no obligation to take action.

Street Crimes and the Urban Poor

Maintaining law and order was another central function of the colonial state, which worked to keep cities safe as well as sanitary. Urban residents worried about the growing numbers of homeless, unemployed men who flooded the towns during the depression. Newspaper coverage of gang robberies and assaults confirmed readers' latent fears, while headlines stoked the fires of suspicion. "Six Murders in Fourteen Days: Police Deny a New Crime Wave in Perak," proclaimed the *New Straits Times* in the summer of 1939. Journalists highlighted the "general uneasiness" about major crimes, although the fine print in the account tied the rise in crime solely to petty thefts.[25] J. A. Hunter, the Acting Colonial Secretary, warned readers of the *Singapore Free Press and Mercantile Advertiser* of the "many dangerous elements" in Singapore's large "floating population." Stories of riots, attacks, brawls, and demonstrations periodically titillated a public already alarmed by vagrants and unemployed. In the larger cities, where most residents did not know one another, suspicions ran rife. Who was disturbing the public's peace? Even thieves used the growing urban cosmopolitanism to their advantage. Gangs whose members cruised Singapore streets on bikes at night snatching purses allegedly disguised their nationalities by using English, Malay, and Chinese to address victims.[26] In a multi-cultural world which mixed the respectable

---

[24] *The Times of Malaya*, 22 April 1930, 6 October 1930, 2 November 1931, 13 December 1935 quoted in Ho, *Ipoh*, pp. 591–595
[25] *The New Straits Times*, 19 June 1939, p. 7
[26] Serious crimes, such as murder, robbery, and gang robbery, doubled in the Federated Malay States during the peak years of the depression (1929–1932). See P. T. Bauer, "Some Aspects of the Malayan Rubber Slump, 1929–1933," *Economica*, Vol. 11, No. 44 (August 1944), pp. 193–194; *Singapore Free Press and Mercantile Advertiser*, 29 August 1936, p. 6, and 24 July 1939, p. 3

and the rough from dozens of nationalities and linguistic groups, a line between friend and potential foe was hard to draw.

Under these circumstances, the police, who constituted a visible presence in the towns, took on the job of guaranteeing safe streets. Their numbers were sizable: in 1931, over 100 British officers led a force of about 4,000 constables and 240 detectives to serve the Federated Malay States, and an additional 4,000 constables served in the Straits Settlements. Communicating by telephone, police patrolled the streets in vans, motorcycles, and bicycles, and central offices could rush squads to the sites of trouble. Armed Sikhs recruited from India handled riots and public disturbances. Aided by a fingerprint bureau and a registry of "bad characters," police kept tabs on known offenders whom the courts had placed "under supervision," and they carried out sentences of banishment and deportation, which courts regularly imposed on vagrants and others deemed to threaten public order. Detectives monitored organized crime, and in the Straits Settlements, Special Branch units investigated "subversive Chinese activities" linked to the secret societies or political groups.[27] Colonial police forces snooped, harassed, and intervened when a group was deemed threatening or subversive. This invasive and regulatory style of rule functioned primarily in towns, where the numbers of police gave them the personnel to meddle effectively. It was much less in evidence in rural areas, where the scanty numbers of police avoided what they saw as lawless zones and where village headmen in remote areas sometimes served as local patrons of criminal gangs.[28] Photographs of town streets in the early twentieth century show uniformed constables, operating from stations sited along town greens and main roads, standing tall to direct traffic and guard intersections (see Figure 7.2). They were a public presence in central spaces, which reassured some and no doubt unsettled others. European officers imposed a quasi-military discipline on police, who were drilled and inspected using the model of the Indian constabulary. The idealized result: teams of smartly dressed, efficient public servants

---

[27] Malays formed the bulk of the constables in rural areas, while Indians were preferred for the towns. Chinese were hired only as detectives, but not as ordinary police from fear that they would be closely linked to the secret societies and gangs blamed by colonial administrators for urban crime and disturbances. A. Caldecott, *Annual Report on the Social and Economic Progress of the People of the Federated Malay States for 1931* (Kuala Lumpur: Federated Malay States Government Printing Office, 1932), p. 64; "Annual Report for 1935," in Robert L. Jarman, *Annual Reports of the Straits Settlements, 1855–1941*, Volume 10: 1932–1935 (Archive Editions, 1998), p. 463; Wilfred Blythe, *The Impact of Chinese Secret Societies in Malaya: A Historical Study* (London: Oxford University Press, 1969), p. 321; "[Police] Equipment," *Annual Departmental Reports of the Straits Settlements for 1938* (Singapore: Government Printing Office, 1940), pp. 402–403, 409

[28] Cheah Boon Kheng, *The Peasant Robbers of Kedah 1900–1929: Historical and Folk Perceptions*, 2nd ed. (Singapore: NUS Press, 2014)

Figure 7.2 Hugh Low Street, Ipoh, being widened in 1920. The street is crowded with autos, rickshaws, and a steam roller. Standing in a small shelter, a policeman directs traffic.

who combined obedience to colonial orders with local knowledge. Officers saw themselves as guarantors of a *Pax Britannia*, which required vigilance throughout the colony. Commanders routinely cultivated local Malay and Chinese leaders, whom they visited to trade information over plates of curry and rice and to give visible evidence of British watchful authority.[29]

The range of activities police monitored was wide. Murders, armed robberies, and assaults were only the tip of a vast iceberg of illegalities that extended to arson, extortion, gambling, rape, and dozens of other forbidden exploits. Police worried about traffic violations as well as traffickers of drugs, women, and smuggled goods. Penal and municipal codes proscribed hundreds of actions ranging from practicing dentistry without a licence to "unnatural offences." Participating in an illegal demonstration, having an unlicensed dog, or obstructing a street could bring citation or arrest. Statistics of reported offences make clear, however, that police paid more attention to some problems than to others. In 1937,

[29] R. H. de S. Onraet, "The Malayan Security Service and the Chinese Secretariat," 28 February 1946, pp. 1–2; "The Importance of Inspections," 28 February 1946, pp. 1–7, Papers Relating to the Malayan Police, BAM V, Crime, file 5, Microfilm No. 2230c (Cambridge University Library, Cambridge)

the Singapore police issued over 17,000 citations to street hawkers for violating market regulations but paid little attention to people who left property that blocked traffic or the 5-foot covered walkways, which lined the streets in front of shops and homes. Very few were arrested for rape or sodomy, but thousands found themselves charged with assaults of various sorts. Whatever the letter of the law, offences had first to be reported to the police and then accepted by them as a pressing concern before they leaped into action.[30]

Official statistics and reports are faulty indicators of criminality, but they reveal the public preoccupations of police and the outlines of their activities. High-profile crimes such as murder and gang robbery got a great deal of attention. Ridding the colony of marauding gangs was a high-priority activity, reassuring to a public raised on stories of larger-than-life thieves who eluded police. One of the worst, a Cantonese named Chan Lung terrorized small towns in the Kinta Valley from 1915 to 1919. After cutting telephone lines and knocking out streetlights, the well-armed gang would shoot the local constables and then proceed to rob the biggest shops. Police eventually captured Chan and secured his conviction on minor charges, lacking witnesses willing to link him to multiple murders. One of Chan's henchmen, "Handsome" Lung Weng, returned to Kinta in 1925 and 1929, recruiting former cronies for robberies and a revenge killing. Finally in 1931, an almost blind, opium-addicted Lung Weng died fighting when an extortion attempt failed. The police, who had not managed to find him, proudly announced the end of robber gangs in the state of Perak. Nevertheless, arrest statistics for Perak in 1930 and 1931 indicate that gang robbery posed a continuing problem there, as well as in rural areas of Kedah.[31]

Police had better success in efforts to control everyday petty crime, whose perpetrators did not have a gang of armed accomplices to threaten witnesses. In 1931 in the port town of Teluk Anson, police picked up Tamil, Chinese, and Malay men regularly for being drunk and disorderly in public or for starting fights. A regular stream of men were hauled into the Magistrate's Court, accused of assault or carrying dangerous weapons. Shopkeepers and homeowners reported thefts, giving lists of stolen goods, which helped police find the culprits. A Malay, Pandak bin Uda Kapak, was arrested a few days after he stole a bicycle from the house of

---

[30] R. H. de S. Onraet, *Annual Report on the Organisation and Administration of the Straits Settlements Police and on the State of Crime for the year 1937*, Straits Settlements, *Paper No. 103 laid before the Legislative Council* (Singapore, 1938), Schedule E, pp. 52–63
[31] Patrick Morrah, "A History of the Police in Malaya, XXI: The Kinta Gangs," *Malayan Police Magazine*, Vol. XXIII, No. 1 (March 1957), pp. 12–16; Caldecott, *Annual Report*, p. 26; Cheah, *Peasant Robbers*, pp. 25–33

Tang Lim Cheng. He put up bail, but was convicted and sentenced to a day in jail and fined $10. Mr Tang got his bicycle back. Even a missing chicken or a couple of pounds of pilfered rubber warranted an investigation, charges, and sometimes restitution. Both the poor and the police took stolen property seriously, and one can imagine neighbours gossiping, pawnbrokers questioned, and patrols put on alert. The concreteness of a particular gold bracelet or a bundle of familiar shirts gave focus to community-wide inquiries.[32]

The apparently cooperative relations between Teluk Anson police and local inhabitants over the question of property rights has to be balanced against a much more adversarial set of interactions over public behaviour. Police sometimes took sides in squabbles between market vendors and street hawkers or rickshaw pullers and clients, and they exercised great power over conduct in public spaces. Municipal laws permitted much police discretion, and men on patrol had constantly to draw the line between what they found acceptable and the potentially illegal. Which strangers would be permitted to sit or stroll along town streets? Constables regularly picked up suspicious looking men and charged them with "failing to give a satisfactory account of themselves." Poor wanderers could be taken to jail for sleeping beneath the arches of the 5-foot ways. Police arrested people whom they deemed vagrants, but how did they select the few who were rounded up? They regularly charged certain rickshaw pullers with obstructing public streets. Yet in small towns with narrow thoroughfares and limited parking space, how did police distinguish those men from all the rest? Banging gongs and drums in public without written approval from the cops could also lead directly to jail, but how difficult was it to get permission, and how loud would noises have to be to become unacceptable? Occasionally a constable chose to make an issue of animal rights: Ng Yew, a Cantonese, was arrested and later fined 50 cents for "carrying a fowl in such a manner or a position as to subject it to unnecessary pain and suffering." One wonders what distinguished Mr Ng's method of chicken transport from those of his neighbours.[33] In practice, police had enormous amounts of discretion, which permitted favouritism and vindictive targeting.

---

[32] These examples are drawn from the 424 cases that came to trial in the Magistrate's Court in Teluk Anson in January and July of 1931; they make up a sample of about 1 in 10 of the total number processed during that year. Information on names, nationalities, the charge, and the disposition of the cases was recorded. Most of the cases were petty crimes, and the few more serious crimes of violence were referred to a higher court for trial. "Register of Cases, Magistrate's Criminal Court, Teluk Anson, Perak," P/KH 10/11, No. 1173/30, No. 1174/30, No. 1175/30, No. 1180/30 (Arkib Negara, Kuala Lumpur)

[33] "Register of Cases, Teluk Anson," P/KH 10/11, No. 22/31; No. 54/31, No. 55/31 (Arkib Negara, Kuala Lumpur)

Traffic control was another arena of coercive but flexible police power (see Figure 7.2). Much attention went into monitoring new drivers and the jumble of bullock carts, rickshaws, motorcars, busses, vans, motorcycles, and bicycles that moved around the towns at different rates of speed, competing with pedestrians. While the requirements for licensing and for following the limited number of rules of the road offered the police clear guidelines, the most common traffic violations in Teluk Anson were committed by young men on bicycles, cited for pedalling at night without a light, for carrying a second passenger, or for not sitting properly on the seat. All of these offences brought fines if proven, and the constable's word carried more weight than that of the accused. Chinese and South Asian boys, presumably out to have fun, could find themselves hauled into court for the most modest of misbehaviours.[34] Perhaps they got caught while showing off or they just happened to catch the eye of an angry cop. Unfortunately, little evidence about these encounters remains; words exchanged and voice tones cannot be retrieved from the archives. Racial profiling, personal animus, or an attempted shakedown surely sometimes came into play. The net result was probably suspicion and dislike on both sides in towns where ordinary people were just becoming used to the speed and the freedoms embedded in modern transport.

Crimes that did not threaten property or safety on the streets got uneven amounts of attention. Stopping the many forms of gambling absorbed much time and effort. Although it was illegal, town residents bet on horses and cock fights; they bought lottery tickets, and they played games with cards and dice. Although petty gambling went on everywhere, police targeted the biggest operations, carrying out dozens of nighttime raids and making hundreds of arrests annually. Chinese detectives and European officers staked out suspected sites of games and urban betting parlours for weeks in advance, carefully timing busts to snag big dealers. They relished the excitement of bursting into circles of avid players and hauling them off to jail. Suppressing gambling operations, which police linked to secret societies and gangs, was part of a wider war against organized crime.[35]

Police were extra-vigilant, too, about collective action that could turn violent. They worried about street fights. They intervened directly or found headmen who mediated quarrels. They monitored demonstrations, arresting leaders and watching participants. When Chinese in

---

[34] "Register of Cases, Teluk Anson," P/KH 10/11, No. 2/31, No. 3/ 31, No. 6/31, No. 37/ 31, No. 707/31, No. 708/31

[35] Police in the larger cities of the Straits Settlements had gambling suppression units during the 1920s and 1930s. Onreat, "Unusual Gambling Raid," in "Papers Relating to the Malayan Police," pp. 1–4, 6–10

Melaka attacked a shop suspected of selling Japanese goods in 1931, constables broke up the group. In the eyes of police, the line between criminal and political activities was quite blurry, and they distrusted rising Asian nationalisms, which they did not want to sprout in British Malaya.[36] In January of 1938, Singapore police rounded up participants in an illegal procession organized by the Anti-Enemy (Japanese) Backing Up Society, and then had to cope with demonstrators who were throwing bottles and blocking traffic near the Central Police Station. Branding the group's leaders as Communists, the Singapore Inspector General of Police arrested many in the crowd and pursued the convictions of 100 people.[37] As international politics became more sinister, authorities in British Malaya cracked down harder on anyone they suspected of radical sympathies or connections.

In contrast to the energetic suppression of games of chance and disturbances, sex crimes and marital problems got much more ambivalent and limited responses. The Teluk Anson police charged only one man with rape and another with procuring during a two-month period in 1931, whose records I tallied. Moreover, they reported no cases of intra-family violence. The beating of wives and children seems only rarely to have been treated as a crime, although newspaper reports allege that it occurred regularly. Missing wives and daughters, when brought to the attention of police, triggered arrests and fines of men convicted of enticement.[38]

Female sex for sale did not count as criminal activity, as long as a girl was over 16 and had agreed in some fashion to work as a prostitute. Although protests in Britain had led to the domestic repeal of the Contagious Diseases Acts and their abolition in most of the Empire in 1888, colonial officials permitted the Straits Settlements to continue to register and license brothels. Government doctors worked for private brothel clubs, where they examined women and hospitalized those with venereal diseases. By the twentieth century, very little had changed in Singapore, Kuala Lumpur, Hong Kong, and other Asian imperial outposts, despite the international agitation by social purity feminists,

---

[36] Straits Settlements, *Annual Departmental Reports for 1931* (Singapore: Government Printing Office, 1933), pp. 431–432

[37] Straits Settlements, "Crime," in *Annual Departmental Reports for 1938* (Singapore: Government Printing Office, 1940), pp. 406–407; "156 Demonstrators Charged," *Morning Tribune*, 11 January 1938, p. 2

[38] Most of the cases involved Tamil women who ran away from their husbands with another Tamil man. Sometimes the cases were settled out of court, but it was possible for a husband to get a conviction of his rival and force either a fine or a jail sentence. See "Register of Cases, Magistrate's Criminal Court, Teluk Anson," P/KH 10/11, No. 4/31, No. 18/31, No. 48/31, No. 544/31, No. 628/31, No. 674/31. Family law for Muslims was under the control of a kathi court.

determined to fight the "double standard" at home and abroad. Thousands of poor women were regularly brought from South China and northern Japan to the brothels of Singapore, Penang, and the Federated Malay States after being sold to a procurer or accepting debt bondage. Authorities worried primarily about the spread of diseases among males, not about issues of servitude, forced sex, or human rights.[39] Major towns in British Malaya continued to have red light districts where brothels operated freely, although colonial officials, empowered by a Women's and Children's Protection Act, would occasionally arrive and question inmates about ages, personal histories, and consent, removing into state-run homes those who did not meet the low standard set for legal sex workers. Police accepted prostitution as a normal urban activity to be regulated, not suppressed.

Between 1927 and 1933, international pressures to end the trafficking of women and children mounted, and medical treatments of venereal diseases improved. As a result, British colonial authorities throughout Malaya became more aggressive in their approach to the sex trade. They blocked the immigration of known prostitutes and ended the licensing of brothels. Aiding, abetting, or compelling prostitution became illegal, as did soliciting. Known houses of prostitution were closed, driving the sex trade underground. "Sly prostitutes" who roamed the streets or worked as bar and club hostesses became the norm. At the same time, economic depression pushed more women into prostitution. Tipped off by informants, police detectives raided lodging houses looking for self-employed prostitutes and their clients. Police normally sent the young women who were rounded up to reformatory homes, where they were married off to willing Chinese men. Convictions of pimps and landlords did little to curb the sex trade. In 1930, constables along with the Protector of Chinese raided the Nam Chau lodging house in Kuala Lumpur, arresting seven young women as well as the house manager on suspicion of violating the law against using a boarding house as a brothel. Fifteen-year-old Wong Chhing told police that she had been sold at age five to a woman who raised her and then forced her to earn money via prostitution. After several weeks working in a club serving wine and sex to clients, she was handed over to an older woman, who ran a group of young girls out of local lodging houses. Clients paid the room rent, managers got 20 per cent, and the procuress got most of the rest with little given to the girls. In

---

[39] Levine, *Prostitution, Race & Politics*, pp. 92–95, 98, 126–129; "Letter G. T. Hare, Secretary of Chinese Affairs to the Resident General, Federated Malay States, 8 August 1902," in "Lock Hospital and Private Medical Exams for Inmates of Brothels," Selangor Secretariat, 1714/1902; 1957/00117 (Arkib Negara, Malaysia)

this case the boarding house manager was fined $500 and sentenced to two months in prison, and the procuress was ignored. Girls in the sex trade had limited options, whether under the control of parents, procurers, police, or protectors. As definitions of crimes shifted, so did police tactics, but prostitution continued. The more the trade was driven underground, the less control police exercised over it.[40] Abolitionist laws seem to have had limited impact on the availability of prostitutes, although they ended the aggressive, compulsory medical treatment of women for sexually transmitted diseases. Using the example of Bombay, Ashwini Tambe argues that colonial legislation abolishing prostitution during the 1920s and 1930s gave the "illusion of action" without the sting of heavy, consistent enforcement. A politically correct response to middle-class public opinion, abolitionist laws co-existed with flourishing sexual commerce, only cursorily curbed by the police.[41]

Constables combined intolerance for riot, robbery, and disturbances of the peace with uneven enforcement of the hundreds of laws whose impact on public order or political climate was negligible. Efforts to combat street crime seem to have been more strenuous than pursuit of illegal behaviours from embezzlement to soliciting. Occasionally a cop or a clerk was arrested for taking a bribe or skimming cash from coffers, but these discoveries seem to have been random rather than the result of widespread campaigns against corruption. Much police activity focused on public spaces, which they had a mandate to survey and where their disciplinary powers could be exercised easily. Yet, as Brenda Yeoh reminds us, colonial control of public space was regularly contested by inhabitants who in their everyday behaviour evaded laws and asserted alternative understandings of municipal environments.[42] Boys riding bicycles without lights or making noise as they marched along the streets were part of a public negotiation between subjects and their colonial rulers over rights to urban spaces and appropriate use of them. Governing colonial cities centred not on voting men into office who had the power to act, but on setting norms which were quietly tested and

---

[40] League of Nations, Committee on Traffic in Women and Children, *Abolition of Licensed Houses* [C.221.M.88. 1934.IV/Series IV. Social.1934.IV.7] (Geneva: League of Nations, 1934); W. D. Horne to the Resident of Selangor, "Minutes of Evidence under Inquiry into Section 11 Women and Girls' Protection Enactment No. 2 of 1914," 29 April 1930, Selangor Secretariat, HQ 1957/ 0303879; "Anonymous Complaint that certain hotels in Kuala Lumpur are being used as brothels," 31 October 1931, Selangor Secretariat G. 2468/1931; 1957/ 00146 (Arkib Negara Malaysia); Warren, *Ah Ku*, pp. 167–177

[41] Ashwini Tambe, *Codes of Misconduct: Regulating Prostitution in Late Colonial Bombay* (Minneapolis: University of Minnesota Press, 2009), pp. 122–123

[42] Brenda Yeoh, *Contesting Space*, pp. 313–315

sometimes publicly challenged. Colonial rule operated through negotiations between police and citizens, between sanitary board members and their constituents, and among a range of interest groups and administrators. Although the inhabitants of British Malaya lacked representative political institutions, a growing number voiced opinions about public policies or flouted the letter of the law to make their points. Since sovereignty in the colony was divided and layered, they could choose among authorities to consult and networks to engage.

Underground Governance

For all its surface solidity, British control of the towns was only partial. Indirect rule rested on top of a generally unacknowledged realm of competing groups and powerbrokers. British urban governance was weak and was informally shared with men powerful in local Chinese and Malay communities. To go beyond its sphere of influence, the colonial government required the help of culture-crossing intermediaries and the tolerance of competing authorities, who have left only modest traces in colonial archives. Both parties to transactions benefitted from silence. Although, after 1901, British authorities in the Federated Malay States no longer formally appointed headmen to run their ethnic groups, the informal leaders of clans and dialect associations retained much stature and practical influence well into the 1930s. Local Malay headmen continued to direct kampongs or villages, backed up by state appointments as penghulus.[43] While the formal control of law and order in the Straits Settlements and the Federated Malay States rested with the police and colonial courts, keeping the peace often required intervention by leading Chinese men or Malay elites. But to delegate power, civil servants and police officers had to know the right intermediaries, and information about certain types of power brokers was in short supply. Some of the most successful were the least visible to British authorities.

On town streets as well as rural plantations, underground bodies competed with police to wield power over people. Neighbourhoods had their gangs. Immigrants from China joined their Triad brotherhoods. For men separated from family and home who knew neither Malay nor English, brotherhoods offered protection, help with employment, and a

---

[43] Wilfred Blythe, *The Impact of Chinese Secret Societies in Malaya: A Historical Study* (London: Oxford University Press, 1969), p. 290. Craig Lockard has identified a similar pattern in Kuching, where indirect rule worked through the leaders of ethnic communities. Separate Malay and Chinese courts handled much of their groups' legal affairs. See Craig A. Lockard, *From Kampong to City: A Social History of Kuching Malaysia, 1820–1970* (Athens, Ohio: Ohio University for International studies, 1987)

quasi-kinship group that proclaimed the goals of self-defence and mutual aid. Chinese immigrant labourers who had virtually no influence, money, or contact with the colonial state found in the brotherhoods a structure to organize their daily lives. Such groups had local authority, which they extended over newcomers. Their organizations existed alongside local Chinese gangs and clan associations that controlled particular territories or trades.[44] In December of 1913, a Hokkien noodle seller working in Ipoh, Kho Tiau Kee, went to the office of the Protector of Chinese to complain about a Hokkien gang which had assaulted him after he refused to join their group and pay protection money. The society they represented offered him security if he agreed to be initiated (at a cost of $8), to pay "dues" ($2 per month), and to join them in street fights. Kho was not happy with the deal, and his employer nudged him to go to the authorities by reminding Kho that he would be in big trouble if colonial officials found out he had joined the thugs' "secret society." In this case, the police managed to arrest the group's leader. Nothing more about its clumsy attempt at extortion appears in surviving records, but similar gangs escaped detection and flourished for long periods of time in both urban and rural areas.

Since they arrived in the region, British authorities had worried about the loyalty of local Chinese societies, identifying them with the Triad brotherhoods, which had a history of opposition to Qing rule in China. They labelled such groups "secret societies" and stressed their illegal activities – primarily smuggling and gambling – to brand them as gangsters. A long history of bloody street riots between rival Chinese associations pushed officials in the Straits Settlements to monitor their leadership and locations. After 1869, all societies in the Straits Settlements with more than ten members had to register with the colonial government, listing their offices, objects, and premises, and it became illegal for British subjects to belong to a non-registered society. Nevertheless, these "secret societies" continued to flourish among Chinese immigrants, and authorities opposed their sponsorship of illegal gambling. In 1890, shortly after William Pickering, the Protector of Chinese, was seriously wounded by a Chinese man linked to Ghee Hin leaders, the state replaced its limited toleration of such associations with active suppression. All societies except those organized for recreation, charity, religion, or literary studies had to register. Any denied permission to operate became illegal, and members could be deported. The other western Malay states passed similar legislation. Those groups that the British had already identified as "Dangerous Societies" – for example, the Ghee Hin or the Ghee

[44] Blythe, *Chinese Secret Societies*, pp. 1–3

Hok – were dissolved and their properties distributed. Anyone who joined or tried to organize such a group in defiance of the law faced stiff fines and jail time, or they were exiled from the colony.[45] Nevertheless, similar groups sprouted like mushrooms in the privacy of town lodging houses and jungle clearings, when the hope of advantage outweighed the fear of detection. Authorities in Penang and Singapore regularly discovered new groups whose leaders they arrested and banished – if the men were born outside the colony and if colonial police could secure sufficient evidence. Illegal societies continued to form in the Kinta Valley tin-mining towns as well as in Negeri Sembilan and Pahang.[46]

During the twentieth century, waves of repression followed evidence of resurgence, as the police attempted to remain one step ahead of what they viewed as criminal activity in the towns and larger villages. After 1890, periodic raids of initiations and meeting rooms drove any remaining illegal societies even farther underground, and banishments of leaders reduced the power of fledgling groups. As a result, many of the welfare and social functions of the early brotherhoods shifted to legal, registered groups, while non-registered societies drifted farther into illegality. To support themselves, the "secret societies" ran gambling games, sold drugs, and extorted protection money from prostitutes and coolies. The Peace on Land and Water Society (aka the "Coffin Breakers") specialized in robbing ships' passengers, but it moved in the longer run to more clandestine forms of skulduggery.[47]

Red and White Flag societies, which organized Malay labourers in self-defence, also proved impossible to eliminate. Despite being banned by state sultans, they remained powerful in Penang, Kuala Kangsar, Bruas, Sitiawan, and Teluk Anson, as well as in dozens of villages along the Perak River. Mahani Musa finds them to have been "deeply rooted" in north-west Malaya, constituting the "unofficial government" of the Islamic community for at least a century before the Japanese invaded in 1941. Although British officials paid relatively little attention to the flag societies, perhaps thinking them benign, Mahani Musa links them to the same

---

[45] Irene Lim, *Secret Societies in Singapore* (Singapore: National Heritage Board, 1999), pp. 25–26; "Anonymous Petitions B: 1914, Perak Files," No. B4, Blythe papers, Box 6, Folder 23, p. 24, PP MS 31 (SOAS Archive, London)

[46] Over 100 secret society leaders were banished from the Straits Settlements in 1910. C. J. Saunders, "Annual Report of the Chinese Protectorate for 1910," quoted in Blythe papers, Box 1, Folder 4, p. 21, PP MS 31 (SOAS Archive, London)

[47] The one exception to registration was the Freemasons, a largely European and loyalist group. After 1890, the government could also dissolve any group they considered a threat to the public order. Blythe, *Chinese Secret Societies*, pp. 46–49, 152, 225, 291; Lim, *Secret Societies*, pp. 20–29

set of illegal activities – riots, street fights, gambling, and theft – that characterized their Chinese counterparts, who in fact also joined the flag societies. Police in Perak reported on their revival in 1902, 1912, 1917, 1922, 1928, and 1931, but could not do much to stop their operations. While police suspected several village headmen and known society members of masterminding an attempted murder in Kuala Kangsar in 1927, police found it virtually impossible to get witnesses to confirm flag members' participation in that or other local crimes.[48]

Chinese societies continued to reappear in the Straits Settlements and in the Federated Malay States during the early twentieth century. Periods of high immigration brought in more recruits, while unemployment triggered by economic decline in the rubber and tin industries increased the appeal of alternative, gang-related forms of money making. Police worked for decades to control the Ban An T'ai group (Hokkiens and Teochews) and its rival, the Khien Khoon or Heaven and Earth Society. Although based in Penang, both also spread among agricultural workers in Province Wellesley, creating an urban and rural network allegedly involved in opium smuggling and other forbidden activities. Between 1910 and 1912, authorities prosecuted dozens of unlawful societies in the Straits Settlements, blaming them for multiple robberies and street fights and banishing 247 of their members in that brief period.[49] In Teluk Anson in January 1913, thirteen shopkeepers sent a petition to the Protector of Chinese, which charged that "ferocious ruffians are causing troubles to the commercial class" by bullying and robbing people on the streets and driving away customers. They gave details on the organization of the San Yi Hing Society, which had enrolled between 100 and 200 men who met in a palm leaf house near a burial ground and in town eating houses. Many members were said to be Cantonese carpenters and sawyers who worked at the Thung Fat Saw Mill. Townspeople apparently thought they were troublemakers long before the police were informed of the group's existence. When San Yi Hing gangs started to harass street hawkers, steal into theatres for free, and break into brothels, local men decided they had had enough. Armed with the names of headmen and their addresses, the police raided a meeting and soon they had secured convictions of five men. Although police identified Ng Iu Chhung, an elderly shopkeeper and mill owner, as the headman, and supplied documentary evidence of his leadership, colonial authorities were reluctant to

[48] Mahani Musa, *Malay Secret Societies in the Northern Malay States, 1821–1940s* (Kuala Lumpur: Malaysian Branch of the Royal Asiatic Society, 2007), p. 5; "Extracts from the Bain Report on Banishment," Blythe Papers, Box 6, Folder 23, pp. 113–117, PP MS 31 (SOAS Archive)

[49] Blythe, *Secret Societies*, pp. 284–294

arrest or charge Ng, whom they called "a man of some means." They decided to let Ng know that "a Damoclean sword is hanging over his head" if any more trouble erupted within the next six months. Police, as well as the Protector of Chinese, reacted when prodded into action by townspeople, but in this case they seem to have been content to monitor, rather than to upset, local power structures as long as leaders prevented major breaches of the public peace.[50] It was easier to crack down on street fights and robberies than on the large-scale smuggling and gambling operations that funded the illegal societies and lined the pockets of their leaders.

During the 1920s and 1930s, the colonial police reorganized themselves: they added more Chinese detectives, multi-lingual interpreters, and specialized investigation units to increase their ability to monitor the immigrant Chinese population. Fingerprints and photographs helped them keep track of miscreants who crossed state lines and changed their names, and an armed detail of Sikhs took on the task of suppressing riots and demonstrations. Nevertheless, societies continued their extortion rackets in all the major towns of the Federation and the Straits Settlements. Where police were thin on the ground, Triad societies successfully initiated members and used their full range of rituals to bind newcomers. Wei Kei societies, well known for their gambling games, flourished among the Cantonese, while the Sin Ghee Hin (New Ghee Hin) organized many Hokkien, and the Hok Tio Kheng attracted Teochew. While maintaining divisions among the dialect groups, the Chinese societies sometimes joined with Malay flag societies to form grand coalitions of local workers to defend whatever turf they had staked out. In the on-going battle of wits between society leaders and cops, alliances shifted as did temporary advantage, but skirmishes continued.[51] Colonial police were unable to eliminate these rival centres of power, which had long existed under indirect rule and layered sovereignty.

It is difficult to assess the size and influence of the secret societies. Police suspected that the societies had spread among government employees – constables, forestry agents, village penghulus, and court officers, for example – who tipped off their comrades and hindered investigations, but they rarely could secure convictions in the courts. Probably the most powerful and effective societies stayed in the shadows, outside the gaze of colonial officials. Historians can see some of the information that flowed into police departments because it survived in

---

[50] "Teluk Anson, 1913," A 80, Blythe Papers, Box 6, Folder 23, pp. 20–3, PP MS 31 (SOAS)
[51] Blythe, *Secret Societies*, pp. 295, 320–321

archives or in court records. Nevertheless its authors had their own agendas. Anonymous petitioners and informers made specific charges, but what were their motives and expectations? Although seized registry books list hundreds of members, they reveal nothing about participation or commitment. For rulers, these mysterious societies raised the question of loyalty, but the concept of a single allegiance does not work well for a mobile, transnational population. Loyalties were multiple and contingent, and allegiances could shift according to circumstances. Colonial subjects could sometimes back the gangs and sometimes support official authorities. They could uphold both of them in different fashions.

Illegal societies remained alive and active throughout the entire period when the British controlled Malaya, and they proved impossible to exclude from either the plantations or the towns. While police managed from time to time to shut down individual groups in particular places, similar factions regenerated easily among male workers who felt a need for more protection and community than distant British rulers could provide. While proud of successful suppressions, colonial officials had few illusions about their ability to crush the societies. In 1932, John Dalley, Police Superintendent in Kuala Kangsar, complained that he could not get society members to give evidence against a group "because it would be made impossible for them to continue living in the district." Society men were "rarely convicted" of any crimes they committed, leading citizens to conclude that "the Government, meaning the Police, is incapable of taking any definite or serious action against any member of these branches of the society."[52] Although frustrated, Dalley did not challenge their conclusion. The societies successfully inserted themselves between the population and British authorities in the towns as well as the countryside of British Malaya, substituting an alternative vision of law and order for that of a police-protected state. Whatever ambiguities existed about strength and influence, the societies represented alternative centres of power that both undermined and stabilized colonial rule.

***

Despite the growing scope of urban government, the British did not attempt to build a unified political community in Malaya in the 1920s and 1930s. Indirect rule, layered sovereignties, restricted rights, and linguistic differences helped to maintain the ethnic and class compartments recognized, and partly created, by the British. Urban workers had no recognized voice in local politics, and in any case Triad and flag

[52] "Extracts from the Bain Report on Banishment," Blythe Papers, Box 6, Folder 23, p. 123, PP MS 31 (SOAS)

societies offered more visible protection and immediate responses. Activism within the growing cosmopolitan civil society produced pressure for inclusion, but it was not sufficiently strong to extract concessions from a colonial administration not interested in power sharing. A local nationalism, which could have overridden differences of class and culture to mobilize unity through opposition to British rule, remained very weak in Malaya, in comparison with such movements in India, Burma, Indonesia, and the Philippines before 1941.[53] Members of the cosmopolitan, educated urban population in Malaya found themselves pulled in multiple directions. They wanted a voice in local governance to parallel their growing economic stake in the country, but transnational ideologies and organizations linked them to compelling political and religious conflicts elsewhere. All local populations belonged to diaspora scattered around the Indian Ocean and South China Sea. In a frontier colony where immigrants, creoles, and "natives" of various sorts jostled for position, transnationalism was the norm, not an exception. Residents learned to shift their political tongues as well as verbal languages, sliding among allegiances easily. The early twentieth century in Southeast Asia was a time and place, to quote Tim Harper, "in between empire and nation."[54] The compatibility of empire and alternative loyalties held together uneasily, but it survived until the Japanese invaded in 1941.

---

[53] Paul Kratoska, "Nationalism and Modernist Reform," in Nicholas Tarling, ed., *The Cambridge History of Southeast Asia*, Vol. 3, Part 1 (Cambridge: Cambridge University Press, 1999), pp. 245–320

[54] Tim Harper, "Singapore, 1915, and the Birth of the Asian Underground," *Modern Asian Studies*, Vol. 47, No. 6 (2013), 1782–1811

8   Multiple Allegiances in a Cosmopolitan Colony

Between 1900 and 1941, people in many societies had to declare their political allegiances and identify themselves with one particular party or faction. Did they support the Qing emperors or their political opponents? Would they back the revolutionary parties in Russia or defend the Czar? Did their loyalties lie with the Allies or the Axis powers during World War II? Anti-imperialists and nationalists mobilized masses of people in India, Turkey, Austria-Hungary, and Japan to demonstrate their common commitments. In contrast, inhabitants of the British Empire could choose to identify themselves as British subjects, a category compatible with other classifications and nationalisms. In British Malaya, maintaining multiple political and cultural loyalties was not only possible but also was supported by law, custom, and daily experience. Consider the case of Tan Kah Kee, who was born in China but became a naturalized British subject in 1916 after building a highly successful business career in Singapore. Tan willingly became part of the colonial administration of Singapore, serving as a justice of the peace and a member of the Chinese Advisory Board. Moreover, he actively supported the British war effort in World War II, and gave his younger sons, who were raised in Singapore, bilingual educations at Anglo-Chinese schools and Raffles College. At the same time, Tan Kah Kee was a socially conservative Chinese who had studied the Confucian classics. He organized his social and cultural life within the Singapore Chinese elite, its clubs, and its business groups. Tan committed major amounts of time and money to the Singapore Hokkien community and its association, the Hokkien Huay Kuan, which ran multiple schools, cemeteries, and welfare associations in the city for its members. A third set of loyalties for him multiplied during the later 1920s, when he became an active but non-partisan Chinese nationalist, heading the Shantung Relief Fund and later the Singapore China Relief Fund. A known opponent of Japanese expansion in China, he supported a series of charities and schools in China without aligning himself with either the Communists or the

278

Kuomintang before 1949.[1] Tan Kah Kee circulated within several political and cultural networks, moving among them seamlessly. His commitments were contingent and contextual, rather than absolute. Within the British Empire in the early twentieth century, allegiances of the ruled cannot be simplified into any stark choice between a pro- or anti-British position. Multi-ethnic, immigrant populations had ties to political groups and regimes scattered around Eurasia and the Americas, and their loyalties were correspondingly complicated and flexible. Imperial cosmopolitanism shaped not only consumption choices in Malaya, but also the political sympathies of British subjects and British protected persons, who supported a range of seemingly contradictory causes. The issue of self-identification and loyalty in the British Empire during its later years has to be seen within the context of the transnational networks built by immigrants and their rulers.

Flexible Subjecthood

The question of exactly who was "British" on the Malay Peninsula in the early twentieth century was complicated to answer. Legal definitions pointed in one direction, prejudice and practice in others.[2] The British Nationality and Status of Aliens Act of 1914 confirmed the principle that every individual born in British-ruled territory acquired British nationality by virtue of birth or the treaties that incorporated new lands into the Empire. All would be considered "British subjects," their status equal to that of all the millions of others who owed allegiance to the British monarch, wherever they lived and whatever their rank or income. Not until 1948 did the language of citizenship replace that of subjecthood in British law, and even then an imperial set of categories, rather than national ones, organized the vast populations ruled by the monarch.[3] Subjecthood derived from the European feudal tradition that promised protection – and little else – in return for loyalty. For those living within the British Empire, it offered a transnational form of belonging that

---

[1] C. F. Yong, *Tan Kah-Kee: the Making of an Overseas Chinese Legend* (Singapore: Oxford University Press, 1987)

[2] For a more detailed discussion of this issue, see Lynn Hollen Lees, "Being British in Malaya, 1890–1940," *Journal of British Studies*, Vol. 48 (January 2009), pp. 76–101

[3] The British Nationality Act of 1948 distinguished four categories of Imperial citizenship: Citizens of the United Kingdom and Colonies, Citizens of independent Commonwealth countries, British subjects without citizenship, and British protected persons; Reiko Karatani, *Defining British Citizenship: Empire, Commonwealth, and Modern Britain* (London: Frank Cass, 2003), p. 116; Andreas Fahrmeir, *Citizens and Aliens: Foreigners and the Law in Britain and the German States, 1789–1870* (New York: Beacon Press, 2000); John Mervyn Jones, *British Nationality Law and Practice* (Oxford: Clarendon Press, 1947)

transcended particular territories and ethnic or religious groups. It was publicly defined in Malaya in ways calculated to reassure British subjects, whatever their race or religion, of their equal status in a powerful global community. Subjecthood seemed to smooth out the practical differences that divided imperial populations without guaranteeing individuals any of the growing array of political and social rights offered by European nation states to their citizens. The concept allowed the British state to maintain a legal commitment to equality of status, while in practice following "the rule of colonial difference" which permitted unequal standards at home and abroad.[4]

The concept of subjecthood helped to hold the British Empire together in an era of growing nationalism. The equality it seemed to guarantee was splintered, however, through the legal manoeuvres of British Dominions, particularly Canada and Australia, as they worked to control the immigration of non-European populations. In 1911 and 1914, the Dominions and the London government finally agreed that Dominions could enact their own nationality laws and differentiate between types of British subjects who would be permitted to gain local residence and naturalization rights. As the self-governing Dominions turned British subjects into local citizens, they limited the rights of colonial subjects from other parts of the Empire to settle in their territories. Moreover, they divided British subjects into favoured and non-favoured groups, in practice according to race.[5] They also created within modern British law the important principle of dual nationality. Canadians could be both Imperial subjects and Canadian citizens. They did not have to choose, for Britishness was compatible with other political identities.

In multi-ethnic Malaya, virtually the entire population had several political allegiances, which produced complicated affiliations as well as loyalties of varying strengths. Any person born in the colony of the Straits Settlements (Singapore, Penang, Melaka, Province Wellesley, and the Dindings) counted as a British subject, as did newcomers to the Malay peninsula from other parts of the Empire. Hundreds of thousands of Indian and Ceylonese immigrants retained their British subjecthood when they moved to Malaya, a status inherited by their children. At the same time, travel back to ancestral villages reinforced family and regional attachments to territories of origin and to a second set of local political allegiances. Malays, if born in one of the "protected" states on

[4] The phrase is used by Partha Chatterjee, *The Nation and Its Fragments: Colonial and Postcolonial Histories* (Princeton: Princeton University Press, 1993), p. 10

[5] Karatani, *Defining*, pp. 75–80, 94–96; Marilyn Lake and Henry Reynolds, *Drawing the Global Colour Line: White Men's Countries and the International Challenge of Racial Equality* (Cambridge: Cambridge University Press, 2008)

the peninsula, were formally subjects of those territory's sultans. Those born in the Netherlands Indies who had moved to the peninsula from Sumatra or other Indies islands were Dutch citizens. Yet they also merged into the local "Malay" population and were deemed "British protected persons," having a right to a British passport. Over time, the British Foreign Office tended to merge the status of British protected person with that of British subject, since both were entitled to the same set of privileges and protections when travelling outside the Empire. Sir Edward Grey's opinion in 1912 that subjects of the Malay states "should be treated in a similar manner as British subjects" continued to be quoted and used in Foreign Office documents in the early 1920s. Between 1912 and 1955, Chinese emigrants to Malaya and their locally born descendants retained Chinese nationality because Chinese citizenship was conferred by inheritance, not by residence or birthplace. As a result, Chinese residents of Malaya held multiple nationalities until that principle was abrogated by the post-revolutionary Communist government.[6] According to these rules, over 90 per cent of the Eurasian, Ceylonese, Indian, and Malay residents of Malaya in 1931 counted as British subjects or British protected persons, and a minimum of 31 per cent of the ethnically Chinese population belonged in those classifications.[7] Cosmopolitan people living in Malaya had options given to them by their multiple legal statuses, despite the rising barriers among states generated by war and economic depressions in the twentieth century. They could move among different political categories, choosing one or another according to sentiment, opportunity, or advantage.

Residents of the peninsula who most aggressively asserted their British subjecthood were Anglo-Chinese businessmen who travelled outside the colony. Claims by Straits-born Chinese for protection as British subjects when living in China arose as early as 1851 and continued into the early twentieth century. Periodically, Anglo-Chinese merchants and ship owners ran into trouble with Chinese authorities, who chose not to recognize their assertion of British status.[8] British officials, who were willing to defend the group's rights but who were confused when asked to identify particular individuals, launched elaborate discussions within the Foreign Office and the Colonial Office about rules governing British status and

[6] CO 273/383/33127; CO 717/28/ 45218 (National Archives, London); Man-Houng Lin, "Overseas Chinese Merchants and Multiple Nationality: A Means for Redesigning Commercial Risk (1895–1935)," *Modern Asian Studies*, Vol. 35, No. 4 (2001), pp. 995–996; see also Ann Dummett and Andrew Nicol, *Subjects, Citizens, Aliens and Others: Nationality and Immigration Law* (London: Weidenfeld and Nicolson 1990)

[7] C.A. Vlieland, *A Report on the 1931 Census* (London: Crown Agents for the Colonies, 1932), pp. 69–72

[8] CO 273/253 (National Archives, London)

legal help. The position which they reached was a discriminatory one. To establish their rights, Anglo-Chinese had to accept restrictions and to produce evidence of their status that went well beyond those levied on other residents of the Straits Settlements. A Costume Regulation issued in 1867 required that Chinese claiming British subjecthood in China dress differently from Chinese subjects, although no consensus was ever reached on an acceptable dress code. Should they adopt European dress? Ought they cut their queues or wear a badge? Each of those choices had connotations that were unacceptable to some.[9] After 1882, passports granted in the colonies of residence served as proof of British subjecthood, and British consuls in Chinese treaty ports developed a clumsy registration system, which required birth certificates and local interviews, to make sure that they knew the people for whom they were responsible.[10]

By the late nineteenth century, the Straits Chinese routinely and actively proclaimed their Britishness in many contexts. In 1899, the *Straits Chinese Magazine* answered the question "Are the Straits Chinese British Subjects?" with a resounding YES, basing their opinion on several centuries of English common law. "*Civis Britannicus*" was the pseudonym of one of their number who in 1902 wrote a strongly patriotic, pro-imperialist account of the South African war and the impending coronation of Edward VII.[11] Leaders of the Straits Chinese community demanded equal treatment and opportunities because of their status as British subjects. In particular they insisted on their right to serve in the local military, the Straits Volunteers.[12] Whenever possible on public occasions, leaders of the Singapore Chinese Chamber of Commerce and the Straits Chinese British Association affirmed their patriotism and their British nationality.

The British Foreign Office accepted the claims of the Anglo-Chinese when in China to be given "all the rights" of British subjects. They

---

[9] CO 273/34/5509; CO 273/253 (National Archives, London)

[10] Regulations issued in 1867 and recognized by the Chinese government identified as "Anglo-Chinese" four categories of people: 1) those resident in Hong Kong or Kowloon when ceded to Britain and their children; 2) naturalized British subjects of Chinese origin and their children; 3) ethnic Chinese born in a British possession and their children; 4) children born out of wedlock to British fathers and Chinese mothers. Each was entitled to different levels of British protection. Naturalized Chinese, the British-born children of Chinese subjects, although legally British, could not claim that status in China. Mixed-race children born out of wedlock were not entitled to the rights of British citizenship in China unless their parents subsequently married and they wore European dress.

[11] Song Ong Siang, "Are the Straits Chinese British Subjects?" *Straits Chinese Magazine*, Vol. 3, No. 9 (1899), pp. 61–66; Civis Britannicus, "The King and the Empire," *Straits Chinese Magazine*, Vol. 6, No. 23 (1902), pp. 106–113

[12] Song Ong Siang, *The Straits Chinese and a Local Patriotic League* (Singapore, 1915)

reaffirmed this position regularly, although changes in governments and local instability intermittently hindered renegotiation of the policy with Chinese authorities.[13] Their defence of the Anglo-Chinese, however, had its limits. Married women took on the nationality of their husbands, rather than that of the land of their birth; illegitimate children did not acquire their father's political status unless parents subsequently married. To be protected effectively, Anglo-Chinese had to have a colonial certificate of nationality, to be registered as a British subject, and to renew annually a passport for travel in China. In 1898, Khung Yiong, a Straits-born Chinese was imprisoned in Amoy, but the British Consul there refused to recognize his nationality because he was not wearing Western dress.[14] The British Consul in Peking, Sir Claude MacDonald, ordered the British Consul in Amoy not to shield him from Chinese authorities because he considered his to be "a particularly flagrant case of a British subject of Chinese race enjoying all the privileges of a Chinese subject by concealing his British nationality until he found it expedient to take advantage of it in order to obtain immunity from offenses committed by him." This decision was protested by the governor of the Straits Settlements, who championed the letter of the law over character issues, but his position was overruled by the Foreign Office, the Prime Minister, and the Secretary of State for the Colonies, Joseph Chamberlain, who was not willing to grant Anglo-Chinese travelling outside British Malaya unconditional British protection. He suggested that the Straits Settlements should "exercise great care" in issuing passports to Anglo-Chinese to "prevent as far as possible [their] improper use."[15] The passport issue was only one of several areas in which the legal rights of British subjects in Malaya to travel abroad were circumscribed on racial grounds in the early twentieth century. The Straits Chinese British Association protested this and similar cases, demanding protection from British officials. They demanded an end to "diplomatic uncertainty" through the issuing of "unqualified British passports, [to] every Chinese born in the Colony because he is a natural-born British subject, whether traveling to China or elsewhere."[16] They recognized that British subjects were not treated equally in practice, whatever imperial propaganda proclaimed, and they deeply resented their inequality.

Nevertheless, the Straits Chinese publicly cast their lot with the British Empire when the opportunity to signal enthusiasm arose. They, as well as

---

[13] CO 717/28/45218 (National Archives, London)
[14] CO 273/390 (National Archives, London); see also, *Straits Chinese Magazine*, vol. 1, No. 1 (1897), p. 156
[15] CO 273/2, pp. 64–65 (National Archives, London)
[16] Song Ong Siang, *One Hundred Years' History of the Chinese in Singapore* (Singapore: Oxford University Press, 1984), pp. 370, 549, 489–490

hundreds of thousands of their compatriots, mobilized in appreciation of empire, using a language of loyalty which circulated among all ethnic groups in Malaya and which created a common ground among them.

Performative Britishness

Thousands of people in British Malaya trumpeted enthusiastic support for the British king using forms and language developed during the reign of Queen Victoria. Rituals of royal celebration, carefully choreographed in London for dramatic impact and favourable publicity, spread widely through the Empire via print, radio, and film, which local officials could then copy on a smaller scale. Elaborate ceremonies to award imperial honours, such as the Most Excellent Order of the British Empire or the Royal Victorian Order drew enthusiastic crowds to see local rulers dressed in silken regalia transformed into British peers.[17] By 1936, when King George V celebrated twenty-five years on the throne, Jubilee celebrations using well-established forms such as parades and patriotic addresses of allegiance multiplied throughout the Straits Settlements and the Federated Malay States. An Ipoh primary school teacher, Sangara Pillai Rajaratnam, recorded the Jubilee in Perak, publishing an official account under the pseudonym, "Loyalty."[18] His friends around the state gave encouragement and sent him newspaper clippings and photographs, which permitted him to chronicle how "every town, hamlet, and kampong in the State did something to celebrate the memorable day." The events in Kampar illustrate what had become a familiar format, combining those of earlier royal festivals with local traditions of celebration. Syed Noordin, a Muslim who was the chief local administrator, worked with a planning committee that included one Tamil Chettiar, three Englishmen, and several Chinese notables. Official photos of the organizers show an ethnically diverse group of men, mostly but not all in Western dress, staring proudly at the camera. Aiming to draw in the entire population, they sponsored Malay dances, Chinese operas, and band concerts, to give everyone a good time. Businesses and shops closed to give workers a holiday, and

---

[17] David Cannadine, "The Context, Performance and Meaning of Ritual: the British Monarch and the 'Invention of Tradition,'" in Eric Hobsbawm and Terence Ranger, eds., *The Invention of Tradition* (Cambridge: Cambridge University Press, 1983), pp. 101–164; David Cannadine, *Ornamentalism: How the British Saw Their Empire* (London: Penguin Press, 2001), pp. 94–99

[18] Rajaratnam is a good example of a border-crossing British citizen. Born in Ceylon, he was brought to Malaya as a child, where he attended local English-language schools. After graduating from a teacher training college, he made his career teaching in English-language secondary schools in Perak. One of his major projects was the development of a public library in Ipoh, Perak, with the aid of the local Rotary Club. He was also a justice of the peace. See E. C. Hicks, *History of the English Schools in Perak* (Ipoh, 1958), pp. v–vi

Figure 8.1 The Pei Yuan Chinese School and the Hock Kean
Association celebrating the coronation of King George VI and Queen
Elizabeth in Kampar, 1937

even town mosques held celebratory services. Students competed in a
football match and other outdoor games. One evening, twenty-nine
clubs, guilds, and schools paraded through the streets, waving paper
lanterns and symbols of fealty. Rajaratnam claimed that most houses had
hung Union Jacks and banners so that residents could express their appreciation of the British king, whose long life and lack of political power made
him a non-threatening symbol of a stable, benevolent empire.[19] In Kampar
at the Jubilee, the British flag was displayed next to the flag of Perak and the
Chinese National Sunshine Flag, to indicate multiple loyalties. The rajas of
the Federated Malay States sent an address to George V in which they
proclaimed themselves to be Malays, as well as His "Majesty's subjects."
Britishness was a capacious identity that drew together many groups
residing in the Straits Settlements and Federated Malay States.

The crowning of George VI in 1937 produced even more elaborate
performances of Britishness (see Figure 8.1). Civic celebrations centred
on the public reading of a declaration of loyalty to the monarch by a local
worthy, usually translated into multiple languages to reach a wide popular
audience. In Singapore, all the leading civil and military officials of the

---

[19] Loyalty (Sangara Pillai Rajaratnam), *The Jubilee Anniversary Book of Perak* (Ipoh: Times
of Malaya Press, 1936), pp. 75–79

Straits Settlements gathered on the stage at the Victoria Memorial Hall to hear the speech of allegiance and to listen to a 160-voice, white-robed choir sing "God Save the King." For the crowds who could not get tickets inside, loudspeakers broadcast the ceremony into the adjoining park, and throughout the week Singaporeans who did not own radios could listen to public rebroadcasts of the London ceremony and other metropolitan observances. Calling itself the "City of Carnival," Singapore threw a week-long party, complete with fireworks and parades for all major communities and religions. Protestant churches, Malay mosques, Hindu and Buddhist temples, Jewish synagogues, and Sikh gurdwaras held services of Thanksgiving. Costumed children from the English-speaking schools presented "Empire Tableaux" at a Festival of Youth. One evening, several thousand Chinese carrying lanterns and driving decorated cars paraded slowly from Chinatown through the centre of the city. Some groups dressed as American sailors; others wore lion costumes. Crowds of labourers, rickshaw pullers, and shop assistants could listen to drummers and to jazz musicians along the route. Men, women, rich, and poor witnessed a cultural pot pourri dedicated to imperial loyalty and British subjecthood. Led by men carrying a Union Jack and the Turkish Star and Crescent flag, a parade of Malays proclaimed their support for good relations between the King and his Muslim subjects. Moving from Kampong Glam down Arab Street into the heart of the colonial city, young men in mock military dress enacted historical battles and scenes of pre-colonial Malaya, while thousands cheered from the sidelines. Chettiars and other South Asian groups organized a procession behind their silver temple cart, which led devotees around the town. As the parades wound through the streets, they linked ethnic neighbourhoods symbolically to the colonial heart of the city. Union Jacks, royal portraits, crowns, and crests signalled a common vocabulary for expressions of loyalty to the king, which rang out around the globe from Melbourne to Kuala Lumpur to Bombay, Gibraltar, and London. At the Ramakrishna Mission, Sikh, Sinhalese, Tamils, and Indian Muslims issued a declaration: "We gather together ... to acknowledge a new King and to proclaim our own sense of citizenship and our membership in the far-flung Empire ... We are all members of one family." How deeply felt or long lasting were these patriotic sentiments is unknowable, but royal celebrations periodically mobilized at least the urban populations of the Straits Settlements and other parts of Malaya into extravagant, empire-wide expressions of loyalty, which Asians planned, funded, and joined in large numbers.[20] They

[20] *Singapore Free Press and Mercantile Advertiser*, 6 April 1937, p. 3; 10 April 1937, p. 1; 6 May 1937, p. 9; 12 May 1937, p. 2; 14 May 1937, p. 9

adopted imperial forms of allegiance, inflecting them with local rituals and images to produce a multi-cultural performance of Britishness. These ceremonies expressed contextual commitments, which were seen as legitimately compatible with loyalties to other rulers and polities.

The group most heavily represented in these self-proclaimed crowds of British subjects were male city dwellers. Newspaper accounts identify Jubilee organizers as socially prominent men drawn from the British, Chinese, Malay, and South Asian "communities," although school children, workers, and local villagers attended the events. Most of the active participants were men and boys, drawn from various clubs, schools, and skilled occupations. Although Malay and Chinese schoolgirls joined in children's sporting contests or parades, they were a minority. While dozens of European women danced, prayed, and dined in public to celebrate royal longevity, Asian females, for the most part, did not. Nevertheless, the large crowds that flocked to see fireworks and many free entertainments included women and family groups, who walked from their homes to the ceremonies in familiar urban public spaces. How such spectators interpreted these events is not known, but they were happy to participate and to be counted among the celebrants.

British patriotic performance widened socially during the 1920s and 1930s in terms both of class and of gender. Telok Anson's Jubilee parade in 1936 included wharf labourers, forest labourers, and small shopkeepers, as well as people of higher social status. A local Malay club, an Indian association, several Chinese clubs, and a convent that taught Chinese and Malay girls were illuminated, alongside government buildings and schools.[21] These events spread well beyond the colony's elites to urban workers and ordinary residents. As education became more widely available and the celebration of events such as Empire Day spread, more women were exposed to the language and symbols of Britishness. Jubilee speakers urged loyalty on girls, as well as boys, as they praised King George V and his "wise government." In the small Perak town of Batu Gajah, girls from a Chinese school sang and danced as part of a celebratory Jubilee show. In Kampar, Mrs C. P. Lee and Madam Lee Soon Ho of the Public Chinese Girls' School helped to plan the official sports day, and the former was photographed with the Kampar Jubilee Executive Committee.[22] By the mid-1930s, Asian females had taken on a larger part in official ceremonies; Lady Chulan, wife of the heir to the Perak sultanate, gave prizes at a Jubilee celebration sports day in the town of Grik.[23]

---

[21] Loyalty, *Jubilee Anniversary Book*, p. 88
[22] Loyalty, *Jubilee Anniversary Book*, pp. 70, 74, 76–77
[23] Loyalty, *Jubilee Anniversary Book*, p. 38

Mrs Tan Chay Yan, the owner of rubber estates in Melaka and Johore, was awarded a Silver Jubilee medal in 1935 and profiled in Melaka's royal coronation souvenir booklet in 1937 as a patron of girls' education and of the Portuguese Church.[24] Being female became compatible with the public expression of political loyalty.

Yet what sort of Britishness was being celebrated? The British king was a constitutional monarch without political power, someone representing no specific party or ideology, whose role was to solidify imperial patriotism. To populations unsettled by World War I and by party conflicts, depressions, floods, and famines, the British monarch offered a symbol of stability and a romanticized life of duty to his people. Moreover, the language of British subjecthood was that of promised equality throughout the Empire. Sangara Pillai Rajaratnam maintained that all peoples of the peninsula had lifted themselves above "colour, creed, language, custom or religion" to participate in the Jubilee. His statement highlighted a message of political equality among all ethnic and social groups. Rajaratnam had long made similar arguments, and he saw British subjecthood as guaranteeing equality of political status. The Empire was a "federation of free nations" whose members agreed to stand together out of fellowship and self-interest, and he gave equal weight and importance to their multiple religions, traditions, and literatures. He wrote in 1926,

The poorest and the weakest are the children of the Empire just as much as the richest and the strongest. Whether we come from the interior villages and Kampongs or from the towns, whether we live in the humble attap sheds in a far away Ulu or in high, stone-walled mansions in the pecan, whether we walk about on foot or drive about in thick cushioned and balloon tyred cars, whether in the train of life we are passengers in the third class or first class, we are proud sons and daughters of the British Empire, which fact brings us to the same level after all.[25]

His comments asserted social equality within Malaya, challenging local elites as well as British overlords on the issue of status. These were radical claims in the context of colonial Malaya both in 1926 and 1936, when imperial rule rested upon ethnic inequalities and British privilege. Rajaratnam had taken the language of subjecthood and turned it effectively against the racial and economic hierarchies that divided the Empire.

---

[24] P. V. Gopalan, *Coronation Souvenir of the Settlement of Malacca, Undertaken with a View to Foster an Everlasting Inter-Racial Harmony and Amity among the Heterogeneous Folks of this Historic Settlement* (Kuala Lumpur: Commercial Press, 1937), p. 166

[25] S. Rajaratnam, "The Significance of the British Empire: Thoughts on Empire Day for School Children," *The Pedagogue*, Vol. 1, No. 1 (1926), pp. 27–30

The rhetoric of royal ritual openly challenged prevailing assumptions of difference based on both class and race. At the Silver Jubilee Thanksgiving Service in Teluk Anson, Reverend Hamilton Aikin told the multi-ethnic audience, "You and I are citizens of the Empire," and he identified the monarchy with "principles of equity, purity, and righteousness." As subjects, they received justice and "a square deal." The official Coronation Souvenir booklet for Melaka, produced by bi-lingual Tamil teacher and headmaster P. V. Gopalan, proclaimed, "Nor colour, clan, nor widening waves/Shall cleave the Commonwealth." An egalitarian language that mixed subjecthood with citizenship circulated in the virtually independent, democratized sections of the Empire and was sometimes used in Malaya by both Asians and British.[26] The overriding public message that circulated during the Jubilee in Malaya was one of civil and social equality, whatever the daily practices of colonial rule.

Of course Gopalan and Rajaratnam were aware that Britishness could be, and usually was, defined more narrowly. Anthony Stockwell has described Europeans' social behaviour in Malaya as "white tribalism," based on belief in the cultural and biological inferiority of Asians to those of Caucasian descent. Even Sir Hugh Clifford of the Malayan Civil Service, who spent most of his adult life championing Malay rights and culture, wrote of the "hopeless limitations of the brown people." He saw the Asian subjects of the British Empire as "alien folk" who could not follow the moral rules of the English.[27] While there was much variation in the racial attitudes of English residents of Malaya, heavy-handed statements about racial differences circulated freely, undermining official messages of imperial community and equality. Residents of British Malaya confronted multiple definitions of Britishness, which could not be reconciled. Nevertheless, imperial ritual and rhetoric gave them a public platform for challenging the "white tribalism" of their rulers, which they did with both loyalty and defiance as they reminded colonial rulers that subjecthood entailed equality.

Performative Malayness

Abdul Majid bin Zainuddin was a devout Muslim and proud Malay who faithfully observed Ramadan and paid his respects to his sultan on appropriate occasions. Educated both in Malay and in English, he worked as a teacher, as the assistant inspector of Malay vernacular schools, and, later, as a pilgrimage officer in Jeddah, representing the Federated Malay

[26] Loyalty, *Jubilee Anniversary Book*, pp. 92–93; Gopalan, *Coronation Souvenir*, p. 3
[27] A. J. Stockwell, "The White Man's Burden and Brown Humanity: Colonialism and Ethnicity in British Malaya." *Asian Journal of Social Science*, Vol. 10, No. 1 (1982): 44–68; Lees, "Being British in Malaya," pp. 76–101

States. Abdul Majid easily shifted cultural styles as he moved from setting to setting. Abdul Majid had two great enthusiasms: the Malay language and sports, particularly football and billiards. He taught Malays English and the English Malay, encouraging all to leap over linguistic barriers. At home, he insisted on following Malay customs and forms, but at school, he organized football leagues and lectured boys on "the sporting spirit."[28] Abdul Majid saw no contradiction between his reverence for his sultan and service to the British colonial administration. A socially conservative but modern-minded Malay, he moved easily in the transnational networks fostered by the British Empire.

Indirect rule assumed the compatibility of British and Malay loyalties. The British monarch served as the overlord of the Malay sultan, who maintained his court and ritual importance. Malays could honour both and give each his due, since sovereignty was formally divided, albeit unequally. What it meant to be Malay, however, was debated in the early twentieth century. The Malaysian constitution defines Malays as Malay-speaking Muslims who follow a "Malay way of life." But neither language, nor religion, nor traditions are straightforward guides to self-definition and allegiance in a world where the Malay language served as a *lingua franca*, where long-distance migration of Muslims was common, and where customs varied village to village. Exactly who was Malay and what that label meant at different dates has remained open to question. Although Leonard Andaya sees the beginnings of a Malay identity as early as the seventh century in the in the area of Melaka, the term was rarely used in pre-colonial times. It gained a following in the nineteenth century, when colonial hard-edged categorization of peoples spread. Nevertheless, its boundaries have remained fuzzy: some see an amorphous Malay-Polynesian world stretching from Thailand to Hawaii, while others tie it to cultural discourse in the regions of Melaka and Johore. Whether local Muslims of Arab or Indian descent were "real Malays" led to conflict during the 1920s and 1930s among intellectuals jostling for the right to represent the group. Rather than debate the issue, British amateur ethnologists opted during the colonial period for a simplistic description: Malays were brown-skinned peasant farmers who lived in wooden houses on stilts in rural areas and who dressed in sarongs. Finding the term useful to characterize a range of local people different from themselves, they saw Malayness in life choices which flowed into loyalty to a local sultan.[29]

---

[28] William R. Roff, ed., *The Wandering Thoughts of a Dying Man: the Life and Times of Haji Abdul Majid bin Zainuddin* (Kuala Lumpur: Oxford University Press, 1978), pp. viii–xiii, 83–84, 130, 144

[29] Leonard Y. Andaya, "The Search for the 'Origins' of Melayu," *Journal of Southeast Asian Studies*, Vol. 32, No. 3 (2012), pp. 315–330; Anthony Milner, *The Malays* (Chichester:

Discussion of what it meant to be Malay spread only after outsiders appeared, bringing with them very different ideas about self-definition and belonging, ones in which "race" placed a large part.

Among local people, Malayness was tightly bound to the political idea of *kerajaan* – rule by a raja who was "God's Shadow on Earth." Malays "defined themselves as subjects of a sultan" to whom they owed unquestioning loyalty. Lacking a tradition of political participation, Malays substituted a system of hierarchy based upon reputation (*nama*) and officially granted honours. Rajas, whose major activities were ceremonial rather than administrative, created and ratified social distinctions based upon titles, dress, and precedence. Sumptuary legislation decreed who could wear silk and who could carry an umbrella. How head scarves were tied proclaimed status and allegiance. Identifying Malay kingdoms as "theatre states" understates the importance of military power and wealth, but that term recognizes the importance of ritual and reputation at the royal courts. Sultans controlled people and relationships, rather than a particular, bounded space. The people (*rakyat*) had duties, rather than rights: "Whoever be king, my hands go up to my forehead," declared a nineteenth-century Malay proverb. Not only could possessions, labour service, and income be commandeered in pre-colonial times, but debt bondage produced a type of slave status, which was inherited by children. Those who objected could migrate elsewhere, leaving the polity largely untouched by their resentments. Not without reason, British officials described these relationships as autocratic and feudal, but they took advantage of the structure of *kerajaan* and its public display for their own ends as they built modern administrations.[30]

When British residents arrived to "advise" the Peninsula's sultanates, they broadened royal rituals to give themselves a central place in ceremonies of allegiance and honour. In 1874, after a small-scale civil war broke out in Sungai Ujung over succession issues, the British Resident, Captain P. J. Murray, supported the accession of Antah, the more popular candidate for sultan. As part of Antah's installation, the new ruler (the *yam tuan*) toured his state with the British Resident. At the formal ceremony of investiture, Murray initially took the central chair, with the prospective raja and other chiefs arranged around him according to precedence. After agreements of accession and confederation were read, Murray shook

Wiley-Blackwell, 2008), pp. 5–15; Ariffin Omar, *Bangsa Melayu: Malay Concepts of Democracy and Community 1945–1950* (Kuala Lumpur: Oxford University Press, 1993), pp. 16–17

[30] Clifford Geertz, *Negara: The Theater State in Nineteenth-Century Bali* (Princeton: Princeton University Press, 1980); Sir Richard Winstedt, ed., *Malay Proverbs* (London: John Murray, 1950), p. 49; Anthony Milner, *The Invention of Politics in Colonial Malaya* (Cambridge: Cambridge University Press, 1995), pp. 21–27; Milner, *The Malays*, pp. 66–70

hands and gave up his central seat to Antah, while police shot their rifles into the air. Murray's farewell address, which consisted largely of patronizing advice, was answered by similar statements from the chiefs, thanking their "friend" for his "assistance" and pledging to keep the peace. A language of cooperation and friendship masked differences in power, but the centrality of the British role was unmistakable.[31] A new style of Malay rule was formed under the umbrella of British protection, and its leaders, some of whom wore European-style dress uniforms, acknowledged their fealty to the British. Over time, installations became much more elaborate, mixing older Malay rites with western-style banquets, fireworks, and toasts to Queen Victoria.[32] Malay traditions were reinvented in a new idiom that reaffirmed royal prestige while acknowledging British supremacy (see Figure 8.2). The arrangement both masked and rationalized the almost complete transfer of power to the British, despite the fiction of continued Malay sovereignty. The contrast between Malay traditionalism and a broader British modernity was exploited by sultans and colonial officials to justify themselves. Both parties gained from the bargain.[33] The losers were the ordinary people, who were expected to remain in their villages and pay their taxes without complaint.

Chances to proclaim Malayness through performance multiplied under British rule. Audiences and obeisances, childbirths and funerals brought subjects face to face with royalty. Automobiles and yachts ferried sultans in style through their districts to meet their people. Dressed in gold-embroidered sarongs and silk headscarves folded into crowns, they greeted petitioners in elegant reception halls and invited thousands to sumptuous wedding parties in new palaces stuffed with European goods. A lucky few went to London for Victoria's Diamond Jubilee, where they were required to wear "traditional" Malay dress to contribute to the Empire's parade of exotica. The sultans personified Malayness, but a new variety infused with European modernism in which they were seen to embrace "progress." Sultans' visible presence at key state and imperial events assured their subjects of the continuity of Malay sovereignty, while concealing the effective transfer of power to the British. For the sultans, Malay "tradition" meant survival and continued influence, whatever changes the colonial political economy brought to their realms.

[31] The district which became Negeri Sembilan had been settled by migrants from Sumatra, primarily Minangkabau Muslims who had their own set of ruling families, customs, and feuds. The resulting confederation of nine mini-states became part of the Federated Malay States in 1896, and it still exists as part of Malaysia; Donna J. Amoroso, *Traditionalism and the Ascendancy of the Malay Ruling Class in Colonial Malaya* (Petaling Jaya and Singapore: Strategic Information and Research Development Centre of Malaysia and NUS Press, 2014), pp. 26–29
[32] Amoroso, *Traditionalism*, pp. 81–86   [33] Amoroso, *Traditionalism*, pp. 6–7, 11, 23

Figure 8.2 Sultan Alang Iskandar and his entourage with Sir Hugh Clifford, High Commissioner of the Federated Malay States, in Kuala Kangsar, 1928

Sultan Idris Shah, who ruled between 1887 and 1916 in Perak, the richest of the Malay states, helped reconcile his people to British ways. His installation, where he was presented with an ancient Perak sword and seal, progressed to a seventeen-gun salute and the playing of "God Save the Queen." An early supporter of English-language education and of cooperation with the British, Sultan Idris won great favour with his pro-imperial attitudes and activities and earned English chivalric honours, as well as visits by touring royals. In 1913, Edward VII made him Knight of the Royal Victorian Order, sending him its large and lavish Grand Cross, a bejewelled and enamelled silver star with a Tudor crown in its centre. To confer it, his staff cooperated with British colonial officials to organize a week of celebrations in his capital, the riverside town of Kuala Kangsar. After a royal barge brought the silver star up the Perak river, seventy-seven howdah-capped elephants carried it through the decorated streets of the town, while Malays in sarongs and songket caps cheered. Gongs and tom-toms marked the beat of the slow parade. Investiture took place in the palace throne room decorated in royal yellow, where the sultan and his court sat under ceremonial umbrellas, surrounded by guards with glittering swords and krises. Watched by British officials and leading citizens, Malay chiefs made ceremonial homages, and communal leaders offered formal addresses of congratulation.[34]

However striking the Malay packaging of the event, its imperial frame-work was unmistakable. The local Chinese community framed its response as "pride and pleasure . . . on the bestowal . . . of this additional mark of the confidence of your Overload and Protector . . . this mark of favour from the Great White King beyond the seas." Many of the elephants had been contributed by a British District Officer, Hubert Berkeley, who used them for local transport in northern Perak. Moreover, the overall list of events scarcely differed from those mounted by town committees for British coronations and ritual events: sports days, fireworks, and military drills with added Asian touches in the form of lantern parades, rongkeng dancers, and shadow puppets. As the Malay State Guards paraded, mixed crowds of Europeans, Malays, Chinese, and Tamils wandered through city streets and parks. None seemed to object to the intermingling of Malay and British styles of celebration.[35] Indirect rule in practice assumed the com-patibility of dual loyalties.

Cosmopolitan Commitments and Multiplying Allegiances

Although British subjects regularly proclaimed loyalty to the English king and British protected persons honoured their sultans, news of political alternatives drifted into the peninsula from outside and stretched the

[34] *Malay Mail*, 25 September 1913, p. 9; 26 September 1913, p. 9; *Malay Daily Chronicle*, 24 September 2013, p. 7; 26 September 1913, p. 7
[35] *Malay Mail*, 25 September 1913, p. 9; 26 September 1913, p. 9; *Malay Chronicle*, 26 September 1913, p. 7; Amoroso, *Traditionalism*, pp. 81–82

allegiances of the local population. Political exiles from failed uprisings and civil wars went not only to London, Paris, and Tokyo, but also to Penang and Singapore, settling long enough to convert local contacts. Sun Yat Sen, who became the first president of the Republic of China, settled in Penang for six months in 1910, actively spreading a gospel of nationalism and democracy among Chinese emigrants to the peninsula and raising money for his revolutionary allies.[36] Although there was no active domestic political scene, literate Malays found it difficult to ignore the winds of political controversy that swirled into the Indian Ocean world from the rest of Eurasia and Africa. Newspapers covered the Boer War and Sino-Japanese battles in lurid detail and discussed Ottoman troubles, exposing the fault lines of rickety empires. They became even more complicated when imperial powers began a world war that forced citizens to take sides. Soldiers and civil servants were sent out to fight in the broader conflict, whose ideological repercussions bounced back to the peninsula. Effective imperial governance entailed managing cosmopolitan people, some of whom accepted anti-colonial arguments and political causes.

Empires fostered connections among dissident students, sailors, Sufis, and spies. The sea lanes along which troops moved between Calcutta, Singapore, and Hong Kong were also used by Indian revolutionaries travelling around Asia. Steamers from the United States to Singapore employed Indian sailors and labourers radicalized by time spent among socialists and trade unionists in North America. Enthusiasts smuggled into Singapore and Penang the weekly paper *Ghadar* (meaning mutiny or rebellion in Urdu), published in San Francisco and later in Canada by Punjabi nationalists. It then circulated to North Indian soldiers via the Sikh gurdwaras that they visited. Several hundred subversive South Asian travellers stopped in Singapore and Penang in 1914 and 1915 on their way to various destinations around the Indian Ocean region, where they planned to encourage simultaneous mutinies by Indian regiments.[37] Ports carried on a free trade of ideas as well as goods in the years before passports and heavy tariffs effectively inhibited global exchanges. During World War I, globalization spread revolutionary ideas as well as conservative nationalism.

---

[36] Marie-Claire Bergère, *Sun Yat Sen*, Translated by Janet Lloyd (Stanford: Stanford University Press, 1998)

[37] R. W. E. Harper and Harry Miller, *The Singapore Mutiny* (Singapore: Oxford University Press, 1984), p. 9; Maia Ramnath, *From Haj to Utopia: How the Ghadar Movement Charted Global Radicalism and Attempted to Overthrow the British Empire* (Berkeley: University of California Press, 2011)

As part of their plan for victory in World War I, the German and Ottoman governments encouraged rebellions among the Muslim populations in opponents' empires by calling for a jihad against infidel rulers. Would Indian Muslim soldiers fighting for Britain attack Ottoman troops defending the Caliph? Pan-Islamic sentiments, which circulated through the Middle East and Northern Africa in the early twentieth century, signified sedition in colonies where conservative Muslim rulers pledged their allegiance to a British overlord.[38] Pro-Ottoman propaganda slipped into Malaya via the Netherlands Indies and Muslim travellers. A few months later, in February 1915, those efforts bore fruit in Singapore when the Indian Fifth Light Infantry, the city's main garrison force, mutinied. A regiment of Punjabi soldiers seized guns and marched around the city while trying unsuccessfully to raise a rebellion. The Muslim troops in the infantry unit attacked civilians and soldiers, killing 47 men. Fearing a repeat of the 1857 Indian Mutiny, European women and children fled in panic to steamships in the harbour. After two days, however, loyal soldiers aided by local volunteers and troops sent by the Sultan of Johore suppressed the uprising and captured most of the dissidents. Over two hundred men were jailed, transported for life, or executed by firing squad in a gruesome public display of retribution for what at the time seemed a major threat to imperial security. A Muslim merchant, Kassim Ali Monsoor, who had entertained troops and officers of the Fifth Infantry and whose ties with Indian nationalists were known, was arrested and executed. Although an official inquiry blamed ineffective commanders and poor discipline for the mutiny, other explanations seem more convincing. Some of the regiment had been attending a local mosque whose imam had urged rebellion against the British, and others had easy access to anti-British pamphlets that circulated in the city. On the day of the outbreak, rumours that the regiment was being sent west to fight Turkish troops raised discontent. Although officials both in Singapore and in London took pains to deny the broader significance of the mutiny, they also moved quickly to expand political intelligence networks in the region, and they worked with the Dutch to track radicals of various stripes who moved across porous imperial borders.[39] Subversion

---

[38] G. F. Abbott, "A Revolt of Islam?," *Quarterly Review*, Vol. 222, No. 442, Part I (December 1914), pp. 68–69; Francis Robinson, "The British Empire and the Muslim World," in William Roger Louis and Judith M. Brown, eds., *The Oxford History of the British Empire*, Vol. 4, *The Twentieth Century* (Oxford: Oxford University Press, 1999), pp. 398–420

[39] Tim Harper, "Singapore, 1915 and the Birth of an Asian Underground," *Modern Asian Studies* Vol. 47, No. 6 (2013), pp.1782–1811; Heather Streets-Salter, "The Local Was Global: The Singapore Mutiny of 1915," *Journal of World History*, Vol. 24, No. 3 (2013), pp. 89–100; R. W. E. Harper and Harry Miller, *Singapore Mutiny* (Singapore: Oxford

by militant nationalists worried colonial administrators, and they never managed to stop the flow of anti-British propaganda into the peninsula. In comparison with concurrent anti-imperial activities in India, Burma, Egypt, Palestine, and other parts of the Middle East, the mutiny seems a very small crack in the loyalist carapace of British Malaya. Yet it surely signalled the effective infiltration of the colony by subversive ideas from outside.

By the 1930s, Indian nationalists regularly visited British Malaya, and news about campaigns for more home rule in India spread in the peninsula. Anarcho-syndicalists, Theosophists, conventional nationalists, Hindu reformists, and Muslim modernists carried their patriotic messages to Malaya, but in the cosmopolitan world in which they moved, these ideas proved complementary rather than contradictory.[40] Tolerance for political differences pervaded the pages of *The Indian*, an English-language newspaper published in Penang and Kuala Lumpur between 1935 and 1941, which aimed to foster "harmony in its communal life" and refused to identify with any political cause or ideology. Readers were urged ambiguously to "do their duty to … their country and … to Malaya," conspicuously giving pride of place to India, however remote the tie. Yet the pressure of multiple loyalties of ambiguous strength and meaning was their major message.[41]

While syndicalists and would-be revolutionaries had to keep low profiles and flee when necessary, other Indian visitors made triumphal tours that spread complicated transnational, anti-colonial messages. Rabindranath Tagore, who won the Nobel Prize for Literature in 1913, visited Malaya in 1916 and in 1926 as he travelled east to lecture in Japan and the United States. Journeying north in triumph from Singapore to Penang, Tagore stopped in Kuala Lumpur and seven other cities, where eager crowds surrounded and garlanded him. Officials, teachers, students, merchants, storekeepers, drivers, and diplomats flocked to hear his comments on the unity of mankind. Tagore wrote of his travels as a "pilgrimage to see the signs of the history of India's entry into the universal," and he probed Asian cultures and religions for traces of cross-fertilization with India. Tagore's well-known attacks on nationalism

University Press, 1984), pp. 2, 8–9; Kees van Dijk, "Religion and the Undermining of British Rule in South and Southeast Asia during the Great War," in R. Michael Feener and Terenjit Sevea, eds., *Islamic Connections: Muslim Societies in South and Southeast Asia* (Singapore: Institute of Southeast Asian Studies, 2009), pp. 109–133; Leon Comber, "The Singapore Mutiny (1915) and the Genesis of Political Intelligence in Singapore," *Intelligence and National Security*, Vol. 24, No. 4 (2009), pp. 529–541

[40] Sugata Bose, *A Hundred Horizons: The Indian Ocean in the Age of Global Empire* (Cambridge, MA: Harvard University Press, 2009), pp. 149–151

[41] "Looking Forward," and "Notes of the Week," *The Indian*, 28 December 1935, p. 8

functioned, therefore, within a deep attachment to the culture in which he was born. Sugata Bose describes Tagore as inhabiting a "cosmopolitan thought zone" in which love of the universal coexisted with Indian patriotism. Tagore's defence of humane values used a language of self-confident Indianness that resonated with nationalists, while confirming in his audiences the legitimacy of their own pluralistic, hybridized world. At the same time, he strengthened anti-colonial sentiments with his opposition to the violence embedded in imperial rule.[42] Tagore reinforced Indian pride in ways that did not force expatriates to choose among their multiple communities, and he spoke with them in English, an immediate sign of the transnationalism of his message and of his appeal to educated, bilingual South Asians.

Indians who appreciated Tagore also rushed to welcome Jawaharlal Nehru, then President of the Indian National Congress, when he and his daughter toured west Malaya in 1937. Local enthusiasm ran wild for one whose name was proclaimed "a household word." A "mammoth crowd" greeted them in Seremban and threw rose petals and flowers as they arrived. In Klang, over 3,000 were said to have come to hear him speak. After Indian hosts honoured his patriotic work and wished him success in his "fight for Indian freedom," they donated money to the cause. But the nationalism that all embraced was neither hard-edged nor exclusive. It, too, was framed in English, in this case to ease communication between a Kashmiri Brahmin and his Tamil supporters. Nehru told his audiences that they were "the children of Malaya," whose interests were "wrapped up in the future of [that] country" with only sentimental ties to India. His nationalism, he said, was "based on an internationalism ... No country or people can isolate themselves from the rest of the world." Although Nehru proclaimed he was not anti-British and issued no calls for freedom fighters or violent resistance, he wanted to change the British Empire's political structure and radically improve the position of plantation workers, a message not lost on his audiences, who cheered him roundly. Nehru denounced "subjection imposed from above."[43] He called for trades unions to be formed by Indian labourers and recommended that they be given full civil and citizenship rights in Malaya.[44] The Indian National Congress regularly sent speakers who combined calls for political rights in India with backing for reforms in British Malaya. Their visits both raised money for nationalist campaigns and generated enthusiasm among emigrants for social changes in their new home.

[42] Bose, *Horizons*, pp. 245–260
[43] *Malaya Tribune*, 1 June 1937, p. 4; 3 June 1937, p. 1; 4 June 1937, p. 1
[44] Michael Stenson, *Class, Race and Colonialism in West Malaysia: The Indian Case* (Vancouver: University of British Columbia Press, 1980), p. 47

Straits Chinese also absorbed dual messages about political allegiances and activism. Leaders of the Singapore Chinese community contributed money and service as soldiers to the British side during World War I, but also demanded political changes in the Qing Empire. Dr Lim Boon Keng, a leader of the Straits Chinese British Association who was later appointed to the Legislative Council of the Straits Settlements, was an early supporter of Sun Yat Sen and the *T'ung Meng Hui* (the Revolutionary League), which worked to overthrow the Chinese emperor. An illegal, unregistered society, the *T'ung Meng Hui* set up reading rooms in over fifty Malayan towns and cities to cover its work, and it sponsored several newspapers that supported Sun Yat Sen's brand of democratic republicanism. Its leaders, drawn from the wealthier, better-educated China-born with a sprinkling of Straits Chinese, became stalwart organizers for the next two decades of the Republican cause, which they found compatible with their British loyalties.[45]

The level of Chinese expatriate engagement with Chinese politics rose significantly higher after the founding of the Republic of China in 1912. Multiple branches of the Kuomintang (Nationalist Party) opened in the cities of the Straits Settlements and the many towns of the Federated Malay States, enrolling members from all the major dialect groups – both the China-born and those who were British subjects. The first legal political party in Malaya, it gave thousands of political activists a channel for their Chinese nationalism and raised significant funds for Sun Yat Sen and, later, Chiang Kai Shek, as they struggled to maintain control of the new state. Local branches published newspapers, imported books and pamphlets from China, and then circulated partisan documents within the many Chinese vernacular schools in Malaya, building support among teachers and pupils. They organized demonstrations and parades by students and local members (see Figure 8.3). As the Japanese seized more Chinese territory, the party provided leadership for boycotts of Japanese goods and funds for social welfare projects. British efforts to suppress the Kuomintang were intermittent and ineffective, although the party was officially banned in 1925 and again in 1930 because British administrators saw it as a threat to British control, fearing its support for trade unions and its cooperation with communists.[46]

The compatibility of loyalty to British rule in Malaya and support for an independent, unified China was demonstrated repeatedly by Chinese nationalists in Malaya who had worked to create a Chinese republic

[45] C. F. Yong and R. B. McKenna, *The Kuomintang Movement in British Malaya, 1912–1949* (Singapore: Singapore University Press, 1990), pp. 12–16
[46] Yong and McKenna, *Kuomintang*, pp. 74–76, 83–84

Figure 8.3 A Chinese procession in Sitiawan in support of Chiang Kai Shek and the Kuomintang, 1928. Women and children are among the crowd.

since early in the century. Teo Eng Hock, a Teochew British subject who became wealthy as a cloth merchant and rubber manufacturer in Singapore, belonged to the T'ung Meng Hui and later to the Kuomintang, working actively for Chinese nationalists and for the British in Malaya, where he was appointed a justice of the peace in 1925. He and others like him moved back and forth from China to Malaya, taking up administrative jobs in both places and strengthening Sino-Malayan civil society by funding newspapers and schools. Choosing between China and Malaya was not necessary for more moderate nationalists, who cultivated colonial ties as well as republican ones. Tan Kah Kee, the Singapore philanthropist and entrepreneur whom the British viewed as "non-partisan" despite his fervent nationalism and long-term linkage to Kuomintang projects, was allowed to raise funds in Malaya for relief projects during the Sino-Japanese War in 1937.[47] His friend, Dr Lim Boon Keng, who had received the coveted Order of the British Empire, spent much of the 1920s and 1930s as president of Amoy (now Xiamen) University, serving at the request of Sun Yat Sen. Many of the Kuomintang leaders and sympathizers in Malaya led

---

[47] Yong and MacKenna, *Kuomintang*, pp. 96, 99, 115, 190–191; C. F. Yong, *Tan Kah-Kee: The Making of an Overseas Chinese Legend*, rev. ed. (Singapore: World Scientific, 2013)

transnational lives, taking on the political colouration of the political community around them.[48]

Transnational allegiances among Muslims in Malaya were less overtly political than those among Chinese expatriates, but no less important. Generations of Hadrami sayyid immigrants, who had married Malay women and settled into port towns, kept their Yemeni identities alive through their inherited names and genealogies that traced back to the Prophet Mohammed. While their strong British loyalties made them valuable to colonial authorities in times of political need, they cultivated Islamic connections through pilgrimages to Mecca and Sufi grave-shrines in Yemen. Sons were sent to Mecca to study or to the Hadramaut to live among relatives. The combination of multiple marriages among merchant families created a web of kin stretching from East Africa through the Netherlands Indies, a transnational community that existed within global empires. Some of the most wealthy Straits landlords, merchants, judges in the Islamic courts, and leaders of the Islamic community in Penang and Singapore belonged to this Hadrami diaspora, honoured as "good Arabs" by their British hosts.[49]

Other Muslim communities had similarly far-flung ties, reinforced by immigration and religious practice, but some of them became entangled with anticolonial, anti-British politics in the early twentieth century. British Muslims' respect for the Ottoman caliph became seditious after the outbreak of World War I. Fearing non-Muslim control of Mecca and Medina, Indian Muslims based in London, Cairo, and Singapore – probably a very small number – organized to support Ottoman rule and to undermine the loyalty of British Indian soldiers in the Middle East. After 1919, threats to the continuation of the caliphate led many Indian Muslims to oppose the dissolution of the Ottoman Empire. While the centre of the Khalifat movement lay in Northern India, Indian Muslim leaders in Singapore set up a Khalifat committee in 1922 and circulated

---

[48] Dr Lim Boon Keng, one of the first Queen's Scholars, earned a medical degree at the University of Edinburgh before returning to Singapore and becoming a leader of the Straits Chinese community there. His lectures from 1917, "The Great War from a Confucian Point of View and Kindred Topics" (1917) signal his continued sense of his Chinese background as well as a commitment to a cosmopolitan world federation centred around a reformed empire. See Tim Harper, "Globalism and the Pursuit of Authenticity: The Making of a Diasporic Public Sphere in Singapore," *Sojourn: Journal of Social Issues in Southeast Asia*, Vol. 12, No. 2 (1997), pp. 261–292

[49] Enseng Ho, *The Graves of Tarim: Genealogy and Mobility across the Indian Ocean* (Berkeley: University of California Press, 2006) pp. 253, 272–273, 322; Khoo Salma Nasution, *The Chulia in Penang: Patronage and Place-Making around the Kapitan Kling Mosque, 1786–1957* (Penang: Areca Books, 2014), pp. 258–259. The sayyids' privileged status bred resentment among less well-connected Malays who used their transnational ties as a weapon against them. See Omar, *Bangsa*, p. 16

the Pan-Islamic paper, *Khaliafat-i-Usmania*. Early leaders of the group couched their protests within a framework of British loyalty, but their alliance with Gandhi and the Indian National Congress pulled them toward the Indian nationalism and a stronger anti-colonial stand.[50] Religion drew Indian Muslims in Penang and Singapore into multiple global movements that complicated their allegiance to the British Empire. Although Pan-Islamic activity declined in the region after the abolition of the caliphate in 1924, Pan-Islamic congresses in Mecca and Jerusalem during the later 1920s and 1930s kept the movement alive and before the eyes of enthusiasts.[51]

Educated Muslims in Malaya maintained deep connections to Middle-Eastern and South Asian religious teachers and leaders. Not only did Malay men go to Cairo, Mecca, and India to study, but the international mails brought a wealth of Islamic publications from around the Muslim world into Malayan towns in exchange for local periodicals. The reformist Ahmadiyya movement, which spread from the Punjab into cities throughout Southeast Asia and Britain, used the printing press to launch what it called an intellectual jihad for purifying Islam. In the 1920s, texts in Arabic, Malay, English, and Urdu spread the ideas of Mirza Ghulam Ahmad widely around the Netherlands Indies and the Malay Peninsula, recruiting local followers and sparking debate about what constituted the "true" Islam.[52] *Genuine Islam*, an English language publication, circulated from 1936 into 1939 as a vehicle for exchanging the views of Asian and European Muslims and introducing readers to Islamist intellectuals, such as Muhammed Iqbal. It also featured the multi-lingual Indian Muslim teacher and reformer, Muhammed Abdul Aleem Siqqidi. He made multiple visits to Singapore, where he helped to organize the All Malaya Muslim Missionary Society and to promote the global unity of Islam.[53] In the towns of the Straits Settlements, where there was free trade in religious ideas, Islamic scholars from Arabia, Egypt, India,

---

[50] M. Naeem Qureshi, *Pan-Islam in British Indian Politics: A Study of the Khilafat Movement, 1918–1924* (Leiden: Brill, 1999), p. 61; Khoo Salma Nasution, *Chulia*, pp. 374–375

[51] Jacob M. Landau, *The Politics of Pan-Islam: Ideology and Organization* (Oxford University Press, 1994)

[52] Mirza Ghulam Ahmad (1835–1908) was a Punjabi religious leader who founded the Ahmadiyya movement. He claimed to be the Messiah or Mahdi and advocated a reformist style of Islam; Iqubal Singh Sevea, "The Ahmadiyya Print Jihad in South and Southeast Asia," in Feener and Sevea, *Islamic Connections*, pp. 134–148

[53] I would like to thank Terenjit Sevea for the reference to *Genuine Islam*; the publication was funded by Dato Syed Ibrahim bin Omar Alsagoff, a leading merchant and British loyalist of Arab descent, who served as a justice of the peace in Singapore, as well as municipal commissioner, and president of the All Malay Muslim Missionary Society during the 1930s. See http://eresources.nlb.gov.sg/infopedia/articles/SIP 1623 2009-1 2-31.html

brutality and sexual exploitation, venting long-standing grievances.[59] Understanding the depth of the challenge, the colonial government and employers pushed back hard. Special Branch officers arrested strike leaders in Selangor and Negeri Sembilan; troops and police broke the Batu Arang miners' strike. In a second wave of agitation, during 1939 and 1940, clashes at the Singapore Harbour Board Dockyard, at pineapple canneries, and on rubber estates ended brutally with casualties, arrests, and multiple deportations.[60] In workplaces and plantations, colonial rulers turned openly violent in the late 1930s, determined to defend existing political and social inequalities.

Over a relatively short time, tens of thousands of workers went from quiescence to militancy. No longer did Indian labourers appear always docile and the Chinese segregated and disciplined. When anger and energy produced a united front, ethnic and language divisions faded. Although leaders of the Malayan General Labour Union were Chinese, they called for common action, and they drew on Marxist rhetoric to reinforce their appeal. Moreover, class lines blurred as several middle-class organizations such as the Central Indian Association of Malaya, the Malayan Indian Association, the Chettiar Chamber of Commerce, and Tamil teachers unions protested against the poverty of Indian labourers and pushed the colonial government aggressively on their behalf. In several districts, clerical staff and middle-ranking estate employees decided they had to work together and enrolled Asians from multiple ethnicities.[61] Some of this broadened activity came from communist pressures, but not all of it. The economic pressures of the 1930s pushed Malayan workers into new alignments and mobilized them against employers. Colonial authorities, however, continued to equate labour organization with political subversion and rejected demands for economic and social reforms.

As Japanese aggression in China widened, the influence of the Malayan Communist Party deepened. Not only did it have small footholds in the towns and villages of the peninsula, but it had some support in the mines, plantations, and ports of the colony. The party was weakest among Malays and strongest among the Chinese, having broadened its leadership from the Hainanese to include other dialect communities and joining

---

[59] The demands of the Klang District Indian Union in 1940 and 1941 also included the firing of brutal managers, an end to sexual exploitation of women workers by European staff, and the right of workers to remain on bicycles when passing European managers and Asiatic staff. Stenson, *Class*, p. 64

[60] Yong, *Origins*, pp. 211–234; Stenson, *Class*, pp. 60–70; K. S. Jomo and Patricia Todd, *Trade Unions and the State in Peninsular Malaysia* (Kuala Lumpur: Oxford University Press, 1994), pp. 58–61

[61] Stenson, *Class*, pp. 80–81

a broad range of political groups in the united front against the Japanese. Although it probably counted only 5,000 members late in 1941, its allied Anti-Enemy groups enrolled almost 40,000 members and could mobilize perhaps ten times as many sympathizers. An estimated 50,000 had jointed the Malayan General Labour Union by May of 1940. Gathering support within the labour movement and among Indian workers, the communists were becoming a mass organization capable of opposing colonial rulers, whether European or Japanese. C. F. Yong argues that after the British ran from their Asian conquerors in 1941, the Malayan Communist Party became the "only effective political and military power" that could confront the Japanese during their wartime occupation of the peninsula.[62] Conventional nationalism proved less able to mobilize the mass of the population against the new invaders than the Chinese-dominated Communist party, which had established its anti-Japanese credentials during the 1930s.

In December of 1941, the Japanese launched coordinated attacks on Pearl Harbor, Hong Kong, the Philippines, and Malaya, overwhelming opponents with their organization and speed. When Japanese ships landed in southern Thailand and northeastern Malaya, their army had at least three advantages: surprise, excellent roads on which to travel, and British unwillingness to believe that the war had come to the region. Equipped with bicycles, Japanese soldiers sped south along the west coast of the peninsula, outflanking and outsmarting their unimaginative and ill-equipped British opponents, who failed to launch counter attacks in time and who abandoned supplies and equipment as they retreated. Penang burned after it was attacked by waves of Japanese bombers, which had earlier sunk British warships and blown up aerodromes and their planes. Within a few days, British commanders decided not to defend the island. They quietly evacuated all the Europeans, leaving Asians behind. So much for the equality of British subjects! As the Japanese moved relentlessly down the peninsula, Australian and Indian troops slowed their advance. Meanwhile thousands of refugees and defeated regiments poured into Singapore, where they hoped for safety. British commanders had maintained a naïve faith in the heavy guns of "Fortress Singapore," but its defences were designed to repel attacks from the sea, not a land invasion. Since Winston Churchill and the War Cabinet had decided months before that no reinforcements could be sent to Malaya because of military needs in the Middle East, the colony was left to fend for itself with few planes and no tanks. As bombs rained down on the city, those who could do so fled to Sumatra or Java. Many of the remaining

[62] C. F. Yong, *Origins*, pp. 234, 241–242, 268

Epilogue: Representing Empire, Remembering Colonial Rule

At the end of World War II, British enthusiasm for the sultans and aristocrats temporarily dimmed in light of Malay wartime cooperation with the Japanese, which they compared unfavourably to the anti-Japanese resistance of many Chinese and South Asians. After Allied troops reoccupied the peninsula and the British resumed political control, officials tried unsuccessfully to centralize the colony and to abandon indirect rule. They wanted the Straits Settlements, the Federated Malay States, and the Unfederated Malay States to become a unified polity called the Malayan Union, which offered citizenship to anyone born there, irrespective of ethnicity or religion. Strong opposition by elite Malays, who quickly organized into the United Malays National Organization or UMNO, eventually blocked the Malayan Union proposal and forced the British to abandon their support for a unified state that guaranteed equal rights to all. Eager to retain political control, Malay aristocrats joined forces with the sultans to demand the construction of a federated state, which elite Malays would run. Together they made the case that loyalty to the nation meant support for UMNO, Islam, and the rajas, and the British bought the argument. Meanwhile, the outbreak in 1948 of a major anti-colonial uprising ("The Emergency") led by Chinese Communist guerrillas pushed the British to adopt violent counter-terrorist tactics. To defeat the insurgents, the British forcibly resettled tens of thousands of rural people into guarded and fenced "New Villages." The "Emergency" gave new life to the more conservative politicians of all ethnicities, who decided to work together in their mutual interest. After the Malayan Chinese Association and their Indian counterparts from the Malayan Indian Congress threw their lot in with UMNO, the resulting coalition (the Alliance) built an electoral majority that has lasted until the present time.[1] The newly independent nation passed into the hands of

---

[1] Barbara Watson Andaya and Leonard Y. Andaya, *A History of Malaysia*, 2nd ed. (Houndsmill: Palgrave Macmillan, 2001), pp. 264–269, 274–278; see also T. N. Harper, *The End of Empire and the Making of Malaya* (Cambridge: Cambridge University Press, 1999); Ariffin Omar, *Bangsa Melayu: Malay Concepts of Democracy and*

conservative Malay politicians and the sultans, who remain the most powerful political figures in Malaysia.

The pattern of indirect rule in which Muslim rajas retained formal sovereignty carried over into the newly federated state of Malaysia, whose nine sultans take turns serving as king (*Yang di-Pertuan Agong*). Malaysia's national rituals rest on Malay traditions and a Malay political vocabulary.[2] Nevertheless, more than 150 years of British colonial rule have left a heavy imprint on Malaysia. Not only do state institutions – parliament, judiciary, and constitutional monarchy – derive from British models, but so does the country's legal system. Malaysia chose to join and to remain within the Commonwealth. The state has been built upon its colonial past as much as upon its pre-colonial heritage.

This book has argued that the British Empire created a transnational, multi-cultural society in Malaya where the denial of political rights to inhabitants was coupled with a rhetoric of equality that was belied by social experience in the colony. Indirect rule kept the formal power of the sultans intact while it eviscerated it in practice. Powers informally delegated to the Chinese during the nineteenth century encouraged the survival of Chinese communal institutions and brotherhoods that infringed on state sovereignty and perpetuated social divisions. On rural plantations, colonial rule rested on racial hierarchies and authoritarian expectations, whose models reached back to the slave societies of the Caribbean. Its costs were devastating to the individuals trapped by indenture contracts and low wages. The plantation regime softened, however, during the rubber era, when the state's commitment to public health and to workers' welfare led to improvements in housing, sanitation, and family incomes. Colonial urbanization created a world parallel to, but contrasting with, the plantations. Urban cosmopolitan communities fostered growing middle groups and a multi-ethnic civil society. Townspeople broadened their horizons through urban cinema, ceremony, and a flood of new consumption goods. Print culture gave the literate access to international information and permitted on-going contacts with China, India, Britain, and the Netherlands Indies. British subjecthood, granted to those born in a British colony, was compatible with other religious, cultural, and political commitments nourished in the towns. Loyalties remained multiple and contingent, rather than unitary and absolute. As individuals moved within British Malaya, they crossed not only political and economic frontiers, but also cultural divisions blurred by

Community, 1945–1950 (Kuala Lumpur: Oxford University Press, 1993); A. J. Stockwell, *British Policy and Malay Politics During the Malayan Union Experiment, 1942–1948* (Kuala Lumpur: Malayan Branch of the Royal Asiatic Society, 1979)
[2] Donna J. Amoroso, *Traditionalism and the Ascendancy of the Malay Ruling Class in Colonial Malaya* (Petaling Jaya: Strategic Information and Research Development Centre, 2014)

(1956), describes local people trapped between the demands of the colonial police and Communist guerrillas in a confused world of "cruelty, obtuseness, violence, hypocrisy, courage and devotion." In the novel, British officials who cannot distinguish between truth and falsehood jail the wrong people, reward the better liars, and force thousands into prison-like camps. Anthony Burgess worked in the British Colonial Service as an education officer and a teacher in Perak and Kelantan between 1954 and 1958. His novel, *Time for a Tiger* (1956), depicts a colonial world dominated by bumbling, drunken, philandering expatriates who run the local police force and an elite boarding school. Headmaster Boothby, whose efforts to control his staff always fall short, is described as an "imitation lion" with false teeth and cardboard claws. Teachers at his school predict that after retirement to Britain, Boothby would "bore people with his unintelligible talk about a country he could never learn to understand." Both Han and Burgess, who not only lived in the colony but had sustained experience of British officials, portray an empire defined by casual racism and rampant ignorance.[30] As the British Empire was collapsing, novelists living in British Malaya joined the mounting chorus of political criticism that was reshaping international views of imperialism.

In the post-colonial period, writers continue to remind readers of the harsh side of imperial rule, although Asians have pushed Europeans to the margins of their tales. Chuah Guat Eng tells a story of coerced sex, murder, and family secrets, which begins on a British-owned rubber plantation before World War II. The action of *Echoes of Silence* follows a Chinese and a Eurasian woman as they live out the consequences of Europeans' decisions to take Asian mistresses or to allocate vulnerable women to local men for their protection.[31] Amitav Ghosh's widely read book, *The Glass Palace*, follows Rajkumar Raha, Dolly Sein (maid to the Queen of Burma), and Saya John (a teak merchant) as they move around the British Empire and establish their families. While much of the story tracks upward mobility and survival, the implications of colonial rule lie close to the surface. Using interviews of former labourers in Malaysia,

---

[30] Han Suyin, a Eurasian doctor, lived and practised medicine in Johore and in Singapore during the early 1950s during the period of guerrilla warfare. She was a strong supporter of the Chinese Communist party. Han was married to Leon F. Comber, Assistant Commissioner of Police in the Malayan Special Branch. John Anthony Burgess taught at the elite Malay College in Kuala Kangsar and, later, at a teacher training college. He was fluent in Malay. Han Suyin, *And the Rain My Drink* (New York: Signet, 1960), p. 228; Anthony Burgess, *The Long Day Wanes: a Malayan Trilogy* (New York: Norton, 1964), p. 159; see also Elleke Boehmer, *Colonial and Postcolonial Literature: Migrant Metaphors* (Oxford University Press on Demand, 2005)

[31] Chuah Guat Eng, *Echoes of Silence* (Kuala Lumpur: Holograms, 1994)

Ghosh has them talk of plantation "slavery," where the men found "every action constantly policed, watched, supervised." Ghosh's target is colonialism rather than the actions of individual Europeans. When the soldier Arjun advocates loyalty to the British rather than support for the Japanese, as his nationalist friends want, he is told, "There are no good masters and bad masters, Arjun – in a way the better the master the worse the condition of the slave, because it makes him forget what he is."[32] Europeans play bit parts in a novel that worries more about Asians and their dignity than about direct abuse, but colonial exploitations drive the narrative forward. Drawn from both history and memory, his stories reach out to an international audience whose members incorporate them into their own store of colonial tales.

The difficulty of finding direct testimony from ordinary men and women who lived under colonial rule enhances the importance of literary reconstructions of such experiences. Multiple writers with roots in Canada, the Caribbean, France, and South Asia have followed and reinterpreted the post-slavery Indian diaspora of Indians. One of the most eloquent, Khal Torabully, a writer from Mauritius of Indian, Malay, and Jamaican descent, has worked with the historian Marina Carter to combine letters and archival sources with poetry and theory to recreate the sensibility of emigrant plantation workers. Torabully seeks to "Word me/ Soul me/ Humanize me/ Man me." Using the concept of *Coolitude*, he combines the assertion of dignity with that of oppression:

> I am the banished, excluded, exiled
> Who decided to lose myself in the anonymity of indenture
> Between the recruiter and the consular agent
> Between Protector of Emigrants and torturing settlers
> I had already lost my way amid droughts
> In the heart of the canefields.

Torabully's films and two books of poetry bring to life the Indian people who moved globally into plantations during the colonial period.[33] Anticolonial literature, of course, has developed a global audience in postcolonial times. It reminds forgetful readers of the grossly uneven costs and

[32] Amitav Ghosh, *The Glass Palace* (New York: Random House, 2002), pp. 378, 449–450, 471–472
[33] Khal Torabully, a Mauritian poet and filmmaker, comes from a family with roots in Trinidad, Malaya, and India. He now lives and publishes in France. His concept of Coolitude self-consciously echoes Aimé Césaire's idea of Négritude, intended to foster the self-awareness of blacks and their cultural values. See Marina Carter and Khal Torabully, *Coolitude: an Anthology of the Indian Labour Diaspora* (London: Anthem Press, 2002), pp. 91, 144–145, 226

benefits of empire, and it highlights the deep interweaving of colonialism and violence.

In the period before 1940, much less lethal violence erupted in British Malaya than in neighbouring colonies. Nevertheless, the British struck opponents hard during the few attacks carried out by British troops on the peninsula. After the British Resident J. W. W. Birch was murdered in Perak in 1875, troops arrived from Hong Kong and from India to pursue the killers in Perak, and other regiments moved against possible conspirators in Johore and Sungai Ujung. After the tiny and easily defeated Singapore Mutiny of 1915, thirty-seven men were publicly hanged or shot, seventy-seven were transported, and twelve jailed.[34] Moreover, violence takes many forms, most not lethal. In the towns, police regularly raided unlicensed gambling houses and opium dens, forcing underground all competition with the licensed activities that fed state budgets. They inspected brothels and forced prostitutes into lock hospitals and vagrants into jails. Police courts harassed and fined young men for loitering and rickshaw pullers for obstructing public streets.[35] As plantation records and government inquiries demonstrate, casual violence was endemic on sugar and rubber estates. Police constables chased after plantation runaways and brought them back for punishment. Martin Thomas argues persuasively that before World War II, colonial governments throughout Asia, Africa, and the Caribbean commonly used police to control labour. In British Malaya, constables were part of a surveillance regime that limited unrest directly through strike breaking and crowd control, but also indirectly through inspection, fines, and enforcement of contracts.[36] Colonial rule was fundamentally coercive in its structures and in its basic premises.

Even if subdued in comparison to levels in nearby colonies, anti-colonial violence occurred repeatedly throughout British Malaya. During the early years of British rule, disgruntled chieftains attacked British-supported rajas and their followers. Resentment of tax and land policies triggered other clashes, as did quarrels over local authority. Bandits who attacked landlords and officials had reputations as Malayan Robin Hoods who defended

---

[34] C. M. Turnbull, *A History of Singapore, 1819–1988*, 2nd ed. (Singapore: Oxford University Press, 1989), p. 127. By the early twentieth century, an Indian army unit was regularly stationed in Singapore; Keith Jeffery, *The British Army and the Crisis of Empire 1918–1922* (Manchester: Manchester University Press, 1984), p. 3

[35] See Chapters 3 and 7.

[36] Martin Thomas, *Violence and the Colonial Order: Police, Workers and Protest in European Colonial Empires, 1918–1940* (Cambridge: Cambridge University Press, 2012). See also Elizabeth Kolsky, *Colonial Justice in British India: White Violence and The Rule of Law* (Cambridge: Cambridge University Press, 2012)

the poor against oppressors.[37] Well before labour unions and nationalist political groups multiplied during the later 1930s, local police and plantation owners knew that deference sometimes shifted to defiance. Whether such actions erupted from individual grievances or more considered partisan arguments is usually very difficult to determine, but surely the personal slid easily into the political in an imperial setting.

Representing empire has generated a multi-vocal conversation in Malaysia among contending parties and contradictory stories, all shaped by present needs. Both the official narrative and the accounts that challenge it, however, raise the issue of entitlement and belonging. Who can legitimately call themselves Malaysian? How can descendants of immigrants earn a place in the polity? Heritage societies point to the built environment, which bears the imprint of multiple ethnicities and religions, as evidence that all must be acknowledged. The desire to control space and to mark it as one's own lies behind many efforts to earn a place in Malaysian public memory and public space. Under the threat of eviction and unemployment, Tamil estate workers in the state of Selangor now defend local temples and schools as communal possessions, and they seek to retain the right to live together in places that give meaning to their lives in defiance of the local property market.[38] Who has the right to remain on the land: Sri Mariamman's devotees or the clients of Malay housing developers? Communal self-defence goes hand in hand with workers' determination to control some of the soil on which they laboured. These workers' protests and legal cases recast plantations as *their* heritage, which they earned through labour and longevity. These claims, as well as the legal mechanisms through which they are being settled, are both imperial legacies. The British Empire not only brought Tamils to till Malayan fields, they also imported concepts of customary use, public domains, and procedures of legal appeal that are available to all. The inconsistencies within the colonial heritage provide opportunities for subalterns to organize in self-defence.

Chinese immigrants and their descendants have also staked claims to Malaysian land, but in ways that reflect the realities of the land market and their communal hierarchies. Hillsides throughout the western part of the peninsula are dotted with granite tombs, which have become sacred spaces for Chinese patrilineages. They are sited according to the principles of feng shui to maintain harmony between society and the physical landscape, and they may not be moved. Every year in early April at the

---

[37] Cheah Boon Kheng, *The Peasant Robbers of Kedah 1900–1929: Historical and Folk Perceptions*, 2nd ed. (Singapore: National University of Singapore Press, 2014)

[38] Andrew C. Willford, *Tamils and the Haunting of Justice: History and Recognition in Malaysia's Plantations* (Honolulu: University of Hawai'i Press, 2014)

Qingming festival or Tomb Sweeping Day, families visit gravesites to clean graves and to present offerings to their ancestors. Several patriarchs of the Lee family of landlords in Batu Kawan are memorialized in large, curvilinear tombs, their names and dates boldly emblazoned in stone. They occupy the high ground, looking downhill toward fields and riverside, remembered by local people.[39] Chinese community associations buried ordinary workers on lower ground and gave them wooden markers. But they also provided proper funeral rites to permit spirits to move safely through the underworld. Although the labourers occupy much less auspicious land, they remain in communal memory. A small cemetery in Bukit Tambun shelters the graves of Chinese immigrants who worked on the Batu Kawan sugar plantations. A committee and resident caretaker look after the site, and they conduct the yearly memorial rites for workers who left no descendants. They sweep walkways and leave fruit and flowers at a central altar. Each stone has a full cup of incense sticks that reveals past visitors and the expectation of those to come. Recently, the association paid for dozens of new granite stones to replace crumbling wooden plaques. One keeps alive the memory of Liu A Sao, a Teochew from Pu-Ning, who died in 1854, and another memorializes Zhen Yu Tou, a Hokkien from Tong An, who was buried in 1889. Mr Huang, whose parents gave him the name "Pig Shit" to shield him from the wrath of the gods, lies nearby. He died in 1892, presumably alone and unmarried, but his grave is kept clean.[40] These men and hundreds of others like them are remembered in a sacred space close to the sugarcane fields. Their graves remind visitors that not only Europeans planted empire in Malaysian soil.

British colonization of the Malay Peninsula began with the founding of sugar plantations, and it ended as the dominance of natural rubber faded after World War II. The link of the Ramsden family to Malayan plantations ended violently about a century after it had begun. John St Maur Ramsden, grandson of John William Ramsden and heir to the family's vast estates and the baronetcy, lived on the Penang Rubber Estates intermittently after 1945. Acting as their general manager, he helped to restore buildings and replant fields damaged during the Japanese occupation. Ramsden lived in the elegant "House of the 99 Doors," where he and a small staff of Malays and Tamils treated local planters

---

[39] I would like to thank Chew Joo Leong and his son Elwynn Chew, who kindly gave a wandering historian knocking unexpectedly at their door not only a terrific meal but a tour of the village, temple, and gravesites. They keep alive memories of Batu Kawan's plantations, where their family has held land since 1841. See also Brenda S. A. Yeoh, *Contesting Space: Power Relations and the Urban Built Environment in Colonial Singapore* (Kuala Lumpur: Oxford University Press, 1996), pp. 290–296

[40] I would like to thank Law Siak Hong for his expert interpretive help and company in Bukit Tambun, as well as for his translations.

to feasts of beef and beer on weekends. On the evening of 7 June 1948, Ramsden was walking up the central staircase of his bungalow when two shots rang out and hit him in the back of his head, killing him almost instantly. Although Chinese insurgents were active in the area, the police stated that it was not a political assassination. After a brief investigation, they arrested two Malay men – Embi Bin Hashim, who had been Ramsden's driver, and Mohamed Zain bin Ramjan, a twenty-seven year old local Malay who also worked at the plantation. They charged the latter with murder. Several months later, the Nibong Tebal coroner concluded that Ramsden "had been shot by an unknown person." Both Embi and Mohamed Zain were soon released because proof of their involvement was insufficient.[41] Since the timing of the murder coincided approximately with the beginning of guerrilla war in the area, initial suspicions in London ran high that Ramsden's death was an attack on European planters by Chinese revolutionaries. No evidence of that theory was ever presented, however.

Anti-colonial politics can be personal, as well as nationalist. Even fifty years later, men and women living near the Caledonia plantation have sharp memories of Ramsden and his death. At a small Indian tea stall in Nibong Tebal where I stopped in 2009 to get directions to the Ramsden plantations, two young men rushed over when they heard the name. "Ah, Ramsden – the man who was murdered. I know where," one said, and he immediately hopped on his motorbike to show the way. Their parents and relatives had worked on one of the Ramsden rubber estates, and they had grown up with tales of the big house and its inhabitants. They led me down a rutted dirt road shaded by rubber trees to a huge, decaying mansion. Laundry hung outside on sagging lines, while skinny dogs and chickens wandered about during my visit. Graffiti and missing plaster marked the open entryway and the staircase where Ramsden fell. An elderly widow, Muniammah, who had worked on the Caledonia estate since adolescence, lived alone in a corner of the virtually abandoned mansion. Muniammah described John St Maur Ramsden as "a nice man" who gave children on the estates chocolate and rides to school in his car. She also remembered the private golf course and airfield that adjoined the big house, signs of privilege now long gone. She talked energetically about Ramsden during his last days. Muniammah told of a Malay woman who lived in the big house, whom she said Ramsden had taken as a mistress. She was the sister of one of the plantation's young

---

[41] *The Times*, 10 June 1948, p. 4; *Straits Times*, 16 June 1948, p. 1; *Straits Times*, 10 July 1948, p. 7; *Straits Times*, 1 September 1948, p. 6; *Straits Times*, 3 September 1948, p. 10; *Straits Times*, 17 September 1948, p. 5

male employees, who resented her liaison with Ramsden. Other local people said that Ramsden was gay and said he only employed young, handsome Malay houseboys, the sort who had been arrested by the police. All remembered that no one had been convicted of his murder, and they did not seem to care.[42] These divergent stories clearly coupled sex and death against a background of inequality and colonial privilege. The Ramsden family's connection with plantations that began in 1850 with Edward Horsman's purchase of Malayan land ended in a violent response to an employer and a way of life, probably not in a nationalist confrontation. Local memories clearly set the story of Ramsden's death within a context of privilege and retribution – a comment on colonialism rather than the international political conflicts of the mid-twentieth century.

The Penang Sugar Estates helped to plant empire on the Malay peninsula, and their story can remind us of the British Empire's complex legacy there. Today the elegant manager's house stands derelict and empty; yet Tamil workers still live in the estates' "coolie lines." Plantations that once grew sugar and rubber now produce palm oil from the fruit of trees tended by immigrant labourers, reproducing patterns of ethnic inequality and privilege that date to British colonial times. The plantation complex has outlasted the regime that gave it birth. Sugar and rubber plantations have left multiple legacies to the estates that have replaced them. The question of how best to remember the Ramsden-properties in Malaysia remains unanswered. How should the story of Ramsden's murder be told? Should the "House of the 99 Doors" be restored and repurposed or torn down and forgotten? The multiple versions of Ramsden's life and death mirror the fractured reflections on British colonial rule that circulate in Malaysia today and in colonial archives. The lack of a single story reflects not only the range of experiences remembered but also the varied political needs of a population that has never accepted a common narrative of the Malaysian past.

---

[42] Interview of Muniammah, 4 January 2009, Caledonia plantation, Nibong Tebal (Perak Oral History Project); interview with Tang Tsen Tsen, 11 January 2009, Nibong Tebal, Perak (Perak Oral History Project)

Select Bibliography

Archives and Libraries

American Philosophical Society
Arkib Negara, Malaysia (Kuala Lumpur, Kedah, Perak, Pulau Penang)
Bodleian Library, Oxford
British Library, London
Buckinghamshire County Record Office, Aylesbury
Cambridge University Library
Cumbria Archives, Whitehaven
Guildhall Library, London
Library of Congress
London School of Economics Archive
Missions Étrangères de Paris
National Archive, London
National University of Singapore Library
Rhodes House, Oxford
School of Oriental and African Studies Archives and Special Collections
Singapore National Archives and Library
United Methodist Archives and History Center, Drew University
Van Pelt Library, University of Pennsylvania
West Yorkshire Archive (Leeds and Huddersfield)

Newspapers and Periodicals

Bintang Timor
The Eurasian Advocate
The Indian
Journal of the Malaysian Branch of the Royal Asiatic Society
Journal of the Straits Branch of the Royal Asiatic Society
Lat Pau
Malay Tribune
Perak Pioneer

The Planter
Roda
Saudara
Straits Chinese Magazine
Straits Echo
Straits Times

Printed Primary Sources

Abdul Majid bin Zainuddin. *The Malays in Malaya by One of Them*. Singapore: Malaya Publishing House, 1928.

Ainsworth, Leopold. *The Confessions of a Planter in Malaya: A Chronicle of Life and Adventure in the Jungle*. London: H. F. & G. Witherby, 1933.

Balestier, Joseph. "View of the State of Agriculture in the British Possession in the Straits of Malacca." *Journal of the Indian Archipelago* 2 (1948): 139–150.

Begbie, Peter James. *The Malayan Peninsula, Embracing Its History, Manners and Customs of the Inhabitants, Politics, Natural History etc. from Its Earliest Records*. Oxford: Oxford University Press, 1967. https://archive.org/stream/malayan peninsul00banegoog#page/n6/mode/2up

Belfield, H. Conway. *Handbook of the Federated Malay States*. London: Edward Stanford, 1904.

Birch, E. W., and revised by H. Conway Belfield. *The Orders of H. H. the Sultan of Perak in Council, 1877–1895, Vol. II*. Taiping: Perak Government Printing Office, 1896.

Bird, Isabella. *The Golden Chersonese: Malayan Travels of a Victorian Lady*. Singapore: Oxford University Press, 1983.

Blythe, Wilfred. *The Impact of Chinese Secret Societies in Malaya: A Historical Study*. Oxford: Oxford University Press, 1969.

Burns, P. L., ed. *The Journals of J. W. W. Birch, First British Resident to Perak 1874–1875*. Kuala Lumpur: Oxford University Press, 1976.

Burns, P. L., and C. D. Cowan, eds. *Sir Frank Swettenham's Malayan Journals, 1874–1876*. Kuala Lumpur: Oxford University Press, 1975.

Cameron, John. *Our Tropical Possessions in Malayan India*. Kuala Lumpur: Oxford University Press, 1864.

Clayton, R. J. B. *Recollections of R. J. B. Clayton: District Officer in Perak and Pahang 1898–1926: Twelve Tales of Events and Incidents*. Singapore: University of Singapore Library, 1984.

Cochrane, Charles Walter Hamilton. *Law for Planters*, 2nd rev. ed. Kuala Lumpur: Federated Malay States Government Printing Office, 1929.

Collins, W. L. *Directory of Commerce, Retailers, and Residents, Straits Settlements*. Singapore: Far East Publishing Syndicate, 1935.

The Colonial Directory of the Straits Settlements for 1875. Singapore: Mission Press, 1875.

Committee of the Singapore Bar, eds. *Straits Settlements Law Reports*. Singapore: Straits Times, 1893–1940.

Crawfurd, J. A. *Descriptive Dictionary of the Indian Islands and Adjacent Countries*. London: Bradbury and Evans, 1854.

Dennys, N. B. *A Descriptive Dictionary of British Malaya.* London: London and China Telegraph Office, 1894.

Dossett, J. W. *Who's Who in Malaya.* Singapore: Methodist Publishing House, 1918.

Earl, G. W. *The Eastern Seas or Voyages and Adventures in the Indian Archipelago in 1832–33–34.* London: W. H. Allen and Co., 1837.

Evans, W. J. *The Sugar-Planter's Manual: Being a Treatise on the Art of Obtaining Sugar from the Sugar Cane.* London: Longman, Brown, and Green, 1847.

Federated Malay States. *Federated Malay States Government Gazette.* Kuala Lumpur: FMS Government Printing Office, 1909–1930.

———. *The Law Reports of the Federated Malay States.* Kuala Lumpur: FMS Printing Office, 1924.

———. *The Laws of the Federated Malay States in force 31 December 1934.* Compiler, William Sumner Gibson, rev. ed., 4 vols. London: C. F. Roworth, 1935.

———. *Report of the Commission Appointed to Enquire into the Conditions of Indentured Labour in the Federated Malay States, 1910.* Kuala Lumpur: Government Printing Office, 1910.

Foo Choo Choon. *The Opium Traffic in Perak.* Ipoh, Perak: The Times of Malaya Press, Ltd., 1907.

Fox, Thomas. *The G.C.V.O. Week: An Account of the Celebrations at Kuala Kangsar from September 21st to September 28th, 1913 to Mark the Presentation to His Highness the Sultan of Perak of the G.C.V.O.* Ipoh, Perak: The Times of Malaya Press, Ltd., 1914.

Freir, F. W., ed. *"The Colonizer": Travellers' Handbook for British Malaya.* London: The Colonizer, 1939.

German, R. L. *Handbook to British Malaya.* London: Malayan Information Agency, 1929.

Gopalan, P. V. *Coronation Souvenir of the Settlement of Malacca, Undertaken with a View to Foster an Everlasting Inter-Racial Harmony and Amity among the Heterogeneous Folks of This Historic Settlement.* Kuala Lumpur: Commercial Press, 1937.

Green, Lewis B. *The Planters' Book of Caste and Custom.* Colombo: Times of Ceylon, 1925.

Harrison, Cuthbert Woodville. *An Illustrated Guide to the Federated Malay States.* Singapore: Oxford University Press, 1985.

Ho, Ruth. *Rainbow Round My Shoulder.* Kuala Lumpur: Eastern Universities Press, 1975.

"Indian Labour in Ceylon, Fiji, and British Malaya." *International Labour Review* 42 (1940): 57–76.

Innes, J. R. *Report on the Census of the Straits Settlements Taken on 1 March 1901.* Singapore: Government Printing Office, 1901.

Jarman, Robert L., ed. *Annual Reports of the Straits Settlements, 1855–1911.* London: Archive Editions, Ltd., 1998.

Keaghran, T. J. *The Singapore Directory for the Straits Settlements, 1877.* Singapore: Government Printing Office, 1877.

Khan, Munshi Rahman. *Autobiography of an Indian Indentured Labourer.* Delhi: Shipra Publications, 2005.

Kidd, Benjamin. *The Control of the Tropics.* London: Macmillan Company, 1898.

Kyshe, John William Norton. *Cases Heard and Determined in Her Majesty's Supreme Court of the Straits Settlements (1808–1884)*. Singapore: Singapore and Straits Printing Office, 1886.

Leech, H. W. C. "About Kinta." *JSBRAS* 4 (1879): 21–33.

"About Slim and Bernam, Part II." *JSBRAS* 4 (1879): 34–45.

Logan, J. R. "Plan for a Volunteer Police in the Muda Districts, Province Wellesley, Submitted to the Government by the Late J. R. Logan in 1867." *JSBRAS* 16 (1885): 174–202.

Low, James. *The British Settlement of Penang*. Singapore: Singapore Free Press, 1836.

"Loyalty" [S. Rajaratnam]. *The Jubilee Anniversary Book of Perak*. Ipoh: Times of Malaya Press, Ltd., 1936.

Mallal, Bashir Ahmed, and Nazir Ahmed Mallal, eds. *Malayan Cases, Being a Collection of Old and Important Cases Which Are Still Law*. Singapore: Malayan Law Journal Office, 1939.

Marjoribanks, N. E., and Ahmad Tambi Marakkayar. *Report on Indian Labour Emigration to Ceylon and Malaya, Parts I and II*. Madras: Government of India, 1917.

Marriott, Hays. *Report on the Census of the Straits Settlements Taken on March 10, 1911*. Singapore: Government Printing Office, 1911.

Maxwell, W. E. "A Journey on Foot to the Patani Frontier in 1876." *JSBRAS* 9 (1882): 1–67.

Maxwell, William George, compiler. *The Laws of Perak From 11th September, 1877 to 31 December, 1903*. 2 vols. with a supplement for 1904. Kuala Lumpur: F. M.S. Government Printing Office, 1905.

McNair, Fred. *Perak and the Malays: Sarong and Kris*. London: Tinsley Bros., 1878.

Moore, A. "Rubber-Growing: Elementary Principles and Practice." In *Planting Manual, Small Holders Advisory Service, 7*. Kuala Lumpur: Rubber Research Institute of Malaya, 1938.

Nathan, J. E. *The Census of British Malaya, 1921*. London: Waterlow & Sons, Ltd., 1921.

Newbold, T. J. *Political and Statistical Account of the British Settlements of the Straits of Malacca*. London: John Murray, 1839.

Perak, State of. *Laws of Perak: Orders in Council and Enactments, 1877–1896*. Taiping: Perak Government Printing Office, 1899.

Perak Government Gazette and Supplements. Kuala Lumpur: FMS Government Printing Office, 1888–1930.

Prinsen Geerligs, H. C. *The World's Sugar Cane Industry: Past and Present*. Manchester: Norman Rodger, 1912.

Purcell, Victor. *The Memoirs of a Malayan Official*. London: Cassell, 1965.

The Queen's Empire: A Pictorial and Descriptive Record. London: Cassell and Company, 1897.

Rajaratnam, S. *Ipoh: Where and What It Is*. Ipoh: Times of Malaya Press, Ltd., 1938.

Ramsay, Christine Wu. *Days Gone By: Growing Up in Penang*. Penang: Areca Books, 2007.

Rathborne, Ambrose B. *Camping and Tramping in Malaya: Fifteen Years Pioneering in the Native States of the Malay Peninsula*. Singapore: Oxford University Press, 1898.

Richmond, Broughton. *Directory of Malaya, 1927*. Singapore: C.A. Ribeiro & Co., 1927.

Rigby, J. "Law. Part II. The Ninety-Nine Laws of Perak." *Papers on Malay Subjects*. Kuala Lumpur: J. Russell at the F.M.S. Government Press, 1908.

Saravanamutter, Manicosothy. *Sara Saga*. Penang: Areca Books, 1937.

Sasreen, T. R. *Secret Documents on the Singapore Mutiny 1915*. New Delhi: Mounto Publishing House, 1995.

Sastri, Right Honourable V. S. Srinivasa. *Report on the Conditions of Indian Labour in Malaya*. New Delhi: Government of India Press, 1937.

Sim, Katherine. *Malayan Landscape*. Singapore: Asia Pacific Press, 1946.

Singam, S. Durai Raja. *Malayan Street Names: What They Mean and Whom They Commemorate*. Ipoh: Mercantile Press, c. 1939.

The Singapore and Malayan Directory. Singapore: Fraser & Neave Ltd., 1929–1940.

Singapore and Straits Directory. Singapore: Singapore and Straits Printing Office and Fraser & Neave, Ltd, 1885–1911.

Siow Choon Leng, ed. *The Chinese Commercial Directory and S. S. & F. M. S. Trade Register*. Singapore: Siow Choon Leng, 1919.

Song Ong Siang. *One Hundred Years' History of the Chinese in Singapore*. Singapore: Oxford University Press, 1984.

⸻. *The Straits Chinese and a Local Patriotic League*. Singapore: Straits Albion Press, Ltd., 1915.

⸻. *Straits Almanac and Directory for 1861*. Singapore: S. Bateman & Son, 1869.

⸻. *The Straits Calendar and Directory for the Year 1865*. Singapore: Commercial Press, 1865.

Straits Settlements. *Annual Report of the British Resident of Perak for the Year 1894*. Singapore: Government Printing Office, 1894.

⸻. *Blue Book*. Singapore: Government Printing Office, 1890–1930.

⸻. *Papers Laid Before the Legislative Council of the Straits Settlements*. Singapore: Government Printing Office, 1876–1883, 1937.

⸻. *Report of the Commission Appointed to Enquire into and Report on the Question of the State of Labour in the Straits Settlements and the Protected Native States, 1890*. Singapore: Government Printing Office, 1890.

⸻. *Straits Settlements Government Gazette*, Singapore, Government Printing Office, 1885–1910.

Sweeney, Amin, and Nigel Phillips, eds. *The Voyages of Mohamed Ibrahim Munshi*. Kuala Lumpur: Oxford University Press, 1975.

Swettenham, Sir Frank. *The Real Malay: Pen Pictures*. London: John Lane, The Bodley Head, 1900.

⸻. *British Malaya: An Account of the Origin and Progress of British Influence in Malaya*. London and New York: John Lane, 1907.

⸻. *Footprints in Malaya*. London: Hutchinson, 1942.

Thomson, J. *The Straits of Malacca, Indo-China, and China or Ten Years' Travels, Adventures, and Residence Abroad*. London: Sampson Low, Marston, Low & Searle, 1875.

Vaughan, J. D. *Manners and Customs of the Chinese of the Straits Settlements*. Singapore: Mission Press, 1879.

Khor, Neil Jin Keong, and Khoo Keat Siew. *The Penang Po Leung Kuk: Chinese Women, Prostitution and a Welfare Organization*. Kuala Lumpur: MBRAS, 2004.

Kidambi, Prashant. *The Making of an Indian Metropolis: Colonial Governance and Public Culture in Bombay, 1890–1920*. Aldershot: Ashgate Publishing, 2007.

Kidd, Alan, and David Nicholls. *Gender, Civic Culture and Consumerism: Middle-Class Identity in Britain, 1800–1940*. Manchester: Manchester University Press, 1999.

King, Anthony D. *Colonial Urban Development: Culture, Social Power, and Environment*. London: Routledge, 1976.

Kolsky, Elizabeth. *Colonial Justice in British India: White Violence and the Rule of Law*. Cambridge: Cambridge University Press, 2010.

Kratoska, Paul H. "Rice Cultivation and the Ethnic Division of Labour in British Malaya." *Comparative Studies in Society and History* 24, no. 2 (1992): 280–314.

——— ed. *Honorable Intentions: Talks on the British Empire in South-East Asia Delivered at the Royal Colonial Institute, 1874–1928*. Singapore and New York: Oxford University Press, 1983.

——— *The Japanese Occupation of Malaya, 1941–1945*. London: Allen & Unwin, 1998.

Lee, Edwin. *The British as Rulers: Governing Multiracial Singapore, 1867–1914*. Singapore: Singapore University Press, 1991.

Lee Kam Hing, and Chow Mun Seong, eds. *Biographical Dictionary of the Chinese in Malaysia*. Petaling Jaya: Pelanduk Publications, 1997.

Lee Kam Hing, and Tan Chee-Beng, eds. *The Chinese in Malaysia*. Shah Alam: Oxford University Press, 2000.

Lee Poh Ping. *Chinese Society in Nineteenth Century Singapore*. Kuala Lumpur: Oxford University Press, 1978.

Legg, Stephen. "Foucault's Population Geographies: Classifications, Biopolitics, and Governmental Spaces." *Population, Space, and Place* 11, no. 3 (2005): 137–156.

Levine, Philppa. *Prostitution, Race, and Politics: Policing Venereal Diseases in the British Empire*. New York: Routledge, 2003.

Leichty, Mark. *Suitably Modern: Making Middle-Class Culture in a New Consumer Society*. Princeton: Princeton University Press, 2003.

Lim Heng Kow. *The Evolution of the Urban System in Malaya*. Kuala Lumpur: Penerbit Universiti Malaya, 1978.

Lim, Patricia Pui Huen. *Wong Ah Fook: Immigrant, Builder, and Entrepreneur*. Singapore: Times Editions, 2002.

Lim, Teck Gee. *Peasants and Their Agricultural Economy in Colonial Malaya, 1874–1941*. Kuala Lumpur: Oxford University Press, 1977.

Lockard, Craig A. *Chinese Immigration and Society in Sarawak 1868–1917*. Sibu Sarawak: Sarawak Chinese Cultural Association, 2003.

——— *From Kampung to City: A Social History of Kuching, Malaysia, 1820–1970*. Athens, Ohio: Ohio University Center for International Studies, 1987.

Loh, Francis Kok Wah. *Beyond the Tin Mines: Coolies, Squatters, and New Villagers in Kinta Valley, 1880–1940*. Singapore: Oxford University Press, 1988.

Lubis, Abdur-Razzaq, and Khoo Salma Nasution. *Raja Bilah and the Mandailings in Perak: 1875–1911.* Kuala Lumpur: MBRAS, 2003.

Mahayudi, Haji Yahaya. *Sejarah Orang Syed Di Pahang.* Kuala Lumpur: Dewan Bahasa dan Pustaka, 1984.

Mak Lau Fong. *The Sociology of Secret Societies: A Study of Chinese Secret Societies in Singapore and Peninsular Malaysia.* Kuala Lumpur: 1981.

Mamdani, Mahmood. *Define and Rule: Native as Political Identity.* Cambridge: Harvard University Press, 2012.

Manderson, Leonore. *Sickness and the State: Health and Illness in Colonial Malaya, 1870–1940.* Cambridge: Cambridge University Press, 1996.

Maniam, K. S. *The Return.* Kuala Lumpur: Scoob Books, 1993.

Manjit S. Sidhu, and Gavin W. Jones. *Population Dynamics in a Plural Society: Peninsula Malaysia.* Kuala Lumpur: UMCB Publications [University of Malaysia Cooperative Bookshop Pubs.], 1981.

Mazumdar, Sucheta. *Sugar and Society in China: Peasants, Technology and the World Market.* Cambridge: Harvard Asia Center, 1998.

McIntyre, William David. *Commonwealth of Nations: Origins and Impact, 1869–1971.* Minneapolis: University of Minnesota Press, 1977.

Metcalf, Thomas R. *Ideologies of the Raj. The New Cambridge History of India*, vol. 3, no. 4. Cambridge: Cambridge University Press, 1994.

Imperial Connections: India in the Indian Ocean Arena, 1860–1920. Berkeley: University of California Press, 2007.

Milner, Anthony C. *The Invention of Politics in Colonial Malaya: Contesting Nationalism and the Expansion of the Public Sphere.* Cambridge: Cambridge University Press, 1995.

Kerajaan: Malay Political Culture on the Eve of Colonial Rule. Tucson: University of Arizona Press, 1982.

The Malays. Chichester: Wiley-Blackwell, 2008.

Morris, R. J. "Cities and Civil Society." In *Representation in British Cities: the Transformation of Urban Space, 1700–2000.* Eds. Andreas Fahrmeir and Elfie Rembold, pp. 48–64. Berlin: Philo, 2003.

Musa, Mahani. *Kongsi Gelap Melayu Di Negeri-Negeri Utara Pantai Barat Semenanjung Tanah Melayu 1821–1940 an.* Kuala Lumpur: MBRAS, 2002.

Nonini, Donald M. *British Colonial Rule and the Resistance of the Malay Peasantry, 1900–1957.* New Haven: Yale University Southeast Asian Studies, 1992.

Noor, Farish A. *The Other Malaysia: Writings on Malaysia's Subaltern History.* Kuala Lumpur: Silverfish Books, 2002.

Nordin Hussein. *Trade and Society in the Straits of Melaka: Dutch Melaka and English Penang, 1780–1830.* Singapore and Copenhagen: NUS Press and NAIS Press, 2007.

Northrup, David. *Indentured Labor in the Age of Imperialism, 1834–1922.* Cambridge: Cambridge University Press, 1995.

Ong, Aihwa. *Flexible Citizenship: the Cultural Logics of Transnationality.* Durham, NC: Duke University Press, 1999.

Ong, Aihwa, and Donald M. Nonini, eds. *Ungrounded Empires: the Cultural Politics of Modern Chinese Transnationalism.* New York: Routledge, 1997.

CPSIA information can be obtained
at www.ICGtesting.com
Printed in the USA
LVHW052022260722
724434LV00001B/135